Department of
Law Enforcement
and Corrections
Pennsylvannia State
University

DANIEL KATKIN

DREW HYMAN

JOHN KRAMER

Juvenile Delinquency and the Juvenile Justice System

Duxbury Press

North Scituate, Massachusetts

Photograph Credits

Page 15: Photo courtesy of *The Boston Globe*
Page 26: Photo courtesy of Eugene Richards
Page 28: Photo courtesy of *The Boston Globe*
Page 47: Photo courtesy of G. D. Hackett
Page 54: Photo courtesy of Eugene Richards
Page 55: Photo courtesy of United Press International
Page 96: Photo courtesy of Eugene Richards
Page 111: Photo courtesy of *The Boston Globe*
Page 134: Photo courtesy of Wayne Miller/Magnum Photos
Page 184: Photo courtesy of Eugene Richards
Page 192: Photo courtesy of United Press International
Page 205: Photo courtesy of Eugene Richards
Page 212: Photo courtesy of Eugene Richards
Page 218: Photo courtesy of Eugene Richards
Page 231: Photo courtesy of *The Boston Globe*
Page 262: Photo courtesy of Camerique
Page 301: Photo courtesy of Wayne Miller/Magnum Photos
Page 342: Photo courtesy of Charles Harbutt/Magnum Photos
Page 371: Photo courtesy of *The Boston Globe*
Page 374: Photo courtesy of Eugene Richards
Page 382: Photo courtesy of Eugene Richards
Page 389: Photo courtesy of *The Boston Globe*
Page 431: Photo courtesy of Eugene Richards
Page 437: Photo courtesy of Eugene Richards

DUXBURY PRESS

A DIVISION OF WADSWORTH PUBLISHING COMPANY, INC.

Juvenile Deliquency and the Juvenile Justice System was edited and prepared for composition by Jane Lovinger. The interior design was provided by Dorothy Booth, and the cover was designed by Joseph Landry.

L.C. Cat. Card No.: 75-41972
ISBN 0-87872-104-5
Printed in the United States of America
1 2 3 4 5 6 7 8 9 10 — 80 79 78 77 76

Contents

Foreword
Preface

Part One   *1*

Foreword

By Gilbert Geis

"Juvenile delinquents" is what we call youngsters in this country who violate the codes that define their legally permissible behavior. The words are heavy and graceless. Most nations do better in coining less pretentious terms for youngsters who do not do what those making the rules wish they would. The French label them *blousons noirs* ("black jackets"). To the Germans they are *halbstarke*, or "half-strong," and to the Swedes *skinnknutte*, or "leather jackets." In England, they are "teddy boys" and in Australia "bodgies" and "widgies." Perhaps Americans still have not come to either social or linguistic ease with the phenomenon of youthful transgression. To a country with so intense a concern about young persons, delinquency is a particularly threatening form of behavior.

There is a prevalent belief throughout our society that childhood and adolescence are periods of freedom and joyfulness, however much youngsters at those ages might dispute this idea. Parents are inclined to stress that life never again will be as attractive as when one is young. Such a belief is, of course, neither true nor false. It represents an emphasis on certain values. The opportunity to work afforded adults can be viewed as an exciting chance to be creative and independent and to gain financial rewards with which to purchase desirable things. The same opportunity can also be seen as a tedious burden, restricting pleasure. Each view (regardless of the nature of the precise job) can amply be supported; neither is "correct."

Certainly, the cosmetics and hairdressing industries, the incessant stress on youth in advertising, and similar items indicate clearly that, given the choice, Americans prefer to prolong as long as possible the illusion of their own youthfulness and the pleasures believed to be associated with this stage of life. And clearly, one of the results of this emphasis is that juvenile delinquency — the falling away of some youngsters from social expectations — is taken very seriously.

Delinquency thus seems to challenge commitments at the core of adult existence. In fact, though, many juvenile delinquents may be attempting to achieve those very things that adults value, in deed if not necessarily in dictum, and they may be using tactics that many adults, if they were not afraid of being caught, would themselves employ. The novelist Joyce Carol Oates offers a telling insight into the essentially conforming behavior of middle-class college students in matters that "count," though it may appear on the surface that they are in rebellion. Of one such student, Ms. Oates writes that she is "dressed in the familiar slovenly style of the neighborhood, a shapeless dress and bare legs and sandals. But, like the rest of the students who played at being poor, she had good teeth; being poor stopped at teeth."

There are many other reasons why delinquency is considered a serious problem in the United States today, beyond its possible defiance of important articulated principles. Certainly, it represents a not inconsiderable threat to the physical and material well-being of members of the society who feel that they are entitled to protection and security. Individuals may be willing to tolerate placidly more serious threats to their existence — such as those involved in air pollution, the use of cigarettes, and highway hazards — but this paradox hardly undercuts the fact that they are with reason concerned about juvenile behavior which is marked by violence and depredation.

Other roots of adult concern with delinquency have also been suggested. William Kvaraceus observes that there is a certain emotional release involved in fiery agitation against delinquents. "The young law violator," he notes, "tends to siphon off much of the adult frustration that abounds in the complexities of everyday living. The irritating delinquent serves admirably as a handy hate target. He is a perennial and classical institutional scapegoat". Kvaraceus goes on, not without a certain scapegoating zest himself, to underline his point:

> In the sanctimonious clucking of many parents can be heard a half-concealed vicarious thrill and delight in the escapades of youth. One can almost sense the adult smacking his lips as he bemoans the "awful" norm-violating conduct of the less-inhibited young. If delinquency is to be prevented and controlled, it will be necessary for many adults to inspect their own problems, and even their own pleasures in the delinquency phenomenon.

To the items of fear and threat involved in delinquent acts and those of vicarious satisfaction and catharsis in assailing manifestations of delinquency, Erik H. Erikson adds a poignant third source of adult discomfort at youthful waywardness: guilt. "A peculiar guilt can haunt those of the older generation — the guilt over having caused what they cannot guide to a foreseen completion," Erikson writes, indicating the sense of responsibility which American parents often assume for the fate of their children's lives, even though they are unable to control or to manipulate most of the major ingredients conditioning that fate. "This can make them look at youth as a cast of characters looking for a scenario not yet written; or worse, a cast populating a play with a scenario already in production and badly in need of rewriting."

Mostly, of course, juvenile delinquency represents the behavior of young people growing up and floundering about before they come to terms with the demands of society that they must live according to the law, that they must work — often very hard — in order to survive, and that they must learn to exist as best they can on what they legitimately are able to obtain for themselves. Young persons usually also come to accept the fact that for the most part they are going to be anonymous, unattended, and, to some extent, alienated. All of us are; none of us gets enough of everything we would like. For many persons, at least some of the time, there will be anodynic satisfactions in the form of pleasant leisure, interesting jobs, and satisfying personal relationships. For others, things will not be as good. But most of these persons, too, will more or less accept that this is the way it is and this is the way it is going to be. They come to understand and to be influenced by the fact that if they do not settle into the patterns of law-abiding behavior demanded of them, serious consequences are apt to follow; they may be arrested and punished, which might prove much worse than their own problems. Some justify their conformity by maintaining that things are fair. Robert K. Merton reports, for instance, on an elderly woman with a small income and limited education who reaffirms the legitimacy of the social order: "People with good heads deserve more. If my head isn't as good as another one, why should I get the same as you? I didn't try hard enough for it. . . . How do people get rich? They're smarter than we are." Other persons rebel and fight for changes in social structure and personal relationships. Their efforts, if successful, can reduce discontent and delinquency, though they also may increase it — depending upon who gets what and who wants what, and the relationship between these two. Others simply do not question, but do the best they can. Shirley Deane, describing life in an Andalusian village in Spain, offers a striking portrait of such adjustment in the face of terrible deprivation:

In the midst of their poverty — a poverty utter and complete in bad weather, when a day's work can mean the difference between life and death — these people never lose their dignity. They rouse admiration, not pity. They live sometimes ten or fifteen to a room, their children have nits, weak eyes and tuberculosis through overcrowding and under-nourishment, but they are proud and dignified and courteous. Lack of money brings no sense of inferiority, no bitterness or envy. They accept their poverty, though they suffer from it — and the rich accept the poverty of the poor without fear, without guilt. In a society where the classes are so rigidly defined one is, in a sense, less aware of them. The rich man drinks with the poor man in the bar, and they meet as equals, because one fears no change, the other hopes for none. The rich grant the poor their dignity, though they do not grant them bread. It is only in societies where the rich feel guilty or afraid that they flaunt their riches; it is only in societies where the poor have hope that they feel bitterness or envy. Here in Pueblo . . . they shrug and spit on the cobbles.

Students with a background in classical writings might immediately associate Ms. Deane's vignette with the "noble lie" that Plato suggested almost 2,500 years ago as a method for affording opportunities to the able while keeping other people quiescent and conforming. Unlike in Andalusia, the low-born with talent would be able to come forward, while the high-born without ability would sink. But Plato's blueprint leaves as many questions unanswered as it addresses: Who, for instance, is to make the judgment about talent in order to reward it? And how will the nature of such talent satisfactorily be determined? And how could this "noble lie" be made believable to the people? It was, all in all, no more than an idle thought by a philosopher daydreaming about an ideal society. As Plato put it, the scheme would work in the following manner:

"All of you in the city are certainly brothers," we shall tell them, "but the god, in fashioning those of you who are competent to rule, mixed gold in at their birth; this is why they are most honored; in auxiliaries, silver; and iron and bronze in the farmers and other craftsmen. So, because you're all related, although for the most part you'll produce offspring like yourselves, it sometimes happens that a silver child will be born from a golden parent, a golden child from a silver parent, and similarly all the others from each other. Hence the god commands the rulers first and foremost to be of nothing such good guardians and to keep over nothing so careful a watch as the children, seeing which of these metals is mixed in their souls. And, if a child of theirs should be born with an admixture of bronze or iron, by no manner of means are they to take pity on it, but shall assign the proper value to its nature and thrust it out among the craftsmen or the farmers; and, again, if from these men one should naturally grow who has an admixture of gold or silver, they will honor such ones and lead them up . . . believing there is an oracle that the city will be destroyed when an iron or bronze man is its guardian.

Fundamentally, then, the basic equation says that delinquency is behavior engaged in because the person desires something that he or she cannot or is unwilling to do without and which cannot or will not be achieved in a legal manner. The desires can be a lust for power and continuing prestige, such as that which apparently drove the Watergate conspirators; a quest for goods and excitement that will send youngsters on shoplifting expeditions in supermarkets and department stores; or a desire for surcease from humiliation that propels youngsters into physical confrontations with teachers who reinforce students' feelings of inferiority and academic ineptness.

As the labeling theorists and critical criminologists point out (and this book does an exceptional job in setting forth the new and intellectually exciting ideas of these schools of thought), many now unobtainable things that persons desire are legitimate human aims, and it is unpardonable to suggest that the total focus ought to be on the individual's adjustment to the status quo while ignoring the possibility of rearranging the system so that people's reasonable desires can be realized legally. This position offers a vigorous counterbalance to those who insist that the only — or the best — means of dealing with delinquency is to locate policies that guarantee that the perpetrators and those likely to behave as they did adjust to the laws. Often either the laws or the conditions that led to their violation demand remediation. Such theorists might regard the Andalusian peasants as benighted rather than as the admirable persons Ms. Deane believes them to be. Similarly, labeling theorists would emphasize that most persons ultimately will behave decently if they are not reinforced in undesirable patterns by punitive and discriminiatory patterns of response, patterns which often single them out for retaliation while ignoring similar actions by persons better off in terms of social position.

The problem will remain, however — labeling theory beliefs notwithstanding — that, for various reasons, different people come to desire different things and to develop varying tolerances of doing without them. Many youngsters who seemingly have satisfying present lives and very attractive futures nonetheless engage in serious forms of delinquency. Sometimes their motivations seem to be more subtle than we can readily understand. John Steinbeck, for instance, has offered a taste of the complexity of those things which contribute to making us the kinds of human beings we become:

And as a few strokes on the nose will make a puppy head shy, so a few rebuffs will make a boy shy all over. But whereas a puppy will cringe away or roll on its back, groveling, a little boy may cover his shyness with nonchalance, with bravado, or with secrecy. And once a boy has suffered rejection, he will find rejection even where it does not exist — or, worse, will draw it forth from people simply by expecting it.

Similarly, there is not apt to be any society which will evenly reward all in the manner they might hope for. Margaret Mead has tellingly illustrated, for instance, that persons who are born with or who learn traits that Americans value and reward will have considerable difficulty if they are Arapesh. Some Arapesh children, she notes, are capable of clear thinking and score very well on the Stanford-Binet intelligence test. These individuals, however, become "deviants" in Arapesh society, because their traits prevent them from dealing effectively with the "soft, uncertain" outlines of the culture, one in which no one does skilled work. So too, if manual dexterity or musical ability were more valued in the United States than verbal and writing ability and interpersonal manipulative skills, we might create a very different group of successful and esteemed persons and a very different cadre of juvenile delinquents and adult criminals.

Juvenile delinquency, it can be seen, is a phenomenon intimately tied to the nature of our social system. In some regards it reflects our freedom; in others our injustice and our tyranny. There are no easy answers about its causes, and no easy approaches to its control. But the pages that follow offer a comprehensive and sophisticated review of information and insights about juvenile delinquency and about the juvenile justice system that has been mounted to deal with the behavior. I would attend to its observations carefully if I wanted to understand delinquency and, in the process, to better understand myself and the world in which I live. If I were a student using this book, I'd also remember its cogent observations about the prosecution of witches in colonial times in Salem. From that material I would develop a criticality, a belief that some things that we think are true today may later turn out to be no different than the mythic superstitions of our ancestors. So I would read skeptically. This is what education should be: an important topic, a fine book, and a learning and questioning student.

Preface

Systems are generally thought to be ordered, rational, and cooperative. Justice is generally thought to be equitable, moral, fair, and right. The juvenile justice system, however, is rarely ordered, rational, and cooperative; nor is it consistently equitable, moral, fair, and right. Nevertheless, the interacting agencies, individuals, and institutions that work with children in trouble can usefully be conceptualized as a system; and the goal of that system can reasonably be conceptualized as justice.

The purpose of this book is to examine this paradox so as to explicate the truth it contains. A systems approach is employed because it focuses on the interrelationships among the programmatic efforts designed to help young people; thus, it facilitates a more complete understanding of each such program.

Traditional analyses have focused on such major components of the juvenile justice system as the police and the courts. In executing their duties, however, those agencies interact not only with each other, but also with schools, correctional institutions, probation officers, child welfare departments, and a wide range of other community agencies, as well as with parents and other concerned individuals. (Indeed, it may well be that larger numbers of delinquents are dealt with more effectively — and more justly — by individuals and other community agencies than are processed by the police and the courts.)

The total number of agencies interacting with young people who offend against the law is great. The goals of these agencies are varied and sometimes conflicting. But the existence of each agency defines the alternatives and limits the resources available to all the others. This book seeks to describe not only the agencies, but also their interactions, both cooperative and competitive.

This systems perspective requires analysis of the interactions of these many agencies, programs, and individuals in terms of the goals toward which they strive. In reality, there is no single goal of the juvenile justice system. Actors throughout the system are likely to contend that they seek to achieve justice for children, but "justice" is a highly subjective concept. Many in the community believe that justice requires punishment for those who violate the law. Many lawyers believe that justice requires due process in adjudicatory hearings — a belief which can conceivably result in the acquittal of a factually guilty youngster on technical grounds. Social workers tend often to believe that justice requires the provision of regenerative treatment to youngsters who need it, without regard to issues of factual guilt or innocence. Not only do the interpretations of "justice" abound; they are often contradictory. Thus, actors pursuing justice by their own lights may, in the judgment of others, be perpetrating injustice. All these interactions, whether cooperative or conflict ridden, have great significance for the futures of many young people.

This book seeks to describe the juvenile justice system and to analyze its varied and ever-changing nature. It will discuss individual programs and agencies in great detail, but will focus primarily on the patterns of interaction — both cooperative and competitive — within the system. By looking at differences between the components of the system, and by exploring the roots of the conflict that is often generated, this book may serve to broaden the outlook and enhance the understanding of students and professionals in such diverse areas as law, law enforcement, social work, criminology, community mental health, probation, and social planning. That, at any rate, is its goal.

Acknowledgments

As readers of acknowledgments know, authors always acquire intellectual and emotional debts. When three authors work together their indebtedness to others can grow exponentially. We are grateful to three wives and six children who were consistently gracious about our having to work evenings, weekends, and vacations.

Our obsession with this book must have been at least an occasional source of concern to faculty colleagues, many of whom were helpful and encouraging. We are particularly indebted to Dean Donald Ford and to Professor Walter Freeman for creating an atmosphere in which interdisciplinary efforts are fostered and facilitated.

There are many good people at Duxbury Press whose contributions to this book have been considerable. Jane Lovinger and Margaret Kearney were positively invaluable. Ed Francis was almost a fourth collaborator; he provided technical assistance, moral assurance, and a good deal of pressure, none of which we could have done without.

Several people made helpful comments about the manuscript as it developed. They include Professor Gilbert Geis of the University of California at Irvine, Professor Larry Seigel of Northeastern University, Professor Robert Murillo of the University of New Haven, Professor William E. Hemple of The American University, Professor Robert E. Croom of Georgia State University, Professor Frederick G. Barry of Massasoit Community College, Professor Bruce Bullington and Ms. Jan Essman of The Pennsylvania State University.

Part One

The juvenile justice system is characterized by tension, controversy and change. The four chapters in Part I provide an introduction to the divergent theories, philosophies, values, attitudes, and historical events which have contributed to the operation of modern juvenile justice systems.

In Chapter 1 the reader is invited to become engaged directly in considering the nature of delinquency, the magnitude of the problem, and the characteristics of youngsters who ultimately enter the formalized processes of juvenile justice.

Chapter 2 focuses on explanations of delinquent behavior. The discussion of three primary sets of theories about the causes of delinquency is fundamental to understanding the divergent and conflicting programs and orientations which are prevalent in juvenile justice systems.

Chapters 3 and 4 review historical reasons for the establishment of juvenile justice systems; they also explore the extent to which conflicting goals and programs are influenced by such incompatible values and ideologies as protecting individual rights, achieving social protection, and promoting the best interests of the child.

Part One

1 An Introduction to the Juvenile Justice System and the Social Problem to Which It Responds

Youth is a perpetual intoxication; it is the fever of reason.

— *La Rochefoucauld*

With a differing fate, men commit the same crimes: one man gets a cross as a reward of villainy, another a crown.

— *Juvenal*

This is a book about America's system of justice for children. It is about the network of human service agencies that identify, process, sometimes rehabilitate, but all too often exacerbate problems of children in trouble. It is also about the attitudes, values, theories, philosophies and historical events which give direction and character to the juvenile justice system.

Throughout the system there are simultaneous and potentially contradictory calls for more procedural safeguards of the rights of juveniles and for more informality in dealing with delinquent behavior. There is virtual unanimity throughout the nation that the system is undesirably fragmented; but consensus about new directions seems, at present, to be unattainable. From its inception the juvenile justice system has sought to reconcile the conflicting value bases of such diverse professions as law, psychiatry, and social work. Until recently the "reconciliation" has been accomplished by the clear subjugation of such legal values as due process and equal protection. Real reconciliation will be necessary, however, if the nation is to establish a system which deals with juveniles both as children with special needs and as people with equal rights.

Toward that goal, this book seeks to present an ordered and comprehensible image of a social system that is typically disorganized and frequently incomprehensible. Comprehension of the juvenile justice system requires familiarity with its component parts and an understanding of the patterns of interaction among those parts. Figure 1.1 presents a stylized model of a juvenile justice system. It shows the disposition of all persons who are "at risk" for delinquent acts they have committed. The model recognizes that only a small percentage of the total population of misbehaving young people will be processed; more importantly, it reminds us that all youngsters will be returned to a community almost identical to that from which they came.

Dissecting the Juvenile Justice System

For purposes of analysis the juvenile justice system can be studied in five units: (1) causes and prevention of delinquency, (2) identification of delinquents, (3) detention, (4) informal adjustment and adjudication, and (5) disposition. Later chapters of this book discuss each of these functional units in some detail; at this point, however, a brief overview is appropriate.

Causes and Prevention of Juvenile Delinquency

While there is fundamental disagreement about the causes of delinquency, most theories focus on community institutions such as families, schools, subgroups (e.g., peers, neighbors), religious organizations, and the economy. One of the most basic functions of all human communities is the socialization of children; that is, the creation of new generations of mature, responsible adults. To a considerable extent, delinquency may be viewed as the *failure* of agencies and individuals charged with teaching children how to behave.

Communities contribute to the delinquency of their own youngsters in three ways: First, they may create a climate which increases the probability that misbehavior will occur; poverty, neglect,

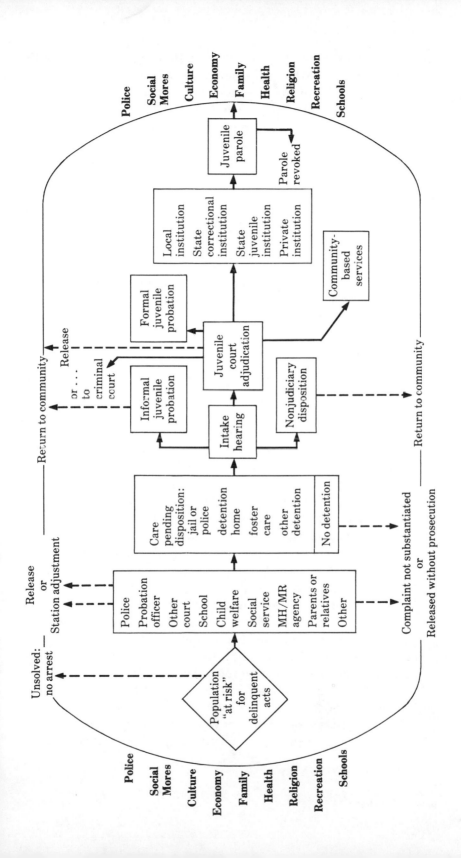

and racism, for example, may incline youngsters towards "acting-out" behavior, behavior designed to express rebellion against the society. Second, they may fail to provide adequate opportunities for education, recreation, employment, and self-fulfillment; unresponsive schools, unrewarding jobs, and inadequate recreational programs may generate pressures toward antisocial behaviors. Finally, communities contribute to the problem through intolerance and fear; that is, they expend resources primarily to isolate small numbers of children from the community rather than to develop programs for large numbers of children in the community. Throughout the nation, programs of delinquency prevention suffer from inadequate funding while hundreds of millions of dollars are spent on facilities for youngsters whose delinquency could conceivably have been prevented. The activities of the juvenile justice system are a response to the failure of communities to socialize children and provide them adequate opportunities for personal growth and development.

Identification of Delinquents

This task involves the process of observing, apprehending, and accusing a selected portion of the population of young people who misbehave.

There is a tendency to associate identification of delinquents with the police; in fact, however, a wide range of agencies is involved. Obviously a large amount of delinquency is effectively hidden; that is, it is never observed. A sizable but undetermined percentage, however, is known to child welfare workers, public and voluntary social service workers, mental health and retardation workers, teachers, doctors, parents, peers, and, of course, victims. These agencies and individuals make decisions about whether to notify appropriate authorities or to proceed "informally." In subsequent chapters, the extent to which youthful misbehavior is ignored, and/or responded to outside the justice system (that is, handled informally), will be examined in detail. At this point it is sufficient to note that public officials and private citizens know about much more delinquency than they choose to report. This is true for the police, too; they are also aware of more delinquency than they choose to recognize formally.

The police, then, function in a dual capacity: they identify delinquents directly, and they receive referrals from others. In any given case the police have a range of behavioral options available to them. They may "divert" a youngster by ignoring the delinquency or by dealing with it informally (e.g., by calling on parents or by threatening repercussions "next time"); if the police choose not to divert the youngster, they will refer the case to juvenile court.

The discretionary power of the police — and of the other community agencies involved in the identification process — is such that the decision to process a case formally is based on many factors other than the nature of the offense. These factors include the child's previous record, his family situation, and his attitude and demeanor; other influencing factors (which are even less appropriate) include social class and race.

Detention

This aspect of the juvenile justice system involves the temporary suspension of a youngster's right to freedom, and of his parents' right to custody, pending disposition.

Detention is an exceptionally problematic stage in the procedure of the juvenile justice system for two basic reasons: first, because it involves deprivation of liberty *before* a finding of delinquency; and second, because detention facilities are notoriously inadequate.

A child being placed in detention has not been legally defined as a delinquent. Therefore legal safeguards ought to be present to ensure that a juvenile is not detained if: (1) he has not violated the law; or (2) despite alleged law violation, he is clearly not dangerous; or (3) he does not, himself, need to be protected from danger. Capricious use of detention would contradict the juvenile justice system's philosophy of doing that which is in the best interests of youngsters in trouble. While detention decisions are generally made by the police, most states require judicial review to determine the legal and moral appropriateness of detention in any particular case.

The second critical issue concerns the quality of detention care in most jurisdictions. Most juveniles who are detained are held in local jails that also house adults. If jails were adequate institutions, this might not be so deplorable; but jails generally represent the worst physical facilities as well as the worst rehabilitative services within the criminal justice system.

Informal Adjustment and Adjudication

This component of the juvenile justice system involves decisions by juvenile court personnel about a child's guilt or innocence, and about his future. Informal adjustment involves "treatment" without a full hearing and without a formal finding of delinquency. Adjudication involves a formal hearing, before a judge, and may result in a formal finding of delinquency and quite possibly in commitment to an institution.

The goal of the juvenile court is "rehabilitation" rather than punishment; that is, the court's focus is supposed to be on helping the child rather than on exacting retribution. Nevertheless, probation officers and judges often emphasize to the child and his family the negative consequences of delinquency to underline the seriousness of the situation.

In operation, the juvenile court is a hybrid: part court of law, part social service agency. The first stage in the adjudicatory process involves review of the case by an "intake officer" who talks to the youth, to his parents, and in some cases to school officials, neighbors, or other involved persons. From this "assessment" of the youth's social and psychological environment, the intake officer determines whether to handle the case informally, by himself, or to send it on for a court hearing. An informal adjustment often involves supervision by a probation officer (typically for a period of six months); in other cases the "adjustment" may involve some form of restitution to the victim.

When a decision is made (usually by a probation officer) that the youth should have a hearing, it is generally on the grounds either of a claim of innocence, which requires a testing in court, or of the seriousness of the offense, which seems to require judicial review.

Referral to court, however, does not necessarily indicate that an adversarial proceeding will occur. The court has a traditional philosophy of trying to "help" the youngster and has not, therefore, typically tried to emulate the proceedings of a criminal court (a court for adult offenders); thus, it does not bother itself with the empaneling of a jury, presentation of evidence, and testimony of witnesses. More commonly, the concern of the court is with the child's "condition," the reasons for his behavior, and the type of "help" he needs.

It was not until 1967 that the Supreme Court held that juveniles have the right to a defense attorney and to the cross-examination of witnesses. Even now, however, defense attorneys are frequently absent; even when they are present, the therapeutic ideology of the court works to discourage them from a vigorous performance of an adversarial role. The same problem exists for prosecuting attorneys (in fact, many states do not provide for any attorney to serve as prosecutor), and consequently probation officers frequently perform this function.

It is difficult to seek a youngsters conviction while simultaneously pursuing his "best interests." Thus, the juvenile court is caught in the dilemma of attempting to serve both informal welfare concerns and formal legalistic concerns. The resulting conflict often places considerable strain on court personnel and youngsters alike.

Disposition

The final functional component of the juvenile justice system which we shall study involves the network of organizations and institutions that provide care, custody, and treatment to adjudicated delinquents. Programs range from community-based services, such as probation and day treatment centers, to secure institutions in which children are held for indefinite periods of time (generally not to exceed their twenty-first birthday).

For the comparatively small percentage of misbehaving youngsters who are eventually adjudicated delinquent, a range of dispositions is available. The most common is probation, which involves formal supervision of the youngster by an officer of the court hired to counsel youngsters and to help them "to stay out of trouble."

After probation, the next most commonly used and discussed disposition is institutional commitment. Institutionalization involves incarceration in a correctional facility which may be a forestry camp or an open, nonwalled, cluster of buildings (appearing to be much like a small college campus), or a secure prison-like facility — in some cases attached to an adult prison. No matter how homey institutions are made to appear (and the majority are not), they nevertheless remove youngsters from the community environment and the ongoing socialization processes which their peers experience.

Eventually, the institutionalized youngster is returned to his home community, one which is often unenthusiastic about accepting him back. His time in the institution has left him somewhat behind his classmates both socially and academically; but he is more knowledgeable about the ways of crime. He has learned how to gain status among other antisocial youths, and perhaps he has acquired greater expertise in the commitment of delinquent acts; thus, he is susceptible to further delinquency.

Institutions do succeed in safeguarding the community by removing delinquents for a period of time, but they may also exacerbate delinquency problems by returning children who may have become more prone to antisocial behavior.

The Nature and Extent of Delinquency in America

The juvenile justice system has been described as a succession of decision-making stages, at each of which a large number of youngsters who commit delinquent acts are either "diverted" from the formal proceeding of the juvenile justice system or are "encapsulated" further into the system.

Diversion and Encapsulation

Throughout this book, diversion and encapsulation will be important concepts. They are defined as follows:

> **Diversion:** A decision process by which people who have identified youthful misconduct seek to resolve such incidents without recourse to formal adjudication. The goal of diversion is to handle cases informally, thus, reducing as much as possible the probability that a youngster will be labeled delinquent.

> **Encapsulation:** A decision process by which people who have identified youthful misconduct seek to resolve such incidents by drawing the alleged offender into the workings of the juvenile justice system. Encapsulation occurs when an agent of the community takes some action that starts a youngster toward the formal process of adjudication. Any number of turn-offs from the road to adjudication exist: each is a form of diversion.

Diversion and encapsulation are in no sense mutually exclusive concepts. They are the concepts identifying the poles of a continuum: most decisions involve elements of both concepts. For example, assume that a youngster drinking beer has been observed by a police officer. If the officer decides that this youth should go to court he can refer him there. That would be the most encapsulating reaction available to the officer — because it leads to more formal handling as well as to greater likelihood that the community will become cognizant of the youth's misconduct and will consequently label him a delinquent and reduce his access to legitimate jobs and to nondelinquent peers. On the other hand, the officer might "divert" the youngster by ignoring the offense altogether, or by stopping the youth to warn him of the potential consequences of continued drinking, or by taking him to the stationhouse and then releasing him to his parents with no referral to court. These options represent various degrees of "diversion" and therefore, various degrees of "encapsulation." An officer who ignores the youth is, in effect, making a decision not to invoke the formal process of the juvenile justice system at all (all diversion, no encapsulation). An officer who stops and warns the youth is using the power vested in his role not only to point out the potential impact of continued drinking but also to become familiar with the youth; if the officer should observe that youth misbehaving again, the likelihood of formal action against the youth is greater. (Thus, even though this decision is primarily "diversionary" in nature, it also contains aspects of encapsulation because it increases the chances of more severe reactions later. In fact, it is rare that a juvenile is responded to formally by the police the first time he is encountered violating the law. A more usual scenario involves a series of legal contacts in which the reactions become more and more encapsulating.)

The extent to which diversion can be said to be the rule is underscored by the fact that practically every youngster in America commits acts for which he or she could be apprehended and subjected to the adjudicatory process. Furthermore, juvenile court statistics indicate that roughly one out of five boys, and one out of twenty girls, will appear in court before they reach their eighteenth birthday.[1] In highly urbanized inner-city areas, the percentage may rise to above one in three.[2] The remainder of this chapter discusses the magnitude and seriousness of delinquency in American society. You are asked to consider the extent of delinquency, to participate in considering its potential impact on you, and to consider the characteristics of young people who are diverted or encapsulated.

Types of Crimes Committed by Youngsters

F.B.I. arrest statistics indicate that young people are responsible for a substantial part of the national crime problem. The offenses for which youngsters are arrested are often very serious. Let us consider the statistics for 1973 for example: One out of four persons arrested (25.6%), was under eighteen years of age (these figures reflect an impressive rise from about 20% in 1965). People under eighteen represented 68.9% of all vandalism arrests, 58.4% of all arson arrests, 56.5% of all auto theft arrests, 53.8% of all burglary arrests, and 43% of all larceny arrests. Juveniles constituted a significant percentage of all persons arrested for crime involving violence or the threat of violence.

Almost 20% of those arrested for forcible rape were under eighteen years of age, as were 17% of those arrested for aggravated assault, and 10.3% of those arrested for murder. In addition, young people were arrested for many "victimless" crimes; they made up 26.3% of arrests for narcotic law violations, 40.6% of liquor law arrests, and 22.4% of disorderly conduct arrests.[3] The amount of harm perpetrated by "juvenile delinquents" is clearly considerable.

You and the Population At-Risk

You are now invited to participate in an attempt to determine the nature and extent of juvenile delinquency; you will undertake this study in ways that are meaningful, relevant, and perhaps even enjoyable. This is a venture which requires you to reflect with honesty and candor about some of your own life experiences and then to consider the consequences for others. To begin this interactive process, it is necessary for you to respond first to the questions posed in Table 1.1.[4]

One more thing: from time to time throughout the book we will reach out in this form to "tap you on the shoulder." We thus interrupt our development of an idea because we want to focus your attention on a special issue, or to ask you to reflect on some personal experience, or just to remind you about something that is appropriate.

The probability is that you know people who have committed many of these acts at least once and some who have done them more times. Let's turn the light on you now. Examine the same list again (Table 1.2), but this time respond in terms of your own behavior. It does not matter whether you are honest in sharing this information with anyone else; but if you are going to understand the material in this book, you should be honest with yourself.

Affirmative answers to any of the questions means that your acquaintances (Table 1.1) or you (Table 1.2) have committed delinquent acts. You may be struck by the breadth of the definition of the term "delinquent"; it encompasses some of the most serious and some of the most trivial behaviors. You may also have begun to notice that the commission of delinquent acts is quite commonplace. In fact, the term

TABLE 1.1. Do you know anyone who has . . .

	Never	1 time	2 times	3-4 times	5 or more times
Run away from home?					
Used force to take money or valuables from another?					
Visited a house of prostitution?					
Used or sold narcotic drugs?					
Taken things of large value (more than $50)?					
Broken into & entered a home, store, or building?					
Defied parental authority to their faces?					
Taken a car for a ride without owner's permission?					
Started a fist fight?					
Purposely damaged or destroyed public or private property?					
Taken things of medium value ($2.50 to $50)?					
Skipped school?					
Carried a concealed weapon?					
Taken things worth less than $2.50?					
Drunk alcoholic beverages (under legal age)?					
Engaged in premarital intercourse?					
Smoked or possessed marijuana?					
Attempted rape?					
Attempted homicide?					

is so broad that there are very few young people in the United States (or elsewhere for that matter) about whom it can be said: "He has never committed a delinquent act."

TABLE 1.2. Have you ever . . .

	Never	1 time	2 times	3-4 times	5 or more times
Run away from home?					
Taken money or valuables by force?					
Visited a house of prostitution?					
Used or sold narcotic drugs?					
Taken things of large value (more than $50)?					
Broken into & entered a home, store, or building?					
Defied parental authority to their faces?					
Taken a car for a ride without owner's permission?					
Started a fist fight?					
Purposely damaged or destroyed property of others?					
Taken things of medium value ($2.50 to $50)?					
Skipped school?					
Carried a concealed weapon?					
Taken things worth less than $2.50?					
Drunk alcoholic beverages (under legal age)?					
Had premarital intercourse?					
Smoked or possessed marijuana?					
Attempted rape?					
Attempted homicide?					

Furthermore, the pervasiveness of delinquent behavior may cause you to wonder what it means to say of someone: "He is a juvenile delinquent." Presumably there are some differences between the huge numbers of young people who commit delinquent acts and the infinitely smaller number who are adjudicated "delinquent."

Succeeding sections of this chapter will focus, in turn, on: (1) the ambiguity about the definition of delinquency, (2) the true extent of delinquent behavior, and (3) the relationship between official and unofficial delinquency.

Ambiguity About the Definitions of Delinquency

Initially it must be noted that there is *no* ambiguity about the status of "delinquent": it applies only to children. An adult who commits robbery is a criminal, but a child who commits the same act is a delinquent. The difference in labels attached to people for similar acts is significant because punishment for a *crime* is generally much more severe than treatment for *delinquency;* moreover, society has established distinct "systems" to deal with the people who commit these acts. In fact, it will be seen that a major justification for the creation of juvenile justice systems is to protect troubled children from the punitive operation of the criminal justice system and from the stigmatizing effects of being identified as a "criminal".

While it is absolutely clear that only children can be "delinquent," there is some ambiguity about the age at which an individual ceases to be a "child." In most states, offenses are treated as "delinquent" rather than "criminal" if committed by a person under the age of 18. In some states the maximum age of a "child" has been set as low as 15.[5]

The very fact that the status "delinquent" is intended to protect children has contributed to ambiguity. Having determined that delinquent children ought to be provided with regenerative treatment and services, the law was then required to define "delinquent." Statutes throughout the nation mandate that children who commit acts that would be crimes if committed by adults be treated as delinquent. Other children, however, may also receive the label. In fact, the term has been defined so broadly that any of the following noncriminal acts may form the basis for adjudication of delinquency:[6]

* violation of *any* law or ordinance
* habitual truancy from school
* association with vicious or immoral persons
* incorrigibility
* behavior that is beyond parental control
* absence from home without consent of parents

* growing up in idleness or crime
* deportment that injures or endangers the health, morals, or safety of self or others
* use of vile, obscene, or vulgar language in public
* entering or visiting a house of ill repute
* patronizing a gaming place
* patronizing a place where liquor is sold
* wandering in the streets at night, not on lawful business (curfew violation)
* engaging in immoral conduct at school or in other public places
* engaging in an illegal occupation
* involvement in an occupation or situation dangerous or injurious to self or others
* smoking cigarettes or using tobacco in any form
* loitering
* sleeping in alleys
* use of intoxicating liquor
* begging
* running away from a state or charitable institution
* attempting to marry without consent, in violation of law
* indulgence in sexual irregularities

Noncriminal behaviors which are legally sufficient to sustain a finding of delinquency are generally referred to as "status offenses." Such behaviors are entirely permissible if performed by adults; they are impermissible for children. In twenty-five states, status offenders are classified as delinquents and are subject to the same dispositions as children who have committed criminal acts.[7] In the remaining twenty-five states (Alaska, Arizona, California, Colorado, Florida, Georgia, Hawaii, Illinois, Kansas, Maryland, Massachusetts, Nebraska, New York, North Carolina, North Dakota, Ohio, Oklahoma, Pennsylvania, Rhode Island, South Dakota, Tennessee, Vermont, Washington, Wisconsin, Wyoming), and the District of Columbia, status offenders receive special quasi-delinquent labels such as "child-in-need-of-supervision" (CHINS), "person-in-need-of-supervision" (PINS), "incorrigible child," or "deprived child."[8]

The national trend is toward the increased use of quasi-delinquent labels for status offenders (there is also a movement to eliminate status offenses from consideration as crimes or delinquencies altogether). Let us contrast relevant sections of Minnesota's Juvenile Court Law and Pennsylvania's Juvenile Act.

JUVENILE COURT LAW: MINNESOTA

260.015 Definitions. Subd 5. "Delinquent Child" means a child:

(a) Who has violated any state or local law or ordinance; or

(b) Who has violated a federal law or a law of another state and whose case has been referred to the juvenile court; or

(c) Who is habitually truant from school; or

(d) Who is uncontrolled by his parent, guardian, or other custodian by reason of being wayward or habitually disobedient; or

(e) Who habitually deports himself in a manner that is injurious or dangerous to himself or others.

JUVENILE ACT OF 1972: PENNSYLVANIA

Section 2. Definitions. — As used in this act:

(1) "Child" means an individual who is: (i) under the age of eighteen years; or (ii) under the age of twenty-one years who committed an act of delinquency before reaching the age of eighteen years.

(2) "Delinquent act" means: (i) an act designated a crime under the law of this State, or of another state if the act occurred in that state, or under Federal law, or under local ordinances; or (ii) specific act or acts of habitual disobedience of the reasonable and lawful commands of his parent, guardian, or other custodian committed by a child who is ungovernable. "Delinquent act" shall not include the crime of murder nor shall it include summary offenses unless the child fails to pay a fine levied thereunder, in which event notice of such fact shall be certified to the court.

(3) "Delinquent child" means a child whom the court has found to have committed a delinquent act and is in need of treatment, supervision or rehabilitation.

(4) "Deprived child" means a child who: (i) is without proper parental care or control, subsistence, education as required by law, or other care or control necessary for his physical, mental, or emotional health, or morals; or (ii) has been placed for care or adoption in violation of law; or (iii) has been abandoned by his parents, guardian, or other custodian; or (iv) is without a parent,

guardian or legal custodian; or (v) while subject to compulsory school attendence is habitually and without justification truant from school.

Section 24. Disposition of Deprived Child
    (b) Unless a child found to be deprived is found to be delinquent he shall not be committed to or confined in an institution or other facility designed or operated for the benefit of delinquent children.

Children may come to the attention of the juvenile justice system not only to answer for the commission of crimes or status offenses, but also because they have become "dependent" and/or are the victims of "neglect." A dependent child is one who has no parent or guardian, or whose parent or guardian is physically or mentally incapacitated, or whose parent or guardian "with good cause" wishes to give up his responsibilities for the child.[9] A neglected child is one "whose environment is injurious to his welfare;" or whose parent fails or refuses to provide "care necessary for his health, guidance, or well-being;"[10] or "who suffers or is likely to suffer serious harm from the improper guardianship" of his parents.[11]

In some respects neglect and dependency cases are very different from cases involving allegations of delinquent and quasi-delinquent behavior. In all such cases, however, the juvenile justice system's concern is with providing helpful services to a troubled child. As it happens, there are frequently elements of delinquency, quasi-delinquency, and neglect in a single case.

> A child who steals can be adjudicated delinquent; but if his failure to respect the property of others is accompanied by a "lack of moral supervision" at home . . . then he [may] also [be] "neglected." So too, if he is an habitual truant from the same family then he may be a person-in-need-of-supervision as well as a neglected child. It would appear, therefore, that when the entire family situation is brought into view in a delinquency or semi-delinquency case, there may be grounds for proceeding against the parents in a neglect petition in addition to or in lieu of a delinquency charge.[12]

Juvenile justice systems, then, are involved in the lives of children who assault others and in the lives of children who may be the victims of assault. Children who commit murder, robbery, and rape are processed through the same agencies as children who skip school, drink beer, smoke marijuana, and defy parental authority. The institutions that house such children may also house youngsters who have never committed any offense but whose parents have proved unable or unwilling to care for them properly.

Neglected and dependent children are never classified by the law as delinquent; but their presence in juvenile courts, probation offices, and state institutions for children contributes to the existing ambiguity about the meaning of the term "delinquent." Throughout this book only occasional reference will be made to neglected and dependent children. Our focus is on the ways in which communities respond to youngsters who commit crimes and status offenses; that is, on the system of justice for delinquents and quasi delinquents. You have already seen that legal definitions of those terms are so broad that nearly all children could be brought within the juvenile court's jurisdiction if a judge were willing to listen to accounts of their lives.

The True Extent of Deliquency

Consider your answers to the delinquency questionnaires you filled in at the beginning of this chapter. If you reported for yourself the commission of crimes or status offenses, you are part of a large majority of young people who commit delinquent acts. A number of studies have utilized similar questionnaires. Some of those studies have involved high school students,[13] youngsters in correctional institutions,[14] college students,[15] and youngsters selected off the street.[16] Such studies indicate that approximately eighty to ninety percent of the respondents have committed at least one such offense.[17] Thus it is known that most young people could be adjudged delinquent.

The first self-reported delinquency study was administered by Austin L. Porterfield in the 1940s. Questionnaires were administered to 200 precollege men, 100 college men, and 137 precollege women. Every respondent reported having committed at least one criminal act or status offense.[18] The precollege men averaged almost 18 offenses each. The college men averaged about 11 offenses each. The women averaged almost 5 offenses each.[19] You might want to compare your own history of delinquency, or your class' self-reported history of delinquency, with Porterfield's findings. (See Table 1.3[20])

The commission of delinquent acts is so common and so

TABLE 1.3. Self-Reported Delinquency of 200 College Men and 137 College Women.

Offenses by Type	Percentage of Students Reporting the Offense		
	Precollege		
	Men	Women	College Men
Acts of public annoyance:			
Disturbing church	7.0	2.9	2.0
False fire alarms	8.5	3.5	0.0
Tripping trolleys	13.5	0.7	0.0
Disturbing (miscellaneous)	26.0	8.8	8.0
Throwing at cars	28.0	7.4	16.0
Shooting staples	35.0	0.0	8.0
Driving noisily by schools, churches	37.0	4.4	13.0
Shooting in the city:			
A "nigger shooter"	39.5	6.6	10.0
An air rifle	45.0	5.1	12.0
Fireworks in public buildings	49.5	8.8	42.0
Spitwads at others' displeasure	77.0	29.9	20.0
Violations of traffic laws:			
Drunken driving	22.0	0.0	18.0
Hanging on cars, trucks	46.5	12.4	25.0
Reckless driving	51.5	22.6	30.0
Speeding	67.5	46.0	55.0
Miscellaneous	67.5	51.8	61.0
Malicious mischief:			
Setting fires in buildings	13.0	1.5	14.0
Breaking furniture	27.5	6.6	18.0
Breaking fences, doors	29.0	5.8	18.0
Breaking windows	36.5	2.2	11.0
Painting, flooding rooms	40.0	17.5	36.0
Miscellaneous	42.5	10.2	35.0
Breaking street lights	47.0	8.7	13.0
Encroaching by—			
Tampering with property	21.0	2.9	6.0
Prowling	29.5	9.5	16.0
Trespassing	57.5	16.7	28.0
Slipping into theater	62.5	10.2	29.0

Offenses by Types	Percentage of Students Reporting the Offense		
	Precollege		
	Men	Women	College Men
Personal affronts and injuries (except homicide):			
Extortion threats	0.5	0.0	0.0
Assault (clubs, knucks)	3.0	1.0	0.0
Ordinary fighting	61.5	5.8	25.0
Abusive language	79.0	36.5	80.0
Vagabondage:			
Suspicious character	0.0	0.0	0.0
Vagrancy	4.0	0.0	4.0
Begging	5.5	0.0	3.0
Peddling, no license	5.5	0.0	5.0
Runaway, wandering	14.5	4.3	2.0
Stranded transiency	14.5	0.0	12.0
Truancy	42.5	34.3	28.0
Loafing in a pool hall	48.0	0.0	46.0
Liquor violations:			
Illegal manufacture	8.0	0.0	0.0
Illegal possession	35.5	2.9	47.0
Buying as a minor	38.0	2.2	53.0
Drunkenness	39.0	2.9	43.0
Theft:			
Auto theft	0.5	0.0	0.0
Bicycle theft	0.5	0.0	0.0
Theft of tools, money	5.5	0.0	1.0
Burglary	7.5	0.0	4.0
Shoplifting	10.0	1.5	5.0
Miscellaneous, petty	23.0	8.8	11.0
Stealing melons, fruit	69.0	16.0	15.0
Dishonesty (other than stealing):			
Forgery	2.5	5.1	1.0
False collection	8.0	2.2	10.0
Possessing stolen goods	20.0	3.6	14.0
Passing slugs, bad coins	24.0	0.0	14.0
Gambling	58.5	17.4	60.0

TABLE 1.3, continued

Offenses by Types	Percentage of Students Reporting the Offense		
	Precollege		
	Men	Women	College Men
Sex offenses:			
Attempt to rape	5.5	0.0	3.0
Indecent exposure	24.5	2.2	23.0
Extramarital coitus	58.5	0.7	59.0
Other cases:			
Carrying concealed weapons	14.0	0.0	0.0
Homicide, murder	0.5	0.0	0.0
Homicide, negligent	0.5	0.0	0.0
Incorrigible	0.0	0.0	0.0
Neglected, abused, etc.	0.0	0.0	0.0

Source: Austin L. Porterfield, *Youth in Trouble* (Fort Worth: Texas Christian University Press, 1946), p. 41.

widespread that the word "delinquent" and the word "child" may almost be said to be synonymous. Yet we reserve the term "delinquent" for only those children whose misbehavior results in adjudication; we do not apply it to every child who commits an offense. Hence, the concept, "delinquency," seems to defy precise definition. Paul Tappan, a thoughtful scholar, has offered the following definition, which may well be the best available:[21]

> *The juvenile delinquent is a person who has been adjudicated as such by a court of proper jurisdiction* though he may be no different up until the time of court contact and adjudication at any rate, from masses of children who are not delinquent. *Delinquency is any act, course of conduct, or situation which might be brought before a court and adjudicated* whether in fact it comes to be treated there or by some other resource or indeed remains untreated. It will be noted that under these definitions adjudicatable conduct may be defined as delinquent in the abstract, but it cannot be measured as delinquency until a court has found the facts of delinquency to exist.

> *If a society is concerned with control of youngsters it considers troublesome, or if it views most such acts as "kids will be kids," such an ambiguous definition is desirable. But a society concerned with issues of law and individual rights would demand a much more explicit definition.*

The commission of a delinquent act, then, is a necessary but not sufficient condition for a finding of delinquency. The vast majority of young people commit acts sufficient to sustain a finding of delinquency, but comparatively few are formally identified. It is therefore important to examine the mechanisms of selection of some youngsters for the label delinquent; that, in fact, is a central objective of this book, in particular the chapters in Part III. A preliminary overview is appropriate here, however, because the purpose of this chapter is to explore generally the meaning of the term delinquency.

Official and Unofficial Delinquency: A Process of Identification

Frequency and Severity of Offenses

The most reasonable assumption that might be made about the relationship between official and unofficial delinquents is that the former commit a greater number of offenses or more serious offenses. A significant body of research indicates that the self-reported delinquency of most young people, while considerable, invariably involves the commission of fewer delinquent acts, especially fewer of the serious delinquent acts, than are self-reported by officially recognized delinquents.[22]

It is important to recognize, however, that there is considerable overlap between the self-reported delinquent histories of official and unofficial offenders: some adjudicated delinquents have committed fewer and less serious offenses than other youngsters with unblemished records. Sociologists James Short and F. Ivan Nye compared the self-reported histories of adjudicated and nonadjudicated youngsters:

> Comparisons of . . . instututionalized and non-institutionalized boys and girls on the delinquency items [similar to those in Table 1.1]

indicate that significantly higher proportions of the "official delinquents commit virtually all of the offenses and commit them more often, than do the high school students. . . . In spite of the statistical significance of these comparisons, however, it is apparent that there is a good deal of "overlapping" between institutionalized and non-institutionalized boys and girls in the frequency of commission of our delinquency items.[23]

Notice that Short and Nye compared institutionalized youngsters to high school students. It is reasonable to assume that the delinquency reports of noninstitutionalized delinquents are even more similar to those of the high school students — that is, that there is more overlap between the noninstitutionalized delinquents and the high school students.

Frequency of offense and severity explain some *but not all* of the difference between adjudicated and nonadjudicated delinquents. It is important, then, to explore other variables which may help to explain why some misbehaving youngsters are officially processed while others go undisturbed. In the remainder of this chapter we shall explore three potentially significant variables: (1) public expectations about delinquents, (2) race, and (3) socioeconomic status.

Public Expectations about Delinquents

Thus far discussion of the term delinquent has focused on the ambiguity that pervades the law. But we must realize that many members of the public have a clear subjective image of the delinquent.

What about it? Do you generally conceptualize delinquents as good or bad, gentle or vicious, clean cut or greasy, sick or healthy, rich or poor, educated or uneducated, black or white, disrespectful or polite, decent or nasty?

When a member of the general public observes the commission of a delinquent act, he will respond to that act not on the basis of the act itself but on the basis of what he perceives to be the characteristics of the offender; that is, the more nearly a misbehaving child fits the popular image of a delinquent, the more likely it is that his misbehavior will be noticed and punished. Most of you have avoided serious involvement with the juvenile justice system despite the commission of delinquent acts. No doubt that is due in part to the fact that your indiscretions have been comparatively few and minor. Quite likely, however, it is also due in part to the fact that you have generally been perceived as bright, clean, middle-class, decent, and respectful young persons. Your ability to project an image of yourself as something other than "a real delinquent" may well have contributed to your lack of involvement with formal agents of the juvenile justice system.

This phenomenon is discussed at some length in Chapter 9.

A youngster who is unable to project a positive image of himself because his peer group has a bad reputation or because of psychological problems or physical characteristics or poverty or racial prejudice may be at a significant disadvantage in encounters with agents of the juvenile justice system.

Race

The percentage of minority-group members in the total number of youngsters involved with the juvenile justice system is far higher than the percentage of minority-group members in the general population. This fact suggests the existence of institutional racism. While such racism certainly exists, it is probably not the controlling factor. A study comparing self-reported and officially recognized delinquency in Flint, Michigan, found that blacks reported the commission of more

numerous and more serious delinquent acts than whites.[24] Obviously, blacks are more likely than whites to be arrested and referred to court for such acts. The data indicate, however, that blacks who commit a crime are more likely to be apprehended and convicted than are whites who commit the same crime.[25] That situation is probably accounted for by the fact that police surveillance in any inner-city ghetto is more intensive than it is in the middle-class suburbs. It may also be that policemen, most of whom are white, use their discretion more benevolently in interactions with whites. There is even evidence that, when the offender is black, citizen complainants may be particularly adamant in demanding that the police make an arrest rather than an informal adjustment.[26]

There is a strong correlation between minority-group membership and poverty in America. And there is evidence that an offender's socioeconomic status may influence the way in which the offender is perceived and processed.

Socioeconomic Status

Delinquency among lower-class youngsters (of all races) is more extensive and more serious than among their middle-class counterparts. The Flint, Michigan, study referred to in the preceding section found that the ratio of low-status to high-status boys with official records was 5 to 1: on the basis of self-reports it should have been 1.5 to 1.[27] Even when the offenses were matched for frequency and seriousness of offenses, the ratio of low- to high-status boys was more than 3 to 1.

The overrepresentation of youngsters from the lower socioeconomic classes in the juvenile justice system may have several explanations. It may be that middle-class children have more to lose, hence, the risk in being caught may be greater; consequently they may perform delinquencies in relative isolation so that the police or witnesses who would report it are less likely to see the behavior. Further, the middle-class juvenile has an advantage of greater privacy in which to commit his delinquencies. The basement, the family room, and the car provide opportunities to conceal delinquencies that the lower-class youngster does not have. Kids in overcrowded slums are forced out into the street both for recreation and for escape from the crowded conditions of their apartments; thus, they are subject to greater visibility than their middle-class counterparts. The police, because of the high reported crime rates in poor areas, conduct more

intense surveillance of such neighborhoods. It may also be that witnesses, whether police or members of the general public, are more likely to protect the middle-class child because he is not seen as needing treatment. For whatever reason, it is less likely a middle-class youngster will be caught — and less likely, if caught, that he will be sent to a correctional institution for juveniles.

Conclusion

Delinquency is not an either/or proposition: it is a human variable that ranges from the small minority of juveniles who never commit acts of delinquency to the small minority who commit frequent and serious offenses.

Most juveniles fall somewhere in between, sometimes engaging in a delinquent offense, but most of the time conforming to society's expectations. There are few absolute delinquents who reject the basic values of our social system. And even the most troublesome delinquent engages in delinquency only a small percentage of his time; most hours and minutes are spent in conforming activity. Most delinquencies are situational, with very little planning (which may explain why juveniles are more likely than adults to be caught) and take only minutes to complete. Truancy, it is true, provides eight hours of delinquency, but most other delinquencies are quickly concluded. It is interesting to note that a behavior that takes less than one percent of a juvenile's time is given so much importance in determining what is wrong with him and what should be done for him.

The point of this chapter should be clear: Delinquency is not inherent in an act, for too many "delinquent" acts are perpetrated by youngsters not defined as delinquent. The juvenile justice system acts as a sieve that screens for labeling a select minority of those who violate the delinquency statutes. The purpose of this book is to examine the system of selection much more closely. The system generated to deal with the problem must be understood if the true nature and parameters of the problem are to be understood. Thus, this book will focus on such issues as who operates the system, what are their values, attitudes, and aspirations, how they make decisions, whom they select for treatment, and what they do for (to) those selected. Chapter 2 will review existing knowledge about the causes of delinquency so that the system can be evaluated in terms of its relationship to explanations of delinquent behavior.

References

1. *Task Force Report: Juvenile Delinquency and Youth Crime* (Washington, D.C.: U. S. Government Printing Office, 1967), p. 1.

2. Michael Lalli and Leonard Savitz, *Interim Report: A study of Delinquency and Criminal Careers* (Washington, D.C.: National Institute of Law Enforcement and Criminal Justice, January 1972), p. 7.

3. *Uniform Crime Reports, 1973,* issued by Clarence M. Kelley, Director, F.B.I. (Washington, D.C.: U. S. Government Printing Office, 1972), p. 128.

4. Items in this questionnaire were selected from these studies: Robert A. Dentler and Lawrence J. Monroe, "Social Correlations of Early Adolescent Theft," *American Sociological Review* 26 (October 1961): 733 - 43; F. Ivan Nye and James F. Short, Jr., "Scaling Delinquent Behavior," *American Sociological Review* 22 (June 1957): 326 - 31.

5. Mark M. Levin and Rosemary C. Sarri, *Juvenile Delinquency: A Comparative Analysis of Legal Codes in the United States* (Ann Arbor, Mich. National Assessment of Juvenile Corrections, 1974), p. 13.

6. See Sol Rubin, *Crime and Juvenile Delinquency: A Rational Approach to Penal Problems,* 2nd ed. (New York: Oceana Publications, 1961),

p. 49; also see Ruth S. Cavan, *Juvenile Delinquency,* 2nd ed. (New York: J. B. Lippincott, 1969), p. 25.

7. Levin and Sarri list 26 states in this category *(Juvenile Delinquency,* p. 12); however, Pennsylvania has recently enacted a new juvenile act with different provisions.

8. Levin and Sarri list 24 states in this category *(Juvenile Delinquency,* p. 12), but Pennsylvania with its new law, belongs here.

9. See, for example, the Ill. Juv. Ct. Act, Section 702-5.

10. Colo. Children's Code, Section 21-1-3 (19) (a), (d), (e).

11. McKinney's New York Family Court Act, Section 312 (b).

12. Sanford J. Fox, *The Law of Juvenile Courts in a Nutshell* (St. Paul, Minn.: West Publishing Co., 1971) pp. 59 - 60.

13. See, for example, John P. Clark and Eugene P. Wenninger, "Goal Orientations and Illegal Behavior Among Juveniles," *Social Forces* 42 (October 1963): 49 - 59.

14. See, for example, F. Ivan Nye, James F. Short, Jr., and Virgil J. Olson, "Socio-economic Status and Delinquent Behavior," *American Journal of Sociology* 63 (January 1958): 381 - 9.

15. See, for example, Austin L. Porterfield, "Delinquency and Its Outcome in Court and College," *American Journal of Sociology* 49 (November 1943): 199 - 208.

16. James F. Short and Fred Strodtbeck, *Group Processes and Gang Delinquency* (Chicago: University of Chicago Press, 1965).

17. Martin Gold, *Delinquent Behavior in an American City* (Belmont, Calif.: Brooks/Cole Publishing Co., 1970).

18. Austin L. Porterfield, *Youth in Trouble* (Fort Worth: Leo Potishman Foundation, 1946), p. 38.

19. Ibid.

20. Ibid., p. 41.

21. Paul Tappan, *Juvenile Delinquency* (New York: McGraw-Hill, 1949), p. 30.

22. For an excellent discussion, see Roger Hood and Richard Sparks, *Key Issues in Criminology* (New York: McGraw-Hill, 1970), pp. 61 - 3.

23. Thus the juvenile, while frequently given a "break," also can have the treatment philosophy backfire on him by extended jurisdiction under the court. See *In re Gault* as a case in which two juveniles received a sentence for up to six years' jurisdiction under the juvenile court which would be punished by 30 days in jail for an adult.

24. Gold, *Delinquent Behavior,* p. 79.

25. Ibid., p. 81.

26. Donald J. Black and Albert J. Reiss, Jr., "Police Control of Juveniles," *American Sociological Review* 35, no. 1 (February 1970): 63 - 77.

27. See Hood and Sparks, *Key Issues in Criminology,* p. 58, for an interpretation of Gold's study.

2 The Causes of Delinquency

Contemporary criminology has been dominated by a philosophy rooted in the belief that delinquents are radically different from other youngsters, and that these differences, whether genetic, social, or psychological, constitute the causes of criminal behavior.

Some theorists identify this philosphy as criminological positivism. That, however, is a bit confusing as there are two possible uses of the term "positivist." Scientific positivism is a philosophical school which holds that knowledge must always be based on observable data rather than on faith, intuition, or pure reason. Historically, the first positivists in criminology studied differences between individual criminals and noncriminals; and the term "positive criminology" has come to be applied to theories which locate the causes of crime in individual differences. Some criminologists subscribe to rigorous scientific method but deny the importance of individual differences; they may consider themselves positivists, but not criminological positivists.[1] In this chapter the term positivism refers to criminological positivism, that is, to schools that focus on individual differences.

While this individual-oriented approach has had the most influence on the development of programs for the treatment and prevention of delinquency, it has long competed with a community-oriented approach which has sought to find explanations of criminality in social conditions rather than in personal pathologies.[2] Both orientations have traditionally accepted the assumption that there are fundamental differences between delinquents and nondelinquents; they differ only on the issue of whether those differences inhere in the individual or in his social experiences.

In recent years a fundamentally different orientation, called either the labeling perspective or interactionism, has begun to emerge.[3] Drawing partially on data yielded by self-report studies of the type included in Chapter 1, labeling theoreticians have argued that delinquents and nondelinquents behave in very similar ways and that the postulated differences between them are clearer in textbooks than in reality.

In each of the following sections we will try to point out the potential utility and the clear weaknesses of each theory. Bear in mind that delinquency is a complex phenomenon, and no single explanation is likely to be totally comprehensive.

Individual-oriented (positive) criminology has held that the proper focus of inquiry is the delinquent himself, in whose motivational and behavioral systems the explanation of crime is believed to reside. Community-oriented criminology has maintained that the focus must be widened to include examination of the impact of social environment. Labeling theory argues that acts do not become delinquent until reacted to by agencies of social control; thus it suggests that these agencies (the police, the courts, and even the substantive criminal law itself) are the proper foci of scientific investigation. Each of the first two orientations tends to ask why a delinquent child behaves as he does; the third asks why some children are labeled delinquent while so many others who behave similarly are not.

The differences among these competing orientations are neither inconsequential nor "purely academic." They are of great importance in the day-to-day operations of the juvenile justice system, and to all its personnel. The decision to offer help must always wait upon a determination of what type of help is needed. It is exactly on this point that the orientations differ; and the matter is complicated because even *within* each camp there are significant differences of opinion.

Within the individual-oriented camp there are deep schisms between the geneticists, the psychologists, and the sociologists; and even within those subgroups there are major disagreements. Community-oriented theoreticians cannot agree over the definition of relevant communities, let alone over the significance to be attributed to different components of community structure. The labeling perspective is fairly new; thus, there has not been sufficient time for major internal differences to appear. There does, however, seem to be utility in dividing the labeling approach into two perspectives: one social-psychological, and the other political.

This chapter does not attempt to discuss all existing theories of delinquency (which probably could not be done in less than an entire book), but rather presents an overview of the differences and conflicts within and among these major orientations. Our goal is to allow the reader to begin to make personal judgments about the nature of delinquency — judgments that he is obliged to make before he can determine what a good juvenile justice system *ought to do* about delinquency.

The Individual-Oriented Camp

Individual-oriented criminology relies heavily on positivism, a philosophy of knowledge developed in the nineteenth century and nurtured in the twentieth. Positivism views worthwhile knowledge as that which can be supported by concrete evidence, and tends to look disapprovingly upon "knowledge" which is based on faith, intuition or pure reason. Pure positivists are not inclined to believe in anything unless its existence can be verified empirically — that is, through the collection of sensory data.[4] Clearly then, early positivists were in sharp conflict with the religious attitudes that dominated nineteenth-century society. In that context Charles Darwin emerges not only as a brilliant scientist, but also as an important positivist philosopher. His contribution to the development of positivist respectability was the successful amassing of empirically obtained data in a manner which made it possible to answer questions about the origins of biological species which men had previously answered only through faith in the account provided in the story of Genesis.[5]

Darwin's influence in biology was obviously very great; however, his influence in other disciplines cannot be minimized. He set creative thinkers in many fields to the task of paralleling his genius — that is, to amassing evidence that would allow men to be certain (positive) about how things come to exist. In criminology, the relevant question was: How does crime come to be? Given the specific content of Darwin's work, it is not surprising that answers to this query were first sought in the field of biology.

Biogenetic Explanations of Delinquency

The biogenetic school has never claimed the ability to explain all deviance. Its earliest and most prominent theoretician, an Italian physician named Cesare Lombroso (1835 - 1909), claimed that his theoretical model explained only about one-third of all crime.[6] While that model has been thoroughly discredited, it is quite likely that a more modest biogenetic thesis is still useful in explaining some (probably small) amount of crime and delinquency.

Lombroso's "Born Criminal"

Drawing heavily on Darwin's thinking about the evolutionary descent of man from earlier ape-like species, Lombroso postulated that criminals are throwbacks to earlier, more primitive types of men. The theory came to him as a consequence of observing and examining inmates in Italian prisons. Lombroso argued that inferior physical and mental inheritances cause some individuals to be "born criminals." More specifically, he maintained that such criminals are possessed of inferior biological and neurological features similar to those found in apes and lower primates, and that these traits are accompanied by a tendency to behave in the same manner as ancestral (and presumably vicious) types of man. It was clear to Lombroso that such inferior, pathological individuals would be unable to conform to the rules and expectations of modern civilized societies.[7]

These ideas came to Lombroso as a consequence of observing and examining inmates in Italian prisons. Apparently the whole theory "jelled" while Lombroso was performing an autopsy on the body of a particularly infamous offender. Opening the skull, he found a strange depression on the interior of the lower back part which reminded him of similar features on the skulls of lower animals. This observation apparently had the force of revelation for Lombroso; from it, and "corroborating" observations of seemingly innocent facts he took a mighty (and perhaps far-fetched) intellectual leap. Consider his own words:

> At the sight of that skull, I seemed to see all of a sudden, lighted up as a vast plain under a flaming sky, the problem of the nature of the criminal — an atavistic being who reproduces in his person the ferocious instincts of primitive humanity and the inferior animals. Thus were explained anatomically the enormous jaws, high cheek-bones, prominent superciliary arches, solitary lines in the palms, extreme size of the orbits, handle-shaped or sessile ears found in criminals, savages, and apes, insensibility to pain, extremely acute sight, tattooing, excessive idleness, love of orgies, and the irresistible craving for evil for its own sake, the desire not only to extinguish life in the victim, but to mutilate the corpse, tear its flesh, and drink its blood.[8]

The intellectual atmosphere in those years just after the publication of Darwin's most important works was such that Lombroso's ideas received more widespread acceptance than they probably would have at any time before or since that era. The scientific tenor of the time required that those who objected to Lombrosian notions develop empirical support for their arguments. The concept of the born criminal was refuted in two principal ways. One approach was simply to observe large numbers of criminals and systematically record the incidence of the physical characteristics described by Lombroso; two such studies yielded no support for Lombroso's assertions. The major refutation of Lombroso of this type was published in 1913 by an English prison doctor, Charles Goring.[9] Evidence derived from his compilation of 3000 cases indicated that the enormous jaws, high cheek-bones, huge eyes, and sessile ears characteristic of Lombroso's "criminal man" simply did not appear with sufficient frequency. In 1924 another Englishman, Cyril Burt, demonstrated that delinquents in London did indeed have different physical characteristics than the general population, but that these differences (delinquents tended to be shorter, less intelligent, and less healthy) were attributable to social factors such as poverty and malnutrition.[10] Thus, the Lombrosian position was further weakened.

The other major strategy of refutation involved the study of twins. Fraternal twins (from two separate egg cells) are no more alike (except, of course, in age) than usual siblings, but identical twins (from a single fertilized egg cell that splits) result in two biogenetically identical persons.[11] Now, if criminality (or delinquency) is genetically determined, then *every* identical twin who is a criminal ought to have an identical twin who is also a criminal, while the concordance of criminality among fraternal twins need not be expected to be very great at all. A study of all the twins born in Denmark between 1890 and 1910 (6000 pairs) demonstrated that the concordance rate among identical twins was only 36 percent.[12] True, that's high; but anything less than 100 percent indicates that genetic inheritance *alone* cannot explain the propensity to crime; there must be additional social or psychological factors of relevance. However, the finding that the concordance rate among fraternal twins was only about 12 percent[13] indicates that the genetic component of criminality cannot be dismissed outright. If biology is not a determinant of criminality, how can it be explained that the concordance rate amongst genetically identical twins is so much higher than among genetically nonidentical twins?

Theoreticians firmly committed to the view that biological factors are of no relevance (those who believe that criminality is determined entirely by environmental factors) sometimes argue in this vein — that monozygotic (identical) twins have more nearly identical environments than dizygotic (fraternal) twins. Because monozygotic twins always look very, very much alike, it is possible that they get treated more similarly (more nearly identically) than other twins. Having more nearly identical environments, they may be more likely to develop very similar behavior patterns; and that, it is argued, may explain the higher incidence of two-twin criminality among identicals.[14] This theory seems plausible, but not altogether convincing.

An additional factor may help to resolve the issue. Some types of unusual crimes seem to be committed by individuals with mental abnormalities. Crime among middle-aged prosperous men, for example, is relatively uncommon (with, perhaps, the exception of white-collar crime). Psychiatrists are generally of the opinion that such unusual occurrences are indications of pathological conditions;[15] and there is solid evidence for the proposition that some such abnormality may be genetically determined.[16] Thus one might expect that among monozygotic twins rates of concordance in crime would be greatest when atypical crimes are involved. That is exactly what the study in Denmark found.

Chromosomal Anomalies

Long before most of the readers of this book were born, criminologists had come to accept that whatever the influence of biology might be, the Lombrosian concept of "born criminals" was just plain wrong. Then, in the late 1960s the idea experienced a brief renaissance when genetics researchers found a chromosomal anomaly (imperfection) which seemed to correlate with certain types of criminality. The potential significance of XYY chromosomes seemed to some, for a fleeting moment, to be very great.[17]

Chromosomes are threadlike bodies located in all living cells, which carry genes in some linear order. Genes, of course, are the bits of matter through which inheritable traits are transmitted from one generation to the next.

Sexuality, for example, is an inherited trait, determined at the moment of conception by the combination of genes found in the fertilized egg. In humans the cluster of genes which determine sexuality are carried in every cell by chromosomes that actually look like the letters X and Y. Every female has two X chromosomes; and every male has one X chromosome and one Y. Egg cells and sperm cells have only one such chromosome apiece. Because a woman has only X chromosomes, her egg cells can contain only X chromosomes. Because a man has both an X and a Y chromosome, his sperm cells may have either. Thus, the sex of a newborn child is determined at conception by the "accident" of whether an X-carrying or a Y-carrying sperm cell reaches and fertilizes the egg first.[18]

It happens from time to time that an embryo is conceived of normal parents, but with a chromosomal abnormality. Sometimes, for example, a child is born who has in every cell in its body only a single sex-determining chromosome. Such children are afflicted with a disorder called Downes Syndrome, or mongolism; they are characterized by a wide, flat skull, narrow slanting eyes, and greatly impaired intelligence.[19]

In the late 1960s it was demonstrated that men are sometimes born with an extra Y chromosome (XYY), and that the incidence of this disorder was greater among men found in institutions for the criminally insane than in the general population.[20] Note that the evidence was not that all, or even most, such inmates have the XYY anomaly, but only that there are more XYYs per thousand people in penal institutions than there are per thousand in your home town, or in your dormitory. The disorder, which is exceedingly rare in society, is merely *quite* rare in hospitals for the criminally insane. If all, or even most, of the examined inmates had turned out to have the extra chromosome, the "born criminal" concept would have resurfaced with force. The fact that the vast majority of examined inmates are genetically normal, combined with the fact that some XYYs are not criminally insane, kept the Lombrosian model from being significantly revitalized.

The likeliest explanation of the relationship between XYY chromosomes and crime is that the genetic anomaly is associated with physical and neurological conditions which make it unlikely that the afflicted individual will be able to compete successfully. XYYs tend to be very tall but badly coordinated. They seem generally to be of subnormal intelligence; and they seem to have low tolerance for frustration.[21] Uncoordinated, comparatively unintelligent individuals who are easily frustrated are quite likely to be separated out for ridicule, deprived of access to rewarding behavior, and perhaps even goaded into committing antisocial acts. They are most likely to be found at the periphery of society rather than in positions of respect or authority. Prisons, mental hospitals and reform schools are places in which societies store such peripheral people. The defect does not compel individuals to turn to crime, but it does make it likely that they will not achieve success in conventional ways. What's more, it probably ensures that if they do turn to crime, they will fail at that too, and will wind up apprehended.

The XYY anomaly is not *the* explanation of criminality, nor even *an* explanation; but neither can it be regarded as irrelevant to criminology. This marginal but undismissable assessment is generally a fair one to apply to theories stemming from the biogenetic approach.

Thus, while Lombroso's explanation of the relationship between biology and crime seems plainly to have been wrong, and his estimate of the importance of genetic factors seems plainly to have been exaggerated, the significance of biogenetics cannot be dismissed outright.

Psychological Explanations of Delinquency

Positive criminology has generated a broad range of individual-oriented explanations of crime. The unifying theme that can be found in all positivist theories is that delinquents are meaningfully different from non-delinquents, and that the differences are determined by factors which are *beyond individual control.* The theories diverge on the question of causes — what types of factors actually determine delinquency. Lombrosians, with their emphasis on inherited physical traits, exist at one pole of the positivist camp. At the opposite pole are found sociologists and social psychologists who, while still focusing on individuals, seek the determinants of human behavior in the social environment. Between these poles of positivist thinking, there exist two main schools of psychological theory — behaviorism and psychoanalysis. The behaviorists, with their heavy emphasis on psychophysiology, are closest to the biogeneticists. The psychoanalysts (used here to mean all humanistic clinical psychologists as well as Freudians) are closest to the social environmentalists.

Behaviorism

Much of current behaviorist psychology stems from the concept of conditioning which was first developed in work with dogs by the Russian scholar, Ivan Pavlov. By ringing a bell just before feeding his dogs, Pavlov was able to demonstrate that after a while they would salivate automatically at the sound of the bell, even when no food was presented.[22] The dogs' future behavior had become predetermined by learning from past experience. Similar conditioned responses can be demonstrated in human beings. If every time a bell is rung, a puff of air is blown in your eye, you will soon start blinking at the sound of bells, even if you don't want to.[23]

It is certainly plausible that much more complex forms of human behavior are determined by similar mechanisms. One theory, for example, asserts that infants acquire the self-restraint which underlies all social conformity through a process of conditioned avoidance; that is, learning (being conditioned) to avoid situations and behaviors that cause us to experience pain or fear. Screaming, punching, pulling hair, and urinating on the cat are youthful behaviors that are generally followed by slaps or other punishments that result in fear or pain (or both).

> Thus, frequent repetition of punishment, by means of the conditioning mechanism, gradually establishes an automatic conditioned reaction of anxiety and withdrawal in the face of situations liable to provoke bad behavior. The process is aided by a characteristic of conditioning, known technically as generalization, whereby avoidance responses readily become linked with a wide range of associated stimuli. Furthermore, in humans, because of the ability to increase associations by the use of language, and in this context to define a wide range of behavior as bad, conditioned avoidance reactions can be greatly reinforced and extended.[24]

Conditioning of the type done by Pavlov is fairly easy to extinguish (undo). If you ring the bell a few times without presenting food, the dogs soon cease to salivate at its sound. Similarly, people who have been conditioned to blink at the sound of a bell (or at any other stimulus) soon stop if the stimulus is presented without a puff of air.[25] All that is required for the extinguishing of a Pavlovian response is an opportunity for new learning. But avoidance conditioning (the second type mentioned) is much harder to extinguish, precisely because its very nature makes new learning unlikely.[26] A child who has been successfully conditioned not to punch his sister will go on not punching her; thus, he will not have an opportunity to punch her and escape punishment, which presumably would weaken the conditioning. Avoidance conditioning, once completed, tends to be self-perpetuating.

Both the ease with which such conditioning takes place and its persistence vary from individual to individual. An experiment performed with puppies is illustrative. A group of young pups were conditioned to avoid a particular dish of food; whenever they approached it, they were swatted with a piece of newspaper. Later, with the experimenter absent but observing, the puppies were put back into the room with that dish. Some overcame their conditioning speedily. Others whined and complained for a while, but finally got down to eating. Some fasted for so long that they had to be rescued from the situation.[27]

In attempting to explain such behavioral differences, psychologists tend to express themselves in biological terms, for it is probable that the variability in the persistence of conditioned responses is related to inborn differences in physical, neurological mechanisms. In short, humans, like puppies, are probably born with differing capacities to become and remain conditioned. As anyone who has ever raised puppies will know, some can be conditioned to avoid behaviors (such as jumping on the sofa) with very little punishment, while others require an ongoing struggle. Similarly, some of us will be conditioned to blink at the sound of a bell after only a very few puffs of air, while others will be able to resist blinking for a longer "training" period.

Perhaps it is obvious by now that the criminological theory that all this is leading toward is simply that delinquents are individuals who fail to learn social expectations because of inborn neurological deficiencies in their capacity to develop and retain conditioned responses.[28] The prominent English psychologist, H. J. Eysenck, claims that research with the most extreme of the badly behaved delinquent types shows that they are both slow to develop conditioned responses and fast to lose them.[29] Similar findings have been produced in research with badly behaved, poorly socialized brain-damaged children.[30]

Eysenck's position is not that criminality is caused solely by neurological difficulties in conditioning, but rather by a cluster of physical, physiological, and psychological traits, all of which are determined to some extent by heredity. According to this behavioristic view, criminals are mesomorphs (people with muscular, sturdy body types, neither frail nor flabby) who are not only resistant to conditioning but also clumsy in performing psychomotor skills (such as moving a pencil through a printed maze without touching any of the printed lines marking the border of the maze). In addition, they are extroverts (cheerful, outgoing, sociable individuals), and tend to be neurotic (emotionally unstable in the face of stress).[31]

While there is some research that tends to confirm the existence of these traits in delinquent populations, it can hardly be said to be conclusive. First of all, while such individuals are found in prisons and reform schools, so too are they found outside; and even inside institutions, there are many other types of inmates. In fact, quiet introverted types seem especially common among repeated offenders. Another weakness in the research is that it focuses on known delinquents. The results tell us nothing about the psychophysiological characteristics of individuals whose law-breaking behavior never comes to the attention of the authorities. It is at least conceivable that such behavioral traits as psychomotor clumsiness correlate not so much with the commission of delinquent acts as with the propensity to be caught for them.

Psychodynamic Explanations

Humanistic psychologists (those interested in the internal dynamics of human personality) disagree with the behaviorists not so much on the adequacy of their evidence as on their dismissal of such important human characteristics as love and hate. The behaviorists, in turn, reject the humanistic approach because of its emphasis on unconscious mental processes, which by their very nature are incapable of being directly observed or measured. Essentially, the behaviorists take the position that unobservable and unmeasurable phenomena fall within the scope of philosophy or theology rather than science.

Without entering into the argument about whether the psychodynamic approaches are scientific, it can nevertheless be asserted that they are products of the intellectual revolution called positivism. Like all positivist approaches to the study of crime and delinquency, humanistic psychology asserts (1) that there are significant differences between delinquents and nondelinquents, (2) that these differences can be demonstrated through rigorous observation and study of individuals, and (3) that criminality is caused (determined) by these differences.

The schism between the geneticists and psychophysiologists on the one hand and the humanistic psychologists on the other resides in their beliefs about the nature of these crucial individual differences. The psychoanalytic view has been succinctly stated by Franz Alexander and Hugo Staub:

> The majority of criminals are not different physically and grossly psychologically from the normal individual; the deviation from the normal is a matter of development, which depends more on the life history of the person than upon heredity; in other words, the greatest number of criminals could under different circumstances have developed into normal individuals.[32]

There is a broad range of humanistic approaches associated with such outstanding psychologists as Erik Erikson,[33] Harry Stack Sullivan,[34] Karen Horney,[35] Carl Jung,[36] and many others, which attempt to understand individual behavior as determined by life history. At the root of all these, however, are the psychoanalytic theories developed by Sigmund Freud. The purpose of this chapter is not to catalog *all* existing relevant theories about the cause of delinquency, but only to reflect on the main elements of criminological theory; thus, it seems reasonable to examine the humanist camp by drawing two examples from Freudian psychology: neurotic delinquency and psychopathic delinquency. First, however, it may be necessary to review the basics of psychoanalytic thinking.

Humanistic psychology has been very influential in the development of programs for the treatment and prevention of delinquency. It is important to be familiar with psychoanalytic contructs, even if you don't like them, because many professionals who work with delinquents have been trained in

*the humanistic psychological tradition, and a
significant number of programs are based on the
image of man pioneered by Freud.*

Freudians posit that human personality is composed of three main forces: id, ego, and superego.[37] The id, which is with us from birth, seeks pleasure; it drives us to satisfy primitive instincts. In its pursuit of gratification it is unconcerned about the rights of others; indeed, it may even be unaware of the existence of others. Early in infancy, however, we begin to learn about an external reality with which we must cope. There are other people who can provide or deny food, cuddling, and other types of satisfaction; there are physical barriers (such as the sides of cribs) which, if ignored, can cause pain. Thus, even in very young children there is a psychological force that is very much in touch with the outside world; this force is called ego. Superego, the third force, develops later in childhood. Essentially, it is the conscience developed in response to demands made by others. As children begin to exert control over themselves and to internalize the standards of the adults they love, superego emerges. Generally all three of these forces exist in full bloom by age six or seven. From then on every human action is a compromise between the desire for pleasure (id), the sense of guilt (superego), and the mediating influences of the ego.

It sometimes happens, however, that an individual suffers an imbalance among the forces in favor of the superego. Such a person endures a constant feeling of guilt, even though his behavior may be exemplary, because he cannot tolerate the existence of his aggressive and sexual desires. Because his guilt feelings derive from normal impulses (normal in the sense that we all have them) rather than from deeds actually committed, such a person is said to be neurotic. If the guilt feelings become overwhelming it can become necessary for the person to commit an act that will result in punishment — because only punishment can expiate his feeling that he deserves to be punished. Thus, neurotic criminality is motivated not by lust or greed, but by guilt.[38] This dynamic may be clearly seen in, for example, the case of the affluent, middle-aged housewife who shoplifts items she could easily afford to buy.[39] Arguably, a good deal of delinquency is similarly motivated.

Psychopathic criminality is of a somewhat different order. Whereas the neurotic is guilt ridden even before he misbehaves, the psychopath is guiltless even after. His superego is weak and unformed; thus, his instinctual impulses are restrained only by considerations of what he can get away with — and sometimes not even by that. The psychopath is a totally antisocial character: self-centered, overbearing, unable to delay gratification, and capable of lying or stealing or cheating without remorse. Perhaps most important, he lacks the capacity to form the loving, stable attachments to others which provide most of us with the incentive to behave in considerate and even altruistic ways.[40]

As different as these two disorders seem to be, they have one thing in common. They are both developmental in nature, the product of life experiences rather than genetic or neurological defects. Both the guilt of the neurotic and the guiltlessness of the psychopath are seen, by Freudians, to be the product of early childhood experiences. Neurotic conflict is associated with strict and repressive parents whose rigid morality is internalized by the child in the form of a conscience which will not permit the experiencing of aggressive or sexual feelings without guilt or anxiety. Psychopathy is believed to be the product of maternal deprivation in the first months and years of infancy. It is the first relationship, to mother, that forms the prototype for all future relationships.

> A loving relationship acts as a powerful incentive to conformity, since rebellion or badness risks the withdrawal of love, upon which the child feels utterly dependent. When the maternal relationship is less close, as for instance if the parents are over-burdened, preoccupied, uninterested or neglectful, opportunity to learn and absorb the rules is correspondingly reduced, and the situation is worse still if the parents are inconsistent, sometimes condoning and sometimes punishing a particular act. If mother is positively hostile towards the child, the threat of further rejection loses its force, so the child obeys when under observation, but acquires no internal constraints. In short, unloving, erratic, and neglectful parents, by failing to teach their babies to curb their impulses properly, and by failing to inspire a restraining ideal or superego, leave an indelible mark upon the character of their offspring, who risk growing up into anti-social adults with a permanent incapacity for love and kindness.[41]

The acid test of any theoretical explanation of delinquency is its capacity to describe criminal types that actually exist in the real world. In this regard the psychoanalytic approach, like the genetic and psychophysiological approaches, is less than altogether satisfactory. There are simply too many delinquents who are neither neurotic nor psychopathic; and conversely, there are too many neurotics (and perhaps even a few psychopaths) who seem able to satisfy their impulses and irrational needs without recourse to crime.

The vast majority of delinquents are not sufficiently affectless (emotionless), unloving, and unloved to be considered psychopaths. And the vast majority of crimes are altogether too rational (in pursuit of profit, for example) to be considered neurotic. Psychoanalytic concepts simply do not suffice to explain all delinquency. They do, however, seem especially useful in attempts to understand two elements of delinquency: (1) unusual crimes, and (2) the behavior of persistent and especially troublesome offenders.

Sociological Explanations of Delinquency

As we have seen, positivism has a general meaning (knowledge must be based on empirical, scientific inquiry) and a meaning that is special to criminology (delinquency is caused by harmful individual differences). While sociologists regard themselves as scientific positivists, they generally resist being identified as criminological positivists. Sociology, after all, is concerned not with individual differences, but with the study of groups, communities, and societies. Nevertheless much of sociological criminology proceeds from the positivists' assumption that delinquents are different from nondelinquents, and it does attempt to explain those individual differences. Where Lombrosians find the determinants of delinquency in genetic inheritance, and Freudians find them in intrapsychic conflict, sociologists find them in environmental influences on the individual. The branch of sociology which strives to understand the development of attitudes and values as a function of environmental pressures is best characterized as social psychology. The point has already been made that psychoanalysts are also very concerned about the impact of environmental pressures, because they are thought to guide the development of the ego and superego. There are, however, important differences between these approaches. Psychoanalysis focuses on the early-childhood experiences which form character and personality; subsequent life experiences, which may or may not precipitate specific delinquent acts, are seen as secondary. Social psychologists are not primarily concerned with the formulation of character in infancy because they view socialization as an ongoing process. Their focus is on attitudes and values as they develop and change in response to current life experiences.[42]

The theory of differential association,[43] developed by Edwin

Sutherland, is based firmly on the belief that delinquency is learned in later life rather than induced in infancy. Essentially, Sutherland argues that delinquents are mentally healthy individuals who have learned criminality from interactions with "significant others" in their environment. We all have associations with people we like and respect who teach us restraint as well as with people we like and respect who may teach us that it's okay to bend the rules some. Ultimately, according to differential association, our behavior is determined by the comparative weights of these sets of associations. Youngsters who grow up in poor neighborhoods with bad schools are more likely to have contacts with delinquent peer groups and with older persons of confirmed antisocial attitudes; from these sources they learn both the attitudes and skills associated with delinquency.

> Everyone is to some extent exposed to conflicting possibilities, temptations and restraints, but where the young person perceives or experiences more in favour of crime than against it, he will become delinquent. On this theory, the budding criminal strives for money, status and happiness just like everyone else, but the attitudes with which he has come into contact, especially in his strongest personal relationships, have been such as to teach him unlawful rather than lawful ways of attaining his ends.[44]

There are obvious and important differences between this theoretical model and all the others in the positivist camp. First of all, it regards the delinquent as healthy and normal, afflicted with neither biological nor psychological defects. In addition, it emphasizes, to a much greater extent than any of the other positivist theories, the impact of forces outside the individual. Nevertheless, it satisfies the important requirements of positive criminology: differential association regards delinquents as different (socially, rather than genetically or psychologically) from nondelinquents; and it views these differences (derived from differential associations) as causal or determining.

Theories of this type seem, on first glance to focus primarily on environmental pressures; but in fact, they focus on individual reactions to environmental pressures. This emphasis on the individual's behavior may perhaps be seen most clearly in the theory of gang delinquency developed by Albert Cohen.[45]

According to Cohen, social life is inherently frustrating for lower-class boys because success in education and in the world of work is reserved for youngsters with middle-class ideas, values, skills, and contacts. Middle-class child-rearing practices tend to emphasize am-

bition, self-discipline, and the constructive use of leisure time (for example, piano lessons or the Boy Scouts); thus, they tend to inculcate the skills and attitudes which facilitate the attainment of success in school and in later life. Lower-class child-rearing habits, on the other hand, tend to emphasize freedom and spontaneity rather than self-discipline and ambition; thus, they prepare children less adequately for school and business, both of which are essentially middle-class operations. Contact with the social establishment, both in schools and in the job market, causes lower-class boys to become aware of their inferior status. Some of these boys respond to their discomfort by rejecting middle-class values altogether, and by ridiculing conventional morality and respectability. In delinquent gangs, such boys come together in order to reinforce one another's sense of adequacy by confirming the rejection of middle-class values, and by conferring status on members according to their daring and skill in executing such antisocial behaviors as theft, vandalism, and fighting.

There are weaknesses in both Cohen's and Sutherland's theories. Neither is very satisfactory in explaining middle- and upper-class delinquency, of which there is apparently a significant and increasing amount. Neither does well in explaining why individuals from the same community, who have had very similar life experiences, often pursue very different careers. Both, however, square nicely with the fact that officially recognized delinquency is largely a lower-class phenomenon,[46] and with the fact that neighborhoods (in which social environment is presumably more or less equal for all residents) tend to breed characteristic types of offenses.[47] As with the other positivist theories thus far described, these two do not seem adequate as explanations of all delinquency, but they do appear to have utility in explaining some.

Theoreticians like Cohen and Sutherland stand at the far edge of the positivist camp. Their emphasis on individuals is obviously much weaker than Lombroso's or Freud's.

You might want to think about the implications of all these different theories for social action. While positivist theories differ dramatically about the relative significance of physical, psychological, and social determinants of behavior, all tend to view delinquents as different from ordinary people. This position seems to suggest that intervention in the lives of delinquents is the way to deal with the crime problem. What sorts of intervention would different theoreticians advocate? It is important to think about such questions if one is going to understand how juvenile justice systems function or, more importantly, if one is interested in trying to make them function better.

The next cluster of sociological theories to be examined depart even further from emphasis on individual differences; thus, they fall outside the camp of criminological positivists altogether.

Community-Oriented Criminology

Individual-oriented theories assert that (1) delinquents are different from nondelinquents and (2) criminology is therefore the study of individual differences. Community-oriented theories accept that delinquents and nondelinquents behave differently but holds that these behavioral differences are to so great an extent caused by environmental pressures that criminology ought to concentrate on the study of social conditions rather than on the persons who commit crimes.

The most basic theory of this type links delinquency to poverty. The earliest socioeconomic theories asserted that the degradation of want, unemployment, idleness, and hunger conspires to debase men and destroy their inherent nobility of character, thus forcing them towards savagery and criminality. Early studies attempted to correlate crime rates with fluctuations in the economic cycle. Thus, nineteenth-century economists found that crime rates varied with the price of wheat and rye. The assumption underlying such studies is that as the price of basic commodities rises, relative poverty increases, and men become hungry and crime prone. It is possible, of course, that the assumption is mistaken. In the United States there have been many years in which wages have increased when prices did, and many in which relative poverty appears to have declined despite price increases.

A more impressive study of this type was conducted by the English criminologist Cyril Burt,[48] who demonstrated that 56 percent of London's identified delinquents came from the poorest 30.7 percent of the population. Thus, poor populations seem to be more prone to criminality (or is it only to being caught?) than middle- and upper-class populations. In any event, Burt's study cuts two ways, for it also demonstrates that a significant percentage of criminals come from the ranks of the comfortable classes, thus weakening the argument that poverty is the cause of crime. The argument is further weakened by the knowledge that sometimes even the very rich become delinquent, and that there are some crimes (such as tax evasion, corporate crimes, and even embezzlement) which can be committed only by the affluent.

There are, however, more sophisticated community-oriented explanations of crime and delinquency. In this section, four will be examined: (1) the socioeconomic class theory of Walter B. Miller, (2) Marxist theory, (3) anomie theory, particularly as developed by Robert Merton and Albert Cohen, and (4) opportunity theory, particularly as developed by Richard Cloward and Lloyd Ohlin.

A Theory of Social Class

Miller has theorized that gang delinquency is rooted in the cultural traditions of lower-class life — that is, of those people who are at the bottom of the social heap, and for whom there is little prospect of success. The culture of the lower class is characterized by a complex web of structural elements and "focal concerns."[49]

A major structural characteristic of lower-class life described by Miller is the female-based household, which results from the practice of serial monogamy. In serial monogamy, women become involved in repetitive sequences of mate finding, cohabitation, and desertion or divorce by the male. The children in such a household are likely to be the progeny of several different fathers and are likely to have a strong relationship only with their shared mother. Women in such households provide economic as well as emotional support for the entire family unit.

> For the boy who grows up in the female-dominated family, life is fraught with anxieties about sex-role identification. The young male is assaulted on all sides by verbal assertions that men are "no damn good." From this situation there flows a concern on the boy's part for becoming a "real man" as quickly as possible. The male adolescent peer group, territorially located on city streets, provides the training ground and milieu in which lower-class males seek a sense of maleness, status, and belonging.[50]

Life experiences for young lower-class gang members are shaped by the same "focal concerns" that exist in the larger poverty community. Miller describes these focal concerns as "trouble," "toughness," "smartness," "excitement," "fate," and "autonomy." Trouble refers to the omnipresent anxiety about encounters with the police or other agents of social control. Toughness requires continued demonstration of bravery and daring in order to prove that one is not weak. Smartness refers to the ability to live by one's wits, to earn a living through a "hustle" rather than through hard work. Excitement is Miller's term for the gang members' pervasive concern for seeking out activities that disrupt the monotony of day-to-day life. Fate represents the belief of lower-class individuals that life is dominated by forces beyond the control of individuals (luck or superstition). Autonomy refers to the basic and important need of lower-class individuals to feel that they are not dominated or controlled by others.

Delinquency, then, is seen by Miller as the product of two things: (1) *community structural elements,* which drive young, lower-class males into mutually supporting gangs; and (2) the "focal concerns" of all lower-class people with such things as bravery, independence, luck, and street smartness. Youngsters misbehave not because they are bad or ill, but because they are impinged upon by a complex set of pressures and fears which drive them toward gangs, and which drive the gangs toward acting-out behavior (behavior that relieves tensions by expressing them). It is the culture of the slum, then, that gives rise to the delinquency of its inhabitants.

Several criticisms of this theoretical model are possible. For one thing, it tells us very little about nongang delinquency or about gangs in middle- and upper-class neighborhoods. Further, the theory tells us nothing about varieties of gang behavior: why do some steal while others fight?[51]

Marxist Criminology

Marxist criminologists, such as the Dutchman W. A. Bonger,[52] view delinquency as a problem caused not by the culture of a particular social class, but by the culture of the entire society; more specifically, the Marxist sees delinquency as a predictable response to the pressures generated by capitalist economic systems. To the Marxist it is not poverty that debases a fundamentally noble mankind; rather, it is the profit motive. Capitalist society is organized around the free marketplace, in which the greatest rewards go to the most cunning businessmen. It is argued that the lesson of capitalist institutions to the individuals who live with them is simply this: "Look out for number one. Try to get the best deal you can for yourself because that is what everyone else is trying to do for himself." According to the Marxist, the competition of the free marketplace tends to undermine the higher human values, such as cooperation and altruism. Crime, then, is seen as the natural consequence of an economic system that reinforces the greedy and self-serving aspects of men rather than the generous and selfless.

There are some problems inherent in this approach. Perhaps the most significant is that its obvious implication, that crime will disappear in a Marxist society, does not seem to square with the observed facts. Communist countries tend not to keep very good criminological statistics (or at least not to publish them), so it is impossible to know the extent to which such self-serving acts as theft continue to occur in Russia or in China or in Cuba; there is strong evidence, however, that property crimes (such as resisting collectivization) and political crimes continue to exist. For conspicuous examples one need only read such books as *One Day in the Life of Ivan Denisovitch*[53] or *Gulag Archipelago.*[54]

In any event, whatever the merit of Marxist criminological theories, one must observe that the Marxist approach has never been very dynamic in the West.

Anomie Theory

Anomie theory focuses not just on the nature of a community's economic institutions but on the quality of social life within the community. The term anomie was coined by the French sociologist, Emile Durkheim, to describe a form of social malaise that occurs when the restraining pressures of tradition and social custom are weakened, so that people find themselves uncertain about how they are supposed to behave.[55] In tradition-bound societies everyone knows what is expected of him, and people tend to suffer hardship without protest. In modern industrial societies progress tends to destroy tradition, and the rules of acceptable social behavior change from generation to generation. Increases in social mobility and in affluence create whole new career possibilities; the sons of coal miners can become physicians or physicists or millionaires. Individuals feel that their horizons are limitless, and therein lies the problem; for with limitless ambition the prospects for dissatisfaction, disillusionment, and frustration become great. In anomic societies it can be expected that there will be considerable unrest and delinquency.

Robert Merton, an American sociologist, has taken the concept a step further. He has redefined anomie as a form of social malaise that arises when a society encourages individuals to achieve success but restricts their access to legitimate means of attaining it.[56] In America success has generally been defined in terms of acquisitions. Our television heroes generally live in very comfortable surroundings. Advertisements present expensive cars and clothing as evidence of success and personal worth. To be a success means to own attractive clothing — whether Brooks Brothers' suits or leather cowboy jackets. To be a success means to live in an attractive home — whether opulent and in an expensive suburb or sparce but by a beautiful beach. To be a success means to drive a fine car — whether it is a Cadillac or a Porsche. Even the counterculture has its trappings of success. While some of us may resist the pressure to acquire status symbols, all of us are exposed to it. Access to the socially approved means of attaining success is greater, however, for people in the middle and upper social classes.

According to one's starting position in the social hierarchy, the social system can act as either a barrier or an open door. Young people with poor backgrounds and education are handicapped in the race towards success symbols, although they are under the same pressure to make good. Hence comes the temptation to take illegitimate short-cuts. Merton and Durkheim agree about the danger of unleashing unrealistic aspirations, but Merton goes on to explain why this should happen especially among the lower classes. In effect, his theory suggests that by organizing itself so as to arouse and then to frustrate lower-class aspirations, society gets the criminals it deserves.[57]

According to anomie theory, then, delinquency is a product of social rather than individual pathology. Merton has suggested several ways in which individuals may respond to life situations in an anomic society. Two are of interest here: retreatism and innovation.[58] Retreatists simply contract out of conventional society: they reject not only the means that society approves but also the success goals that society establishes. Vagrants, skidrow alcoholics, and drug addicts fall into this category. Innovators accept the success goals and strive for affluence and status, but they reject the socially approved means. Some innovators embrace criminal life styles in order to increase their chances of becoming rich and powerful.

The frustrations of life in modern technological societies are seen as driving people to drugs and crime. While these frustrations exist in all strata of society, they are obviously expected to be greatest among the poor and the powerless. One possible source of frustration for lower-class youngsters may be their inability to compete successfully in the educational system. That is the view of Albert Cohen, who derived a theory of gang delinquency from Merton's conception of anomie.[59]

Cohen maintains that lower-class boys — because they are not socialized into such middle-class values as ambition, individual responsibility, delay of gratification, courtesy, and control of physical aggression — have difficulty achieving success in schools which are dominated by middle-class teachers. As they discover they are unprepared to compete in a middle-class environment, lower-class youngsters begin to feel rejected and inferior. They strive to maintain their feeling of self-worth by forming associations with similar youngsters, who can provide support and reinforcement.[60]

The delinquent subculture, we suggest, is a way of dealing with the problems of adjustment we have described. These problems are chiefly

status problems; certain children are denied status in the respectable society because they cannot meet the criteria of the respectable status system. The delinquent subculture deals with these problems by providing criteria of status which these children *can* meet.[61]

Gang delinquency is believed by Cohen to be a reasonable, healthy response to an essentially anomic condition. It is not surprising that the behaviors valued by the gang are antithetical to those valued by the schools. Delinquency is seen by Cohen to be a negative, hostile rejection of middle-class values, made in defense of one's own self-concept. Youngsters denied success at school may react by asserting that they do not aspire to such success at all.

Anomie theories such as Merton's and Cohen's may be criticized on several grounds. They do not explain how some poor ghetto

youngsters escape delinquency and drugs, nor why increasing numbers of affluent youngsters are becoming involved in antisocial behavior. These theories focus on the fact that opportunities for legitimate success are denied, but they do not explain how the opportunities for antisocial behavior arise.

Opportunity Theory

Opportunity theory, developed by Richard Cloward and Lloyd Ohlin,[62] is closely related to anomie theory but focuses attention on how youngsters are presented with opportunities for particular manifestations of gang delinquency. Both models attribute delinquency to an imbalance between culturally induced aspirations among lower-class youth and the possibility of attaining them by legitimate means. Where anomie theory sees delinquency as a healthy response to socially created frustrations, opportunity theory sees it as healthy *learned* response. We all desire to make good, and we all learn, by observing the people around us, how to succeed. Youngsters who grow up in comfortable suburbs learn early in life that people achieve success by becoming doctors, lawyers, architects, etc. All they need to do is look around. They do not know that some people make successes of themselves by becoming pimps or gangsters because they do not see such people. Similarly, children in ghettos who see affluent numbers runners, drug pushers, and prostitutes may have no idea what an architect or an engineer is. In the pursuit of success people can learn to do only whatever there is an opportunity to do. The following exchange, between a social worker and a delinquent gang member, may well be the best available synthesis of opportunity theory:

Q: Why don't you get a job?
A: Oh come on. Get off that crap. I make $40 or $50 a day selling marijuana. You want me to go down to the garment district and push one of those trucks through the street and at the end of the week take home $40 or $50 if I'm lucky? Come off it. They don't have animals doing what you want me to do. There would be some society to protect animals if anybody had them pushing those damn trucks around. I'm better than an animal, but nobody protects me. Go away, mister. I got to look out for myself.[63]

Opportunity theory, like anomie theory, seems particularly useful in explaining lower-class delinquency. It does not, however, explain how some poor youngsters go on to achieve success through the legitimate opportunity system while their neighbors and siblings turn to drugs (retreatist subculture), crime (criminal subculture), or fighting (conflict subculture), nor does it explain middle- and upper-class delinquency. In addition, the point must be made that there is not a great deal of empirically obtained factual evidence to support either of these theories in preference to the other, or, for that matter, in preference to any of the other sociological theories discussed in this chapter.

Think about the implications of some of these community-oriented theories for social action. After all, this book's concern is not with abstract discussions of theory, but with the ways in which programs for the treatment and prevention of delinquency operate, and with ways in which they might operate better. Unlike the positivist approaches, these theories seem to suggest that it is society rather than individuals that must be changed in order to eliminate delinquency. Or is that so? Can you imagine programs designed to provide services to individuals that might be supported by the proponents of these community-oriented theories? What other kinds of programs can you imagine? What might a social action program try to do in order to deal with the problem of delinquency? Subsequent chapters of this book will deal with these questions, but it might be helpful to start thinking about them now.

The Labeling Perspective

There is a clear and important difference between labeling theory, on the one hand, and all the positivist and community-oriented theories on the other: labeling theory holds that there are *no* significant differences between delinquents and nondelinquents. Thus, labeling theoreticians would turn the focus of criminological inquiry away from the study of delinquents and towards the study of the social institutions that define delinquency and process so-called "offenders."

A case example drawn from Kai Erickson's excellent book, *Wayward Puritans*,[64] may prove useful. In 1692 a witchcraft hysteria began in Salem, Massachusetts. The generally good and pious folks who lived in that early New England settlement became convinced that the devil had sent emissaries to live among them in order to destroy that foothold of Christianity in the pagan wilderness. Between June 10 and September 22 of that year, nineteen persons were executed as witches, and one other was pressed to death under a load of rocks in an unsuccessful attempt to extract testimony from him. Obviously, witchcraft was a very serious crime in Salem. Suppose there had been criminologists there; how would they have attempted to explain the phenomenon of so many persons being identified and dealt with as witches?

Presumably, a Lombrosian would have inquired into the biogenetic inheritances of the accused, individuals who had allegedly reverted to vicious and uncivilized standards of behavior. A Freudian might have attempted psychoanalysis in order to understand the witches' innermost psychic tensions. Sociologists might have explained the propensity to witchcraft as the product of differential associations, or of peer pressures, or of bad social and economic conditions. All such lines of inquiry, however, make sense only if one assumes that those poor souls hanged in Salem really had made bargains with the devil and were practicing witchcraft. If one does not believe in the existence of witches, then all the questions raised by traditional criminologists would seem a bit silly. The important questions to ask would be: What were the forces operating in that community which caused a witch-hunt to take place? Why did those people believe in witches? How did community institutions determine which individuals would be selected out to be affixed with the label *deviant?*

In our own society we are inclined to believe that individuals selected out to be processed as deviants really are different from the rest of us. But there's not a lot of evidence to support that belief. All the research done by positivist and community-oriented criminologists who believe in the existence of significant biological or psychological or sociological differences between delinquents and nondelinquents has failed to yield any important information on what the nature of such differences might be.

Perhaps it can be argued that even if we don't understand the nature of the differences between delinquents and nondelinquents, at least we know that they behave differently. But it's not clear that that's true either. Think back to the self-report study included in the first chapter. There's an overwhelming likelihood that you, or your friends, or at least your acquaintances, have engaged in (and probably continue from time to time to engage in) delinquent acts. There is hardly anyone whose behavior is so exemplary that he could not, if caught at a bad moment, be sentenced to prison or reform school. In thinking about this line of argument, remember that the vast majority of criminal acts are against property and do not involve either violence or the threat of violence.[65] Consider how many respected, law-abiding citizens also "offend" against property. Tax evasion provides an interesting example. Literally millions of individuals and businesses defraud the government by lying to the Internal Revenue Service about their income or deductions. Yet little effort is made to stop such crime, and people who are "caught" are rarely prosecuted.[66] White-collar crime provides another interesting example. Millions of individuals and businesses cheat the public by forming illegal cartels in restraint of trade,[67] by fudging data about the safety of products placed on the market,[68] by charging for work that was never done,[69] and by doing work that never needed to be done.[70] These are all explicitly criminal acts; and it is much more likely that you will lose money to such criminals than to robbers or pickpockets, yet few white-collar criminals are ever caught or prosecuted. In truth, although you are more likely to lose money to businessmen who behave illegally than to burglars or sneak-thieves, you are probably less morally outraged by sharp business practices. And there are probably many types of criminal acts that don't bother you at all, such as taking home supplies from the office in which you work, or flying on someone else's youth-fare card, or getting government food stamps for which you are not, strictly speaking, eligible.

The point of all this is not to suggest that any reader of this book is really a terrible, awful person, who ought to be institutionalized, but only to assert that people labelled "delinquent" have no monopoly on the commission of delinquent acts. This line of argument, that delinquents and nondelinquents are really very similar, is enhanced by two further considerations. First, the absolute, total delinquent just doesn't exist. Even the most hardnosed offenders behave like "normal" people most of the time. They eat with knives and forks, they generally refrain from kicking dogs and little old ladies, they probably do not jaywalk or spit on the sidewalk just for the fun of making trouble. Second, the definition of deviance changes from time to time and from society to society. Thus, individuals whose moral character *we* may respect and whose behavior *we* may consider exemplary may be identified as criminals in their own societies. Christ and Socrates, for examples, were both criminals. Contemporarily we may note that literary geniuses in the Soviet Union who might be rich and respected here are sometimes treated as criminals in their homeland. Even here, it must be noted, Nobel Peace Prize winner Martin Luther King spent a fair amount of time in Southern jails, and other black activists and antiwar campaigners who are regarded as heroes by some have been regarded as criminals by others.

Consider, then, that sometimes the best among us act in specifically criminal ways, most of the time even the worst criminals amongst us behave in very normal ways, and on top of that, it is probably impossible to get a broad consensus about what type of behavior ought to be considered deviant in the first place. What is deviance? The labeling perspective offers a straightforward answer: deviance is any behavior that is so labeled by the dominant groups in a society.

> Deviance is not a property *inherent in* any particular kind of behavior; it is a property *conferred upon* that behavior by the people who come into direct or indirect contact with it. The only way an observer can tell whether or not a given style of behavior is deviant, then, is to learn something about the standards of the audience which responds to it.[71]

The best statement of labeling theory may have been written by the novelist, William Faulkner:[72]

> Sometimes I ain't so sho who's got ere a right to say when a man is crazy and when he ain't. Sometimes I think it ain't none of us pure crazy and ain't none of us pure sane until the balance of us talks him that-a-way. It's like it ain't so much what a fellow does, but it's the way the majority of folks is looking at him when he does it.

Thus, labeling theory suggests that the focus of criminological inquiry ought to be on community institutions that deal with crime. The study of delinquency becomes, then, not so much the study of delinquents as the study of the juvenile justice system. Labeling theorists are not primarily interested in why delinquents behave as they do; they are interested in the way in which communities decide how to select out of the total body of persons who break the law the small number who are to be called delinquent. The words of Kai Erikson are instructive:

> It is important to notice that the people of a community take a number of factors into account when they pass judgment on one another which are not immediately related to the deviant act itself: whether or not a person will be considered deviant, for instance, has something to do with his social class, his past record as an offender, the amount of remorse he manages to convey, and many similar concerns which take hold in the shifting mood of the community. Perhaps this is not so apparent in cases of serious crime or desperate (mental) illness, where the offending act looms so darkly that it obscures most of the other details of the person's life; but in the day-by-day sifting processes which take place throughout society this feature is always present. Some men who drink heavily are called alcoholics and others are not, some men who behave oddly are committed to hospitals and others are not, some men with no visible means of support are charged with vagrancy and others are not — and the difference between those who earn a deviant title in society and

those who go their own way in peace is largely determined by the way in which the community filters out and codes the many details of behavior which comes to its attention.[73]

This assertion, that deviants behave much as everyone else does, raises several important questions: How does the labeling mechanism work? Is there some reason it operates as it does, rather than some other way? What impact, if any, does the labeling process have on the individuals who come to be identified as deviant? The first two questions are essentially sociopolitical in nature; the last is social-psychological.

The Political Perspective Within Labeling

Labeling theoreticians are sometimes accused of favoring the underdog. The position that delinquents and nondelinquents are very similar is certainly conducive to the belief that harsh penalities imposed on delinquents are inappropriate and unfair. And labeling theorists do tend to view the social mechanisms for defining deviance and those for processing deviants as biased against minority-group members and the poor.

This line of argument begins with the assertion that the written criminal law is merely a political document which codifies the values and attitudes of the middle- and upper-class individuals who write it. If poor people wrote the law, there might be fewer tax loopholes and more strict prohibitions against sharp business practices. The great American criminal lawyer Clarence Darrow wrote:

> That certain things are forbidden does not mean that these things are necessarily evil, but rather that politicians believe there is a demand for such legislation from the class of society that is most powerful in political action.[74]

The law reflects political power rather than God-given wisdom — a fact we can see proved when we observe how the laws change as different coalitions attain power. Within only a little more than a decade, alcohol, for example, was prohibited and then repermitted in the United States. A more recent fluctuation in our balance of political power has resulted in liberalized abortion laws, but they may well be modified if a conservative coalition reattains dominance. And it is worth noting that the movement for legalization of marijuana has coincided with greater use of that drug by middle- and upper-class youngsters.

As poor people and minority-group members are rarely able to exert considerable political power, they generally have little influence over the ways in which the law gets written. Consequently, labeling theorists argue, justice systems begin with a built-in bias against the interests of the poor.

In addition, the machinery of law enforcement is less likely to come down hard on the comparatively affluent. Middle- and upper-class lawbreakers are likely to be ignored or treated leniently. Tax evasion, for example, is a crime that is available only to members of the comfortable classes; and it is no surprise to any of us that little police effort is expended in trying to achieve deterrence. Similarly, white-collar offenses, which are definitionally available only to members of the middle and upper classes, rarely result in arrests or convictions. On the other hand, offenses which are arguably no more noxious, but which are engaged in by members of the lower class (such as prostitution, vagrancy, public drunkenness, petty larceny, and burglary) receive much more police attention.[75]

The way in which the criminal law is written and enforced may explain why so few affluent people appear in criminal court; and even when they do, it is with the distinct advantage of good counsel. A man who can hire a first-rate lawyer has a much better chance of acquittal than a man who is dependent on a public defender; even if the public defender is competent, he is very likely also to be overworked.[76] Money talks, even in the halls of justice.

The mechanism of selection for determining who will be labeled deviant and who will be ignored seems to be related to social class, according to the labeling theorists. Delinquents are those who are less fortunate than the rest of us. It is not so much what a person does as who he is, and how he does it, that determines whether it is appropriate to call him a "deviant."

But why should that be?

The answer developed by interactionists (labeling theorists) is that societies need deviance in order to define the boundaries of socially acceptable behavior. According to this view, communities exist only when individuals have shared expectations about the ways in which they are supposed to behave. Group membership requires adherence to some set of social rules. One cannot be an Orthodox Jew and eat pork; one cannot be a monk and also a nudist. Most group rules are more subtle than these examples; but the point is that groups generate rules which members *must* learn. But how does this learning take place?

> To begin with, the only material found in society for marking boundaries is the behavior of its members — or rather, the networks of interaction which link these members together in regular social relations. And the interactions which do the most effective job of locating and publicizing the group's outer edges would seem to be those which take place between deviant persons on the one side and official agents of the community on the other. The deviant is a person whose activities have moved outside the margins of the group, and when the community calls him to account for that vagrancy it is making a statement about the nature and placement of its boundaries. It is declaring how much variability and diversity can be tolerated within the group before it begins to lose its distinct shape, its unique identity. . . . (0)n the whole, members of a community inform one another about the . . . (range of acceptable behaviors) by participating in the confrontations which occur when persons who venture out to the edges of the group are met by policing agents whose special business it is to guard the cultural integrity of the community. Whether these confrontations take the form of criminal trials, excommunication hearings, courts-martial, or even psychiatric case conferences, they act as boundary-maintaining devices in the sense that they demonstrate to whatever audience is concerned where the line is drawn between behavior that belongs in the special universe of the group and behavior that does not. In general, this kind of information is not easily relayed by the straightforward use of language. Most readers of this paragraph, for instance, have a fairly clear idea of the line separating theft from more legitimate forms of commerce, but few have ever seen a published statute describing these differences. More likely than not, our information on the subject has been drawn from publicized instances in which the relevant laws were applied. . . .[77]

It can be argued, then, that the labeling of deviance is a process by which the in-group in a society defines its own boundaries. The interaction between deviants and agents of social control demonstrates the limits of the range of behaviors available to individuals who do not wish to become outcasts, outlaws, or outsiders of any type. Thus, the identification of deviants in any society is a reflection of the values and concerns of that society's most powerful elements. In theocratic states, religious conformity is valued, and deviants are recruited from the ranks of the least religious. In authoritarian states, political conformity is valued, and deviants are selected from the ranks of the dissident. In capitalist states, personal wealth is valued, and deviants are selected from the ranks of the poor. In all societies, criminals are valuable social resources because they provide the contrasting background against which shared values can be clearly seen.

The Social-Psychological Perspective Within Labeling

The political argument that societies need deviants raises an intriguing question: do societies actually behave in ways designed to create deviants? Labeling theorists are inclined to answer yes. Indeed, they may even suggest that the creation of deviants is the "real" social function of prisons. Consider that prisons (and reform schools) are places in which marginal people are gathered into tightly segregated groups in which they have the opportunity to share knowledge and skills in the ways to perform illegal acts, and in which they become increasingly alienated from the mainstream of the larger society while simultaneously being exposed intensively to persons with whom they can readily identify in terms of experience and expectations.[78]

Nor are prisons the only social institution that creates and perpetuates deviance. The job market, for example, tends to discriminate against "ex-cons" — despite the touting of the belief that a man who has paid his debt to society deserves a fair chance — and the inability to find work makes crime increasingly attractive as a way for the ex-con to make a living.[79] Perhaps most pernicious of all, the very process of labeling may cause persons for the first time to think of themselves as deviants; thus, the label may become a self-fulfilling prophecy.

In his book, *Delinquency and Drift,*[80] David Matza argues that differences between delinquents and nondelinquents don't begin to exist until the labeling takes place. All youngsters "drift" around illegitimate activities; they experiment with a range of more and less acceptable behaviors. Youngsters who are caught in the commission of a delinquent act and who are processed by social control agencies begin to develop deviant self-concepts and become more deeply enmeshed in patterns of lawbreaking behavior. Juveniles who do not become so labeled have a greater chance of eventually settling into the patterns of behavior that are generally viewed as acceptable. Thus, the psychological perspective within the labeling approach is distinctly antipositivist in nature. Individual differences are seen not as a cause of delinquency but as a consequence of being labeled delinquent.

Reflections on the Labeling Perspective

As with all the theories discussed in this chapter, there are important critical comments that have to be made about the labeling approach. It does not seem, for example, to be a wholly satisfactory explanation of all types of deviance. It tells us something about the importance of social class differences in the selection of individuals for the label "deviant," but very little about the occasional middle- and upper-class persons who also become enmeshed in the justice system. Labeling theory suggests that the fact of being labeled is what drives people to careers of crime. But we can't help thinking that surely some professional criminals exist who have never been caught and thus never labeled. And, if being labeled is what drives people to criminal life styles, how is it that many people who get caught and convicted manage to "go straight"?

Perhaps the most trenchant criticism of labeling is that it is almost entirely a theoretical perspective. There is very little empirical research which tests hypotheses derived from the labeling perspective. And there are some criminologists who are inclined to believe that the complexity of developing experimental tests of the labeling theory is so great that proving (or disproving) it is virtually impossible.

It may be that the greatest utility of the labeling perspective is not so much as a comprehensive explanation of delinquency, but as a far-reaching and potent critique of the assumptions about individual differences which underlie traditional positivist and community-oriented theories. If we cannot be sure that labeling theory is true, at least its existence forces us to the realization that in the area of criminology it is unsafe to assume that traditional "knowledge" and beliefs are true either.

The labeling approach insists that the phenomenon of delinquency can be understood only if one understands the society in which it exists and the particular social institutions in that society which define delinquency and which process individual delinquents. The focus of this book is on those institutions; thus, it may be seen as having derived from the labeling perspective.

At earlier points in this chapter we suggested that you put down the book for a while in order to think about the implications of specific theoretical orientations for strategies to treat and prevent delinquency. That would be a good and useful exercise now, too. Suppose you were convinced by the labeling perspective, what would you want to do? What kinds of programs and strategies might seem appropriate?

Might you just ignore delinquency? Would you seek to deal with delinquent youngsters in any new and different ways?

What you do about a problem depends on what you think causes it. This book is not about delinquency, but about the agencies and programs that deal with it. It is what juvenile justice systems do, and what they ought to do, that is of interest here. But remember, what they do reflects theoretical conceptions about the nature and causes of delinquency, and what you think they ought to do reflects your own theoretical conceptions about those things.

References

1. See generally David Matza, *Delinquency and Drift* (New York: John Wiley & Sons, 1964), pp. 3 - 11.

2. For an excellent collection of readings dealing with cultural and social approaches to the study of delinquency, see Donald Creesey and David Ward, *Delinquency, Crime and Social Problems* (New York: Harper & Row, 1969).

3. For important and interesting conceptual works, see Kai Erikson, *Wayward Puritans* (New York: John Wiley & Sons, 1966); and Howard Becker, *Outsiders: Studies in the Sociology of Deviance* (New York: Free Press, 1967).

4. Webster's New World Dictionary defines "positivism" as "a system of philosophy basing knowledge solely on data of sense experience; especially, a system of philosophy originated by Auguste Comte, based solely on observable, scientific facts and their relations to each other: it rejects speculation about or search for origins."

5. See Charles Darwin, *The Descent of Man, and Selection in Relation to Sex* (New York: D. Appleton, Publishers, 1876). The conflict between religionists and positivists has often been fiery and intense. In 1925, for example, the State of Tennessee enacted legislation prohibiting the teaching of Darwin's theories in public schools. John Scopes, a teacher who violated the law, was prosecuted. He was defended by a team that included Clarence Darrow; the prosecution was assisted by William Jennings Bryan, who had four times been the Democratic candidate for the Presidency of the United States. An interesting account of this exciting trial may be found in L. de Camp, *The Great Monkey Trial* (Garden City: Doubleday, 1968).

6. For an excellent review and commentary on Lombrosian thinking, see Marvin Wolfgang, "Cesare Lombroso," in *Pioneers in Criminology,* 2nd ed., ed. H. Mannheim (Montclair, N.J.: Patterson-Smith, 1972), pp. 257 ff.

7. Ibid., p. 247.

8. Cesare Lombroso, "Introduction" to Gina Lombroso-Ferrero, *Criminal Man According to the Classification of Cesare Lombroso* (New York: G. P. Putnam & Sons, 1911), p. xii.

9. Charles Goring, *The English Convict* (London: H. M. Stationary Of-

fice, 1913); see also J. Michael and M. Adler, *Crime, Law and Social Science* (Montclair, N.J.: Patterson-Smith, 1971), pp. 150 - 2.

10. See Michael and Adler, *Crime and Social Science,* pp. 155 - 7.

11. See J. McCary, *Human Sexuality,* 2nd ed. (New York: D. Van Nostrand, 1973), pp. 137 - 9.

12. See Nigel Walker, *Crime and Punishment in Britain,* 2nd ed. (Edinburgh: Edinburgh University Press, 1968), pp. 49 - 50.

13. Ibid., p. 50.

14. See M. F. Ashley Montagu, "The Biologist Looks at Crime," in *Readings in Criminology and Penology,* 2nd ed., ed. D. Dressler (New York: Columbia University Press, 1972), pp. 250 - 67.

15. Manfred S. Guttmacher, "The Psychiatric Approach to Crime and Correction," in Dressler, *Readings in Criminology,* pp. 294 - 300.

16. Irving Saranson, *Abnormal Psychology: The Problem of Maladaptive Behavior* (New York: Meredith, 1972), pp. 538 - 41.

17. See, for example, "Born Bad?" *Newsweek,* 6 May 1968, 71:87.

18. See McCary, *Human Sexuality,* pp. 38, 71, 72 - 3.

19. J. Thompson and S. Thompson, *Genetics in Medicine,* (Philadelphia: W. B. Saunders, 1966).

20. E. Hook, "Behavioral Implications of the XYY Genotype," *Science,* 73:179, pp. 139 - 50.

21. E. Hook and D. Kim, "Height and Anti-social Behavior in XY and XYY Boys," *Science,* 71:172, pp. 284 - 6.

22. Ivan Pavlov, *Conditioned Reflexes* (New York: Dover Press, 1960).

23. See, for example, H. Braun and R. Geiselhart, "Age Differences in the Acquistion and Extinction of the Conditioned Eyelid Response," *Journal of Experimental Psychology,* 57:1959, pp. 386 - 8.

24. D. J. West, *The Young Offender* (Baltimore: Penguin Books, 1967), p. 140.

25. For a readable introduction to conditioning concepts, see H. Rachlin, *Introduction to Modern Behaviorism* (San Francisco: W. H. Freeman, 1970). The concept of extinction is discussed at pages 66 - 9.

26. Ibid., pp. 151 - 3.

27. These experiments, performed by R. C. Solomon at Harvard University, are discussed in H. Eysenck, *Crime and Personality* (London: Routledge and Kegan Paul, 1964), p. 117.

28. See Gordon Trasler, *The Explanation of Criminality* (London: Routledge and Kegan Paul, 1962); and Gordon Trasler, "Socialization," in *The Formative Years: How Children Become Part of Their Society,* ed. David Edge (New York: Schocken Books, 1970).

29. See West, *Young Offender,* p. 141.

30. Ibid.

31. Ibid., pp. 142 - 5; also see Eysenck, *Crime and Personality.*

32. Franz Alexander and Hugo Staub, *The Criminal, the Judge and the Public* (New York: Collier Books, 1962), p. 51.

33. See, for example, Erik Erikson, *Childhood and Society* (New York: W. W. Norton, 1963).

34. See, for example, Harry Stack Sullivan, *The Interpersonal Theory of*

Psychiatry (New York: W. W. Norton, 1953); also see Harry Stack Sullivan, *The Psychiatric Interview* (New York: W. W. Norton, 1954).

35.   See, for example, Karen Horney, *Our Inner Conflicts* (New York: W. W. Norton, 1945); also see Karen Horney, *Neurosis and Human Growth* (New York: W. W. Norton, 1950).

36.   See, for example, A. Read, M. Fordham, and G. Adler, eds., *The Collected Works of Carl G. Jung* (Princeton: Princeton University Press, 1970).

37.   For a very lucid and readable introduction to the principles of Freudian psychology, see Calvin Hall, *A Primer of Freudian Psychology* (New York: New American Library, 1954). Readers who are interested in the personalities of the great men who created the psychoanalytic movement or who would like to develop an understanding of the historical context in which psychoanalysis was conceived and nurtured might enjoy William McGuire, ed., *The Correspondence Between Sigmund Freud and C. G. Jung* (Princeton: Princeton University Press, 1974).

38.   Franz Alexander and Hugo Staub, *Criminal, Judge, Public,* pp. 113 - 27; for an interesting case record of one such criminal-out-of-a-sense-of-guilt, see pp. 156 - 61.

39.   David Reuben, "Why So Many Women Shoplift," *McCall's,* 97:44, (September 1970), pp. 41 - 3.

40.   See R. Hare, *Psychopathy: Theory and Research* (New York: John Wiley & Sons, 1970); also see W. McCord and J. McCord, *Psychopathy and Delinquency* (New York: Gruen & Stratton, 1956).

41.   West, *Young Offender,* p. 150.

42.   "Social Psychology is the scientific study of the experience and behavior of the individual in relation to social stimulus situations." M. Sherif and C. Sherif, *Social Psychology* (New York: Harper & Row, 1969), p. 8.

43.   See Edwin Sutherland and Donald Cressey, *Principles of Criminology,* 6th ed. (Philadelphia: J. B. Lippincott, 1960), pp. 77 - 80.

44.   West, *Young Offender,* pp. 84 - 5.

45.   Albert Cohen, *Delinquent Boys: The Culture of the Gang* (Glencoe, Ill.: Free Press, 1955).

46.   West, *Young Offender,* p. 99.

47.   Ibid., p. 99.

48.   Cyril Burt, *The Young Delinquent* (London: University of London Press, 1965), pp. 69 - 93.

49.   See Walter B. Miller, "Lower Class Culture as a Generating Mileu of Gang Delinquency," *Journal of Social Issues* 14, 3 (1958): 5 - 19.

50.   Don C. Gibbons, *Delinquent Behavior,* (Englewood Cliffs, N.J.: Prentice-Hall, 1970), p. 122.

51.   For a good discussion, see ibid., p. 123.

52.   W. A. Bonger, *Criminality and Economic Conditions* (Bloomington: Indiana University Press, 1969).

53.   Alexandre Solzhenitsyn, *One Day in the Life of Ivan Denisovich* (New York: Dutton Press, 1963).

54.   Alexandre Solzhenitsyn, *The Gulag Archipelago, 1918 - 1956* (Paris: YMCA Press, 1973).

55. See Emile Durkheim, *Suicide: A Study in Sociology* (Glencoe, Ill.: Free Press, 1951).

56. Robert Merton, "Social Structure and Anomie," in *Social Theory and Social Structure,* ed. Robert Merton (Glencoe: Ill.: Free Press, 1951).

57. West, *Young Offender,* p. 88.

58. Merton, "Social Structure and Anomie."

59. Cohen, *Delinquent Boys.*

60. Ibid., pp. 25 - 30.

61. Ibid., p. 121.

62. Richard Cloward and Lloyd Ohlin, *Delinquency and Opportunity: A Theory of Delinquent Gangs* (New York: Free Press, 1960).

63. President's Commission on Law Enforcement and the Administration of Justice, *The Challenge of Crime in a Free Society* (Washington, D.C.: U.S. Government Printing Office, 1967), p. 279.

64. Erikson, *Wayward Puritans.*

65. Consider the following data from the *1972 Uniform Crime Reports* (Washington, D.C.: U.S. Government Printing Office, 1973), pp. 1 - 25:

Crimes Involving Violence or the Threat of Violence

Murder and Nonnegligent Manslaughter	18,520
Forcible Rape	46,430
Robbery	374,560
Aggravated Assault	388,650
Total	828,160

Crimes Involving Neither Violence nor the Threat of Violence

Burglary	2,345,000
Larceny — $50 and over	1,837,000
Auto Theft	881,000
Total	5,063,800

The data indicate that 14 percent of the most serious crimes committed in the United States involve violence or the threat of violence. If less serious offenses such as the possession or use of drugs, public intoxication, prostitution, and petty larceny were added to the list, the percentage of crimes involving violence would be considerably smaller. It is quite likely that the number of nonserious offenses committed annually is 50 to 100 times greater than the number of serious ones which the F.B.I. indexes. As the nonserious crimes do not involve violence or the threat of violence, it may safely be said that the vast majority of acts are against property or against public morals rather than against people.

66. See, for example, Edmond Cahn, "Cheating on Taxes," in *White Collar Criminal,* ed. Gilbert Geis (New York: Atherton Press, 1968), pp. 194 - 201.

67. See, for example, Gilbert Geis, "The Heavy Electrical Equipment Anti-trust Cases of 1961," in *White Collar Criminal,* ed. Gilbert Geis (New York: Atherton Press, 1968), pp. 103 - 8. Also see Edwin Sutherland, "Crimes of Corporations," in ibid., pp. 57 - 70.

68. For a beautifully written and frightening account of the way in which a major corporation distorted data in order to make a defective braking system for airplanes appear safe, see Kermit Vandivier, "Why Should My Conscience Bother Me?" in *In the Name of Profit: Profiles in Corporate Irresponsibility,* ed. Robert Heilbroner (Garden City, N.Y.: Doubleday, 1972), pp. 3 - 31. Also see S. Sethi, *Up Against the Corporate Wall: Modern Corporations and Social Issues of the Seventies* (Englewood Cliffs, N.J.: Prentice-Hall, 1971).

69. See, for example, "Confessions of a Turnpike Pocket Picker," *Mechanics Illustrated,* 68 (August 1972): 49 - 51.

70. See, for example, Changing Times, "What the Health Hucksters Are Up To," in Geis, *White Collar Criminal,* pp. 268 - 76.

71. Erikson, *Wayward Puritans,* p. 6.

72. William Faulkner, *As I Lay Dying,* cited in Howard S. Becker, *Outsiders* (New York: Free Press, 1963) at the title page.

73. Kai Erikson, *Wayward Puritans,* p. 7.

74. Clarence Darrow, *Crime: Its Cause and Treatment* (London: Watts, 1934), p. 2.

75. See Michael Appleby, "Overview of Legal Services," in *Justice and the Law in the Mobilization for Youth Experience,* ed. Harold Weissman (New York: Association Press, 1969), pp. 25 - 38. Also see *Report of The United States' Attorney General's Committee on Poverty and the Administration of Federal Crime Justice* (Washington: U.S. Government Printing Office, 1963).

76. See Michael Appleby, "The Effect of Legal Counsel on Criminal Cases," in Weissman, ed., *Justice and the Law,* pp. 39 - 51.

77. Kai Erikson, *Wayward Puritans,* pp. 10 - 11.

78. For an interesting and well-written description of this process, see Gresham Sykes, *The Society of Captives* (Princeton: Princeton University Press, 1958). Also see Erving Goffman, *Asylums* (New York: Bobbs-Merrill, 1962).

79. See R. Taggart, *The Prison of Unemployment: Manpower Programs for Offenders* (Baltimore: Johns Hopkins, 1972).

80. David Matza, *Delinquency and Drift.*

An Interview with Charley Baltimore, Executive Assistant of the Center for Community Alternatives

Charley Baltimore is a young man who has, in recent years, worked for two important projects administered by the Governor's office in Pennsylvania. He was a staff member (a telephone ombudsman) of the Governor's Action Center, a state-wide telephone hotline for people with problems of any type. In May of 1975 he left G.A.C. to take a job as executive assistant of the Center for Community Alternatives. The Center is the primary operational arm of the Camp Hill Project, which is currently attempting to close large, secure juvenile institutions in Pennsylvania and to develop community-based programs for "serious" offenders. Charley is a dynamic and concerned young man whose life-long experiences with the juvenile justice system are reflected in the opinions and attitudes which he freely expresses throughout the interview.

Hyman: How did you get into Camp Hill?

Charley: It was two charges: issuing worthless checks and faulty use of credit cards. And, although it didn't come up in my records, they were both drug related.

Hyman: Whose checks and credit cards?

Charley: It was a guy who owns a bar in town. I didn't even steal the cards. I got them from a friend who had just stole them that day.

Hyman: Was that the first time that you were ever picked up for anything?

Charley: No. About three or four times before that. I would go to court and get let off. Also I did county time two or three times.

Hyman: What were the other offenses?

Charley: They were — ok — two times my parents had me picked up; they were saying I was basically unruly. I would stay out late and they couldn't do anything with me and that sort of thing. There was another time when I got arrested for stealing cars and taking the cars to Philadelphia with about four or five other guys.

Hyman: How did you get caught on this latter rap?

Charley: The Philadelphia police have a tendency to pull a car over if there are four or five black people in the car. And there were six people in the car. We happened to get caught that way.

Hyman: How did you get into doing these things? Did you need the money?

Charley: Every summer it was an annual thing. Every July, before the fourth of July, I'd get arrested. We needed something to do.

Middle-Class Kicks and Tricks

Charley: It's not the typical type of story, where you'd find I came from the ghetto family and I had to struggle and that sort of thing. I came from a middle-class family that was well off. There was always food and always clothes and money to go places.

People do try to brand you right away to make you fit

their prejudices. They want to say, "You went out and stole and robbed and did drugs. It was for a reason — because you had a weak father and that kind of thing, ya know." Well it wasn't because I was poor, or black or that book stuff. I just did it because I wanted to do it. And I started to get into drugs around 13. And I just got into everything that was going on. I just wanted to do it.

It was a heavy ego thing. I guess it all revolves around peer pressure. I knew that what I was doing was like the baddest thing. But I just couldn't get out of it.

I was one of those "out-of-sight" guys. Everybody looked up to me — because this guy was sticking needles in his arm; he was one of the best thieves in town, and that kind of thing. There was like a numerous amount of things that I never got caught for — burglaries and things.

Hyman: How about the kids you ran around with? What were your peers like?

Charley: It was a mixture, a good mixture. They were like usual American families — middle-class families. We just hung out.

Hyman: It wasn't just a matter of one middle-class kid and a lot of poor kids?

Charley: No, it was a good mixture. I wasn't born in Suburbia, though; I was brought up right in the heart of the city. And there happened to be like a street, like a middle-class street. It was even black and white and that whole area was like basically middle-class. Around the outside you got into lower income so it was everybody mixed up together. Sort of an average American bunch of kids.

Middle-Class Diversion

Hyman: You indicated that the first couple of times you were caught, you weren't sent to Camp Hill. What kinds of things did the authorities do?

Charley: Well, ok, "Camp Hill" was a big ugly place that your parents would threaten you with. They'd call it "White Hill." When you were bad at home and acting up your mother would say, "If you don't behave, we're gonna send you to White Hill." And you visualize big giant rats biting the shit out of you, and guards beating you up and big dudes trying to rape you all the time — which was true.

You know people really use this kind of threat — especially when you're that young. Even when I went to court, the judge used this threat. The juvenile judge then was Judge ———; he is now the U.S. District Court Judge for this district. He was a pretty fair judge. He very very seldom sent a kid to jail unless it was his third or fourth time.

He tried everything before sendin' me to jail. That was because I had the type of parents that were very concerned. They were there right by my side. They took the attitude like, "We're not defending him. He's messing up. We need some kind of help. Give us another chance." I think the thing that kept me home as many times as it did was that the probation officers saw how concerned my parents were.

There were a lot of guys that their parents didn't give a shit. Their parents weren't always working or anything; they just didn't want to go to court with their kids. And the judge was left with no choice in a lot of those cases but to send them away. That's the main thing that got me off without anything. He didn't even put me on probation.

Probation, Schools, and Community Services

Charley: As a matter of fact, I was in seventh or eighth grade and I decided that I wanted to be on probation. I went down to the probation office myself and I asked them. In fact — I asked to be sent away.

I hated home with a passion. I just wanted to be free and be out, and I knew there were Youth Development Centers. They were known as "schools," known to street people like schools where they had swimming pools and other out-of-sight guys that you could hang around with. And you had freedom. I asked to be sent to one of those. And it turned out that at that point I was put on probation. I was trying everything to get away from home.

Hyman: When you were in seventh grade?

Charley: Yes, seven or eight I'm pretty sure.

Hyman: Did the court or probation officers provide any services?

Charley: No, I just had to report in every week. Then I didn't even get to see my probation officer, except when I'd run into him and he would say, "Hey how ya do'in?" School was a waste of time and I hated living at home. I hated my parents. They were like very strict: my mother was very set in her ways and Dad was stern and I knew he was serious and that type of thing.

I had the type of personality that I just wanted to be out on my own. I couldn't quit school because I was too young and they wouldn't let me leave home. So when I was fifteen and in ninth grade I was doing everything I could to get thrown out of school. I was skipping every class and acting up. I got put out of school.

That's when the probation officer started getting actively involved. He was saying, "You have to get a job. Since you got put out of school you're gonna have to get a job. If you have a job your chances are good that you won't get sent away." So I was like 15 then and in order to get a job I had to lie about my age. I looked a lot older than I was. I got jobs — the Coca Cola Company, the train station, a restaurant, and a shoe factory. I'd get up at 4:00 every morning to go to work and each time my probation officer (he was a teacher and a preacher too), each time he found out where I was working at, he would call the people up and say, "Did you hear that he is only 15?" And the people would say no they didn't and then they would fire me. The last job was at the train station and I had been there for two months and was making like $2.90 an hour and which was like out-of-sight pay for a 14 to 15 year old guy.

I was there for like two or three months. There were like 14 or 15 other guys. I decided not to tell him that I was working there, but once he came in on a bus and the next day I got fired because he said I was not old enough. He was telling me on one hand. "You've got to get a job if you gonna be out of school." On the other hand he would say I was under age. He knew I was 15 and under age. It was like a hell of a mixed message. That's all the probation officer got involved.

Hyman: Did the school try to help?

Charley: No, they wanted to get me out of their hair. They had me in Edison and when I bombed out of there they sent me uptown to a different district, hoping I would make it up there; and I lasted there for like two days then I started getting into trouble. So the schools wanted to get me out of their hair.

Hyman: What kind of trouble in school?

Charley: It was a lot of mischievous shit. It was like I was bringing whiskey to school and getting drunk in the locker room and playing hookey and coming back to school for lunch and the teacher would say I thought you were off and I'd say, "yeah, but I got hungry." It was that kind of thing.

Hyman: Were there other kids doing that type of thing?

Charley: Oh, yeah.

Hyman: Were there any school counselors who tried to help you?

Charley: They never worked with us. The only time they worked with us was when we got the paddle or something. That was about it. I got really no counseling at all.

Of course I wasn't open to counseling. If someone would sit down and counsel me I would just leave. I was looking out the window. I was doing what I thought was right — you couldn't tell me.

Hyman: So they didn't try any of that?

Charley: No.

Hyman: How about any of the social service agencies? Any contact with them?

Charley: No.

Hyman: Do you think you would do it again if you were at that age?

Charley: Oh, yeah.

Encapsulation and Due Process

Hyman: Now, let's talk about the delinquency you went to Camp Hill for — credit cards and checks. How did you get identified, arrested?

Charley: I got put out of school and then after that I got put out of my house. I was fifteen or sixteen when I got kicked out of my house — my parents gave up.
I got arrested with two other guys that were with me. They were just as much in fault as I was, but I took the whole rap.
The police put me in the county prison. Like they were coming out every week to prison to try to find out who else was involved. I just made a big joke out of it.

Hyman: How old were you then?

Charley: I was 17 then.

Hyman: When were you arrested?

Charley: March 5, 1970, at 1:00 p.m.

Hyman: Did they detain you — put you in a detention home?

Charley: They kept me in the county prison. They have a wing, like five cells with juveniles, and I was there in the county jail for 3 months. For those three months I was locked in solitary. I had to stay in my cell 24 hours a day because I hit another guy. So they had to keep us locked up until one of us left. It was like mid-summer, it was as hot as hell, I'd take a shower for about an hour, anything to stay out of my cell.

Hyman: This was before any hearing or trial?

Charley: Yeh, at that point I had a slight drug habit. It wasn't anything really heavy and I didn't even realize I had a habit until I got picked up and started feeling sick and didn't have any appetite.
   It wasn't like the real big thing, like constantly throwing up — ya know, being real fucked up — but I knew I had some kind of habit and I'd ask for help. Right when I got picked up I was starting to get tied into the addictive disease clinic in Harrisburg. That's when methadone was still legal. So when I got into jail and I realized I was feeling kind of sick, I said I might as well take advantage of the legitimate program. I wrote about three letters to the addictive disease clinic. The head guy then was an ex-cop. He was like helping to run the thing. I never got a reply.
   Later on I found out from one of the guards that they were just tearing the letters up and saying I don't need that kind of help. They wouldn't let me place a phone call or anything . . . .

Hyman: The guards in the jail were doing this?

Charley: Yeh. They. . . that was the whole administrative attitude toward the drug problem. Like if a guy came in with real heavy jones they would just throw him in isolation. This one guy beat his head so bad against the wall that they had to take him to the hospital. But they still didn't have any kind of treatment for him. A junky was a junky.

Hyman: Were you in jail for three months before trial?

Charley: I was in the county jail for three months. They were trying to make me crack. Like on TV they wanted me to tell them who was involved and where did they go. One of the guys split and they wanted to know where he was at and how I got involved in it and blah blah blah. That was holding up the whole trial they said, "As soon as you give us the information, we'll send you to trial." I never gave them the information.

Hyman: It doesn't seem right that you were in jail three months before a hearing. Did you have a lawyer?

Charley: I had a public defender.

Hyman: Did you get him right away?

Charley: No. . . . I had been involved with legal services; my family got in touch with them and asked them to help out, . . . [but] they couldn't touch it because mine was a criminal case and they weren't allowed to do anything with it. So I really didn't have an attorney; and the court appointed an attorney about a day or two before I went to court and he just kind of came out, shuffled some papers, and asked some stupid questions, and he didn't even say anything through the whole thing.

Hyman: Then it was like three months before you got an attorney?

Charley: That's right. That's a procedure they go through.

It's just a procedure, it doesn't really do anything, just so the papers will show that you had an attorney.

Hyman: Now, the special wing in the jail — do you know now whether that was legal?

Charley: It's legal because they kept us separate from the adults. It was right up front where the control desk was and they could see the whole block right from the control desk, but in those times you weren't allowed with the adults at any time; you had your separate yard.

One thing was illegal. I was kept over the five-day limit. There was a five-day limit on how long you can retain the juvenile, especially in a facility like that.

Hyman: You were kept there three months?

Charley: Right.

Hyman: Did you know it was illegal at the time?

Charley: No, all I knew then was that I wanted to get out.

Hyman: Do they still keep people over the five-day limit?

Charley: Oh, I'm sure they do. I can't point out any cases, but I'm sure they do.

Hyman: Was there anything called rehabilitation, social services, or recreation in the jail?

Charley: No.

Juvenile Court

Hyman: When you went to court with the probation officer, was there any social study, any psychological testing, or anything like that?

Charley: No.

Hyman: What was the trial like?

Charley: The trial was a trip because I was waiting upstairs in what you call a "bull pen," waiting to go down; and right before me there was a guy, about his twentieth time before the judge; he had spent half of his life in prison. And the judge said, "Well Joe X, I think you need to go to Camp; I want you to learn how to use your hands, so I'm gonna send you to Camp Hill." So the guy said, "I know how to use my hands, you dirty bastard," and jumped on the bench and beat the shit out of the judge. He started hitting him all on his head and I had to go in there right after that.

The first thing I saw when I walked in there was the judge with his face all beat up. "Who's next?" I knew I was gone. I just turned around and said, "I'll see you later." I knew I was gone.

It's a lot different from adult trials. Very very casual. Everybody's just kind of laying there, ya know, "Ho hum." The procedure they have to go through.

Hyman: When did you meet your lawyer?

Charley: I met him about a day or two earlier. He didn't say hardly anything through the whole hearing. He said like maybe a few words, I can't remember what he said. Me too, I hardly said anything through the whole hearing. I didn't want to get sent away but I really didn't give a shit.

Hyman: Were your parents there?

Charley: Yeah, they were there.

Hyman: Did they say anything?

Charley: I can't remember if he asked them anything or not. All I remember from the hearing was the judge; I really felt that he tried to do whatever he could. The probation officer tried to get a lot of angles on the whole thing.

Hyman: What did they do during the trial?

Charley: The only thing the probation officer did was between every sentence (she's still down there, she's one of the classic probation officers, you can't find another one that's more classic than her), in between every sentence that the judge said, she kept saying, "I think you should send him to White Hill, I think you should send him to White Hill. We gave him too many chances before." That's the only thing she said.

There was a guy that came out to talk to me when I was at the county, about going into the Job Corps. And they, the Job Corps, agreed to accept me by the time I went to court, but I had a three- to four-week waiting period. The judge said, "I don't think we should send him to Camp Hill, that's kind of like the last step, let's try him at the Job Corps. He's not really a bad guy." "Well, how soon can he go to the Job Corps?" The representative from the Job Corps said, "Two to four weeks. We have to process the papers and stuff." The judge said, "Why don't we let him go home and wait."

The probation officer said, "NO, no, I don't want him out on the streets. He's not gonna make it anyway. But if you insist, judge, he has to go to Camp Hill to wait."

So he said, "Ok, we'll send him to Camp Hill for the next two to four weeks for diagnostic classification tests." That's when I went to Camp Hill.

Institutionalization: The Old In-Out

Charley: And diagnostic classification is routine. They still have it. It's just like blood tests and shots and all this sort of thing. At first, going to Camp Hill was like going to the Hilton. After leaving the county prison, ya know — being in that one little stinking cell for three months.

You could breathe and see the sun. So it was like a good

change. It kind of gives you an idea the state of mind that you're in. So I ended up being at CH before I went to the Job Corps.

It was a trip from the moment I got in there. Like the first thing they had to do was take blood tests. They couldn't find a vein in my arm. All my veins were collapsed and burnt out and shit. And the nurse is stabbing me. Everywhere in my arm she's stabbing these big horse needles, and the whole time she's cussing me out. "These goddamn junkies. They always come in here and I don't know why we get them all."

And I can't say anything. The guard is standing over there waiting for me to say something smart. Then he can hit me.

So from that point on, it was like a trip. Like, quarantine was like staying in your cell. The only thing you look forward to is coming out to eat. You know, ya just wait and wait . . . [for meals], visits, and stockade an hour a day.

Hyman: Any social workers or psychologists?

Charley: They had counselors up there. The counselors were then and still are a trip. I was there for about two months, then my counselor called me up. Well, I met him when I first got there and he asked me something, he went through some kind of questioning, like four or five questions he had to ask me. Like, "Who do you contact in case of an emergency?" and that sort of thing. Then he did a social history after I was there for about two months. It was like talking to a computer. "What's your name? Who are your parents? Who was the strongest figure in your family?" and blah blah blah. I'm looking out the window the whole time. That was the only time I saw him.

Hyman: He waited two months to do that?

Charley: Yes. So I went to the Job Corps and I was there about for a month, and I got involved in drugs, pulled a bunch of mischief back there and they sent me back to prison. So I just did time out there.

Hyman: How long?

Charley: I did 15 months in CH and I was transferred in the middle of my sentence to a community-based program, Yokecrest. And I did about 16 months there before I was to graduate from that program. So I was about 20, it was about three years in all.

Debilitation and Rehabilitation

Hyman: So what was Camp Hill like then?

Charley: Camp Hill was a thing. So many things. It's like going into another world. That was like my first contact I ever had with Philadelphia guys. Their whole life is gang wars. They talk an altogether different language — what corner you're from and that sort of thing.

You're getting adjusted to the whole prison life and you're getting adjusted to three or four cultural backgrounds. You might enter with a farmer, Philadelphia guys, Pittsburgh guys, your pimps, your drug pushers. I got this attitude that Harrisburg was kind of like a nothing.

It's like a really ugly war, like if you have any feelings. Like I've seen guys get raped, shit like that. Like some of the guys that got raped would have a visitor. He'd be sittin' there with his parents, his girlfriend and that sort of thing. He'd be smilin' and laughin' like nothin' happened and inside he'd be all twisted up and dyin'.

I didn't really have any outstanding type thing. And I more or less stayed to myself. Like I did tons of reading and a lot of writing and that sort of thing and listened to the radio. Kind of stayed to myself.

One thing that happened when I first got there had a big effect on me. There was this kid who was there for about a week and he kind of stayed to himself. He didn't socialize a lot. When we went to the stockade he kind of hung off to the side. One morning we woke up and he didn't come out, so a trustee went in and shoved him to wake him up. He wouldn't get up, so the trustee hit the lights in the cell.

The kid had slashed his stomach, and his chest, right below his heart all the way across his stomach and his arm all the way from his shoulder to his wrist. He had cut himself over the toilet, then he got in bed. He lit a cigarette and just fell asleep. The floor was just covered with blood.

They took him out to the hospital. They thought he was dead, but he was living. And that was like a trip.

What they did was they got him back together, they sewed him up and he was all right, and for the rest of his time they kept him in the hospital — in isolation — locked up in the isolation center. That was his treatment! Because he was bad, he was dumb, he was crazy, you know. They would let him out about an hour a day and bring him to the stockade, and most of the guys (this was the peer pressure thing) the guys would say, "There goes that nut, that crazy guy."

That incident stuck with me. I don't know what happened to him, but they let him get to that point where he cut himself up. That is so easy in an institution, any institution. How do you keep tabs on 1000 guys? And even more so than that was the treatment that he got.

So I was dealing with that and also I was dealing with the fact that this guy was all slashed up. It took me awhile to get over that. But you do see things like that all the time. You see guys cuttin' each other up over cigarettes.

Hyman: How did you cope with such an environment?

Charley: You really have to get yourself into a strange sense of mind. You can't ignore it. You can't just say, "I'll ignore it." To survive, you must get yourself in your own little world. *You* have to settle *yourself* down. Get into the attitude that "I'm gonna be here the rest of my life." Because there is no way you can actually see yourself on the streets again — especially when you first start to do your bit. In fact, that's the one thing that I really concentrated as much energy and as much effort as possible on — getting myself together.

There were many times when I thought of doing myself in

— a real down kind of thing. I'd say, "Is this really happening to me? Am I really here?" Like all your life you develop an attitude, "It can never happen to me. I can never go out and get hit by a car; it always happens to the other guy." So you finally get into that situation — the reality hits you — you wake up and you're still there and you know you are gonna be there. That incident stuck with me, though, and I didn't try it.

To survive in an institution, you must get into the frame of mind, "It looks like I'm gonna be there for the rest of my life." By getting into that attitude, you can start dealing with reality. You can get your head off the street and start becoming adjusted to prison life. You deal with it as you, an individual, can deal with it.

Hyman: Did the authorities — counselors, psychiatrists, treatment people — help you get your head straight?

Charley: Your whole treatment in prison is usually done by yourself, not the people you talk to for therapeutic or counseling reasons. What they do — I know I was turned off and I didn't want to hear anything. I didn't want to go there and talk to a guy who had a Ph.D., and he read about my kind in a book. And he thinks, "Yeah, you qualify; you're type C61 in the book." I didn't want to talk to him. Even if he could help me — but he couldn't 'cause I just shut him out.

So I — most of the time the treatment you receive is the treatment you give to yourself. You start thinking of where your head is going to be at when you get into the street; your success in the prison, your success after you leave the prison, is how well you got yourself together. Which automatically eliminates a lot of people, because there are not too many people who can get you together.

Hyman: A lot of people make statements that institutions are really schools of crime; is that true?

Charley: Definitely! You figure — you have a few guys from all walks of life in prison — all sorts of types of crimes. You get to talk to people about the trials and stuff. And again go back to the peer pressure thing — you may be there for burglary, and you talk to a guy who has been in for armed robbery and got busted with a machine gun, or a safe cracker. You know, the whole group pressure becomes a feeling, you kind of pick up on it. They definitely are schools of crime.

Hyman:　Is there "solitary" in Camp Hill?

Charley:　The county's hole — you couldn't even stand up, it was like four bare walls, and it was like a little cage. You went to the bathroom in a hole in the floor. The temperature stayed about 97 degrees. At Camp Hill the solitary is like a regular cell block, four tiers, but the cells were in the center of the tiers and were facing out. You couldn't see anyone else or talk to them. But what was bad there was you would get your ass beat by the guards. They used anything they could to beat you, anything justifiable in their report. I saw guys that were so bad, you didn't even know who they were. Their heads were like balloons.

　　I also think there's another place, in the basement; there was like a shackle — I never saw, I just heard people talk about it — they supposedly shackle you to the floor and you urinated there and everything.

Getting It Together in a Community-Based Institution

Hyman:　You mentioned going to a community-based institution. How did you get there?

Charley:　Yokecrest is a therapeutic community. Sort of like the Synanon concept. It had like fifteen people and used the family concept.

　　That's what really started to get my head together. That was for me, ya know. I started really getting it together there.

　　The whole thing about treatment is, like, finding the right thing for each guy. A lot of guys who came through that program couldn't make it. They were chopped off like failures and sent back to prison.

But it was for me — like, if I went to Teen Challenge or a regular group-type thing, I would have bombed out. I needed a real strong type of program where people were constantly kicking me in my ass and constantly holding my ideals up to me. It was for me, and the others are right for some guys.

Hyman: How did you go about deciding what kind of program was appropriate for you?

Charley: At the time one of the counselors over there [Yokecrest] — he recommended it for me. They came over to Camp Hill to see who they could get. He told me, "You have to show them that you want help — at the gut level. Show them that." They had an arrangement with the institution. So I got transferred over there.

Hyman: You've made it straight since Yokecrest. What was it about the program that made the difference?

Charley: The thing about Yokecrest that really helped me make it was knowing that people who were sitting behind the desk did the same thing I did. The executive director had done like 10 to 15 years in prisons. Everyone had done some time. So I could sit down and relate to them. They weren't saying, "I read about you on page 13," you know. They could relate to what you were feeling and say, "I did the exact same thing, and I was an asshole; this is what I did." That was the main thing. There was no copout. You can't play any games with somebody who did the same thing.

Making It on the Outside

Hyman: Since you got out of Yokecrest, you've had a couple of fairly good jobs. What were they?

Charley: My first job after leaving Yokecrest was at their summer camp for kids 13 to 17. When I left there I was assistant director to the summer program. Then I went to

Harrisburg State Hospital and was like a therapist up there — had a caseload of mental patients.

Hyman: How did you get your training to become a therapist?

Charley: In Yokecrest. Three, four, five times a week being in encounter groups — all kinds of groups — marathons, the whole wide range. I got my training there.

After I worked in the state hospital for about a year, I started to really burn out. I was really into helping people, and that is a tremendous emotional drain.

I looked around and saw a lot of psychologists and psychiatrists who had been there for years who really didn't want to be there but they had the training. I saw that people who work in the hospital are like an assembly line. It was like there was no feeling there at all. I didn't want to turn into that. I refused to go to school cause I didn't want to turn into a walking book.

So I decided to try to get into something different. I knew most of the people who left therapeutic communities continued to work with therapeutic communities. They stayed in the field of therapy. I really challenged that. Did I really want to do it, to help these people or how much of a crutch was it. 'Cause here I am, an ex-junkie and an ex-con. What other job could I get? So I sort of felt it was a crutch for me.

I decided I couldn't work in direct therapy anymore. I got out of that and I went to work for the Tri-County Council for Addictive Diseases. This was my first administrative job.

I went around interviewing drug and alcohol directors, did program descriptions and that sort of thing. From there I went to work at the Governor's Action Center.

Hyman: At the Governor's Action Center, in the Governor's Office — what did you do there?

Charley: Well, we handled complaints and helped people get services — you know, cut red tape and that stuff. There I started to get involved with the people who are involved in problems with criminal justice — all the officials; and one day Jerry Miller came in and I talked to him.

Hyman: And now you have a job with the Center for Community Alternatives? What is the program of the center?

Charley: Our job is to set up community-based programs for juveniles — to close down Camp Hill first and then the others. Like Jerry Miller did in Massachusetts — that's what we're doing in Pennsylvania now.

Right now I'm working mainly right in the prison, setting up programs in the prison. We have nine people over there, and I try to make it a little more broad and a little more humane until we can get them out of there.

Hyman: It has been illegal for kids to be kept in Camp Hill for several years, hasn't it?

Charley: Yes, and the state hasn't really done anything about it — until this project. I had a big fight with the Attorney General when I worked in the Governor's Office: it was about the conditions in the juvenile institution. We went around about five different things with the juveniles — five or six kids in a cell that is meant for two people tops. Kept illegally in jail for two, three months. Kids getting mixed with adults. Females with adults overnight. We took it to the Governor's close staff and they were very interested and wanted it taken to the Attorney General. But he was too busy with "more pressing" things to talk with us.

So we set up a meeting with his assistant who I think doesn't know shit about law. We were in the office about two seconds and he had to call in someone else. He said, "I don't know about this law, and since this is the judge's decision, you know, we don't want to do anything because it's a judge who makes the decision." We said, "But it's illegal." You never get them to admit directly, he gives you such a bullshit roundabout answer. This confrontation came about this year. He doesn't want to rock the judges' boat. Everybody's like feeding everybody's hand. It's too bad, lots of kids get their whole lives spoiled.

What If . . .

Hyman: One last question. Where do you think you would be if you hadn't gone into Yokecrest?

Charley: Probably still out on the streets. What keeps me going every day is that I drive down the same streets and see the same old people doing the same old thing. Talking the same old shit. I have a feeling I'm not there 'cause it took a lot of time, a lot of work, a lot of people who cared to get it together for me. When I look at them I have a feeling like I can still end up back there.

Hyman: What made the difference between going back on the streets and where you are now? Probation officers? The judge? The institutional program? Or what?

Charley: Definitely the community program. If I came directly out of prison, you know, then I thought I had it together when I left prison. But there was so much stuff I hadn't confronted tucked away — a lot of little stuff you sort of chalk off, and a lot of things about my personality — a lot of things people didn't see. But it was there; I was covering it up.
We all had our images. Like I still have an image. We cover up all inside. As long as you get it open and know it's really inside and you know how to control it, and you're honest about it — you got it made. It's ok. If you keep it covered up and it slips out every once in a while, you can screw people up and screw yourself. Then you end up on the streets again.

Hyman: What would you say to students who are reading this book? What is it like to be subjected to the juvenile justice system?

Charley: It is really hard to understand something if you haven't actually gone through it. Like it is hard for me to understand what a cancer patient goes through 'cause I haven't ever had cancer. Which doesn't mean I can't help the person; but it means I have to be open to people that have gone through it. Like John Mattingly, who is directing this whole program. His whole background is like working with people from the book. That doesn't make him an ineffective administrator, but he realizes that he is weak in one area and strong in another. He's willing to get involved. He also admits his weaknesses. He has asked me to fill in that area. None of us know everything. I don't know everything. But it's kind of pulling together with all kinds of people.

Hyman: You mean, to learn you must also get out and talk to and interact with people who are . . .

Charley: Tell them never to think they know it all.

3 Three Models of Juvenile Justice Systems

---

*One man's justice is another's injustice; one man's
beauty another's ugliness; one man's wisdom
another's folly.*

— *Ralph Waldo Emerson*

In the first chapters of this book two fundamental questions were addressed: (1) What is delinquency? and (2) What are its causes? In this chapter attention begins to focus on a more central question in this book: What ought to be done about the problem?

Disagreement about the goals of justice systems, including juvenile justice systems, is pervasive throughout American society. The fear of crime is widespread, and the public outcry for crime control and social protection has clearly been heard by politicians whose campaigns have reverberated with calls for "law and order." Consider, for example, the following language from a campaign speech by presidential candidate George Wallace:

> If you walk out of this hotel tonight and someone knocks you on the head, he'll be out of jail before you're out of the hospital, and Monday morning they'll try the policemen instead of the criminal. . . . That's right, we're gonna have a police state for folks who burn cities down. They aren't gonna burn any more cities.[1]

Despite the rising fear of crime and the increasingly articulated demands for its repression, there continues to be strong support in most American communities for the proposition that offenders, particularly juvenile offenders, ought to be "helped" rather than punished. This viewpoint was clearly expressed in the preamble to the

1970 Report to President Richard Nixon of the White House Conference on Children.

> As we begin this significant national reassessment, let us remind ourselves of our purpose.
>
> This should be a Conference about love . . . about our need to love those to whom we have given birth . . . and those who are most helpless and in need . . . and those who give us a reason for being . . . and those who are most precious for themselves — for what they are and what they can become. Our children. Let us ask what we want for our children. Then let us ask not less for all children.
>
> We want for our children a home of love and understanding and encouragement. . . .
>
> We want for our children to live under laws that are fair and just and that are administered fairly and justly.
>
> We want for our children to love their country because their country has earned their love, because their country strives to create peace and to create the conditions of a humane and healthy society for all of its citizens and is dedicating the resources necessary to redeem its commitment to these ends. This we want for our children. Therefore this we must want for *all* children. There can be no exceptions. . . . That we are a Nation founded on equality, so must we not tolerate intolerance in ourselves or our fellows.
>
> We must recognize that there is some child in special need. And he especially must be our child.
>
> At a time when it is all too easy to accuse, to blame, to fault, let us gather in trust and faith to put before the Nation that which is necessary and best.
>
> All this we say with the greatest sense of urgency and conviction. Our children and our families are in deep trouble. A society that neglects its children and fears its youth cannot care about its future. Surely this is the way to national disaster.
>
> Our society has the capacity to care and the resources to act. Act we must. . . .
>
> We as Delegates to the 1970 White House Conference on Children do now affirm our *total commitment* to help bring our Nation into a new age of caring. Now we begin.[2]

The proponents of crime-control models of justice are often in conflict with the proponents of treatment models about how best to respond to youthful delinquency. And there is a third model whose adherents are often in conflict with everyone else. This model, which focuses on due process of law, starts from the premise that both those who would punish and those who would cure juvenile delinquents may, through overzealousness, cause more harm than good. Legal systems must, after all, seek not merely to protect the community, nor even merely to help the offender, but also to assure that the innocent can go their own way in peace, free from unjustified intrusions into their lives. This view was eloquently articulated in Mr. Justice Fortas' opinion in *In re Gault:*

> Failure to observe the fundamental requirements of due process has resulted in instances, which might have been avoided, of unfairness to individuals and inadequate or inaccurate findings of fact and unfortunate prescriptions of remedy. Due process of law is the primary and indispensable foundation of individual freedom. It is the basic and essential term in the social compact which defines the rights of the individual and delimits the powers which the State may exercise. As Mr. Justice Frankfurter has said: "The history of American freedom is, in no small measure, the history of procedure." But in addition, the procedural rules which have been fashioned from the generality of due process are our best instruments for the distillation and evaluation of essential facts from the conflicting welter of data that life and our adversary methods present. It is these instruments of due process which enhance the possibility that truth will emerge from the confrontation of opposing versions and conflicting data. "Procedure is to law what 'scientific method' is to science."[3]

The purpose of this chapter is to show how proponents of each of these three models of justice might, in some ideal world of their own creation, undertake to order, structure, and administer programs directed at juveniles. We shall look in turn at what might happen if each of these models were to attain complete dominance in a juvenile justice system. in reality there is no such thing as a juvenile justice system of which the *only* purpose is to achieve crime control, or to provide rehabilitative treatment, or to secure the benefits of due process of law. Chapter Four will examine the actual functioning of real juvenile justice systems in which all these values compete. First, however, it is essential to develop a complete understanding of the implications of each set of values and to see how each would lead to the creation of different institutions, programs, and behaviors.

A Crime-Control Model of Juvenile Justice

Spare the Rod and Spoil the Child

A juvenile justice system based on the crime-control model would seek primarily to achieve the repression of antisocial acts. The delinquency of children would be perceived both as a danger to life and property and as a threat to the survival of important social values. Law and order would be imperative not only because the streets must be safe today but also because children must learn responsibility, diligence, and honesty to keep society from falling into chaos and disorder in the future. Thus, the primary objective of a juvenile justice system based on a crime-control model would be to increase the efficiency with which the process screens suspects, determines guilt, and appropriately disposes of the convicted minors. An efficient system would be one which could apprehend, try, convict, and dispose of a high proportion of the alleged offenders. Speedy and conclusive intervention would be permitted in a broad range of cases.

The Law in a Crime-Control Model

The legal definition of delinquency would be expansive. Crimes with victims, vitcimless crimes, and status offenses would all be maintained on the law books. The law's concern would be not only with children whose behavior was harmful, but also with children whose

behavior indicated a high probability of future harmfulness. Thus, the processing of children who ran away from home, or were truant, or who drank alcohol, or whose moral development was endangered by bad companionship would be permitted.

Police Power in a Crime-Control Model

The police would be important and highly respected participants in the process. The suspicions and conjectures of policemen would be trusted to be based on professional competence and experience, and thus would be viewed as highly reliable.

Policemen have traditionally had great confidence in their ability to make valid and reliable interpretations of the behavior they observe. This self-confidence was nicely described by Jerome Skolnick in his book, *Justice Without Trial:*

> When he (the policeman) sees a black girl and a white serviceman enter a hotel together, he assumes an act of prostitution is in the offing. To him, these are not constitutionally protected citizens, but predictable actors whose misbehavior he usually judges correctly. Sometimes, to be sure, he may be in error. The probabilities, however, are so strong, he feels, that his judgment is rarely going to be wrong.[4]

In a crime-control model of justice, the accuracy of most of the policemen's judgments would be assumed. Arrest on the basis of suspicion (but in the absence of positive proof) would be encouraged. Suspicions would be confirmed or disproven through greatly increased powers to carry out interrogations and gather evidence. Confessions obtained in violation of the right to remain silent (which would no longer be considered to be a right) would be admissible in court provided that such confessions were not obtained under circumstances which indicate a high probability of inaccuracy. Confessions extracted through beatings, starvation, or prolonged deprivation of sleep would be considered unreliable. Searches for evidence would be considered appropriate whenever police suspected the existence of a crime.

Detention in a Crime-Control Model

The use of detention facilities would be very extensive. It would be assumed that youngsters taken into custody by the police had actually committed delinquent acts; and the overriding purpose of reducing crime would justify holding such probably-guilty juveniles in isolation from the community. Detention centers would not engage in either diagnosis or treatment; their purpose would be simple and straightforward — to incapacitate youngsters so that they could not commit additional delinquencies while awaiting trial.

Adjudication in a Crime-Control Model

The hearing would be perceived as as a relatively unimportant part of the entire process.

> In this model . . . the center of gravity for the process lies in the early, administrative fact-finding stages. The complementary proposition is that the subsequent stages are relatively unimportant and should be truncated as much as possible. This, too, produces tensions with presently dominant ideology. The pure Crime Control Model has very little use for many conspicuous features of the adjudicative process. . . .[5]

The assumption that the police have done a fair and efficient job of identifying guilty youngsters would justify informality at the hearing stage. With managerial efficiency as its primary goal (the speedy resolution of cases), the crime-control model would seek to minimize the sources of delay. Defense attorneys would probably be permitted to participate in the process, but their presence would not be encouraged; and legal technicalities would not be of great interest to the court. Virtually all evidence would be admissible without concern for the manner in which it had been collected. Thus, while policemen might still be discouraged from performing illegal searches, illegally obtained evidence would be admissible in court.

Disposition of Cases in a Crime-Control Model

Clearly it would be expected that the punishment fit the crime rather than that the treatment fit the offender. With the repression of crime as its ultimate goal, the juvenile justice system would seek to achieve incapacitation and deterrence.

Incapacitation, deterrence, and other objectives of punishment are discussed at some length in Chapter Eight. At this point it is sufficient to know that deterrence refers to the potential utility that fear of punishment may have in discouraging offenses and that incapacitation refers to the isola-

> *tion of offenders so that they are unable to commit offenses.*

Lenient measures such as probation, foster home placement, and community-based treatment would be infrequently used. While reform schools might still provide education and possibly even treatment, they would be conceptualized primarily as institutions whose purpose would be to demonstrate that *crime does not pay!* Delinquent children would be "put away" both to rid the community of them for at least a while (incapacitation) and to discourage their future waywardness (deterrence). It would be important that the harsh treatment afforded delinquents be highly visible because the theory of general deterrence assumes that other people must know that real punishment will result from misbehavior. Indeed, it is possible that such measures as corporal punishment would be invoked either (1) in institutions (to ensure that they would be so unpleasant that children would not want to come back) or (2) as an alternative to institutionalization in cases in which it was thought best to maintain in the community a child who was nevertheless considered to be deserving of some punishment.

The Crime-Control Model Summarized

This model is concerned primarily with the repression of crime. Thus, efficiency in detecting and processing delinquents is its highest priority. Youthful wrongdoers would be processed quickly and dealt with harshly in an attempt to discourage lawlessness. The operation of a crime-control model has been well described by Herbert Packer:

> The model . . . must . . . (place) a premium on speed and finality . . . The process must not be cluttered up with ceremonious rituals that do not advance the progress of the case. Facts can be established more quickly through interrogation in a police station than through the formal process of examination and cross-examination in a court. It follows that extra-judicial processes should be preferred to judicial processes, informal operations to formal ones. . . .
> . . . (A) successful conclusion is one that throws off at an early stage those cases in which it appears unlikely that the person apprehended is an offender and then secures, as expeditiously as possible, the conviction of the rest, with a minimum of occasions for challenge, let alone post-audit. By the application of administrative expertness, primarily that of the police and prosecutors, an early determination of probable innocence or guilt emerges. Those who are probably innocent are screened

out. Those who are probably guilty are passed quickly through the remaining stages of the process. The key to the operation of the model regarding those who are not screened out is . . . a presumption of guilt.[6]

The word "guilt" is hardly neutral in meaning. It is value laden — charged with connotations of unacceptability and blameworthiness. Thus, when we say that the crime-control model presumes guilt, we mean not merely that it presumes that children brought into the system have actually committed delinquent acts, but also that such acts are evil and that such children are bad.

A Rehabilitative Model of Juvenile Justice

Treat 'em, Don't Beat 'em

The notion of guilt never enters into the rehabilitative model of juvenile justice. Children may commit antisocial, even violent, acts, but they can never be "guilty" because guilt presumes maturity and responsibility.

You might want to look ahead to Chapter 8, in which the underlying assumption of the rehabilitative model — that children are not deserving of punishment because they are not responsible for their behavior — is discussed at some length.

A juvenile justice system based exclusively on the rehabilitation model would seek to provide psychosocial aid and support to children whose development is perceived to be in difficulty or danger. The delinquency of children would be seen primarily as evidence of their need for care and regenerative treatment. The "saving" of children would be justified to a small degree because it can make the streets safe, but mostly it would be justified because it could ensure the future well-being of those children and the society in which they will eventually be adults. Thus the primary objective of a juvenile justice system based on a rehabilitation model is to make it the duty of the state

. . . instead of asking merely whether a boy or a girl has committed a specific offense, to find out what he is, physically, mentally, morally, and then if it learns that he is treading the path that leads to criminality, to take him in charge, not so much to punish as to reform, not to degrade but to uplift, not to crush but to develop, not to make him a criminal but a worthy citizen.[7]

In many respects the operation of the rehabilitative model would be similar to the operation of the crime-control model. In both models it is important to identify delinquents and probable delinquents efficiently and to process them speedily. It is primarily in intent that the models differ.

The Law in a Rehabilitative Model

As in the crime-control model, the legal definition of delinquency would be expansive. Crimes with victims, victimless crimes, and status offenses would all be maintained on the law books. The law's concern would be not only with children whose behavior was harmful, but also with children whose behavior indicated problems of psychosocial adjustment which might result in future delinquency or criminality. Thus, the processing of children who ran away from home, or were truant, or who drank alcohol, or whose moral development was endangered by bad companionship would be permitted. Unlike the crime-control model, the rehabilitative model would justify intervention to help, uplift, and cure delinquent children.

Police Power in a Rehabilitative Model

Police *power* in a rehabilitative model would not be entrusted primarily to the police. Determining the cases in which official intervention would be appropriate would be a job for social workers, educators, and perhaps even clergymen. As the expertise of policemen is limited to crime detection, the police power in a rehabilitative model would be shared with professionals competent in diagnosis and knowledgeable about human growth and development.

The reality that many delinquency complaints are initiated by victims, who must surely be expected to call a policeman rather than a social worker, suggests that a new position in the roster of police personnel would be beneficial: the juvenile specialist. Ideally such an officer would be familiar with social scientific theories about child development and would be trained in psychosocial diagnosis and therapeutic techniques.

Detention in a Rehabilitative Model

Detention facilities would not be used very frequently. They would not exist to protect the community from harmful youngsters whose guilt had not yet been positively proven; instead, they would protect children whose delinquency had not yet been definitely determined but who appeared to be in need of special care and custody. Children who were not welcome at home, or who had no home, or whose homes were abusive and inadequate would be held in detention. As Dean Monrad Paulsen has observed, an adult who can meet bail will be set free: "He can go to a flophouse, he can sleep in the fields. We don't feel a sense of responsibility for him."[8] In the case of a child, however, "We are still likely to worry where he goes and whether he has a home to go to."[9]

While detention centers would probably not have custody of children for extended periods of time, they would be expected to initiate the therapeutic process and to prepare diagnostic reports to expedite the rest of the treatment process.

Adjudication in a Rehabilitative Model

The issue of a child's factual innocence or guilt would not be considered very important in juvenile court hearings. The concern of the courts would focus not so much on what the child had done as on his psychological and social condition. Informality would be the order of the day. As in the crime-control model, all evidence, however obtained, would be admissible. Legal technicalities would not be permitted to stand between a child and the helping facilities of the juvenile court. Defense attorneys would be considered superfluous because the child does not need, and would not benefit from, a defense against help. Fifth Amendment rights would be ignored because a child's silence would hinder diagnostic and therapeutic processes. The denial of constitutional rights to children would be justified on the assertion that due process is designed to protect individuals from a government that wishes to take something from them — for example, liberty; juvenile justice would be seen as a provident, helping, giving social system.

The traditional rhetoric of existing American juvenile justice systems has claimed that constitutional rights are inappropriate in children's courts. Through most of its history the juvenile court has used arguments such as those developed above to justify informal processes. This element of juvenile court history is discussed at length in Chapter 8.

Disposition of Cases in a Rehabilitative Model

The dispositional challenge would be to place delinquent children in the institutional or noninstitutional programs best suited to their needs. A child's delinquency would be seen less as the product of defective character than as the result of imperfect upbringing. The responsibility of the juvenile justice system would be to ensure the existence of a range of treatment strategies responsive to the gamut of needs presented by children. Some attempt might be made to provide services in the home. Homemaker services might be used, for example, when it was believed that simple education might render a child's parents more nearly adequate. Psychiatric counseling would often be used to overcome the perceived deleterious effects of a child's home life. Therapeutic services and supervision in the community might be provided by psychiatric clinics or probation departments. In cases in which a child's home situation was thought to be altogether inadequate, removal from the home would be possible: foster homes, community-based group homes, and major institutions would all be available. Such institutions would be called "training schools" or "reformatories," reflecting their nonpunitive orientation. Anthony Platt has described the actual development of reformatories in the United States as follows:

> Reformatories, unlike penitentiaries and jails, theoretically repudiate punishments based on intimidation and repression. . . . The reformatory system was based on the assumption that proper training can counteract the impositions of poor family life, a corrupt environment, and poverty, while at the same time toughening and preparing delinquents for the struggle ahead. . . . "(This) method of dealing with juvenile crime," wrote William Douglas Morrison, ". . . recognizes the fact that the juvenile delinquent is in the main, a product of adverse individual and social conditions."[10]

A rehabilitative model might encourage the development of a broad range of dispositional services. At one end of a conservative-to-liberal continuum would be programs which seek to change the child so that he may function better in a society deemed equitable and just. At the other end of the continuum, there would be programs designed to organize delinquent youngsters in campaigns for social change in a society perceived to have injured them with such inequities as poverty and racism. An example of such radical "treatment" strategies would be the involvement of delinquent minority-group youngsters in programs designed to develop racial (or ethnic) pride and to foster social change. Middle-range alternatives might involve attempts to change a child's immediate environment without trying to change either the child or the larger community. In Massachusetts, for example, some delinquent children have actually received weekly monetary allowances from the juvenile justice system.[11] However different these programmatic thrusts might be from one another, they share one thing in common: each seeks — or at least claims to seek — to help rather than to punish.

This might be a good time to think about the theories of delinquency discussed in Chapter Two. Each theory implies a different strategy for helping delinquent children. Psychoanalysts and sociologists, for example, might have very different perceptions about what types of programs would actually prove helpful. The impact of theoretical models on social action will be explored in some detail in subsequent chapters.

The Rehabilitative Model Summarized

The basic goal of this model is to provide supportive and regenerative services to children in trouble. The well-being of each child is seen as paramount even to the well-being of the community. The best interests of society, it is believed, will eventually be realized by protecting the best interests of its children. At each stage of the model's operation, attention will focus not on a child's antisocial acts but on his social and psychological condition.

Children whose offenses have been very grave will be treated in much the same manner as children who have offended in only minor ways. It is what the child is, rather than what he has done, that will determine the nature and scope of intervention into his life. This philosophical orientation will effect procedures throughout the system. At intake, adjudication, and disposition, procedures will emphasize informality. The rehabilitative model will "emphasize investigation of the juvenile's background in deciding dispositions, rely heavily on the social sciences for both diagnosis and treatment, and . . . (be) committed to rehabilitation of the juvenile as the predominant goal of the entire system."[12]

In a pure rehabilitative model there would be great confidence in the capacity and effectiveness of the educators, social workers, and juvenile specialists who would provide intake services. At subsequent stages in this model, it would be assumed that children brought into the system were almost certainly in need of services. Accurate determination of innocence or guilt would not be considered overwhelmingly important since the worst that could possibly happen would be that a child who had not committed a delinquent act would be provided with treatment and services that could only prove beneficial. As the crime-control model operates on a presumption of guilt, the rehabilitative model operates on a presumption of neediness.

A Due Process Model of Juvenile Justice

It is Better That a Thousand Offenders Go Free
Than That One Innocent Child Be
Wrongfully Deprived of Liberty

The due process model presumes neither guilt nor need, but innocence. Both of the other models are concerned with efficiency. The crime-control model seeks to identify, isolate, and punish the guilty as efficiently as possible in order to protect the community. The rehabilitative model seeks to identify and provide services to troubled youngsters as efficiently as possible in order to achieve its therapeutic goals. In the due process model accuracy and fairness eclipse efficiency as a value. The virtue of procedure in this model is not that it expedites the handling of cases but that it reduces the probability that decisions will be based on imperfect or inaccurate information.

The due process model is founded on two types of distrust: (1) governmental power is distrusted because the history of man is replete with examples of the powerful using the law to silence those with whom they disagree; and (2) evidence is distrusted because the observations and recollections of witnesses are notoriously imperfect. The second of these concerns is based on recurrent observations of human behavior; the first is based on considerations of philosophy which deserve examination here.

Deprivation of liberty, whether for punitive or therapeutic purposes,[13] is perceived by adherents of the due process model to be stigmatizing and painful to the individual involved.

> Furthermore, the processes that culminate in these highly afflictive sanctions are seen as in themselves coercive, restricting, and demeaning. Power is always subject to abuse — sometimes subtle, other times, as in the criminal process, open and ugly. Precisely because of its potency in subjecting the individual to the coercive power of the stage . . . (a justice system) must, in this model, be subjected to controls that prevent it from operating with maximal efficiency. According to this ideology, maximal efficiency means maximal tyranny.[14]

In large measure the argument that underlies the due process model is that the government must be prohibited from interfering in the lives of even the most culpable, blameworthy, or pathological citizens, unless factual guilt can be *proved* at a fundamentally fair hearing. It is feared that if the government may casually restrict the liberty of "evil men" today, it may also be able to restrict the liberty of "less evil men" tomorrow. Indeed, an evil government would be able casually to restrict the liberty of good men.

This fear of potential abuses of governmental power has been eloquently stated in Sir Robert Bolt's play, *A Man For All Seasons.* The scene quoted below takes place in the home of Sir Thomas More, Lord Chancellor of England. An associate of More's makes thinly veiled threats that he will "injure" More unless More helps him find an important job. More refuses to be intimidated and the associate, Rich, storms out of the house. More's wife, Alice, and his son-in-law, Roper, exhort him to action.[15]

ROPER: Arrest him.
ALICE: Yes!
MORE: For what?
ALICE: He's dangerous!
ROPER: For libel; he's a spy.
ALICE: He is! Arrest him.
MARGARET: Father, that man's bad.
MORE: There is no law against that.
ROPER: There is! God's law!
MORE: Then God can arrest him.

ROPER: Sophistication upon sophistication!

MORE: No, sheer simplicity. The law, the law, I know what's legal not what's right. And I'll stick to what's legal.

ROPER: Then you set Man's law above God's!

MORE: No far below; but let me draw your attention to a fact — I'm *not* God. The currents and eddies of right and wrong which you find such plain sailing, I can't navigate, I'm no voyager. But in the thickets of the law, oh there I'm a forester. I doubt if there's a man alive who could follow me there. Thank God, . . . (he says this to himself)."

ALICE: (exasperated, pointing after RICH): While you talk, he's gone!

MORE: An go he should if he were the Devil himself until he broke the law!

ROPER: So now you'd give the Devil benefit of law!

MORE: Yes. What would you do? Cut a great road through the law to get after the Devil.

ROPER: I'd cut down every law in England to do that!

MORE: (roused and excited): Oh? (Advances on ROPER.) And when the last law was down, and the Devil turned round on you — where would you hide, Roper, the law's all being flat? (Leaves him). This country's planted thick with laws from coast to coast — Man's laws not God's — and if you cut them down — and you're just the man to do it — d'you really think you could stand upright in the winds that would blow then? (Quietly) Yes, I'd give the Devil benefit of law for my own safety's sake.

A Man For All Seasons *is a fictionalized account of the life of Sir Thomas More. It may be of interest to you to know that More fell into the bad graces of King Henry VIII, of whose excess he disapproved. He was removed from his position as Lord Chancellor, one of the two or three most important posts in the realm, and was eventually convicted of treason upon the* perjured *testimony of Rich to the effect that he had publicly stated his disapproval of the King's divorces and remarriages. More was beheaded for his alleged offense, but is remembered kindly by history and indeed has become a saint of the Roman Catholic Church.*

The main characteristic of the due process model, then, is distrust of government. This distrust is peculiar to the due process model; both of the other models are rooted in a deep faith that their goals can be achieved through the exercise of governmental power. Those who would punish all the guilty and those who would treat all the needy stand together, despite their differences, in desiring swift and efficient identification and processing of delinquents. Adherents of the due process model stand alone. Their concern is less with efficiency than with fairness. Their goal is neither the punishment of the guilty nor the treatment of the needy but rather the control of governmental power as exercised in pursuit of a law-abiding community. They believe, along with Mr. Justice Brandeis, that the right to be let alone by one's government is "the most comprehensive of rights and the right most valued by civilized men."[16]

The Law in a Due Process Model

The legal definition of delinquency would be restricted significantly. Victimless crimes and status offenses would quite likely be removed from the law books. Unlike the crime-control and rehabilitative models, the due process model would not tolerate such vague language as that of the California Welfare and Institutions Code, which defines a delinquent child as one "who from any cause is in danger of leading an idle, dissolute, lewd, or immoral life."[17] From the due process perspective such ambiguous statutes tend to make juvenile justice systems repressive both by their vagueness (there is no way of telling in advance what behaviors are prohibited — what, after all, constitutes idle, dissolute, lewd, or immoral behavior?) and by their breadth (anyone could be prosecuted for having done just about anything).

The crime-control model would tolerate such vague statutory language because its concern is not only with the punishment of offenders, but also with the prevention of future offenses. The rehabilitative model would tolerate similarly vague statutes because it seeks to help *all* children in trouble regardless of the seriousness of their antisocial conduct. The due process model, doubting the government's ability to achieve those purposes and fearing the possibility of abuse of power, would demand clear, precise, and narrowly constructed rules defining the behaviors which could result in a finding of delinquency.

Police Power in a Due Process Model

Unlike the crime-control and rehabilitative models, the due process model would be suspicious of any group to which the police power had been entrusted. The crime-control model assumes that the police are efficient in identifying people who are guilty. The rehabilitative model assumes that social workers, educators, and juvenile specialists are efficient in identifying children who are in need of services. The due process model doubts the capacity of all such professions; and furthermore it challenges the notion that efficiency ought to be a goal of justice.[18] A society in which the police power was exercised efficiently might be one in which we would feel secure from criminals; but it is not clear, according to adherents of the due process model, that it would be one in which we would wish to live, because we might not feel secure against governmental invasion of our private lives.

The due process model can be differentiated from the crime-control and rehabilitative models because it is concerned less with the ravages of crime than with the dangers of abusive government. To the adherents of the due process model, every policeman (and perhaps every social worker) has the potential to be the eyes and ears of "Big Brother."

The due process and crime-control models are similar in one regard: in each the police power would be exercised by policemen rather than by social workers, educators, and clergymen. This is because intervention into a child's life would be permitted only upon a showing that he had in fact committed a prohibited act. Delinquency petitions would be initiated by professionals with expertise in the area of crime detection rather than in the area of psychosocial diagnosis.

The fundamental difference between the crime-control and due process models is that the latter is less inclined to trust the ability of policemen to make valid and reliable interpretations of the behavior they observe. Arrest on the basis of suspicion but in the absence of positive proof would be prohibited. Furthermore, searches in the due process model would be permitted only with warrants issued upon a showing of probable cause. Interrogation would be permitted only in the presence of a defense attorney who could help safeguard the right of the accused to remain silent. At all subsequent stages of the model it would be considered necessary and appropriate to review the way in which police power had been exercised.

Detention in a Due Process Model

The use of detention facilities would probably not be very extensive in a due process model. In this model the purposes of detention would be argued: should it be used only for the protection of the community or only for the protection of the child? In any case, the purpose of detention would be of less interest than the manner in which the detention decision was made. Detention, regardless of the purpose for which it is used, constitutes a deprivation of liberty. The decision to detain, in a due process model, would be made by hearing officers rather than by policemen. At detention hearings children would have to be advised of constitutional rights. And, although the hearing would have to be speedy and less thorough than a full-fledged trial, it would have to provide the child (and his lawyer) with a fair opportunity to argue the merits of the case against detention. In addition, the due process model would be fearful that detention itself might be abused. The right of children to be at liberty would be safeguarded by a provision limiting the length of time for which a child could be restrained in detention; if the delinquency hearing did not begin within a few weeks after arrest, a child held in detention would have to be released and the charges against him dropped.[19]

Adjudication in a Due Process Model

The trial would be perceived as the most important part of the whole process a society uses to deal with law enforcement. This is so for two reasons: (1) it provides an opportunity to review all the evidence collected, which minimizes the possibility of mistaken judgments; and (2) it provides an opportunity to police the operation of the entire juvenile justice system in order to ensure that the government has not abused its power.

The first of these purposes, protecting against mistaken judgments, requires that all evidence obtained by the police and by prosecutors be rigorously evaluated. Defendants would be assisted by lawyers, would be allowed to confront and cross-examine witnesses against them, would be permitted to introduce exculpatory evidence, and would be convicted only if the evidence against them were clear beyond a reasonable doubt. These hurdles to effective prosecution make it quite possible that a factually guilty youngster might nevertheless be found to be "not guilty." This does not mean that Justice in a due process system would be blind, nor necessarily that it

would be a fool; it means only that the due process model would be unwilling to restrict the liberty of youngsters whose guilt was not *absolutely* certain. A finding of "not guilty" would not mean that the court believed a youngster to be "innocent" but only that it believed his guilt had not been satisfactorily proven.

> *Imagine how angry a policeman might be when*
> *a youngster he "knows" to be guilty is acquitted,*
> *not because the court believes the youngster*
> *really to be innocent, but only because it is not*
> *satisfied with the evidence that points to guilt.*

The second of these purposes, policing the police, requires that attention focus not only on the evidence presented in court, but also on the way the evidence was collected. In the due process model it may sometimes be necessary to release a child whose guilt is certain because the evidence has been obtained unlawfully.

(T)he Due Process Model, although it may in the first instance be addressed to the maintenance of reliable fact-finding techniques, comes eventually to incorporate prophylactic and deterrent rules that result in the release of the factually guilty even in cases in which blotting out the . . . (illegally obtained evidence) would still leave an adjudicative fact-finder convinced of the accused person's guilt. Only by penalizing errant police and prosecutors within the criminal process itself can adequate pressure be maintained, so the argument runs, to induce conformity with the Due Process Model.[20]

In summary, the hearing stage in the due process model provides an opportunity to make sure that the police do not do their job by disregarding the rights of citizens. Illegally obtained evidence, coerced confessions, and any other unapproved forms of evidence would be inadmissible. Furthermore, admissible evidence would be subject to careful scrutiny in an adversarial system designed to protect the innocent even at the cost of sometimes letting the guilty go free.

Disposition of Cases in a Due Process Model

The due process model is compatible with either the traditional notion (that the punishment "fit" the crime) or the rehabilitative ideal (that the treatment strategy "fit" the needs of the offender). Attention in the due process model would focus less on the content of dispositions than on the fairness of the decision-making process.

Proponents of the due process model tend to be concerned with disparity in sentencing and with the inequality that results from such disparity.[21] It is conceivable that the due process and crime-control models might converge on this issue: the concern of the former and the methods of the latter could result in a justice system in which all youngsters found to have committed the same offense receive the same sentence. In this combination of the due process and crime-control models the legislature would declare the penalties for all imaginable offenses. All robbers, for example, would receive so many years; all car thieves would receive so many years; etc. Judges would have little responsibility at the dispositional stage. They would merely look to the statutes to determine which punishment to administer in each and every case. This somewhat rigid system, while conceivably undesirable for many social reasons, would have the advantage of minimizing inequities.

Is it fundamentally unfair that some car thieves get sent away for several years while others get probation? Is it reasonable that some youngsters who make obscene telephone calls get sent to institutions while other youngsters who commit assaults are kept at home while receiving

---

Cookbook sentencing (or statute-book sentencing, as the case may be) is hardly a possibility in the twentieth century. Individualized sentencing has emerged as a basic principle of modern penology.[22] In adult as well as juvenile justice systems the judiciary has been vested with broad discretion, and sentencing has become the most difficult and often the only function of the bench.[23] The dispositional arena is one in which the rehabilitative ideal (or at least its rhetoric) has had great influence. The danger in this is that the key variable in sentencing may become the judge; that is, that the sentence a youngster gets may depend less on what he did, or on what his "condition" is, than on the idiosyncrasies of the particular judge who hears the case. How can the due process, concerned with equality, be reconciled with treatment-oriented justice?

There appear to be three resolutions to this dilemma. First, the discretion of judges in a due process/rehabilitative model should not be unlimited. Statutes would be written so as to give judges options in each case but not to give judges total freedom to do whatever they please.[24] Second, the social investigation on which dispositional decisions are based would be open to the juvenile and to his lawyer. Disclosure of the contents of such reports would allow defendants to refute evidence damaging to their chances of obtaining leniency. Furthermore, such disclosure would make the real bases of dispositional decisions more visible and would cause sentencing disparities to stand out comparatively sharply.[25] Finally, in the due process model, appeals from sentencing decisions would be permitted. Appellate courts would be expected to review the sentences of lower courts and would thus be in a position to ensure that sentences would not vary too markedly from court to court.[26]

In short, the due process model would insist either that all similar offenses be similarly punished, or that all similar offenders be similarly treated. Sentencing disparities based on the varied biases and prejudices of judges would be impermissible.

The Due Process Model Summarized

The major characteristic of this model is its lack of concern for efficiency. It is not primarily concerned with the successful identification and processing of large numbers of offenders from whom the community must be protected; nor is it primarily concerned with the successful identification and processing of large numbers of troubled children in need of help. The due process model is concerned with the reliability (that is, the precision, the accuracy) and fairness of the fact-finding procedures which occur prior to a decision to intervene in the life of an individual.

> The aim of the process is at least as much to protect the factually innocent as it is to convict the factually guilty. . . . The Due Process Model resembles a factory that has to devote a substantial part of its input to quality control. This necessarily cuts down on quantitative input.[27]

The fundamental presumption underlying each stage in this model is the presumption of innocence. Intake decisions, whether made by policemen or by social workers, are perceived as potentially inaccurate. The purpose of the trial is to assure that the government, whether it intends to punish or to rehabilitate, can carry the burden of *proving* factual guilt beyond a reasonable doubt. The accused person is to be protected by an array of rights, such as the right to remain silent and the right to be represented by counsel, because findings of guilt may result in substantial restrictions of his liberty.

The due process model does not rest on the notion that the repression of crime is desirable, nor does it rest on the notion that the provision of therapeutic services is desirable. It rests, rather, on the fear that erroneous or even malicious decisions to punish or to "treat" are all too possible in a justice system staffed by imperfect men. If this model gives every advantage to the accused, it is because it sees the individual, even the worst or most pathological individual, as less capable of destroying society than society is capable of destroying any individual.

Reflection: Some Common Ground

Thus far we have focused on differences among the three models. It is essential to note that there are also important commonalities. There are few issues about which all three of the models agree (except perhaps that the state has a right to declare certain behaviors to be a social threat of a nature sufficient to allow the state to deprive an offender of his liberty). There are, however, many areas in which we can identify similarities between any two of the models. Let us consider three issues.

With regard to the importance of *efficiency,* the crime-control and rehabilitative models might be quite similar. Adherents of both models might believe that the goal of their model can be achieved only if large numbers of appropriate children are identified and processed with great speed and at low cost. It is only adherents of the due process model who might disagree about the virtue of efficiency.

With regard to the importance of *social protection,* due process and rehabilitative models might have much in common. In both models the sanctity of the individual would be valued. Only in the crime-control model would the interests of the individual clearly be subjugated to the interests of the community. In the rehabilitative model, the *needs* of the individual would be paramount; in the due process model, the *rights* of the individual would be paramount. In the crime-control model the needs and rights of the *community* would be paramount.

With regard to the importance of *guilt,* the crime-control and due process models would have much in common. Adherents of the due process model would find intrusion into the lives of innocent people to be blasphemous, immoral, wholly unacceptable. Adherents of the crime-control model would find such intrusion to be unfortunate and ineffective, chiefly because the incapacitation of innocent people would not serve to make the streets any safer. Adherents of the rehabilitative model, believing therapeutic intervention always to be helpful, never harmful, would be less concerned about the issue of factual innocence or guilt. Even an innocent person may benefit from treatment; and thus, that person and the community may both gain even if the disposition is based on an erroneous finding of guilt.

Throughout most of this chapter we have spoken about ideal types of models as though they really existed. It is absolutely essential that you realize that *no such models actually exist in the real world.* These models are conceptual tools designed to help you make sense out of trends, tendencies, and conditions that you may find in the real world. Not only will you never find an ideal-type model, you will probably never find an individual who is single-minded in his devotion to such a model. Few, if any, of us are concerned about crime control to the exclusion of concerns about due process and humane treatment. Similarly, few are concerned with due process to the exclusion of concerns about rising crime rates and the needs of children to be properly cared for; and, of course, few are concerned about the rehabilitation of children to the exclusion of concerns about social protection and due process.

In the real world, juvenile justice systems and the people who staff them are full of conflict, ambivalence, and uncertainty. From community to community the relative importance of competing goals may differ greatly. Within a community the values and attitudes of some policemen, and some judges, and some probation officers may differ sharply from the values and attitudes of other policemen, judges, and probation officers. From day to day the attitudes of any given policeman, judge, or probation officer may change. The real world of juvenile justice is in a state of perpetual flux.

These lyrics from the Broadway musical, *West Side Story,* * underline the points made in this chapter: the song, sung by the members of a teenage gang, demonstrates the diverse orientations that exist within juvenile justice systems.

"Gee, Officer Krupke"

All: Dear kindly sergeant Krupke,
      You gotta under stand
      Its just our bringin' up-ke.
      That gets us out of hand.

      Our mothers all are junkies,
      Our fathers all are drunks.
      Golly Moses, natcherly we're punks.

      Gee, Officer Krupke, we're very upset.
      We never had the love that every child oughta get.
      We aint no delinquents, we're misunderstood.
      Deep down inside us there is good.
      There is untapped good.
      Like inside, the worst of us is good.

Skit I

Snowboy: (*Imitating Krupke*)

      That's a touching story.

Action: Lemme tell it to the world.

*WEST SIDE STORY — "Gee, Officer Krupke"
Book — Arthur Laurents; Music — Leonard Bernstein; Lyrics — Stephen Sondheim
Copyright 1957 BY LEONARD BERNSTEIN AND STEPHEN SONDHEIM. USED BY PERMISSION OF
G. SCHIRMER, INC.

Snowboy:	(*Shoving him*)
	Just tell it to the judge.

Action to
Disel:
Dear kindly judge, your Honor,
My parents treat me rough.
With all their marijuana
They won't give me a puff.
They didn't want to have me,
But somehow I was had.
Leapin' lizards.
That's why I'm so bad.

Right, Officer Krupke,
You're really a square.
This boy don't need a judge.
He needs a analyst's care.

It's just his neurosis,
That oughta be curbed.
He's psychologically disturbed.

I'm disturbed.
We're disturbed.
We're the most disturbed.
Like we're psychologically disturbed.

Skit II
Disel: (*Imitating judge*)

In the opinion of this court this child
is depraved on account he ain't had a normal home.

Action: Hey, I'm depraved on account I'm deprived.

Disel: So, take him to a head shrinker.

Action:
My father is a bastard,
My ma's an S.O.B.
My grandpa's always plastered,
My grandma pushes tea.
My sister wears a mustach.
My brother wears a dress.
Goodness gracious.
That's why I'm a mess.

Yes, Officer Krupke
You're really a slob.
This boy don't need a doctor,
Just a good honest job.
Society's played him a terrible trick,
And sociologically he's sick.

I'm sick.
We're sick.

We're sick, sick, sick.
Like we're sociologically sick.

Skit III

Arab: (*Imitating psychiatrist*)

In my opinion this child don't need to have
his head shrunk at all. Juvenile delinquency
is purely a social disease.

Action: Hey, I got a social disease.

Arab: So, take him to a social worker.

Action: (*To Baby John*)

Dear kindly social worker,
They say go earn a buck.
Like be a soda jerker,
Which means like be a schmuck.
It's not I'm anti-social.
I'm only anti-work.
Gloryosky, that's why I'm a jerk.

Baby John: (*Imitating a female social worker*)

Eek.

Officer Krupke, you've done it again.
This boy don't need a job.
He needs a year in the pen.
It ain't just a question of misunderstood,
Deep down inside him, he's no good.

I'm no good.
We're no good.
We're no earthly good.
Like the best of us
Is no damn good.

Judge: The trouble is he's crazy.

Psych: The trouble is he drinks.

Social
Worker: The trouble is he's lazy.

Judge: The trouble is he stinks.

Psych: The trouble is he's growing.

Social
Worker: The trouble is he's grown.

All: Krupke, we got troubles of our own.
Gee, Krupke, we got troubles of our own.

Gee, Officer Krupke, we're down on our knees,
'Cause no one wants a fellow with a social disease.

Gee, Officer Krupke, What are we to do?
Gee, Officer Krupke, Krup you.

References

1. George Wallace in a campaign speech, quoted in George Cole, *The American System of Criminal Justice* (N. Scituate, Mass.: Duxbury Press, 1975, p. 3).
2. White House Conference on Children, *Report to the President* (Washington, D.C.: U. S. Government Printing Office, 1970), p. 4.
3. 387 U.S. 1, pp. 19 - 21 (1967).
4. Jerome Skolnick, *Justice Without Trial* (New York: John Wiley & Sons, 1966).
5. Herbert L. Packer, *The Limits of the Criminal Sanction* (Stanford: Stanford University Press, 1968), p. 162.
6. Ibid., pp. 159 - 60.
7. Julian Mack, "The Juvenile Court," 23 *Harvard L. Rev.* 104, (1909).
8. Monrad G. Paúlsen, "The Changing World of Juvenile Law, New Horizons for Juvenile Court Legislation," 40 *Penn. Bar Assoc. Q.* 30, 34 (1968).
9. Ibid., p. 34.
10. Anthony M. Platt, "The Rise of the Child Saving Movement: A Study in Social Policy and Correctional Reform," *Annals of the American Academy of Political and Social Science* 381 (January 1969): 29.
11. This information was obtained in an interview with Dr. Jerome Miller, former director of the Department of Youth Services in Massachusetts.
12. President's Commission on Law Enforcement and Administration of Justice, *The Challenge of Crime in a Free Society* (Washington, D. C.: U.S. Government Printing Office, 1967), p. 79.
13. See Francis Allen, "Criminal Justice, Legal Values and the Rehabilitative Ideal," *Journal of Criminal Law, Criminology and Police Science* 50 (1959): 226 - 32.
14. Packer, *Limits of Criminal Sanction*, pp. 165 - 6.
15. Robert Bolt, *A Man For All Seasons* (London: Heinemann, 1968), p. 38.
16. *Ohlmstead* v. *U.S.,* 277 U.S. 438, 478 (1928).
17. West's Ann. Cal. Welf. and Inst. Code, § 601.
18. See, generally, Packer, *Limits of Criminal Sanction*, pp. 163 - 73.
19. See, for example, §12 of the Pennsylvania Juvenile Act of 1972.
20. Packer, *Limits of Criminal Sanction*, p. 168.
21. See, generally, D. Katkin, "Presentence Investigation Reports: An Analysis of Uses, Limitations, and Civil Liberties Issues," 35 *Minn. L. Rev.* 15 (1970).
22. Felix Frankfurter and James M. Landis, *The Business of the Supreme Court* (New York: Macmillan, 1927), p. 249.

23. See "Note, Due Process and Legislative Standards in Sentencing," 101 *V. Pa. L. Rev.* 257 (1952).

24. See, generally, Katkin, "Presentence Investigation Reports," pp. 22 - 3.

25. Ibid., pp. 24 - 31.

26. See Note on Sentencing Disparities in M. Paulsen and S. Kadish, Criminal Law and the Processes: Cases and Materials 162 (1962).

27. Packer, *Limits of Criminal Sanction,* p. 165.

4 The Real World of Juvenile Justice

Ius est ars boni et aequi. (Justice is the art of the good and the fair.)

— *Latin saying*

Hogan's r-right whin he says: "Justice is blind." Blind she is, an' deef an' dumb an' has a wooden leg.

— *Mr. Dooley (Finley Peter Dunne)*

The purpose of this chapter is to provide, in an anecdotal manner, a sense of the broad range of cases, procedures, and dispositions possible in America's many juvenile justice systems. The cases discussed are not necessarily representative; indeed, the very point of this chapter is that any of these cases might have been concluded differently had they come to the attention of different policemen, or had they been heard before different judges, or had they involved different lawyers or social workers, or had the children involved had different personalities or social characteristics.

The facts of the cases about to be presented are basically true. In some cases they are embellished, just a little, in order to highlight important theoretical conceptions. Remember that, for purposes of this book, the cases are less interesting for what they tell us about the children involved than for what they tell us about the juvenile justice system.

The Cases

Edwin M.

Fifteen-year-old Edwin M. caused the deliberate, premeditated knife-stabbing death of fourteen-year-old Francisco Sanchez — an act which, had Edwin been an adult, would have constituted the act of murder.

Edwin was identified by witnesses to the homicide and was immediately taken into custody by the police, who brought him to the New York City Youth House, where he was placed in pretrial detention.

A bright, young, aggressive recent graduate of an ivy league law school, working on the staff of Mobilization For Youth, was assigned to the case.

Mobilization For Youth, a fairly radical, activist community organization in New York, is discussed at some length in Chapter 11.

The defense entered a series of time-consuming procedural motions which caused the trial to be postponed for two years. After nine months Edwin was released from detention and remanded to the custody of his parents. During the following year the staff of Mobilization For Youth got him involved in psychotherapy, a special education program, and even a community leadership training project, in all of which he made good progress. When the trial finally began, the defense moved to have the case dismissed on the grounds that the juvenile court had jurisdiction *only* over children who (1) had committed a delinquent act, *and* (2) were in need of supervision, care, or treatment. It was argued that Edwin had received, and would continue to receive, better treatment in the community than the juvenile court could possibly provide. The judge postponed the hearing in order to have time to deliberate whether the court in fact had jurisdiction in this case.

After an eight-month delay, the juvenile court judge issued an opinion stating that the court did not have jurisdiction even though a delinquent act had almost certainly been committed; the judge had decided that Edwin was no longer in need of treatment, care, or supervision. The purpose of the juvenile court, Judge G. wrote, is to provide helping services to needy children; Edwin had already received (and responded well to) better services in the community than the juvenile justice system could have provided. Consequently the charges were dismissed.

It is very important to note that the judge did not first try Edwin and then release him; rather, he decided that because Edwin no longer needed treatment the court was without power even to try him. What do you think about the way in which this case was resolved? How do you suppose the parents of Francisco Sanchez felt? Do you suppose that the same result could possibly have been obtained in a criminal case involving an adult?

Diane M.

Eleven-year-old Diane M. was habitually truant from school, missing as many days as she attended. At school she tended to fall asleep; when awake she behaved badly. Diane ran away from home several times; and there was evidence, although not positive proof, that she engaged in prostitution.

Diane had been known to the juvenile court of Memphis, Tennessee for several years. Indeed, she was on probation because of her habitual truancy. She violated a condition of probation — that she stay home at night — and her exasperated mother complained to the probation department. Diane was brought to the Youth House of Detention while awaiting a hearing on her probation violation.

Mrs. M. waived Diane's right to representation by counsel. At the hearing the facts of the case were told to the judge by a probation officer. Diane was crying and appeared to be frightened; she declined to say anything in her own behalf. The hearing, which took only a few minutes, resulted in a finding of delinquency.

Prior to the hearing, the probation officer on the case had arranged a foster home placement for Diane. The judge was asked to approve the plans that had already been made. Diane was told that she was lucky to be going to a foster home and that a reappearance in court for running away or behaving badly would result in institutionalization.

Randi B.

Sixteen-year-old Randi B. was severely retarded and had a major speech impediment. Randi had gotten onto a bus that stopped for him in the middle of a fairly busy street. He asked the driver, a woman, to wait for a moment so that his lame mother could get to the bus. The driver explained that she would have to pull up to the bus stop at the corner. But, when the bus began to move, Randi became alarmed and frustrated; he yelled at her to stop, then punched her once on the shoulder and once on the head.

A passenger chased Randi off the bus. The driver closed the doors and called for help on a shortwave radio. Within minutes the police arrived and took Randi and his mother, who was brandishing a knife, into custody. That same afternoon Mrs. B. was released on bail and Randi was remanded into her custody by the Pittsburgh juvenile court.

The bus company, upset by the large number of assaults on drivers, sent an attorney to assist in the prosecution. Randi was represented by a Legal Aid lawyer. The bus driver, Randi, and Randi's mother all gave testimony under oath and were subjected to cross-examination. Randi admitted to having hit the driver but claimed to have been provoked by obscene language, which the driver denied having used. After all testimony had been taken, the judge retired to his chambers with both lawyers and the probation officer and discussed Randi's "obvious" need for treatment. A few minutes later, in the courtroom, the judge told Randi that he did not believe the bus driver had shouted obscenities and that, even if she had, it was not a justification for physical violence. A finding of delinquency was entered.

After being given a stern lecture, Randi was told he would be placed on probation. The probation officer was instructed to try to find employment for Randi in a sheltered workshop.

William G.

Fourteen-year-old William G. was charged with having assaulted a minor child, Kathy P., aged three, with the intent to sexually fondle. Mrs. P. claimed to have found passion marks (hickeys) on her daughter's neck and to have been told by Kathy that William, a babysitter, was responsible and that he had "touched her all over."

Mrs. P. complained to William's mother, who became angry and verbally abusive. Incensed by that reaction, Mrs. P. called the police, who brought William to the Memphis Youth House of Detention where he was subjected to extensive psychological evaluation.

Mrs. P. gave conflicting and imprecise statements about the case; she appeared to be an unreliable witness. William denied all the charges; but psychologists and social workers involved in the case felt that William was "severely disturbed," that his problems centered around "sexual orientation," and that it was conceivable that he might have fondled the child.

At the hearing, William's court-appointed Legal Aid lawyer explained that the case might well hinge on the testimony of three-year-old Kathy P.; he suggested that the potential unreliability of such testimony justified a special pretrial meeting. The judge, defense attorney, district attorney, and two probation officers stepped into chambers. Mrs. P. and Kathy were asked in to tell their story. After they left, all parties agreed that the child's testimony was not very useful and that Mrs. P.'s admitted fear of boy babysitters, even before the alleged incident occurred, was suspicious. William was invited in to tell his side of the story. After he left, all parties agreed that he seemed to be a strange, sullen, emotionally disturbed child. The judge said that his primary concern was with helping William. The district attorney said he was willing to settle for an informal adjustment of the case. The defense attorney suggested that William be found "a child in need of supervision," rather than a "delinquent child." Back in court, the judge explained that the delinquency petition was dismissed but that William had been found to be in need of supervision.

The judge explained to William that he did not consider him to be a "bad boy"; nevertheless a serious charge had been leveled against him, and it was clear to all the professionals involved in the case that William would benefit from counseling. The probation department was instructed to provide or secure therapeutic services.

Peter B.

Three-year-old Peter B. lived with his mother. For six months, her boyfriend, whom she planned to marry, lived with them. Ms. B. had taken to asking her boyfriend to assist in disciplining Peter. On one such occasion, when Peter refused to get dressed, the boyfriend became short tempered and beat the child repeatedly around the face and body with a belt. There was evidence that Peter had been severely bruised at least once before.

A neighbor who heard Peter crying and screaming as he was

beaten and who had noticed his bruises on earlier occasions called the police; they took Peter to the emergency room of the local hospital, which called the Department of Child Welfare. A child welfare worker swore out a petition alleging child abuse. Peter was held in the hospital for several days and was then released into the custody of the Department of Child Welfare, which placed him in a foster home pending a hearing on the petition.

At a informal pretrial hearing in chambers, Ms. B.'s privately retained attorney presented a psychiatric report which stated that neither Ms. B. nor her boyfriend were sado-masochistic or otherwise vicious people. The psychiatrist believed that the boyfriend's "overzealousness" in disciplining the child was due to a lack of experience in dealing with children. The boyfriend was not considered to be a future threat to Peter or to any other child. The child welfare worker involved in the case indicated that the department would be willing to have the abuse petition dismissed provided that Ms. B. would accept supervision in the home. The lawyer said that was acceptable, and the petition was dismissed.

Peter was sent home the following day. Ms. B. was told that there would be occasional visits from a child welfare worker over the next year. She was also told that any future incidents would almost surely result in the child's removal from her custody.

Thomas C.

Sixteen-year-old Thomas C. had a "bad trip" on L.S.D. Although he had used that drug and others on earlier occasions without obvious adverse effects, this time he became fearful and hysterical. He was unable to find his home even though he was only a few blocks away. In his frantic search, he knocked on the doors of several strangers who became alarmed by his appearance and called the police; the police found him lying on the street crying frantically; they identified Thomas and inquired of his parents whether he had used drugs before. They were told that he had, which prompted them to take him into custody. A review of police records indicated that Thomas was known to undercover police agents to whom he had allegedly sold L.S.D. Although the police had not intended to charge Thomas with illegal sale of drugs until after "surfacing" their undercover agents, the charge was entered at the time of his arrest. Thomas was held in the Memphis Youth House of Detention while awaiting a hearing to determine whether his case should be waived to the adult criminal court.

At the waiver hearing, Thomas was represented by a young, comparatively inexperienced, privately retained attorney. The district attorney and two high-ranking police officers were also present. The undercover agents to whom the sale of L.S.D. was allegedly made had not yet "surfaced" and thus were not in court. Several members of Teen Challenge, a religiously affiliated drug treatment group, were present; they explained to the judge that Thomas had become involved with them while in detention and asked the court to retain custody so that they could continue to work with Thomas. The judge said that he could not see evidence that "the Lord had come into Thomas' heart" because Thomas was still unwilling to admit his sale of drugs to the undercover agents. Thomas explained that he would not admit to the sale because he was innocent. A probation officer who had been working with Thomas in detention said that he considered the entire issue "irrelevent" because Thomas had admitted to him that he had made other drug sales but merely denied this one.

You might be interested to know that the probation officer prefaced his remarks by saying: "I do not think I am betraying any confidence by telling you this. . . ." Do you think that incriminating remarks made to a probation officer ought to be admissible in juvenile court? How about in a criminal court?

The judge said that the primary issue in the case appeared to be one of factual guilt or innocence. The issue, he thought, could be as well resolved in criminal court as in juvenile court. Citing the seriousness of the allegation, he waived jurisdiction.

Thomas' trial in the criminal court took place several months later. The undercover agents were still involved in street work and were not ready to "surface." In the absence of their testimony there was no competent proof and all charges were dismissed.

Robert S.

Seventeen-year-old Robert S. was asked by a nineteen-year-old friend if he wanted to get some "easy money." Robert agreed to drive to a neighborhood store. Along the way (if not earlier) it became clear that his friend's intention was to commit armed robbery. Robert waited in the car while the robbery was committed. Then he drove to another store where a second armed robbery was committed while he again waited in the car.

The police were notified immediately after the first robbery; the getaway car was described by witnesses who had even noted the license plate number. Within minutes after the commission of the second robbery the car was stopped. The stolen money and pistol were found under the front seat. Robert and his "adult" friend were both taken into custody. Robert was held in the Memphis Youth House of Detention while awaiting a hearing to determine whether his case should be waived to the adult criminal court.

At the waiver hearing, Robert was represented by an outstanding (and expensive) defense attorney. The state was represented by an assistant attorney general. Evidence was presented by a police officer who was examined and cross-examined by both attorneys. The evidence indicated that Robert had certainly driven the getaway car, but there was some possibility that he had done it under duress. The judge suggested a conference in chambers with both attorneys and a probation officer. At the conference, everyone agreed that waiver of the case to criminal court would probably result in a conviction for armed robbery. The defense attorney emphasized the possibility that Robert had been frightened by his compatriot; he spoke eloquently about Robert's future, about his family, and about his suitability for rehabilitation. The attorney general indicated that he was willing to see the case retained in juvenile court but would not like to see the boy placed on probation or in some other noninstitutional treatment program. The defense attorney expressed his feeling that Robert would be much better off if placed in reform school rather than in prison. The judge decided to retain jurisdiction in exchange for a plea of guilty.

The defense attorney told Robert and his parents about the agreement that had been reached. Robert's parents were delighted. The boy, however, protested that he'd driven the car because he had been threatened, that he was innocent, and that he wanted a trial. He shouted at his parents not to accept the deal and then sobbed uncontrollably. Nevertheless, the defense attorney and Robert's parents convinced the judge that the boy was overwrought and confused and that a plea of guilty was agreeable. The plea was accepted and Robert was sent to a reform school for an intermediate period of time not to extend beyond his twenty-first birthday.

Stanley I. and Jane G.

Seventeen-year-old Stanley I. and sixteen-year-old Jane G. engaged in sexual intercourse, as a result of which Jane became pregnant. Without the consent of their parents, they crossed state lines from New Jersey to Maryland where the laws permitted their marriage.

Immediately after their marriage, Stanley and Jane went to Pennsylvania where they resided with relatives of Stanley's until they found an apartment of their own. Shortly thereafter, complaints were filed by Jane's parents in New Jersey. The New Jersey police contacted the police in Philadelphia; although the marriage was legally valid in Pennsylvania, the Philadelphia police abducted the youngsters and returned them to the authorities in New Jersey who placed them in the custody of their respective parents pending a hearing in juvenile court.

Stanley's parents, although unhappy about the marriage, retained a defense attorney. The defense argued that the juvenile court had no jurisdiction over the case because (1) the children were no longer residents of New Jersey, and (2) a legally valid marriage, although it could not have been entered into in New Jersey, could nonetheless not form the basis for a finding of delinquency. The judge denied the motion to dismiss on the ground that a ruling which permitted children to escape the control of their parents merely by going to a state with different laws would be bad public policy. The facts of the case had never been in controversy; the judge concluded that the facts were sufficient to sustain a finding of delinquency.

The judge was unable to annul the marriage because annulment is permitted only when requested by a party to the marriage. He placed the couple in the custody of their respective parents and instructed the probation department to provide them with counseling.

The cases of Diane M., William G., Peter B., Thomas C., and Robert S. were all drawn (with some small modifications) from Juvenile Court, *a documentary film by Frederick Wiseman about the juvenile justice system of Memphis, Tennessee. The film is excellent and presents many cases besides those discussed in this chapter.*

The case of Randi B. was observed by the

*authors in a juvenile court in Pittsburgh. Edwin
M.'s case actually involved several youngsters.
It was heard in the Family Court of New York
City, and is reported under the name In the
Matter of Edwin R., et al., at 323 N.Y.S. 2d 909
(1971). The case of Stanley I. and Jane G. is
reported under the name STATE in the interest
of S.I. at 68 N.J. Super. 598, 173 A. 2d 457 (1961).*

*These cases, taken together, demonstrate the
broad range of problems that may come to the
attention of juvenile justice systems, the myriad
ways in which such problems may be identified,
and the variety of possible responses. Consider
the aggregate of cases we have been reviewing
(see Table 4.1).*

The Relevance of Crime-Control, Rehabilitative, and Due Process Values in These Cases

In this cluster of cases it is possible to see the influence of attitudes and values associated with each of the three ideal models discussed in the last chapter. The release of Edwin M., for example, demonstrates the potential potency of the rehabilitative model. The other serious offenses (Thomas C.'s use and sale of drugs; Robert S.'s participation in an armed robbery) resulted in waiver hearings; the fact that both these offenses were subject to possible consideration by an adult court surely shows the influence of crime-control concerns. In each of these three very serious cases, lawyers were actively involved. Edwin M.'s lawyer was a tough, committed advocate in the finest tradition of the due process model. Robert S. may have hated his lawyer for allowing him to be sent to reform school; but to outsiders Robert appears very lucky indeed to have avoided criminal court and the probability of prison.

The less serious cases were generally less formal, and less legalistic. Lawyers involved in those cases tended to be bargainers rather than adversaries. It is not clear, however, whether an adversarial stance would have served their clients better.[1]

These eight cases are not "representative" of work of juvenile justice systems across the United States; nevertheless, they

TABLE 4.1. Capsule Summary of Eight Cases

	Offense	Intake	Detention	Adjudication	Disposition
Edwin M.	Murder	Police	Youth House — 9 months; custody of parents — 15 months	Case dismissed because no jurisdiction over "cured" youngsters.	Set free
Diane M.	Truancy; Run-away	Probation officer called by mother	Youth House	Delinquent	Foster Home
Randi B.	Assault	Police, called by victim	Custody of mother	Delinquent	Probation
William G.	Child molesting	Police, called by victim's mother	Youth House	Child in Need of Supervision	Probation
Peter B.	Victim of Child Abuse	Neighbor Police Hospital Child Welfare	Foster Home	Case dismissed	Informal supervision of the home
Thomas C.	Use and sale of L.S.D.	Police called by neighbors	Youth House	Waived to criminal court	Case dismissed by Criminal Ct.
Robert S.	Armed robbery	Police called by victims	Youth House	Delinquent	Reform School
Stanley I and Jane G.	Ran away to get married	Police called by parents	Custody of parents	Delinquent	Probation

demonstrate a range of possible offenses, procedures, and dispositions. It is quite likely that any of these cases might have been concluded very differently. Had the murder charge been heard before a different judge, or had the case been prepared by a less talented lawyer, Edwin M. would quite probably have been sent to reform school or perhaps prison. Had Robert S. been represented by a less able attorney, or even had the same lawyer represented him before a different judge, or had Robert's family been less obviously upper-middle-class in demeanor, Robert might well have gone to jail rather than reform school. Stanley I. and Jane G. were actually abducted from Pennsylvania to New Jersey. Some police executives might have refused to let that happen; some judges might have been very upset about it. Had the police behavior come to the attention of different persons in authority, or had Jane's parents been less obstinate, the children would quite likely have been allowed to go their own way unfettered.

Despite their dissimilarities, these cases have something important in common: each came to the attention not merely of the juvenile justice system, but of a juvenile court. Most youngsters who commit murder or armed robbery will become deeply enmeshed in the juvenile justice system. Surely, however, many more children use and even sell drugs than ever come to the attention of the police, let alone of a judge. Similarly, it is exceedingly rare that children who run off to get married wind up on probation. It is important, before ending this chapter, that we put these cases into perspective: juvenile justice systems process far fewer cases than they divert or ignore.

The Real Operation of Juvenile Justice: Diversion

In this section we are going to present data about the operation of the juvenile justice systems in the Commonwealth of Pennsylvania.[2] The data indicate that diversion (that is, the informal resolution of cases at early stages of the system's operation) is the everyday working rule of juvenile justice. The system operates to *exclude* from its processes the vast majority of juveniles who engage in delinquent behavior.

The operating principles which determine whether a child will be processed or diverted are not

obvious; indeed, it may be that decision making
is so idiosyncratic that it defies rational analysis.
In subsequent chapters each of the important
decision-making segments of the juvenile justice
system will be examined in detail in order to
explicate the processes which, in conjunction
with quirks of fate and idiosyncrasies of
personalities, determine the resolution of
individual cases.

In the remaining pages of this chapter, attention will focus on the numbers of cases resolved at each identifiable stage in the system's operation. Perhaps the most striking characteristic of juvenile justice systems is the extent to which they divert young people who have committed delinquent acts from ever experiencing the adjudicatory process. Traditional thinking has generally regarded diversion as a function primarily of a police decision to initiate or refrain from initiating further legal process.[3] This tendency to view diversion as a process of one subsystem (police) rather than as a process of the entire system obscures the effects of all the other components of juvenile justice systems and renders analysis of the criteria for decision making virtually impossible. *Diversion begins when public officials or private citizens decide whether to bring an instance of delinquent behavior to the attention of the police, and it continues throughout the judicial process.*

To appreciate the extent to which diversion exists, one must appreciate the extent to which delinquency exists. Self-report studies reveal that almost 90 percent of all young people have committed at least one act for which they could be brought to juvenile court. One regional study in Pennsylvania, conducted by the National Council on Crime and Delinquency, suggests that every child under eighteen years of age in the region studied could be apprehended and placed in detention.[4] While it is true that many of the offenses for which young people can be charged are relatively trivial (fighting, truancy, running away from home, etc.) the population "at risk" of apprehension is large; 90 percent of the ten-to-eighteen age group represents approximately 1.4 million youngsters in Pennsylvania. Obviously, most juvenile delinquents never come to the attention of the police. In 1971, 92,000 young people[5] were taken into custody by representatives of any of Pennsylvania's more than 4000 police jurisdictions.[6]

What happens to the 94 percent of the 1.4 million youngsters in Pennsylvania who commit delinquent acts but never come to the attention of the police? Almost certainly most of them are never detected by anyone. It is equally certain, however, that many of their delinquent acts are noticed by parents, neighbors, shopkeepers, school teachers, child welfare workers, social workers, and others who decide *not* to invoke the processes of law. There is evidence that far more cases are known to individuals and agencies in the community than are known to the police and juvenile courts.[7] *The process of diversion begins in the community, not in the patrol car.*

The diversion of youngsters from the formal processes of adjudication continues in the police-juvenile interaction. Of 92,000 children against whom proceedings were initiated by the police in Pennsylvania in 1971, 47,000 (52 percent) were released without further referral.[8] It is conceivable, but improbable, that the police decided that more than half of their juvenile arrests were made without cause. It is more likely that police divert known juvenile offenders as frequently as they detain them.[9]

Thus far we have seen that the most important diversionary decisions are actually made by actors in the community who decide whether to refer observed instances of delinquent behavior to the authorities. And, among those children who come to the attention of the police, half will be released and only half will be processed. For those still in the system, the next major decision-making stage involves the use of detention facilities. The most striking characteristics of detention-use patterns is that allegedly neglected children are detained much more frequently than allegedly delinquent children. Among children charged with delinquency, status offenders are detained more frequently than others.

TABLE 4.2. Detention by Offense in Pennsylvania (1971)[10]

Offense	% Detained
Against person	29.1
Against property	22.7
Drug related	24.7
Public order	15.4
Status	33.2
Traffic	10.0
Neglect	58.6

The data suggest that detention facilities are used less for the protection of the public than for the protection of (or provision of services to) comparatively harmless youngsters.

Of the 45,000 youngsters referred to the juvenile courts, about one-third are held in detention. Roughly the same number of youngsters (15,000) are eventually adjudicated delinquent or neglected. There is a considerable degree of overlap. Almost 80 percent of the juveniles detained are eventually found to be either delinquent or neglected. Only about 3000 of the 30,000 youngsters referred to the courts but not held in detention are eventually so adjudicated. Detention decisions and eventual adjudications correlate highly.

What happens to the 30,000 youngsters referred to the juvenile court who are never adjudicated either delinquent or neglected?

45,000 youngsters were referred to the Pennsylvania courts in 1971.

30,000 were not held in detention; of them 27,000 were not adjudicated.

15,000 were held in detention; of them 3000 were not adjudicated.

27,000 plus 3000 gives us a total of 30,000 youngsters referred to the courts but not found to be either delinquent or neglected.

Presumably some of these youngsters are found not to have committed a delinquent act. But it is unlikely that two-thirds of the cases referred by the police would be dismissed for that reason. It has already been noted that 52 percent of all petitions initiated by the Pennsylvania police do not result in referrals to the courts. Theoretically, most factually innocent youngsters are diverted from the system at that point. To conclude that two-thirds of the remaining cases are dismissed on the basis of factual innocence would involve an overwhelming presumption of police incompetence. It is much more reasonable to hypothesize that a large percentage of youngsters referred to the courts are factually guilty; but that despite their factual guilt they are diverted from the system. Indeed, statutes in many states (including Pennsylvania) authorize pretrial hearings at which probation officers are to attempt informal adjustment of cases.[11]

Only one out of every four youngsters adjudicated delinquent or neglected is institutionalized. In Pennsylvania that is about 3750 young people. In other words, only about one-fourth of one percent of all young people who commit delinquent acts are processed through the system to the point of institutionalization. At all stages, more youngsters are diverted out of the system than are sent on for further processing.

Whatever the theoretical models discussed in Chapter Three may say about the ideal goals of juvenile justice systems, the most appropriate motto to inscribe on any component of a real-world juvenile justice system would be:

"DIVERSION IS OUR MOST IMPORTANT PRODUCT."

The figures speak for themselves.

1,400,000 youngsters commit delinquent acts
   92,000 youngsters become known to the police
   45,000 youngsters are referred to court
   15,000 youngsters are adjudicated delinquent and/or neglected
    3750 youngsters are institutionalized

We thought about presenting these numbers on a bar graph. The problem is that if the bar representing the 3750 institutionalized youngsters were drawn to one inch long, then scale could be preserved only by drawing the line representing the 1,400,000 youngsters who commit delinquencies to be more than 400 inches; that bar of the graph would run about 50 pages.

Summary

Diversion, rather than drama, is the everyday working rule of juvenile justice. It is for that very reason — that they were dramatic — that the cases with which this chapter began are atypical. To the extent that we are concerned with developing a comprehensive familiarity with juvenile justice systems, we must study the decision-making processes which result in patterns of diversion. On the other hand, however, to the extent that we are concerned with such basic values as fairness, equity, and humane treatment, it is precisely the atypical cases on which we must focus attention. Decisions to ignore a youngster's misbehavior, or to divert him from the formal processes of adjudication may be standard operating procedures; but decisions to notice misbehavior and to encapsulate youngsters within the system are profoundly important in the lives of individuals.

The challenge to serious students of juvenile justice is to maintain a systems perspective without ever forgetting that this particular system processes people — people as fragile as all humanity is, and younger than most.

A Case Study: The Juvenile Justice System in Operation

The following article from the *New York Times Magazine* provides a dramatic example of what a juvenile justice system may and may not do for young people. The article is highly critical of the present juvenile justice system and of the society which maintains that system. The dramatic presentation of rare but not unique case history creates first a highly emotion-charged reaction to the event, then a challenge to the reader to find creative solutions to the issues raised. The letters to the editor which were written in response to the article give further evidence of the diversity of viewpoints with which the juvenile justice system must deal.

A major issue raised in the article concerns the capacity (or incapacity) of the present juvenile justice system to protect the public from dangerous acts by young people. To a considerable extent the article focuses on prevention and deterrence, but it is also concerned with determining how society ought to respond to unacceptable behavior that can no longer be prevented or deterred: by retribution or rehabilitation? Does it matter if these youngsters were, in their own way, emulating the behavior of a violent society? if they were acting out their rage against a racist social system? if they were manifesting behavior learned in poverty-stricken disadvantaged neighborhoods? Do such circumstances undermine the argument for retribution? If the misbehavior described in this article results from the failure of the education system, religious institutions, and social welfare agencies, is punishment appropriate? Or should society set out to rehabilitate offenders — to transform them into mature, responsible adults? Consider the evidence presented. What success has "the system" had to date with such youngsters?

A second issue raised by the article concerns the identification, arrest, and disposition of people suspected of committing delinquent acts or crimes. The article maintains that the police are restrained by a juvenile justice system that classifies all youthful misconduct as delinquent, not criminal. Should the same label be attached to all youthful misbehavior — from truancy, drinking beer, and writing graffitti on subway walls — to robbery, rape, and murder? This is a serious issue in light of the fact that an increasing proportion of serious crimes are committed by young people. Consider the list of delinquent behaviors presented earlier. In what situations should the police be "turned loose" on youngsters? When should they be restrained? The article describes a juvenile justice system which is virtually incapable of dealing effectively with delinquent youngsters. As you read the article, note the character of the major part of the workload of the juvenile justice system, and note the counterpressures on the judge, the probation officer, and other personnel associated with the court. In particular, be aware of the previous failures of the social welfare, education, and mental health systems to cope effectively with these youngsters. Is it likely that the existing juvenile justice system can carry out its mandate to rehabilitate these youngsters? If it cannot, decide, then, whether you think offenders should be subjected to its inadequacies and failures.

Finally, consider the descriptions of the dispositional alternatives available: probation, institutions, release. How would you determine justice for the perpetrators, the victims, the juvenile justice system, minority groups, the broader community? What disposition would you recommend? How would your disposition affect the individuals involved? others like them? the victims? all young people? Would you seek to make them better people as individuals, or would you act to create a better society? Would your disposition do anything to keep similar events from occurring in the future; or would it just ease the emotions of people regarding this particular crime? Consideration of these issues will test your ability to use the concepts and knowledge from the earlier chapters in considering a real-life situation.

They Think, 'I Can Kill Because I'm 14'

A case study in a juvenile justice system that neither protects the victims nor helps the rising number of violent youth.

By TED MORGAN

On the afternoon of Friday, Oct. 11, two 10-year-old boys left a private school in the Borough Hall section of Brooklyn and went shopping for hockey sticks on Fulton Street, where the big department stores are. Jim Jones was tall for his age, with long blond hair and mild blue eyes. He wore jeans and a football shirt. Bobby Ryan was shorter, quick-gestured, also blond, and wore jeans and a plaid wool shirt. Walking across the sports department of Korvettes, they noticed two black teen-agers bouncing a basketball. A floorwalker retrieved the basketball and ordered them off the floor.

When Jim and Bobby left the store, their new hockey sticks under their arms, the two black youths were waiting for them at the entrance. One pulled a knife and said, "Come around the corner." This was at 4 P.M., in broad daylight in the heart of downtown Brooklyn, on a street crowded with shoppers. Jim and Bobby were relieved of the $6 they had between them. "Get the refunds for the sticks and come back here," the boy who had the knife said. Jim and

Bobby did as they were told. Why didn't they alert a Korvette guard? Or escape via another exit? They remembered their parents' warning: The rule on the street is if you're mugged, give them what they want. Jim and Bobby were too frightened to do otherwise.

They turned over the refund money and the two black youths took them across a parking lot behind Korvettes. The one with the knife, 15-year-old Ken Jordan, tall and lanky, neatly dressed, with a pleasant face and a nice smile, climbed on top of a car. The attendant told him to get off. "These cars belong to everybody," Ken said. "They're not just yours."

"Call that man a nigger," Ken ordered Jim.

"I will not," Jim said.

The knife was at Jim's throat. "Call that man a nigger."

Jim did.

"Ain't these two the *whitest* kids you ever seen," Ken said to the other black youth, short, round-faced Bill Sherwin, who had just turned 14.

They boarded the No. 26 bus with the two 10-year-olds and got off at a construction site at Adelphi and Fulton Streets, on the edge of Bedford-Stuyvesant. It was a 12-story building with cement stairs at each corner. The construction crew had knocked off, and they went to the sixth floor, out of earshot of the guards. They found a pay phone and made Bobby call his parents in Brooklyn Heights. They told Bobby to say that he and Jim had been kidnapped by members of the Tomahawk gang. If the parents left $2,000 on Saturday morning behind May's department store, their sons would be returned.

Bobby's parents called Jim's mother at about 7 P.M. She had already reported her son missing to the police. The divorced mother of three, she said: "I run a very tight

ship here." After the call, Mrs. Jones thought: "This can't be true; this never happens to *your* son, it happens to people you read about in the papers." She began to understand Patti Hearst's parents. "My God," she wondered. "Do I call the police or get my kid back?"

On the advice of a friend, she called the 84th Precinct and said her son had been kidnapped.

At the construction site, the two teen-agers were "having some fun" with the 10-year-olds, as one of them later put it. They defecated on the floor and made the boys pick it up. They tied Jim to a ladder, applied lit matches to his body and set fire to his hair. They tied him upside down to a pulley and immersed him in a barrel of water for a minute at a time. They dangled Bobby, the smaller 10-year-old, out a window, and pretended they were going to drop him.

They broke pieces of plasterboard over their heads. They pounded wedges of wood into their knuckles with hammers. They beat them so badly in the face that a policeman later said, "I have never seen anyone, not even a prizefighter, look like that." They took turns beating each 10-year-old. At one time, Bill Sherwin, the younger black boy, showed a sign of humanity. Pulling his punches, he whispered to Jim Jones, "Yell louder and pretend I'm hitting you harder than I am."

When they were through torturing the boys, they made them lie down on the cement floor and they sodomized them.

Now, with a dim awareness of the seriousness of what they had done, the teen-agers gave up on the kidnapping idea. Prodding them with the knife, Ken Jordan told the boys: "Streak." At about 11 P.M., a group of black men standing on the corner of Fulton Street saw, running toward them, two naked blond boys, their faces like blood pudding. One of them put the boys in his car, took them to the 88th Precinct on the corner of De Kalb and Colson Avenues, dropped them off, and drove away, on the principle that the less you have to do with the police the better.

The parents were alerted, and the boys, wrapped in blankets and in a state of shock, were taken to Cumberland Hospital, where they were treated for multiple contusions and lacerations. They were X-rayed, and the doctors thought Jim had a fractured jaw. Both boys had badly ripped anuses.

When a crime involves a sexual offense, the police give that offense priority over all others except homicide. The case was turned over to two veteran detectives of the Brooklyn sex squad, blond, methodical Hans Fredericks, and his partner, Sandy Johnson, a large jovial black man whose fireplace in Queens is crowded with loving cups won in bowling championships.

Hans Fredericks and Sandy Johnson feel hamstrung when it comes to dealing with juveniles. They point out that no records are kept for youths under 16. (In this article the names of all juveniles have been changed.) "Here is a kid," said Fredericks, "who at the age of 15 is capable of robbing and beating and raping someone at knifepoint, and we're not even allowed to fingerprint him. Say he is sent to a training school; when he comes out, there won't even be a picture of him at B.C.I. [Bureau of Criminal Identification]. At least let us maintain records, so that if those youths become adult criminals, we will know what they look like."

Hans Fredericks feels caught between the conflicting demands of protecting the community and treating juveniles less severely than adult criminals. "A 14-year-old knows the worst that can happen is 18 months in a training school,"

he said. "He thinks, I can kill a man because I'm 14. So you have murderers and rapists returned to the street in no time. If he's older, his parents come in and lie about his age, and say they can't find his birth certificate. They should knock down the whole age barrier, depending on the type of crime and the past history of the kid involved. It should be like intox driving; the first time it's a misdemeanor, the second time it's a felony. The way it is now, it's a big game."

Sandy Johnson agrees. "The law says a child should be treated differently because he can be rehabilitated," he said. "But kids weren't committing the types of crimes you see now when those laws were passed. Kids have changed, and the laws have not kept abreast of the times. A cop kills a 14-year-old, and everybody wants his head. But can't that 14-year-old kill, and when he pulls that trigger doesn't the cop die just as fast? We've found that 13- and 14-year-olds are more likely to kill than adults; they don't grasp the consequences of their acts."

As a result of the rise in violent crimes committed by juveniles, new and tougher laws are being drafted for the next legislative session in Albany. Among these is a law reducing the cut-off age for juveniles from 16 to 14; a law asking for longer sentences for juveniles; and a law allowing for juveniles charged with very serious crimes to be tried in Criminal rather than Family Court. It's too early to tell, however, whether any of these laws has a chance of passing.

The point that all of those connected with juvenile justice agree on is that the violent ones are coming into the system younger and younger. In 1964, in New York City, 1,279 children under 16 were arrested for robbery, 131 for rape and 30 for murder. In 1973, the figures were 4,449 for robbery, 181 for rape and 94 for murder. It is as though our society had bred a new genetic strain, the child-murderer who feels no remorse and is scarcely conscious of his acts.

There are a number of explanatory theories: The kids are affected by periodicals and television; they are learning the lesson of a violent society. There's less and less parental guidance. The policeman is no longer a figure of authority; his role as a deterrent has been eroded by laws protecting the juvenile. Kids exploit the system; they know that if they are under 16 they will be dealt with leniently. "They are emulating adult patterns," says Norman Dix, Deputy Director of the Department of Probation. "In his home the child encounters disapproval in the form of violence, he accepts it and is able to use it, seeing that his elders have found it useful." Charles H. King, director of rehabilitation for the New York State Division for Youth, studied eight boys and one girl, average age 14, who had committed brutal murders, among them a gasoline "torch" burning and a machete dismembering, and found that some of these children had begun to exhibit angry behavior at the kindergarten level. They all came from troubled families, where children were abused and parents displayed unpredictable mood shifts. They learned to distrust their environment and expect harm.

King also found a common educational deprivation. The nine youths were retarded in reading, stunted in language skills, and had what is called dull normal I.Q.'s (92-104). Lacking command of the language, the essential tool to negotiate social transactions, they fell back on what King regards as "inner cues," such as feelings of omnipotence. They grew up emotional loners, whose "I know it all" attitude covered up their actual know-nothingness. To sustain their feelings of omnipotence, wrote King, they reduced the symbols of communication between their world and the real world to primitive speech and action-power. Language became assaultive or provocative: "Make me! F—— you! Who, me? Get off my back!" Such phrases cut off rational discourse. The youths were chronic truants, full of rage at their inability to learn, and seeing the school as a threat to their way of communicating.

In reducing social exchanges to power struggles, other persons became objects, seen only as obstacles. Another person could be killed because he got in the way; he was like a window to be jimmied. He was not a human being, but a target. The child was unable to see people as individuals in a social context. "Forms of communication such as talking and thinking," wrote King, "which imply delay, are perversely experienced as stressful and less tolerable than violence and homicide." The false sense of omnipotence that drove children to kill, King wrote, was in reality a terrible feeling of helplessness. They would kill someone who put them down, and they would feel absolutely no remorse. They would blame the victim — he was stupid to resist. Frozen in their ignorance and family conditioning, the children had become murderers. It was the most extreme form their admission of failure could take.

This was not only a New York City phenomenon. "What I hear from my people, who are checking with judges all over the country," King told me, "is that it's nationwide, although it's more visible in cities where kids are packed together. But all over the country they are getting these kids who reflect a social situation in which only power works, where the only transaction is 'Either you make me or I'll make you.' My impression, based on the ones I've seen in our training schools, is that kids from rural communities are even more wild and impulsive and harder to reach."

When the detectives arrived at Cumberland Hospital around midnight, Jim and Bobby had begun to respond. "Did you know their names?" Fredericks asked.

"Yes, Ken and Bill."

Fredericks said he and Johnson batted those names around, and "there was an officer from the borough anticrime unit who was able to supply four or five Kens and Bills who would have been capable of this. We went to our Youth Records section, where another detective pointed to a Ken and a Bill in the files and said: 'I picked those two up together last year.' That helped narrow it down."

Hans Fredericks and Sandy Johnson had reported for duty at 4 P.M. that Friday, and had seen a group of detectives huddled over some photographs. "Look at this case we got last night," one of them said. "Would you believe it?"

A black woman living with her 13-month-old baby in a second-floor apartment in the Fort Greene section of Brooklyn had been raped by two black youths who had come in through a window. They had forced her at knifepoint to undress and tied her spread-eagled to the bed. While they were robbing her, they found an Instamatic camera and took snapshots of each other molesting the woman. In one picture, the shorter of the two youths had placed two butcher knives on a towel as though he were about to perform an operation, and had put the baby on the woman's belly. There was terror in the woman's eyes. Something happened to frighten the two youths, and they fled through the window, leaving the camera behind. The woman reported the rape and turned the camera over to the police, who developed 8-by-10 color prints of the woman with each of the two youths.

Hans Fredericks and Sandy Johnson decided to concentrate on the Ken and the Bill the detective said he had picked up together the year before. On Sunday morning, they visited Bill's home in a Fort Greene slum. Bill's mother answered the door. She said she did not know where her son was, at the same time indicating that he was hiding in a cockloft, a space between the ceiling and the roof. He finally dropped down, a short, strongly built 14-year-old.

"What are ya' botherin' me for? I didn't do nothin'," he said. "You f—— guys are always after me."

Bill looked familiar to Sandy Johnson. He kept wondering where he had seen him. It came to him — he was the youth in the Instamatic blowups, the one posing in various positions over the woman who had been raped. It was he, right down to the red blotch in his left eye that showed up in the snapshots. Sandy Johnson remembered a question he had asked the 10-year-olds.

"Was there anything peculiar about the two black kids?"

"Yes, one of them had a big red mark in the corner of his eye."

Sandy Johnson went to borough command to get the pictures. Hans Fredericks took Bill and his mother to the precinct. Sandy Johnson showed one of the pictures to the mother, covering the lower half so only Bill's face showed.

"Do you know who this is?" he asked.

"What are you doing with my son's picture?" she said. "You stole it out of my house."

Sandy Johnson exposed the lower half of the picture, showing the naked woman spread-eagled on the bed.

"Who the f—— is that?" the mother asked.

"What do you have to say now?"

Sandy Johnson asked.

"Pictures don't lie," the mother said. Turning to her son, she said: "Who took the pictures, you jackass?"

"Ken did," the boy said.

The next step was positive identification from the 10-year-olds and the raped woman. "You can't put a juvenile on a line-up," Hans Fredericks explained, "and you can't have a photo line-up since we're not allowed to use pictures of other 14-year-olds. The only thing left is a one-on-one. The suspect is brought in and the victim looks at him and says yes or no. In this case we had three separate victims who made a positive identification."

In the meantime, Sandy Johnson had been on the phone to Ken Jordan's mother who said her son had not been home in days. Several days later she called back: "You, Johnson? Will you keep your word? You promise my boy won't be hurt? He just called and said he's coming over for a change of clothes."

Ken Jordan was arrested when he walked in the door, turned in by his mother. A check of records showed that he had 21 Y.D. (Youth Department) cards, meaning that he had been picked up by police that many times, on charges ranging from stealing bus transfer books to raping and robbing a 56-year-old woman.

"Can you imagine how many jobs he did we don't know about," Hans Fredericks said. " In 20 years on the job I've never seen anything like those 10-year-olds beaten and the terrified expression on that raped woman's face."

Ken Jordan was a good example of the turnstile youth, who gets into trouble, falls into the cracks in the system, and is released, until he is picked up again for a new offense. Jordan's father had never married his mother, who was now married to another man. Ken had been in trou-

ble since kindergarten. He had started setting fires at the age of 7. He had killed his mother's pet cat. The mother was conscious of not giving him the attention he needed, but she worked full time, and there were other children, including two half-sisters and an older brother who at the age of 18 was a chronic bed wetter. None of the other children, however, had ever been arrested.

When Ken was 14, his mother brought him to Brooklyn Family Court on a PINS (Person in Need of Supervision) petition. A PINS petition is a mother's admission of failure. She is saying: "I cannot control my child; I am turning him over to the Court."

On the recommendation of Family Court's RIP (Rapid Intervention Psychological) unit, a judge sent Ken to Kings County Hospital for observation. The hospital report, dated Nov. 13, 1973, described Ken as hyperactive with a short attention span. He was defensive, guarded, and he denied there was any problem. His mother was anxious and guilt-ridden at her failure to secure help. She said he had been out of school for two and a half years and had suffered head injuries. His family structure was described as "hysterical." The consequences of his acts had no meaning for him. He had developed a sense of himself as bad. "Somebody who hurts other people ain't got no feelings," he said. His I.Q. was 88 (dull normal). He had a fourth-grade reading level.

Kings County diagnosed Ken as actively psychotic, suffering from chronic childhood schizophrenia. He was placed in Creedmore, a state mental hospital for children, in late November. There, he "acted out," and was put on 50 milligrams a day of Thorazine. He was distant and withdrawn to interviewers but hostile and aggressive on the ward. He etched the words "sly" and "kill" on his forearms. He had auditory hallucinations of his name being called. His insight into his own acts was described as nil.

In January, 1974, he complained to his mother that he had been beaten and sodomized at Creedmore. She signed him out, against the advice of his doctors.

Six months later, on July 10, 1974, he was brought into Family Court again, on a charge of robbery and rape. Again, the court's psychiatrists saw him, reporting that he was angry, guarded and hostile, would not maintain eye contact, and said he could not help himself from stealing. Again, he was sent to Kings County Hospital, where a great improvement in his condition was noted. The hospital recommended a court-supervised day program. While such a program was sought, Ken was placed in his mother's custody. In September, he was back in court on a charge of grand larceny and assault. This time he was sent to Spofford, the city's only lock-up facility for juveniles, but he escaped.

Now Ken was back in Family Court on new and more serious charges. He is part of a growing category of violent and disturbed youths who are showing up in newspaper headlines and in Family Court. But there does not exist a single city or state facility equipped to handle this type of youth. The Family Court judge can send him to a state training school, where he will not get the psychiatric care he needs. Or he can send him to a mental hospital for children, an open facility from which he can easily escape or be released by his parents. Juvenile authorities agree that the most urgent need in the juvenile justice system today is for a secure facility that provides medical and psychiatric care, where children like Ken Jordan can be removed from the community and treated.

The marble facade of Brooklyn's six-story Family Court building on Adams Street has two bas-reliefs of family groups flanking the entrance, over which these words are engraved: "Through the guiding light of wisdom and understanding shall the family endure and children grow strong in the security of the home, for they are the hope of the future."

Inside, one sees not the hope of the future but the lower depths of human behavior, a daily procession of misery and failure and warped children with warped parents. Family Court is a punitive confessional, a laundry where the dirty linen of broken homes is washed, a distribution center for unwanted children. It is an experience of hopelessness that would be hard to match in any society at any time. It is a court for the poor and for the blacks and the Puerto Ricans. It is a court for the ghetto. A 1973 study by the Office of Children's Services of 431 juveniles brought before New York City Family Court showed that 57 per cent were black, 23 per cent were Puerto Rican, 18 per cent were white, and 2 per cent were labeled "other races." Only 21 per cent came from intact families, while 59 per cent of their families were on welfare. Half had been in Family Court before, and more than a third had siblings who had been in Family Court before. One in 10 had a history of psychiatric hospitalization. Of 168 children who had taken I.Q. tests, only 27 had scored over 100. Three out of four children in the over-all sample were truants.

The judges compare themselves to the little Dutch boy with his finger in the dike. They act as social workers, psychologists, marriage counselors and father figures. In a given day, the "all-purpose" judges handle child custody cases, support cases, violations of protection orders, wife-beaters, child molesters, petitions for help and juvenile crimes. They handle as many as 50 cases a day. "We're all on tranquilizers," one judge told me. They are often overcome by a feeling of helplessness as they try to resolve the contradictions of the system, as when a divorced husband charged with failing to pay child support tells the judge he has been fired because he has to come to court so often. At other times, they are like Old Testament judges, making Solomonlike decisions, as in the custody dispute over a French poodle. The judge sent the husband and wife to opposite ends of the courtroom. The poodle was placed in the middle. On his signal, they both called the poodle, which, after some hesitation, made for the husband, thus disposing of its own custody. But cases these days are seldom that comical.

In chambers, between cases, two judges are chatting. One mentions the rise in violent crimes by juveniles. "Last year I had 17 homicides," he says; "I had those two kids who pushed that woman off the roof."

"I had those two girls who killed that 74-year-old man," the other says. "They knocked him out with a lead pipe and filled the bathtub with scalding water and put him face down and drowned him. The girls confessed but it turned out one of them had not been advised of her rights and the charges had to be dropped."

"They call us bleeding hearts," the first one says, "but what can we do?"

"I had a boy last year," says the other, "he'd burned down two synagogues. His father said, 'He's just a little rebellious, your honor.' Because he was white and middle-class he was taken by a private sanatorium."

Such cases are not reported in the press because Family Court proceedings are closed and the records were sealed. For the same reason, statistics on juvenile crime are hard to come by.

The legal policy of separating juveniles under 16 from the adult criminal system is based on the principle that children can be rehabilitated. As Judge Joseph B. Williams, the black, energetic administrative judge of Family Court put it: "We're not punitive; we're just an instrument to move youngsters into a position where they can be treated. But the social scientists can't guarantee an improvement in behavior, and the psychiatrists can't guarantee that a child is cured, so the bottom line is the removal of the child to a new setting. Has that been successful? You can't keep him forever, and he will eventually go back to the same social problems that caused his removal in the first place."

Since juveniles are not treated like criminals, the language and the process of Family Court are special. The juvenile is not a defendant but a respondent. He is not indicted but rather he responds to a petition drawn up at the request of a complainant. There is no such word as guilty in Family Court. If the judge rules that the allegations are proved beyond a reasonable doubt, he makes a finding, rather than reaching a verdict, and decides upon placement, rather than delivering a sentence.

But before a case goes before a judge, it must be screened by a probation officer who decides whether the situation requires court intervention. The officer, who handles five to seven cases a day, must see a juvenile within 72 hours of his arrest. He can send a case to court, adjust it himself or hold it for 60 days. In fact, probation officers adjust about half the cases that come through, cutting the judges' load in two.

As Bernice Raisen, a Brooklyn probation supervisor, explained it: "Let's say it's a first offense, robbery; the parents seem responsible, the kid is contrite and has a good school record and the complainant has his property back and is not eager to press charges. We will take the responsibility of letting the kid go back to the community. But all parties must be satisfied. Any offense can be taken to court if the complainant insists.

"Our function is to divert cases away from the court. Subway graffiti cases, for instance, are almost always adjusted. The kids are given a work appointment; they go to the Transit Authority for four hours and clean up. Of course, if a child seems disturbed, we would refer it to the court so a psychiatric evaluation can be made. PIN's cases are harder to adjust. The parents are at their wits' end; they want the kid out of the house. But we don't take the parent's word, and often the case of the unmanageable child turns out to be the case of the negligent parent."

If the case moves beyond the probation officer, the material obtained by him is given to a petition clerk, who draws up the petition with the help of what is called a corporation counsel, a lawyer who works for the city and who represents the complainant in court. Complainants are not allowed to be represented by private lawyers. Sometimes the corporation counsel, who is in effect the prosecutor, decides that the allegations cannot be sustained and sends the case back. Usually, he draws up the petition, while the respondent is referred to legal aid.

One of the reasons Family Court is so complicated is the number of different agencies it embraces. Each agency has a different interest. As someone who is part of the process put it: "Sometimes the only thing you can hear around here is the sound of axes grinding." Thus, the probation people accuse the legal-aid lawyers of having turned Family Court into an adversary proceeding. Instead of helping the child, it is said, they are acting as lawyers trying to get their young clients released. (In 1967, the Supreme Court ruled that a juvenile charged with an offense that could deprive him of his freedom must be represented by a lawyer.)

Responding to this criticism, Irwin Weissberg, a legal-aid lawyer with long experience in Brooklyn Family Court, said: "I look at the legal-aid lawyer as like a cop in a courtroom. He is there to see that the kid's rights are protected. Many people would prefer a system of a wise and understanding judge, knowledgeable in the mores of the community, who would listen to the problem and resolve it — no such person, of course, exists.

"Can a kid be brought before the judge without a lawyer, represented by his parents, who so often feel that they have been burdened and shamed by their child, and in many instances would be happy to get rid of him? Would you want to be represented by that type of person? What a legal-aid lawyer is supposed to do is not only represent the welfare of the child but also protect his legal rights, and advise him on the law. When we go into the courtroom, the child has a legal and moral right to have his views presented to a judge. I deal with these cases as legal cases. I am trying to get a finding that the petition is not warranted."

After the drawing up of the petition and the assignment of lawyers, the case goes to an "intake" judge, who determines whether the child should be paroled or detained and sets a date for a fact-finding hearing before a second, "all-purpose" judge. In Brooklyn, there are two "intake" parts and eight "all-purpose" parts. Outside "intake," in a large waiting room, respondents and complainants sit on benches, waiting for their names to be called. The courtrooms are small, like offices, with several desks bunched together, and the judge is flanked by a clerk, stenographer and probation officer. Uniformed court officers bring in the parents, who sit on chairs in front of the judge, and their delinquent children, who stand behind them. Sometimes they are so small they can hardly be seen behind their seated parents.

Looking in on an intake proceeding we find Judge Cesar Quinones, a distinguished-looking man with silver-gray hair, presiding. On this particular day, he has a series of petitions involving boys and girls under 16 who are allegedly beyond their parents' control. He studies the language of the yellow petitions in front of him — child a habitual truant, refuses to obey the parent, stays out late, sometimes all night. The judge knows that these petitions can cover up other things. He has seen children who stayed away from home because of a drunken and abusive father. He has seen parents who know that their child has committed a serious crime ask for court supervision as the lesser of two evils. He must decide whether a child should remain with his parents or be placed in an institution.

A mother who has brought a petition against her 13-year-old daughter, who has not shown up, is saying: "She won't go to school, Your Honor. If you'll excuse the language, she said to me, 'Bitch, you don't tell me f—— all.' I don't mind the baby, Your Honor, anybody can make a mistake, but I don't want to put up with that kind of language." Judge Quinones orders a warrant for the girl's arrest.

A very large young woman wearing a rabbit-fur coat is brought in by her equally large mother. "Your honor, in spite of her size," says the legal-aid lawyer, "the respondent has just turned 13."

The respondent is chewing her nails. "Do they taste good?" Judge Quinones asks. The respondent smirks.

"You're keeping late hours," Judge Quinones says. "We'll put a speedy halt to that. Correct?" The girl nods.

"Next time, you won't have to reckon with your mother. You'll have to reckon with me."

"The respondent and her mother have a good relationship, Your Honor," the legal-aid lawyer says. The mother smiles and nods.

Judge Quinones releases the girl in her mother's custody. He may get 10 or 15 of these petition-for-help cases in a single day. For many ghetto parents, Family Court has become part of a disciplinary tactic.

Moving on, we look in on one of the all-purpose hearings, presided over by Judge Gilbert Ramirez, who happens to be blind. His guide dog, Mona, is lying in one corner of the courtroom, and he is reading a braille report. His courtroom is crowded and noisy, like a London magistrate's court in Dickens's day. In his robing room, lawyers are shouting at each other. Judge Ramirez has just told a 14-year-old boy accused of jostling that he is to be remanded to Spofford Juvenile Center until his case is heard. The boy starts crying and says, "Please don't send me back there." The boy's mother is crying too. "Your Honor," she says, "I promise he'll be here on Tuesday." Judge Ramirez asks a probation officer: "Is the mother capable of controlling her son?" The probation officer's answer is inconclusive. The son has several previous offenses. The arresting officer rises and says: "If I may, Your Honor, I have had several conversations with the mother and I believe she is able to bring her son in." Judge Ramirez relents and places the boy in his mother's custody. They are tearfully reunited.

The next case concerns three children abandoned by their mother.

Judge Ramirez is trying to get a supervisor from the Department of Social Services, which had a 1973 budget of $164-million for foster-care services alone, to help finance the care of the three children. Judge Ramirez, after many years in Family Court, retains his capacity for indignation. In his robing room, he explains:

"A kid came in here with two delinquency petitions and there was no father, no mother, no nothing," he says. "We finally located a maternal aunt and she came to court and said she couldn't take care of the kid and that the mother was insane; [the mother] had tried to kill herself 18 times; she had set herself on fire; she was lame as a result of throwing herself out a window. Her three kids were on the street, panhandling and sleeping in subways. A woman in the neighborhood took them in out of the goodness of her heart. But she has three of her own, and she's starving, and someone has to help. I asked the Department of Social Services to send someone but nobody went. I had to issue a warrant for the arrest of a department supervisor to bring her in here to do her job [the warrant did not have to be served. The supervisor was in court]. This situation is an outrage and I want people to know what's going on."

The more serious the offense, the speedier Family Court proceedings tend to be. Within a week of the offense that began at Korvettes, Ken Jordan and Bill Sherwin were charged in an intake proceeding with kidnapping, attempted murder, robbery and sodomy. The two 10-year-old victims and their mothers had to appear at various stages. When Mrs. Jones first saw the smirking, gangling youth who had assaulted her son, her legs began to shake. "What's wrong, Mommy?" her son asked. "I want to kill him,"
she said. "I want to grab a gun and shoot him." Mrs. Jones had never in her life felt such anger. She had gone through the usual sorrows and disappointments of life, buried her parents, been divorced, had financial problems, but she had never felt real fear and the anger that follows fear.

The corporation-counsel supervisor asked her son: "Do you know why you're here?"

"Yeah," Jim Jones said, "and I want those two guys to get the chair."

"You must know that those boys are sick, sick, sick, and you must cast anger out of your heart and feel only Christian love for them."

A two-day hearing was then held before Judge Philip D. Roache, a buoyant and articulate black man, who, like many of his fellow judges, feels frustrated in his task. Before him appear 12-year-old burglars, 13-year-old rapists and 14-year-old murderers. He can send them to a training school for a period "not to exceed 18 months." The length of their stay is determined by the school and, too often, the number of available beds. The training schools are operated by the New York State Division for Youth, and must accept all children placed by the court. When a training school is crowded, there are premature releases, and Judge Roache may see a youth back in court six months after he has been placed. If a Class A or B felony (serious crimes such as armed robbery, assault with a weapon, or arson) has been committed by a 15-year-old, the judge can send him to the adult prison in Elmira for three years, "but we've been reversed so many times by the Appellate Division we hardly ever do it any more." In any case, he knows that feeding juveniles into the adult criminal system is not a solution. He has had roughly this conversation countless times:

Probation Officer: Your Honor, I

recommend parole.

Judge: But he was already on parole and he committed another crime.

Probation: That's true, Your Honor, but every time he goes to a training school he comes back worse.

Judge Roache sees a lot of mentally ill children come through. He knows that the child cannot improve if he stays with his parents, who are often more troubled than he is. If he sends him to a mental hospital, they may refuse to take him. State mental hospitals for children are not supposed to be selective, but they are. They will say that a psychotic child is in a state of remission and refuse to admit him. If they do admit him and he runs away, after a 30-day absence the hospital lists him as discharged, and the court is not even notified.

Time after time, Judge Roache gets a probation report that recommends "therapy in a structured environment," and throws up his hands, because there is no such thing. The closest thing to it are the state's eight training schools, which are not staffed to provide regular psychiatric care.

Whenever he can, he tries to place youths with private agencies run by religious or charity organizations. But he knows from long experience that these agencies, although they are funded up to 80 and 90 per cent with public money, have the right to select the children they want. The children who need help the most are the ones they don't want. The Department of Social Services pays these agencies hundreds of millions of dollars each year to provide day care and resident facilities for children. But which children? Judge Roache knows that a white child with a high I.Q. from an intact family is snapped up at once. But a black child with a low I.Q. and a habit of playing with matches, or a Puerto Rican child who acts up and has committed a crime against a person — forget it. They

would disturb the program. The voluntary agencies are success-oriented, Judge Roache knows; they don't want children who will lower their batting average. As a result, city and state agencies have become places of last resort, with the highest concentration of difficult cases, which makes their programs unworkable.

Justine Wise Polier, who sat on the Family Court bench for 37 years before retiring to head the Children's Defense Fund, said: "There is a growing feeling that there must be some accountability for private agencies receiving public funds. There is no justification in their deciding whom they will or will not take. If they say they're not geared for certain cases and those are the most pressing ones, then I say, let them gear themselves up."

Judge Roache is in a bind. After he has made a finding, he has the right to hold a juvenile for 10 days, with another 10 days continuance for cause. But a placement cannot be made until he has the probation I. & R. (Investigation and Report) and the psychological evaluation report, which can easily take six weeks. Private placement can take three or four months. In principle, after 20 days, the child must be released, even though he presents a danger to the community.

It is one of the Probation Department's functions to find placement, but Judge Roache sometimes has to do it himself. "It's not enough to make a determination of innocence or guilt," he said; "a large part of our day is spent making placement calls. We're not permitted to be judges; we have to be social workers." He gets on the phone and pleads like a fund raiser, asking for placement as a personal favor.

And now Judge Roache had four mothers in his courtroom, each with her son. Two sons from Brooklyn's black ghetto, one of whom had a long record of mental disturbance and arrests. Two sons from affluent Brooklyn Heights, who went to a private school, lived in handsome brownstones and received weekly allowances. The first two had kidnapped the other two. Children preying on children.

There was a problem — the whole case depended on the testimony of two 10-year-olds. Could Judge Roache swear them in? If not, their evidence would require corroboration. The test in former days for children under 12 was belief in God. Today it is up to the judge. Corporation counsel Herb Katz questioned Bobby Ryan along old-fashioned lines.

"Do you go to Sunday school?"

"No."

"Do you say your prayers at night?"

"No."

"Do you believe that if you lie here today God will punish you?"

"No."

"What would your punishment be if you lied?"

"I wouldn't be able to watch Monday-night football."

"I can see these boys are not liars," Judge Roache said, and swore them in.

Bobby Ryan, the smaller of the two, raised his right hand, took the oath, and told the story of the kidnapping. "This was a particularly bright 10-year-old," detective Hans Fredericks said later. "His way of expressing himself was unbelievable. He spoke very matter of factly, as if it had happened to someone else."

His testimony was so complete that when he was through Ken Jordan's lawyer said: "Your honor, at this time the respondent admits to all allegations in the petition except sodomy." Bill Sherwin's lawyer also entered what amounted to a guilty plea.

"Why hold it up?" Judge Roache recalled. "Why put those kids through this excruciating experience? Whether sodomy was part of it or not, I couldn't make my finding more severe."

The victims' mothers agreed. "We didn't want our children to be cross-examined," Mrs. Jones said. "Having to go through it again, subjected to coarse questions."

It was a form of plea bargaining. The sex offense would not be on the record. The maximum punishment was a training school for the 14-year-old "for a period not to exceed 18 months," and Elmira prison for three years for the 15-year-old. But before that was decided, Judge Roache had to wait for the probation report. In the meantime, he remanded both youths to the Spofford detention center. He told Ken Jordan's lawyer that he intended to send Ken to Elmira unless he was certified insane, in which case he would be sent to Creedmore on a two-physician certificate, so that his mother would not be able to sign him out. The lawyer asked for time to obtain private psychiatric evaluation. In return, the lawyer consented that Ken remain in Spofford beyond the legal 20-day period.

Mrs. Jones felt the punishment was too light. "These kids know the system," she said. "They'll do anything because they know they are only going to get 18 months. No one thinks about the victims, what they went through."

A native of Ohio, Mrs. Jones thought seriously of going back there. She liked her life in New York she said, "but why play Russian Roulette with your kids' lives?" She decided to devote her spare time to the reform of the juvenile-justice system and joined a recently formed citizens' group, the New York Coalition for Juvenile Justice and Youth Services, which is now studying such matters as the need for new legislation, the spending of public money, and the problem of inter-agency account-ability.

Spofford Juvenile Center is an eight-story white brick building on 4.5 acres of grounds in the South Bronx, operated by the ubiquitous Department of Social Services. It is the only secure facility for juveniles in New York City, serving the five boroughs. Basically, it's a jail for children, although there are no bars on the windows and the unarmed guards are called juvenile counselors.

It is supposed to be a short-term facility, for children who are being held between arrest and their initial hearing, or between hearings, or between the finding and the place-ment. Since juveniles are meant to be rehabilitated rather than punished, there is a school program. But it's hard to maintain any continuity, with children coming and going for court appearances and conferences with lawyers, so that classes are likely to be poorly attended.

Between 7,000 and 8,000 juveniles flow through Spofford's 13 dormi-tories each year. They are the most serious offenders, those whom judges cannot release in the custody of their parents because they may do harm to others or are likely not to show up in court.

Spofford has room for 286 juveniles, and on the day I visited there were 227 — 187 boys and 40 girls. About half of them were repeaters. It was quite a group, in-cluding about 20 young murderers, kids who were caught running nickel bags (one $5 dose) for heroin wholesalers, 14-year-old transvestites, pregnant 13-year-olds and obviously disturbed youths whom hospitals would not admit. A concentrate, in other words, of the worst things that can happen to children.

Ron Curyla, the superintendent (not warden) is able to keep a lid on the place thanks to locked doors, 24-hour surveillance and an attitude of friendly interest in his wards. Kids who react violently when their parents fail to visit them, or when, for the first time, in the privacy of their cubicles, they face what they have done and go into serious depressions, are isolated from the rest and placed on one-on-one surveillance.

Spofford is a good place to spot trends in juvenile crime. Curyla says that among youths brought there in the last three years the incidence of homicides and other crimes against persons has gone up about 400 per cent. "We used to get one or two homicides a year; now it's 20 or 30. There's a lot more organized street-gang activity. They've all got weapons and they use them." Curyla opened the bottom drawer of his desk, which was crammed with seized contraband — a hunting knife with the word POWER inked in on the sheath, switch-blades, a zip gun, a .22 cartridge, a .30-06 rifle cartridge and a .38 police-revolver cartridge.

Curyla's main problem is juveniles who extend their stay. For one reason or another, they are held longer than the legal period of 20 days. They get bored with the program and become problems. Since Joseph B. Williams became the administrative judge of Family Court, he requires a monthly report listing the children who have been in Spofford more than 30 days, and spurs the judges to action on their cases.

In the report Curyla showed me, 52 children had exceeded the 30-day limit. One youth had been in Spof-ford for an incredible 348 days. Found guilty of homicide, he was in Spofford with his private lawyer's consent while placement with a private agen-cy was sought. They knocked on 21 doors before one opened.

In his Spofford cubicle, 14-year-old Bill Sherwin sat on the floor and stared at the wall. When the juvenile counselors tried to get him out of his room, he shook his fist at them. He refused to talk. He hallucinated, hearing voices and seeing animal shapes. On Nov. 1, he was referred back to Family Court for a psychological evaluation. The psychologist who saw him described him as a cynical and defiant small boy. He said he heard voices telling him to hurt people. He said he might keep hurting others who kept putting him down. He said he wanted to be locked alone in a room with a chair. When he covered his face with his hands and the psychologist pushed the desk aside to see what he was doing, he attacked the psychologist with a sharpened pencil. She concluded that he had a desperado quality and was out of control. He was sent to Kings County Hospital.

Ken Jordan was also under psychiatric observation at Spofford. His supervisor in the A-4 dormitory said he had been displaying homosexual tendencies. But he remained in Spofford while his lawyer sought to obtain an independent psychiatric evaluation. On Dec. 13, he asked Judge Roache for more time, because of the holiday season.

As this article went to press, there had been no final disposition of the case. Ken Jordan, depending on the results of his evaluation, would be sent either to Creedmore or Elmira. Bill Sherwin was committed to Creedmore, but on Christmas day, while awaiting transfer, he escaped from Kings County Hospital and was back on the street. The only other possibility for the two youths would have been the state training-school system.

In its eight facilities the Division for Youth has room for about 900 juveniles. More than half of them are from New York City. Charles H. King, in charge of rehabilitation, said: "We very seldom keep them as long as 18 months. We are under tremendous pressure to take in new kids who are tearing up the community, so we have to release others.

The average stay is about nine months. If we kept them all 18 months we'd need twice as many beds. As it is, we'll fill in behind a kid who's A.W.O.L. If we got back all our A.W.O.L.'s today we wouldn't have room for them."

Most of the training schools are open settings, houses in the country, where the children come and go as they please; one of the biggest is in Warwick, N. Y. Only one facility, the Goshen Center for Boys, about an hour and a half from the city, has maximum security. Goshen, says Charles King, is "a ghetto of explosive kids." Ninety of the 100 boys there have committed crimes against persons. Many have been transferred to Goshen from open settings where they were chronic "breezers," or runaways. But for more than a year now, Family Court judges have been allowed to place juveniles directly into Goshen, in response to the new type of child who is coming into the system. Dr. Denise Shine, head of the Rapid Intervention psychiatrists' office in Brooklyn Family Court, describes these children as showing a "total lack of guilt and lack of respect for life. To them, another person is a thing — they are wild organisms who cannot allow anyone to stand in their way." Goshen is the end of the line — there is no other place to transfer to. It is equipped to handle violent children, with an isolation ward where they can be kept up to 24 hours. They sleep in rooms that are locked at night. A carrot-stick system in enforced. They rise from level D to prerelease, with added privileges at each level, such as TV and canteen, off-gounds activities and home visits.

Leon Herman, the recently appointed director of Goshen, took me on a tour of the place. He is a scholarly looking, bespectacled clinical psychologist who does not believe in long detention for children. Three juveniles were sitting in the dining hall. The walls were covered with Christmas ornaments.

"What do you think of this place?" Herman asked a 17-year-old black youth. (Juveniles who turned 16 in the training schools can be kept there until they are 18).

"This is kiddyland," he said. "This is paradise compared to jail."

"How you doing?" Herman asked a white 15-year-old from Buffalo.

"I'm doin' all right for my second time around."

"Why did you come here?"

"Burglary."

"Just don't come back."

"Not for no third time."

"Why don't you help these younger kids?" Herman asked the black youth. "You've got more experience."

"They young," the black youth said, "so they figure, 'I can mess up two to three more years.' "

In a dormitory, a tall, lanky Puerto Rican youth with shoulder-length black hair, listened to cassettes in a room covered with magazine cutouts. He was 15. Herman asked him what he had done. "Me and another guy," he said, "we're in the Queens Division of the Savage Nomads; we caught a member of the Seven Crowns and beat him and shot him." He said this as if it was a perfectly normal occurrence — like what else are you supposed to do in that type of situation?

He was obviously bright, and had done well at Goshen, rising through the levels in a short time to pre-release, and was due to go home in a few weeks. Maybe you get a better type of delinquent in Queens. Herman asked him about his plans. "I'm not going back to that," he said. "I don't like being locked up." His good intentions sounded a bit forced, but Herman seemed to take him at his word.

Back in his office, Herman explained that his worst problem was mentally disturbed children he was not equipped to handle. "All our kids are disturbed," he said, "but 10 per cent should be receiving intensive medical care. We need in-house psychiatrists, autonomous medical facilities. All we have now is three part-time psychiatrists for a total of 24 hours a week."

Herman refers his seriously disturbed juveniles to Rockland State Hospital, and as often as not, they send the child back with a diagnosis that his psychosis is "dormant." He told me about a 16-year-old he had sent to Rockland that morning, a black youth who had been found guilty of raping 25 women at knifepoint. He had been previously diagnosed as a pseudopsychopathic schizophrenic, Herman said, "whatever that means." In nine days at Goshen he had made four suicide attempts. "He gave me the grounds to send him to Rockland, but they say he's in a state of remission, and they're sending him back. It's always the way."

A car pulled up in the driveway, and Herman said, "There he is, back from Rockland. Look at him grinning; he's glad to be back."

Herman beckoned him. The youth, now sullen-faced, had an afro with a comb stuck in it, and a ring on a chain around his neck. He wore green slacks and a green simulated-leather jacket.

"Well, David," Herman said, "I wish you would find a different way of expressing your bad feelings other than trying to do away with yourself."

"Mr. Herman," the youth said, "I don't trust you no more. I don't even think you a good director no more. You tried to send me to the crazy house."

"Why did you put that thing in your mouth?" Herman asked. (He had cut the inside of his mouth with the end of a wire coat hanger.) "Why did you say you wanted to kill yourself?"

"Who was that worker that lied on me? I swear to my mom I never said nothing like that."

The aide who had brought David in whispered something to Herman about a key ring that had been taken by one of the boys in David's wing. Herman asked David about the key ring.

David shook his head violently. "I don't want to be no dime-dropper [informer]," he said.

"David, I want to refute what you said about not trusting me," Herman said. "Everyone here is interested in you. I only wish you were as interested in yourself. Why are you doing this attempted suicide stuff? You might succeed by mistake."

David was led back to his wing, and Herman said: "He's acting up because he's been locked up for four Christmases. P.S., his mother says she's ill with phlebitis and can't take him."

So there it is. There are hundreds of juveniles like David. He belongs to the Division for Youth because he is a behavior problem and he belongs to the Mental Health Department because he is a mental problem. In fact, neither wants him, and he becomes the victim of interagency squabbles. He falls into the system's cracks. He may be released into the community until the next tragedy occurs. Or he may be in and out of a place like Goshen, a prep school for adult prisons.

There are a great many people belonging to a great many agencies who think they know what is best for juveniles. Some of them agree with Father Flanagan that "there's no such thing as a bad boy." Others hold that you should lock up some juveniles and throw away the key.

The policemen who make the arrests feel juveniles are treated too leniently. The Department of Probation takes the position that once a child is placed, its job is over; so judges have no way of monitoring premature releases or inappropriate placements. The judges have increasing judicial responsibility but cannot provide the required services or impose fixed penalties. The legal-aid lawyers, regardless of a child's need for treatment, see themselves as guardians of his legal rights. The Division for Youth is forced to release juvenile offenders to keep up with intake. The Mental Health Services, a bureaucratic octopus, hands enormous sums of money over to private agencies which then skim the cream of low-risk cases. Small wonder that Family Court judges see the same juveniles showing up again and again.

When Ken Jordan and Bill Sherwin left Family Court after their hearing before Judge Roache, a social worker watched them walking cockily down the hall, after giving the finger to their court officer, and he said, "I'm sure we haven't seen the last of these boys."

Ted Morgan is a frequent contributor to this magazine [The New York Times Magazine].

Letters-to-the-Editor

Now consider the letters which were published in the *New York Times Magazine* a month after the article was published. They manifest a broad range of attitudes and values in the suggestions they propose to deal with these youngsters.

The first letter suggests that the problem is in the society and in how the victims were socialized. Consider the fact that the young victims were so immobilized by fear that they were unable to capitalize on opportunities to run away or alert the police. Why? To what extent was their "fear" a cause of the problem?

The second letter admits the failure of existing individual-oriented techniques of treatment; but it recommends the new "fad" — behavior modification — as a solution. Is society required to develop and use such techniques? Or does the spectre of abuse and totalitarian population control (a la *Clockwork Orange, 1984,* and *Brave New World)* make this the worse evil?

Letters three, four, and five suggest that the problem is not failure of social service programs (as indicated in the article), but chronic underinvestment in these programs and in research and development. To what degree would providing a psychiatrist or child-welfare worker for every youngster prevent such behavior from occurring?

Letters six and seven address the character of a society which perpetuates conditions of poverty and racism, and which thrives on violence. Should such a society condemn 14- and 15-year-old youngsters who act little different from their television and movie heroes, or from people depicted daily in newspaper headlines, magazines, and comics?

Letter eight reflects the anger of the victim's mother. It goes on to suggest that society should repay youngsters who commit such crimes with punishments at least as violent as the crimes. Would that seem to you to be the character of a just society?

The ninth letter raises the issue of individual deviance and societal responsibility. It asks what society is to do to prevent delinquency and to deal with those whom it has failed. Societal factors beyond the immediate event are seen as being embedded in, and caused by, broader societal factors. It recommends action to get to the root causes of racism, poverty, and the anger and frustration which they breed.

The last letter suggests that the problem addressed in this article is atypical, and that the major failing of the juvenile justice system is in its excessively harsh treatment of huge numbers of status offenders and deprived children. The author of this letter feels that the article was suggesting that more vindictiveness may be appropriate; most children in the system, this letter laments, receive "treatment" which is already too vindictive.

Do you think it possible that any juvenile justice system could function in a manner that would be satisfactory to all the people who wrote the letters?

Letters

1

Ted Morgan's article on juvenile crime ("They think, 'I can kill because I'm 14,'" Jan. 19) was shocking and frightening, but is not middle-class response to the situation, as described by Mr. Morgan, also shocking and frightening? Two 10-year-old boys, considered competent by their parents to go shopping alone, were apparently unable to exercise the simplest means of self-preservation. In spite of ample opportunity, they did not run away, phone their parents, alert guards or other shoppers, or appeal to the bus driver. The reason — their parents had warned them: "If you're mugged, give them what they want."

Independence is always accompanied by risk, and parents have always been concerned when youngsters go out on their own. Even in a gentler time there were bullies and even criminals about. Children were certainly taught caution, but instinctive, common-sense response to danger was expected of them.

One wonders, are we now raising a generation of ready-made victims?
Margaret H. McDowell
New York City

2

Ted Morgan dramatically demonstrates the inadequacy and hopelessness in dealing with adolescent crime and deviancy in New York. As a medical student in psychiatry, I've had firsthand experience with young sociopaths at the Meyer

Manhattan State Hospital on Randall's Island. This is where some of the older, more flagrantly disturbed adolescent offenders receive "treatment." They are very much like the younger boys, Ken and Bill, of the article, shaped by their environment, true sociopaths without any conventional moral structure. I'm told their prognosis is poor: either long jail sentences, possibly the zombiesque life of the chronic schizophrenic, or early death. What is to be done?

We can no longer close our eyes to the means afforded us via behavior conditioning. We all blanch at the thought of the Burgess-Kubrick vision of a "Clockwork Orange" conditioning technique, but theirs was only one version. Behavior conditioning with adjuvant social and environmental programs for the patient seems the most effective and cheapest means for change at society's disposal today. Of course, if we could make poverty and the ghetto disappear, we wouldn't have to resort to such drastic and disagreeable methods. But these problems won't go away overnight; neither will today's deviant suddenly become adjusted. The frustrations of these problems have led to a "Death Wish" philosophy that is all too prevalent and acceptable in New York City.

The dangers of behavior conditioning for individuals and the mass society are great, but our systems are collapsing around us. There are more and more victims, more and more deviants. Rarely are either helped. The long-range answers are to get rid of the conditions that create the sociopath. But the immediate answer is to control the deviant and protect ourselves.

Lawrence Diller
College of Physicians
and Surgeons,
Columbia University
New York City

3

There is no doubt that social service agencies are selective and reject the more troublesome children. And state mental hospitals may be similarly selective. But it would be wrong to assume that these practices are the result of a distaste for dealing with seriously troubled children. Most of the selectivity derives from a lack of financial resources, since youngsters with massive problems require manpower in massive amounts.

Both public and private agencies can make a creditable effort in dealing with difficult juvenile cases provided they have resources. Many of us in the youth field were heartened last year when Congress passed the Juvenile Justice and Delinquency Prevention Act of 1974. This would have provided hundreds of millions of dollars over a period of years to public and private juvenile justice and youth agencies starved for funds.

But hopes for better social services for youth died when President Ford signed the bill but refused to ask for new funds to implement its provisions. Too inflationary at this time, he said.

Perhaps it is. But we are also paying a huge price, as Mr. Morgan shows us, when we can't give deeply troubled, even dangerous, youth the help it so desperately needs. To allow them to roam the streets unhelped is to play roulette with the lives and welfare of everyone else.

H. Ladd Plumley
Chairman of the Board,
National Council on Crime
and Delinquency
Hackensack, N.J.

4

Ted Morgan's article is gratifyingly accurate in its presentation of the ideas contained in my study and my interviews with Mr. Morgan. It dramatically speaks to the problems of violence, but, in so doing, it leaves the impression that no one understands, or wants to understand, the most violent amongst them. The sole purpose of my inquiry into the background and circumstances of 10 youths who have committed homicide was to get a better perspective as to what they are like so that we can be more meaningful in what we do to bring about significant change in their behavior. Admittedly, as Mr. Morgan states, current resources in staff, skills, equipment are drastically limited, but we have gained further insights from this study which are helping us to identify more specifically what we need to implement better programs for all our youths, including these.

Charles H. King
Deputy Director
of Rehabilitation,
New York State
Executive Department,
Division for Youth
New York City

5

As horrifying as the vicious attack and violence of Ken and Bill is the utter inability of the juvenile justice system to re-educate and rehabilitate these two youngsters. In this vacuum the reaction will be to "throw the book" at them, which only aggravates the problem.

As there are no ideas for filling this crack in the system, here is one practical immediate possibility:

Since their oppressed and deprived parents cannot care for these youngsters now, we should create an emergency task force to find and train 50 stable foster parents who can discipline and care for these youngsters. These parents should be paid and given ongoing support.

Prof. Howard W. Polsky
Columbia University,
School of Social Work
New York City

6

The first point to consider is who is committing these crimes. Ted Morgan leaves us with the impression that it is primarily poor black and Puerto Rican youths. The statistics he cites concerning juvenile offenders certainly lead to this conclusion. However, these statistics are misleading since they number only those children processed through the juvenile justice system. Thus the statistics in fact count only those too poor to buy their way out, not all offenders.

Therefore, let us not contribute further fuel for racist accusations concerning juvenile offenders. We have no basis for suggesting that nonwhites commit more offenses, only that they are often unable to extricate themselves from the dead-end public system and are unable to afford effective treatment, if they should require it.

Once the poor child steps on the treadmill of the juvenile justice system, he or she may slip into increasingly violent criminal activity. Let us try to understand how this may happen. Consider the reaction of Mrs. Jones, the mother of one of the two 10-year-old victims. Mr. Morgan tells us: "She had gone through the usual sorrows and disappointments of life . . . but she had never felt real fear and the anger that follows fear." She expresses the desire to get a gun and kill her son's torturer. If Mrs. Jones, who has probably led a life

made normal by the comfort of money, can be driven by a single terrible incident to express the wish to murder, then what more can we expect of a poor child, who may have experienced starvation and desperation for most of his or her life, who is consistently brutalized by the system, whose only treatment is to be shot full of Thorazine?

The actions of these juvenile offenders are an abomination but, if blame is to be placed, it is not to the frightened, defiant and angry child that we should look, but to the society that permits the atrocities of the juvenile justice system to continue.

Danielle L. Schultz
Chicago

7

From my experience in representing more than 3,000 indigent slum children in delinquency proceedings, I do not believe that children calculate the risk of penalties when they commit even brutal and violent offenses. By and large, these are children who have little inner control, no hopes for the future, and little incentive to better themselves. To suggest that increasing the penalties would deter juvenile crime is a simplistic notion which will not die, and has not been effective in deterring adult crime. It will be even less effective with children who act on impulse and without an adequate intellectual or moral understanding of what they are doing.

It is too easy to delude the public into thinking that more policemen and stiffer penalties will solve a problem that is rooted in the community and can be solved only by great changes in the social environment and educational system to which these children are subjected.

Judge Lois G. Forer
Court of Common Pleas
Philadelphia

8

When Mrs. Jones, mother of one of the 10-year-olds who had been kidnapped and tortured, sees "the smirking, gangling youth" who has assaulted her son, she cries: "I want to kill him. I want to grab a gun and shoot him." So do I.

When the corporation counsel supervisor sermonizes to one of the victims: "You must cast anger out of your heart and feel only Christian love for them," I would like to ask, "Why? So that they can go blithely on with their murderous activities, secure in the knowledge that there are fools aplenty who will feel only Christian love for them, even if they kill their victims next time?"

Expeditious riddance of these criminals will best serve society, saving human beings the need to expend blood, sweat, tears and money attempting the futile task of rehabilitation.

Mr. Morgan's article gives sound evidence that the present system of handling the problem is deplorable, recognized as deplorable even by those administering the system. A constructive system based on getting rid of the abominations to the general welfare fast is overdue.

The Talmud instructs: "Kindness to the guilty results in cruelty to the innocent."

A.S. Flaumenhaft
Lawrence, N.Y.

9

As teachers in the city's public schools, our response to the Ted Morgan article is a loud, "Hear, hear!" We have felt utter despair at our inability to deal effectively with the child who is so troubled at 5 years of age that we all know he is destined to become a juvenile delinquent. Those of us who daily come in contact with children who are severely disturbed by the time they reach the schools meet with constant frustration. We know these children need help, the administration knows these children need help, the guidance people know they need help — but help is not available. To remove a severely disturbed child from the schools can take between six months to a year, provided the parent will allow the child to be sent to a special class where, one hopes, he will receive some treatment. For many reasons, parents will often refuse help for the child, so back the child comes into the classroom.

Teachers all over the system, if asked, will freely admit that the problem of the "disturbed child" acting out in the classroom is the main problem in our schools. But since the strike of 1965, saying this out loud puts a teacher in a vulnerable position — he or she can be called a racist.

There are so many teachers unemployed who could be retrained to handle a small group of these problem children. There are so many empty classrooms. Why isn't it possible to remove these children to special classes and provide them with teachers who can work with them before they need deep psychiatric help?

Unless society recognizes that it must deal with this problem when it begins, rather than when the problem has reached the violent stage, as in the case of 15-year-old Ken in the Morgan article, we will never be able to cope with it adequately. We are very pessimistic because we see so much that needs to be done in our small school. We feel that our society is seriously threatened by the lawlessness that these children breed, and yet politicians still talk about "crime in the streets" as though it were a problem separate from the rest of society. You can't deal with crime until you deal with these children effectively, and that means when they are 3 or 4 years old. Our priorities need to be reassessed.

Beatrice Schwartz
Barbara Helmers
Brooklyn, N.Y.

10

Except in passing, Ted Morgan has not identified the jurisprudential myth which is the foundation of the present dysfunctional system. Nor has he adequately represented all of its irrationality and unfairness. The depressing revelation that the dangerous twosome he described in his story at present stalk the streets of New York is only one consequence of the myth.

The myth, of course, is that the proper purpose of the juvenile court is *not* to administer a societal response to the criminal acts which some children commit. Rather, the court purports to address the psychological and social deprivations of all children — that is, to "treat" and "rehabilitate" children whose lives are less than optimal. This "treatment" rationale means that the children who have never committed any crime, but who have "problems" (running away from uncaring homes, refusing to attend worse schools) are confined together in the same detention facilities with adolescents who torture, sodomize, rape and murder. Mr. Morgan correctly informs us that the young murderer usually stays no more than nine months in training school. But he does not tell us that the so-called PINS children (Person in Need of Supervision — runaways, truants, etc.) will stay 18 months or longer because their parents, who brought them to court in the first place, do not want them. The young killers who are turned loose make good press. The PINS children who rot in prison (and they account for more than half the nation's child prison population) do not.

Apologists for the present system argue that it is the child, not his actions, which is the court's concern; that the system's present ills would be righted if only there were more money to secure more psychiatrists, more social workers and more and better "treatment" centers for disturbed children. Mr. Morgan reiterates this plaint throughout his piece. As long as this misty-eyed, pious faith in the sanctity of "treatment" and psychotherapy persists as the rationale for the juvenile justice system, the Kens and Bills will continue to return to our midst after a few months and the runaways will continue to be locked up for years.

The length of time that a young criminal is confined ought to be determined primarily by the nature of the offense he has committed, with due consideration for the reduced capacity of children to formulate criminal intent, past records, and the fact that the mere passage of time is more likely to alter the behavior of a 15-year-old than a 30-year-old. Neither the juvenile court nor any agency should have the power to confine any child (with the possible exception of a suicidal child) who has not violated the criminal law, no matter what his problems. For every PINS child who later turns violent, there are hundreds of PINS who never graduate into Kens and Bills. The theory that today's PINS are tomorrow's criminals would also justify the incarceration of all welfare recipients, since poverty is also associated with crime. Most poor people, like most truants and runaways, are not criminals, although the reverse may be true.

Elimination of PINS children from court jurisdiction altogether, and a sentencing system for child criminals which primarily reflects the seriousness of the crimes, are reforms that are long, long overdue. They are vociferously resisted, however, by those misguided humanitarians who insist that the coercive power of a court should be a conduit for social services and that "treatment" is holy.

The tragedy is that sensational articles like Mr. Morgan's serve only to fuel the Legislature to impose vindictive sentences on youths like Ken and Bill (who, despite their rising number, still represent only a small fraction of the juvenile court popula-tion) without paying one whit of attention to the thousands who have committed no crime and are stashed away in the name of treatment.

Rena K. Uviller,
Director,
Juvenile Rights Project,
American Civil Liberties Union
New York City

Source: © 1975 by the New York Times Company. Reprinted by permission.

This case example raises the full range of issues confronting the people who design and operate juvenile justice systems. It suggests that the existing juvenile justice system is incapable of responding adequately to the demands placed on it by individuals who engage in delinquent behavior and by the broader community. The final two chapters of this book will consider what may be done to remedy such a situation. Chapter 11 details major types of prevention efforts and the theories on which they are based. The final chapter discusses three models of juvenile justice and some of the innovative programs now being tested or implemented in various localities. As you read these pages, keep in mind the example you have just experienced as well as the cases presented in Chapter 4.

It is hoped that this case example, the interviews, and the book's other references throughout to the real world problems of juvenile justice will all help you to bridge the gap between the academic world and the arena of action.

References

1. See, for example, W. Vaughn Stapleton and Lee E. Teitelbaum, *In Defense of Youth* (New York: Russel Sage Foundation, 1972).

2. The data used in this selection were collected by the Bureau of Statistics and Evaluation of the Pennsylvania Governor's Justice Commission. We wish to acknowledge the helpful assistance of Mr. Joseph Riggione, Director of the Bureau.

3. Many actors in the juvenile justice system share the somewhat myopic view that discretion is entirely a police function. Even high-quality academic work has sometimes focused on police decision making to the exclusion of diversionary practices of other professionals in the system. See, for ex-

ample, Nathan Goldman, *The Differential Selection of Juvenile Offenders for Court Appearance* (New York: National Council on Crime and Delinquency, 1963).

4. N.C.C.D. Survey Services, *A Feasibility Study of Regional Juvenile Detention* (Hackensack, N.J.: National Council on Crime and Delinquency, 1971).

5. Data provided by the Bureau of Statistics and Evaluation of the Pennsylvania Governor's Justice Commission.

6. This reference is to the total number of different police departments in the Commonwealth — including township, city, county, and state police agencies.

7. Sophia Robinson, *Can Delinquency Be Measured?* (New York: Columbia University Press, 1936).

8. These rates represent a state-wide average; they vary considerably from jurisdiction to jurisdiction within the State.

9. Police decision making of this sort has been explored by such prominent investigators as James Q. Wilson, *Varieties of Police Behavior* (Cambridge, Mass.: Harvard University Press, 1968) and Norman C. Weiner and Charles V. Willie, "Decisions by Juvenile Officers," *American Journal of Sociology* 77 no. 2 (September 1971): 199 - 210. Furthermore, scholarship in the area of police administration has frequently suggested that 50 percent of all cases initiated ought to be resolved in the station house with no need for O/S referrals. See, for example, Jesse R. James and George H. Shepard, "Police Work with Children," in *Municipal Police Administration*, ed. George D. Eastman and Esther M. Eastman (Washington, D.C.: International City Management Association, 1971), pp. 148 - 57. Moreover, the F.B.I.'s Uniform Crime Statistics indicate that the proportion of youngsters referred to court varies from about 30 percent to almost 90 percent (Uniform Crime Reports, 1972).

10. Data provided by the Bureau of Statistics and Evaluation of the Pennsylvania Governor's Justice Commission.

11. See Mark M. Levin and Rosemary C. Sarri, *Juvenile Delinquency: A Comparative Analysis of Legal Codes in the United States* (Ann Arbor, Mich.: National Assessment of Juvenile Corrections, 1974), pp. 52 - 3.

Part Two

Part I provided an overview of fundamental variables and principles which affect the operation of juvenile systems. Part II is a detailed consideration of the actors and processes that divert youngsters from, or pull them into the juvenile justice system. Five processes or "stages" of the system are considered in turn: Identification; Police Decision Making; Detention; Juvenile Court Philosophy and Procedures; and Dispositions. Throughout these discussions, attention is focused on the range of alternatives available at each stage, the nature of community actors involved, systemic factors which condition their operation, and, most importantly, the consequences for youngsters who are or are not made a part of the juvenile justice subsystem.

5 Identifying Delinquents: The Decision to Call (Or Not to Call) the Police

When a child is arraigned in Court, there are always three delinquents: the child, the parent and the community.

Ernest Coulter,
Founder of the Big Brother Movement (1904)

Identification of delinquency is commonly thought to be a responsibility of the police. In reality, however, most police encounters with juveniles result from complaints by individuals or agencies in the community;[1] and there is evidence that these agencies and individuals decide *not* to call the police in many (perhaps even most) cases.[2] Decisions not to bring delinquent acts to the attention of the police are made by victims, parents, schools, and a variety of community agencies; sometimes the police themselves decide not to take official cognizance of observed delinquent behavior.

This chapter is about these community decision makers — about the options which are available to them, about the factors which influence their decision making, and about the consequences of their decisions both for young people (who may either be diverted or sent on for further processing), and for the remainder of those involved in the juvenile justice system.

The Range of Options
Available to Decision Makers
in the Community

People who observe delinquent acts do not think to themselves; "Should I encapsulate or divert?" Rather, they think, "What should I do about this?" One option is to call the police, thus beginning a process of encapsulation into the formal mechanisms of the juvenile justice system. Another option is to ignore the behavior, thus achieving a complete, far-reaching, and effective act of diversion from the formal processes of juvenile justice. This dichotomy, however, is greatly oversimplified because there are various other possibilities available which are neither so completely encapsulating nor so completely diverting. Consider, for example, the possibilities which emerge from the following hypothetical situation:

> It is 5:30 p.m. Mr. Walter Freeman, math teacher at Parsons Memorial High School, is leaving after a faculty meeting. As he walks through the school parking lot, he notices Franco and Zonk, who are on the football team, and two girls — Marilyn, a cheerleader, and Raquel, a high-school dropout — sitting in a parked car. As he waves "Hi," to them, he realizes that they are talking loudly and laughing. He also observes several open cans of beer, and a broken six-pack on the seat. What does he do?

Consider the labeling which is already present in defining the situation: football team, cheerleader, dropout, math teacher.

Clearly, Mr. Freeman must make a decision. First, however, he must define the situation. The way he does that will influence the range of options available to him. Objectively, the situation involves illegal and hence delinquent behavior, which Mr. Freeman may perceive as a violation of the state's teenage drinking laws or as a violation of school rules of some kind. On the other hand, Mr. Freeman may decide that this is just a bunch of kids having some relaxation — probably after a hard practice session or during mid-term examinations. If he perceives the situation as "good clean fun," the youngsters will certainly be diverted; *no* degree of encapsulation will occur. If Mr. Freeman is instead struck by the illegality of the behavior, he must decide how to respond. This initial definition of the situation is to a significant extent a product of the mind and mood and experiences of the observer.[3] It is, nevertheless, the most important decision in the interactional process.[4]

Suppose that Mr. Freeman defines the behavior as delinquent — as a challenge to some legal, moral, or social rules. Does he call the police immediately? Not necessarily; he has several options. He must decide the degree to which he will divert or encapsulate these young people into the processes of the juvenile justice system. At this stage, there are six general options for action. Mr. Freeman may decide to:

1. Ignore the behavior.
2. Talk to them about it.
3. Talk to their parents.
4. Report the incident to the school authorities.
5. Report the incident to other community agencies (drug and alcohol abuse programs, detached street workers, a clergyman, etc.).
6. Report the incident to the police.

This range of options represents varying degrees of diversion and varying types of encapsulation. First of all, if Mr. Freeman decides to ignore the behavior (option 1), he is effecting a complete act of diversion with virtually no degree of encapsulation.

The phrase "virtually no degree of encapsulation" is used advisedly because, in fact, a degree of identification has occurred which will affect future interactions between these actors. The next time he observes similar behavior, Mr. Freeman may decide that there is a pattern which requires intervention.

Although it may seem unusual to suppose that delinquent and illegal acts are typically ignored, that is in fact the case.

If Mr. Freeman decides not to ignore the behavior, he might choose any one, or any combination, or all of the remaining options (2 through 6). Each of these options involves some element of encapsulation because each involves some degree of negative labeling which might be significant at some future time. Each but the last (calling the police) involves some element of diversion because each operates to keep youngsters away from the formal processes of the juvenile justice system. A decision to exercise option six (report the incident to the police), while calling into action the formal law enforcement agent of the community, does not necessarily ensure that further encapsulation will occur. In fact, in a large number of cases, the police choose to take no official notice of delinquent acts which come to their attention. Thus even this most encapsulating option in the identification process generally includes an element of diversion.

The next part of this chapter will involve you in considering the extent to which you and other members of the public (including victims) are prepared to tolerate delinquency. Later sections will consider in turn the decision-making patterns of families, of schools, and of community agencies.

"We, the People:" Perceptions about Misbehavior That "Ought" to be Reported

At the beginning of this book you were asked to complete a self-report questionnaire about delinquent acts which you (and your friends) may have committed. That exercise demonstrated that many more delinquent acts occur (and hence many more "delinquents" exist), than ever come to the attention of the authorities; it showed, furthermore, that most young people who commit delinquent acts are not unlike you. Now it is appropriate to involve you in considering some of the dynamics of identification and reporting of delinquent acts — both those acts you may have committed and those you may have observed.

As a first step in this process, review the answers on your own self-report study in Chapter 1 and indicate in Table 5.1 any of the items for which you recorded positive answers. Then indicate which, if any, were known to someone else (who?).

TABLE 5.1.

Delinquent Act	Observed?		By Whom?
	No	Yes	

Indicate in Table 5.2 which of the options listed on page   were
used. Was the incident reported? If so, with what result?

TABLE 5.2.

Delinquent Act	Option Chosen 1 2 3 4 5 6	If 2-6, to whom did the observer report? With what result?

Now shift the focus from yourself as a subject (or potential subject) of the juvenile justice system, and think about yourself as an
observer — as a member of "the public," much like the rest of us.
Think about the delinquent acts of others of which you reported being
aware (Table 1.1). Indicate in Table 5.3 whether those acts were committed by friends or by other people. Then indicate by a check under
"no" or "yes" whether you reported the incident; and if "yes," to
whom, and with what effect.

We asked students in one class (which is
considered fairly average for a large state
university) to indicate how many had stolen
items worth more than $2.50. Of sixty students,
forty indicated that they had done so. Of
these forty, only five reported that they had
been observed, and only two were reported
to the police — neither were ever contacted.

Now consider the types of delinquent acts which you are or are not
likely to report. Were you more knowledgeable about your friends, but
more reluctant to report them? Did you perhaps notice a tendency not
to perceive some acts as things which ought to be reported to the police
(e.g., skipping school, drinking beer or smoking marijuana, sexual intercourse, defiance of parental orders)? Would you report someone
who had run away from home? Shoplifted? (for objects valued at less
than $2.50? $25? more than $50?) Sold drugs? Purposely damaged a
public restroom?

Questions such as these were probed in a rather extensive
nationwide survey of young people which included both rural and ur-

TABLE 5.3. Delinquent Acts Identified

Delinquent Acts Observed or Otherwise Known	Friends?			Others?		
	Did you report?		If so, to whom? With what result?	Did you report?		If so, to whom? With what result?
	No	Yes		No	Yes	
1. Run away from home						
2. Used force to get money or valuables from another person						
3. Visited a house of prostitution						
4. Used or sold narcotic drugs						
5. Took things of large value (more than $50)						
6. Broke into & entered a home, store, or building						
7. Defied parental authority to their faces						

8. Took a car for a ride without the owner's permission

9. Started a fist fight

10. Purposely damaged or destroyed public or private property

11. Took things of medium value (between $2.50 and $49.99)

12. Skipped school

13. Took things of small values (less than $2.50)

14. Drank alcoholic beverages (under legal age)

15. Engaged in premarital intercourse

16. Smoked or possessed marijuana

ban samples.[5] When asked whose responsibility it is to see that laws are enforced, 64 percent of rural youth and 65 percent of urban youth reported that they consider it a responsibility of public officials such as policemen, judges, and probation officers. Slightly more, however, (67 percent rural, and 68 percent urban) also felt that others (such as themselves, parents, people in the community, and teachers) carry the responsibility as well.[6] Regarding personal feelings of responsibility, the youngsters were asked: "What responsibility, if any, do you feel that you, yourself, have in seeing that the laws are enforced?"

> Young women in both rural and urban areas seem to have a stronger personal sense of responsibility than young men in country or town. Forty-five percent of urban young women and forty percent of their country sisters, as compared to 37 percent of urban young men and 35 percent of their country brothers, believe they personally should see that they, themselves, obey the laws. More young men in rural areas, 21 percent as compared to 18 percent in the city, think they have a personal responsibility to see that others obey the law. Nineteen percent of young women in town and country see it this way.[7]

When the respondents were asked to consider which should be reported to the authorities, the largest percentage thought that stealing should be reported (rural 42 percent, urban 43 percent), although females regarded this less a reportable offense than did males. On dangerous driving, 31 percent of rural youth compared to 20 percent of urban youngsters thought incidents should be reported; here the females surpassed the males in indicating that incidents should be reported. The number of youngsters who thought that other auto-related acts, such as traffic violations and driving without a license, should be reported was, however, negligible. The poll also indicated a reluctance of youth to become involved in reporting acts that caused injury to persons — including fighting, assaults on women, and surprisingly, even murder.[8] Furthermore, only 16 percent of rural youth and 19 percent of the urban youth surveyed thought that "all violations should be reported"; only 2 to 4 percent thought that violations such as disturbing the peace, loitering, and selling liquor to minors should be reported.[9]

It appears then, that young people, at least, are fairly tolerant of much misbehavior. Responses about the types of behavior that *ought* to be reported may vary considerably, however, from *actual* reporting behavior after a delinquent act has been observed. An individual who indicates that the authorities *ought* to be notified about a theft might nevertheless fail to report an offense if it were committed by a friend, or if he were frightened about becoming involved. In light of the fact that a moral "ought" is not always translated into a behavioral "do,"[10] it is appropriate to examine existing evidence about actual reporting behavior in the general population.

"We, the People:" The Public and the Actual Reporting of Misbehavior

A person's awareness of criminal acts may derive either from observations or from the experience of being victimized. The evidence available suggests that victims are more likely to notify the authorities than are casual observers; *but more often than not people decide not to report offenses.*

The Reporting of Offenses by Observers

In an excellent study conducted in Iowa City, incidents of shoplifting were staged under circumstances that assured that they would be observed by casual shoppers.[11] The experimenters, Darrell Steffensmeier and Robert Terry, followed the person who observed the staged "offense" and found that only 29.2 percent notified store employees. During the experiment, an official of the store subsequently approached the 70.8 percent who did not report the crime, inquired if they had seen an offense take place, and pointed out the actor-offender as a person about whom there was suspicion. Even under these circumstances, a significant number of people (23.1 percent of the entire group) refused to report.

In real world situations it is unlikely that such "prompting" would occur; it seems appropriate to conclude, therefore, that only about 30 percent of the shoplifters would have been reported.

Remember that the number of offenses observed is only a fraction of the offenses committed. Some offenses are necessarily going to be observed (robbery, for example, is always observed because it is stealing from, or in the presence of, another person). Other offenses, such as burglary or shoplifting, are less likely to be observed at the time of commission or afterwards. There is no way

Two additional findings of the Steffensmeier and Terry study are of importance in considering public decision making about observed deviance. First, strong differences emerged when the observers were divided into a student group and an adult group. Only 4.8 percent of the student group reported the offense immediately without prompting, while the comparable figure for the adult group was 31.9 percent. Moreover, the student group was virtually unaffected by the prompting encounter with a store employee; 71.4 percent refused to report even after prompting (23.8 did report after prompting). On the other hand, only 17.8 percent of the adults held out and refused to report the offense after prompting. This interesting variation in tolerance for shoplifting between adults and students suggests that the character of the audience observing a delinquent act makes a significant difference in the liklihood of its being reported.

The second additional finding of the Steffensmeier and Terry study concerns the relationship between the characteristics of the shoplifter and the reporting behavior of observers. Two variables were studied: sex and dress style (hippie vs. straight). It was found that the sex of the shoplifter did not significantly affect the likelihood that observers would report; style of dress, however, had a considerable impact.

> [The] shoplifter's appearance provides the potential reactor with information that enables him to locate the actor (shoplifter) on a high-low evaluative continuum. Apparently a hippie appearance constitutes a negative identity that results in a greater willingness on the part of subjects to report the hippie over the straight shoplifter and, by extension, a greater willingness to impute a deviant label to a hippie rather than a straight actor.[12]

While this is a limited study of public reactions to one offense, it does suggest that characteristics of the observer and the offender are important in explaining variations in the reporting of identical offenses.

Data are not available on observer responses to other characteristics. It is interesting to consider, however, what effect variables such as age and race might have on identification.

The Reporting of Offenses by Victims

Victimization studies are investigations asking members of the general public whether they have been victims of criminal or delinquent behavior during some specified time interval (usually one year).[13] Before we study the information derived from such studies, we must first note a serious limitation.[14] Victims frequently do not see the offender (in a burglary or car theft, for example) and even when they do, they would be hard pressed to tell whether he was a juvenile or an adult. Therefore, it is difficult to ascertain from victimization studies the extent of juvenile involvement in the victimizing behavior. Because of these limitations (and in part because of the paucity of more directly appropriate information), victimization studies provide only an inferential base from which to speculate about the role of the public in identifying (or not identifying) delinquent behavior.

To some extent, of course, all the public are victims of crime in at least an indirect way. Consumers, for example, pay a "shoplifting tax" on everything they buy in order to cover what others steal. Victimization studies, however, are concerned only with those who have been the direct victim of a criminal offense, that is, with individuals who have been robbed, mugged, raped, had their cars stolen or their homes burglarized, etc.

Victimization studies help to shed light on identification decisions made by the public. They provide information about the percentage of victims who report offenses to the police and about the relationship between reporting behavior and such variables as seriousness of the offense and victims' attitudes about the police.

Available victimization studies indicate that about half the offenses known to victims are *not* reported to the police.[15] Table 5.4 presents information on reporting of offenses from a national study of victimization done for the President's Commission on Law Enforcement and the Administration of Justice. While an overall average of fifty percent of the offenses were reported, there was considerable variability in reporting from one offense to another. Victims of consumer fraud (dishonesty in the marketing of goods and services), for example, reported only ten percent of the offenses against them, while a vast majority of rape, robbery, aggravated assault, and auto theft victims indicated that they reported the offense to the police. These data led to the conclusion that the more serious the offense, the greater the likelihood that a victim will report it.

TABLE 5.4. Reporting of Crimes by Victims

Crime	Percent of Incidents in Which Police are Notified	Number of Cases in Sample
Forcible Rape	77%	13
Robbery	65	31
Aggravated Assault	65	69
Simple Assault	46	125
Burglary	58	313
Larceny (over $50)	60	198
Larceny (under $50)	37	473
Vehicle Theft	89	65
Auto Offenses	71	144
Malicious Mischief	38	345
Fraud	26	82
Consumer Fraud	10	40
Other Sex Offenses	51	45

Source: Philip H. Ennis, "Criminal Victimization in the United States, Field Surveys II. A Report of a National Survey," *Report of the President's Commission on Law Enforcement and the Administration of Justice*, Washington, D.C.: U.S. Government Printing Office, (1967), p. 42.

A note of caution is appropriate, however; it cannot be concluded that fifty percent of all juvenile offenses are reported. The list of offenses above represents only serious offenses. Many acts for which young people can be arrested (and incidentally for which adults could not be arrested) such as incorrigibility and drinking have only a minimal chance of being reported by the public either because of the absence of a distinct victim or because of the less serious nature of the offense.

An additional factor which may affect the reporting of offenses by victims is their perception of the capability of the justice system to right the wrong. The N.O.R.C. victimization studies asked victims who had not reported to the police for explanations of their behavior. Responses indicate that:

> More than half of the victims (55 percent) have a negative view toward police effectiveness, most of which is a judgment that the police could not do anything about the matter anyway.[16]

This information indicates that victims' decisions to report (or not to report) an offense to the police involved an assessment of the "probable" police response. Many people apparently have little confidence in the police; others probably consider the police adequate but thought that the problem was too insignificant to be brought to their attention; still others thought that the police's hands might be tied because of an obvious lack of evidence,[17] or perhaps because of "crook-coddling" decisions of the Supreme Court.

The preceding paragraphs have pointed out variations among individuals and groups of individuals in their propensity both to feel a responsibility to report, *and* in fact to report observed misconduct. It has also been shown that individuals observing an illegal act do not react mechanically in deciding whether to notify authorities; they go through a complex decision process which involves defining the situation, deciding whether to report, and if so, to whom. In fact, the data on reporting and propensity to report illustrate with clarity that most people are willing to tolerate a significant number of instances of crime and delinquency. Most people, apparently, do not believe it is their responsibility to report offenses to the authorities; indeed, most individuals who observe offenses are strongly inclined to ignore them. Even the victims of crimes are unlikely to complain officially. The public (including victims) constitutes a mighty barrier between the delinquent and the justice system. Diversion is clearly the major response of citizens who, through either observation or experience, know the most about the incidence of crime and delinquency.

The casual observer and the victim, however, are not the only individuals who learn about delinquency and face decisions about whether to report it. Families, school officials, and representatives of community agencies are extensively involved in identifying delinquency and making decisions about the diversion or encapsulation of young people into the juvenile justice system.

Referrals from Families, Schools, and Social Agencies

Traditionally, the family and an extended circle of relatives and neighbors were (and still are to a considerable degree) the community's main agent of socialization and social control. As society becomes more industrialized and complex, however, the immediacy of these institutions in the lives of youngsters is reduced appreciably. Consider that not long ago a youngster would spend perhaps the entire day, every day, surrounded by family and immediate community. Work, play, learning of skills, love, and nurture were all dependent on a close circle of people. Now consider the day of the average teenager in the 1970s. A combination of school, extracurricular activities, community recreation, television, social events, and visiting with peers take up practically every waking moment. And if there does happen to be time that could be spent with the family, parents often have occupational and social activities which take it away. Moreover, responsibilities once the province of family and friends are now the domain of a complex and often depersonalized series of organizations. Theodore Lowi, in addressing some of the problems of control which emerge in contemporary society, has commented that

> almost nothing is left to the family, clan, neighborhood, or guild — or to chance. Even sandlot baseball has given way to Little Leagues, symptomatic of an incredible array of parental groups and neighborhood businesses organized to see that the child's every waking moment is organized, unprivate, wholesome, and, primarily oriented toward an ideal of advancement to adult life of rationality that comes all too soon.[18]

Alain Touraine has called this phenomenon the emergence of a "programmed society"[19] into which each bit and piece must fit. If it does not, it is either rejected or bent, spindled and mutilated. The life of youngsters which once centered around a highly personalized neighborhood is now divided among the domains of a changing family, bureaucratized school systems, and a variety of social agencies. When each of these institutions carries out its responsibility, youngsters presumably grow into mature, responsible adulthood; when they fail, strain is placed on the youngsters involved and on other institutions in the community. This section will consider the activities of families, schools, and social welfare agencies which in large part determine whether youngsters will be touched by the formal processes of the juvenile justice system.

Families as Instruments of Diversion

The report of the 1970 White House Conference on Children noted that the family unit, despite changes in form, continues to function as a "facilitating, mediating, adapting, and confronting system for its members who have differing aspirations, capabilities and potentials."[20]

> The primary tasks of families are to develop their capabilities to socialize children, to enhance the competence of their members to cope with the demands of other organizations in which they must function, to utilize these organizations, and to provide the satisfactions of a mentally healthy environment intrinsic to the well-being of a family.[21]

Family units that perform these functions are invaluable aids in the process of diversion. Troubled families, unable to cope effectively with internal strife and external pressure, may often be a prime force in moving a child toward eventual encapsulation into the juvenile justice system.

A considerable amount of delinquency is actually experienced within the confines of family units. The types of delinquent acts that youngsters commit at home are as minor as disobedience to parental authority and as serious as theft, incest, and assault. Younger siblings who complain to their parents about being punched or slapped repeatedly are involved in a sort of diversion: they do not take their grievances to the police or to court. Older siblings who grumble about money missing from their wallets are also involved in diversion. Parents are quite literally expected to take the law into their own hands in correcting misbehaving children. That we do not normally consider such family activities as part of the process of diversion from the juvenile justice system indicates only that diversion of this type is widespread, approved of, and expected.

Parents and siblings are frequently aware of delinquent acts committed outside the home. Parents frequently suspect (and often know), for example, that their children imbibe alcohol, inhale marijuana, skip school, and engage in premarital sex.[22] In fact, many parents "aid and abet" such acts by serving wine at meals, buying beer for parties, providing contraceptives, and writing to school authorities the "excuses" that are patent lies. It is generally expected, however, that such suspicions or knowledge will not be brought to the attention of the authorities.

In fact, families may shield their children from the justice system in yet another manner. Parents frequently serve as a referral source for neighbors, businessmen, schools, and community agencies that are concerned about a child's misbehavior. Merely by letting it be known that they are concerned about their children's behavior, parents make it possible for teachers, neighbors, social workers, and even policemen to try to have problems resolved at a low level of visibility. A society in which family units were expected to bring misbehavior to the attention of the authorities is conceivable;[23] ours, however, is not such a society.

Families That Fail to Divert

There are several ways in which family units may fail to contribute to the diversion of children. Perhaps the most subtle occurs when parents do not present themselves to the outside world as suitable for referrals. The teacher, neighbor, businessman, social worker, or other individual who perceives that a mother is unconcerned about her child's misbehavior has fewer options available in responding to that misbehavior and may be more inclined to view recourse to the authorities as appropriate. In addition, there is an impressive body of literature which suggests that children for whom the family is not a source of emotional and social support are disproportionately likely to be identified and formally labeled as delinquent.[24] Such youngsters often spend more time on the streets; frequently become socialized into acting-out youth gangs (actually making trouble, not merely striking tough-guy poses); wind up being highly visible to teachers, social workers, and policemen; and thus get into trouble that might otherwise have been avoided.

The failure of a family unit to protect its children — not just from delinquency, but from officials empowered to identify delinquency — may sometimes be active rather than passive. Despite strong social values that families ought to "look out for their own," referrals from families to the juvenile justice system are not uncommon. Court records abound with cases in which parents, generally poor and uninformed, bring their children to the attention of a juvenile court because they know of no other place to which they may turn.

> *The N.B.C. television documentary,* This Child
> is Rated X, *focused attention on the frequency*
> *with which unsuspecting (unsophisticated) well-*
> *meaning parents arrange to have their mildly*
> *misbehaving youngsters sent to reform school*
> *because they believe the experience will be*
> *helpful and pleasant. It is quite likely that middle-*
> *and upper-class, well-educated families make*
> *this type of mistake comparatively infrequently.*

Parents may also bring their children to the attention of the authorities out of anger, frustration, or disapproval. Most complaints about the "incorrigibility" of girls, for example, are made by their parents, typically as a result of teenage pregnancies in lower-class families.

Actively disobedient children (runaways, for example) are successfully coped with in many families; often available resources make it possible for middle- and upper-class families to board such children at private schools, military academies, or mental hospitals, or to maintain them at home in the outpatient care of a psychiatrist or psychologist.[25] Families without such resources must either handle the problem alone or turn to the small number of agencies available to poor families. In the absence of well-developed, highly visible social services, police, probation officers, and others involved in juvenile justice may sometimes appear to such families as the best source of authority and support for the control of their children.

Child Neglect and Abuse

Families may cause their children to be brought to the attention of the authorities in yet another way — by victimizing them. The juvenile justice system is concerned with helping children in trouble. A child's delinquency is merely one manifestation of such trouble. Nondelinquent children in trouble are appropriately the concern of the juvenile justice system if they require protection from neglecting or abusive parents.

There is considerable and increasing concern in the U.S. today for the well-being of abused and neglected children. There is reason to believe that the problem is pervasive throughout all social classes; poor children, however, are involved in most of the cases that come to the juvenile courts. Middle and upper-class families seem able to use

resources to compensate for or conceal abusive and neglecting behavior. It is a distressing paradox of the juvenile justice system that more youngsters are institutionalized for crimes which were committed against them than for crimes they committed against persons or property. Moreover, evidence suggests that more of the abused youngsters will be sent on for further processing than the youngsters apprehended for delinquent activities.[26]

Families — Concluding Comments

The primary characteristic of the relationship between families and the juvenile justice system is diversion. Family units function to keep children away from the authorities. This is the case with much delinquency that occurs in the home, and for much delinquency that is reported to parents rather than the police. Sometimes families fail to divert for these reasons: because of ignorance about the juvenile justice system, or because of inadequate resources with which to utilize diversionary options, or because of frustration and anger. Sometimes families victimize their children, thus opening the possibility of judicial intervention to protect the child. Whatever the situation, when families fail to divert their children from the paths that lead into the juvenile justice system, other institutions of the community are often called upon.

Schools as Instruments of Diversion

Schools are another community institution that identifies and diverts many delinquents from the formal processes of the juvenile justice system. Schools are perhaps the most pervasive social institution in the lives of young people today. Edwin Lemert has noted:

> With the disappearance of neighborhood and community influences, the school becomes the chief democratizing agency for the divergent populations of our society. Because it has contact with the child for a long period during the day and is given prolonged legal jurisdiction over his educational fate, it is often assumed that the school is the logical place to deal with extramural as well as intramural conduct problems. This is emphasized by the strategic positioning of teachers to perceive emerging problems of students, and the *in locus parentis* authority of school personnel to take action.[27]

A considerable amount of delinquent behavior occurs in schools. Smoking in the boys' room, defiance of teachers and administrators, cheating, possession of illegal weapons, fighting, vandalism, alcohol and drug abuse, stealing, and truancy are frequently known to teachers, staff, and administrators. Social interactions that may lead to illicit sex and illegitimacy as well as delinquent gang-oriented activity and distribution of illegal drugs often revolve around school contacts. Films such as *Blackboard Jungle* and *High School* have dramatically depicted conditions which exist in urban schools — and the rising level of crime and violence directed toward schools is a growing national concern. Consider the reprint on the following pages of an article from a recent issue of the *Philadelphia Inquirer*.[28]

Diversion in the Schools

Schools are generally expected to deal internally with a large amount of delinquent behavior, although they may be poorly equipped and reluctant to do so.[29] Nevertheless, there are a variety of official and unofficial ways in which schools shield (and thus divert) youth from the juvenile justice system. Definitive research on the degree to which teachers and other school personnel observe and choose not to take official notice of delinquent behavior is not available. It seems reasonable to infer from self-report and victimization studies, however, that more delinquency is known to school personnel than is reported to the authorities, or even noted officially in school records.

Vandalism in Schools Sweeping the Suburbs

By LINDA LOYD
Inquirer Staff Writer

A 9-year-old boy in Bensalem Township, angry because he got a bad report card last April, hid in his school after classes and set a series of fires — causing $250,000 worth of damage.

The youngster, a third-grade pupil at the Benjamin Rush Elementary School in Bucks County, was apprehended a few weeks later when carrying a can of gasoline near the township's high school. He told police that he was heading back "to finish the job" at his school.

This is not an isolated case of a child who happens to like to burn down schools. It symbolizes an increasingly common, costly and unexplainable problem in America's suburban schools today: Vandalism.

Vandalism is striking white, middle-class schools of the suburbs with the same vengence that has forced urban school systems to bar their windows, hire guards and install blaring alarms.

Anxious parents, many of whom fled from the city years ago in search of quiet country living and safe schools, now are fortifying not only their suburban homes and neighborhoods against rising crime — but their schools . . . as well.

No matter how affluent the school, few escape graffiti on the walls,

broken furniture, doors and handrails, phones stripped of their parts and cracked or gunshot-pocked windows.

Bathrooms, particularly in junior and senior high schools, are a frequent target for vandals. Toilet seats are torn off. Towel racks and soap dishes are torn from the walls. Ventilators are broken and obscene language is scrawled on partitions.

Schools in the Boston area, for instance, recently reported that their repair and replacement costs, due to vandalism, amounted to as much as $10.79 for each pupil.

Of course, stones crashing through windows are nothing new to schools. There has been vandalism as long as there have been rambunctious, growing children. But now it's worse — both in incidence and intensity.

"There's no question that vandalism here has increased in the last year," says Bernard Hoffman, assistant superintendent of the 14-school Neshaminy District in Langhorne.

His school district spends more than $2,000 a month for replacement of broken glass and stolen goods and for repairs of damaged property. And it is not alone.

Hoffman sat in his bright, sunny office the other day, shaking his head in frustration and disbelief: "We're a middle-class, suburban district," he said. "We're not the sort of place where you'd expect explosions and rebellion against the schools.

• • •

What are the causes of vandalism? No one has an answer, only guesses.

Some sociologists and psychologists point to the violence on television and in the media. "I don't think we're any more violent today but we're exposed to it more," says Dr. Robert Sadoff, an associate clinical professor of psychiatry at Penn. "Violence has become a more acceptable way of protest.

Adds Allan Glatthorn, who travels widely as a consultant to schools: "There's a feeling among many kids that we live in a disposable world. You buy stuff, use it and throw it away. Kids in the suburbs have grown up with such a glut of things and money that they really can't believe it's important to take care of things.

Another factor in the rising tide of vandalism is overcrowding in large, impersonal school facilities. Other experts cite the growing number of broken marriages in the suburbs, and the fact that many youngsters go home to an empty house because one or both parents work.

Whatever the reasons, school officials agree that vandalism is part of a much larger picture than just angry children striking back at the Establishment.

"It's a change in the culture pattern," muses Richard Currier, assistant superintendent of the Pennsbury School District in Fallsington, Bucks County. "We've

noticed that parents are much more likely to stick up for their children even when they destroy books or equipment.

"It used to be that parents thought the administration and teachers were always right. Now the attitude of many parents is, 'If something is wrong in school, let's go to the school and find out why THEY'RE wrong.' "

• • •

Here, there and everywhere in the suburbs, as well as in the city, schools are painting, patching and replacing literally thousands of dollars worth of facilities and equipment almost daily. Many officials don't like to talk about it, and some still say vandalism is not a problem.

But it is. An English teacher at Upper Merion High School summed up at least part of the problem recently: "We've lost our sense of mission in the public schools, and we've lost our identity," he said.

"We don't know how much we should be parents or priests or nurses. And we don't have time to sit still long enough to think it through."

Source: *Philadelphia Inquirer*, Vol. 291, No. 154, Dec. 1974. Reprinted by permission.

How many of the behaviors listed in the first part of this section occurred in your high school? How many were known to teachers? To school officials? To what extent did these people:
(1) avoid taking action on the behavior,
(2) deal with it within the school system,
(3) call upon other subsystems of the community — family, social agencies, the police?

When school personnel notice delinquency, they have a variety of options including internal sanctions and positive inducements toward diversion upon which to rely.

Mandatory school laws give teachers and school administrators considerable authority over the daily lives of youngsters. Harsh words, scolding, ridicule before peers, and implied (and often explicit) lowering of grades are effective for controlling most youngsters. Where these fail, detention after school, curtailment of sports and social activities, and even corporal punishment are available sanctions. Suspension may be threatened, and the threat can be executed. Some schools have found it necessary to hire guards or establish hall and washroom monitors in efforts to control unwanted behavior. (See the following pages for an article from the *New York Times.*)

Crime Fighting as Part of Curriculum

By DIANE RAVITCH

Last year, the New York City Police received close to 11,000 complaints of crimes on public school property. They ranged from murder, rape and robbery to false bomb reports. The New York City school system, which only recently began tabulating what it calls "incidents," recorded almost 5,000 for the 1973-74 school year.

The police reports may contain duplicate complaints or false alarms. The school records include only offenses that occur during school hours: and according to the city's Office of School Security are incomplete in any case because many school administrators simply don't report even serious incidents. But no matter how the figures are added up, the total is not reassuring. Juvenile crime is an increasingly serious problem.

It is also one in which the public schools are caught in the middle. The schools are, in effect, called on to reconcile singlehandedly conflicting demands. Law and order advocates want to remove troublemakers and

restore a climate for learning. Advocates of children's rights don't want troubled students isolated or confined.

New Security

Under pressure to provide better protection for students and teachers, the Office of School Security, established in the summer of 1972, has beefed up the school guard system. The city's 96 high schools, each built to hold around 4,000 pupils, now have 950 security guards. The decentralized elementary and intermediate schools average one guard a school, many of whom are women recruited from the neighborhood.

Yet about 900 teachers were assaulted during the past school year, double the number reported only two years ago. Around 640 assaults on students were recorded for the same period. Half the assaults of teachers occurred in classrooms, and school officials have proposed that teachers in the most troubled schools carry portable electronic devices so they can summon help quickly.

The growing consensus is that the problem of crime in the schools is merely one dimension of the far greater problem of juvenile crime. In 1973, over 20,000 children under the age of 16 were arrested in New York

City. Almost 15,000 of those arrests were for felony offenses, an increase of 16 per cent in the last year alone. Ninety-four children aged 15 or younger were charged with homicide, and 181 with forcible rape. In addition, the police issued more than 50,000 "youth delinquent" cards, the equivalent of a warning.

Jeremiah McKenna, general counsel of the New York State Select Committee on Crime, argues that a principal cause of crime in the schools is the presence of a large number of "young criminals" who have received neither sanction nor therapy from the juvenile justice system. Many of the young "murderers, and practically all of the juvenile rapists, robbers, burglars and drug offenders have been released by the courts back into the school system," he wrote recently.

One of the reasons is that about half of all juveniles arrested have their cases "adjusted," or dropped, before they ever get to Family Court. Of those who do go on to court, only 5 per cent are institutionalized for any period of time.

In dealing with juvenile crime, the schools are handicapped by Family Court procedures. By law, the court is not permitted to divulge the disposition of individual cases, and the schools therefore are often not informed of their pupils out-of-school problems. Mr. McKenna, among others, sees one resolution of the problem of crime in the schools in close and confidential communication between the Family Court and the public schools.

Old Services

Barbara Blum, the city's former Commissioner of Special Services for Youth, views the problem from another perspective, that of the children in trouble. Services for the neediest children and neediest families, she feels, are grossly inadequate within the schools as well as without.

Though there are many special education programs for difficult or disturbed children in the school system, their capacity is limited. There are, for example, 18 schools with small classes, generally no more than 15 students, that offer extensive social-psychological services. But they enroll only 7,500 children and have long waiting lists.

Those who have studied juvenile crime have placed the blame on families which do not nurture, communities which lack cohesion, mass entertainment which glorifies violence, and child-care agencies with insufficient resources.

Now some educators are coming to see that the problem of juvenile justice is not limited to any one institution, schools, courts or police. Just as school crime is only a portion of juvenile crime, the schools are only a part of an entire child development network which many feel needs urgently to be rethought and redirected.

Diane Ravitch is an historian who writes frequently on education.

Source: © 1974 by the New York Times Company. Reprinted by permission.

The fact that most youngsters recognize the importance of succeeding in school (and are often subject to pressures from home and peers to do so) renders these sanctions extremely effective as controls on most youthful behavior.

Sanctions and threats of sanctions, however, are not the only means available to school personnel for dealing with delinquent behavior. Counselors are increasingly used to help young people cope with emotional problems and to provide emotional support and encouragement which may not be forthcoming from the family. Clubs and social activities also provide sources of fellowship and support. Special programs on citizenship, alcohol and drug abuse, and sex education are oriented toward specific types of behavior. Special classes and "alternative schools" are often used for disruptive or disturbed youngsters, as well as for slow (or fast) learners, habitual truants, and others with problems which are not handled easily in the routine classroom.[30] There is some evidence that such efforts are useful in dealing with truancy, vandalism, and difficulties with teachers — and that in schools with special programs, there is a lessening of the tendency for administrators to refer problem situations to the police or the courts.[31]

Schools also divert by referring troubled youngsters to other community institutions. When schools cannot deal with behavioral problems, it is generally expected that they will call upon parents. If parental contacts are not sufficient, schools are increasingly likely to turn to community agencies that attempt to help troubled youngsters — mental health, health, welfare, religious, and social service agencies are the primary sources of such aid. Conversely, schools are often called upon for information and advice and even to assist in providing diversionary activities when such agencies identify the youngsters in need of help. Thus schools aid troubled youngsters both by referring to and being a source of referral for community agencies that seek to aid troubled youth.

Schools That Fail to Divert

Despite considerable authority and an impressive array of diversionary resources, schools fail to divert a large number of youngsters, and in fact, may often generate pressures which underlie delinquent "acting out."

The White House Conference on Children states that "more children are committed to some reform schools and mental hospitals during the school year than during vacation periods, with highs at testing times."[32]

Principals, superintendents, and teachers prefer to see themselves as educators rather than socializers; this orientation often means they are often reluctant to deal with problems not related directly to the classroom. Community residents often support and reinforce these attitudes by failing to support, or even directly opposing, the school's involvement in sex education, in social change or political issues, in education about drugs and alcohol, in special and remedial classes, and in counseling programs. In many communities — particularly in inner-city and rural areas — schools that could provide a valuable off-the-streets social and recreational center are kept dark and tightly locked during evenings and weekends when a great deal of delinquent behavior occurs.[33] In the end, though, the underinvestment in quality education creates demands for public expenditures to deal with the troubled children whom the schools failed to divert.

> School officials, who lack training, understanding, and compassion, too often pressure children into failing or dropping out of school. Teacher training remains poor, and pay for elementary school teachers continues to lag behind that of plumbers, carpenters, and other tradesmen. Under-trained or incompetent teachers label some children, ridicule others, and harm them in many other ways. They force youngsters to conform to rigid standards and pay little attention to individual needs or talents. Discipline is usually maintained through punishment and suspension. Schools do not want to cope with children in trouble.[34]

Furthermore, the Task Force on Juvenile Delinquency of the President's Commission on Law Enforcement and the Administration of Justice (1970), suggests that the prevailing emphasis on academic and college preparatory work, combined with the failure of schools to accommodate to the cultural and learning patterns of lower-class and minority groups, often generate the feeling that education is irrelevant, a lack of commitment, educational "failure," and a hostility-misconduct orientation toward the schools. Such conditions put strain on youth, school, and community alike. Moreover, these conditions are exacerbated by inadequate compensatory and remedial education, inferior teachers and facilities in low-income schools, and patterns of economic and racial segregation.[35]

Schools in America typically reflect the white, middle-class orientation of achievement and success through pursuit of high grades, the study of subjects that are for the most part irrelevant to day-to-day living, and preparation for professional-type occupations. In reality, however, a large proportion of young people are oriented to technical or skilled occupations. A large number of studies at the national,[36] state,[37] and local[38] levels document the pressure exerted by school systems on children to get them to achieve high grades; the studies also document the converse of this pressure — the negative labeling of students who perform at lower levels. In such an educational milieu, students who fail are perceived as failures, "slow learners," or "goof-offs," and there are likely to be negative consequences imposed by teachers and even by peers.[39] Such negatively labeled youth are often denied privileges in the classroom, they are excluded from participation in extracurricular activities, and they are objects of negative community and parental sanctions.[40] Such events often set into motion a cumulative cycle of negative interactions involving inner psychological processes as well as social interactions with peers, schools, and community individuals. The student's negative self-concept is reinforced by his experiences; and a pattern of failures can sometimes lead to delinquency.[41] A large body of research suggests that these dynamics of the school system operate to the detriment of lower-income and nonwhite students throughout the United States.[42]

In addition, there is a considerable body of research which suggests that youngsters who have problems with schools have a higher likelihood of becoming *official* delinquents than do other

youngsters. There is also some evidence which suggests that schools which are less academically and middle-class oriented (vocational schools, rural schools, for example) are *less tolerant* of youthful misconduct.[43] It is ironic to consider that the schools which have the opportunity, and indeed the mandate, to provide what would be diversionary support for youngsters are those which are less likely to do so. Thus it is probably fair to conclude that youth who experience problems with both family *and* schools (especially if they come from lower-class or minority groups) are likely to come to the attention of the authorities. Even at this point, however, the police are not the only remaining option; the schools might rather turn to any of a range of agencies in the community which seek to help children in trouble.

Community Agencies as Instruments of Diversion

Many troubled, lawbreaking children are kept from the attention of the juvenile justice system by a network of agencies which constitute an auxiliary system of social services and social control. There are two main channels into which children in trouble may be directed: one channel is the formal processes of juvenile justice; the other is the stream of human services agencies. These two relatively separate systems exist simultaneously; both identify and bring into their organizational domain the same types of youngsters,[44] and they compete both for youngsters and for resources.[45]

The number of young people who reach the formal channels of juvenile justice is generally reported in police and court statistics; the number and types of young people who are handled "informally" by social agencies, however, is relatively undocumented. It is important, nevertheless, to consider the nature of this alternative system (or nonsystem), the range of agencies of which it is comprised, what it does and does not do with children, the extent of involvement with young people, and consequences of its failures for young people and for the juvenile justice subsystem itself.

Who Are the "Community Service Agencies?"

The number, variety, and nomenclature of community service organizations and agencies is so great, and the configuration shifts from locality to locality to such a degree, that this subsystem deserves the label "kaleidoscopic." Consider the "Social Service Organizations" listed in the yellow pages of any telephone book. There are approximately 75 listings for Nashville, 110 for San Jose, 13 for Tallahassee, 70 for Fort Worth, 135 for Akron, 25 for Ithaca, 18 for Concord, Mass., and 10 for Punxatawney, Pa. These organizations operate under the sponsorship of a variety of sources — including private charities; nonprofit corporate groups; local, state, and federal agencies; community organizations; and private profit-making organizations. They provide a variety of services — including emotional support and counseling, child care and substitute parenting, gang work, social and recreational activity, jobs and training for youth, family planning, and crisis intervention.

A first reaction to such a "laundry list" is that these are not in fact services for delinquents or troubled youth, but services for people in general. While that may be true, these agencies process millions of youngsters yearly (an estimated three million in 1970 for child welfare agencies alone).[46] They advertise, solicit funds, and take credit for dealing with delinquent and troubled youngsters. Given the magnitude of self-reported delinquency, it is reasonable to conclude that considerable amounts of diversion occur in these agencies.

Perhaps the best way to resolve the debate over whether such agencies are child welfare agencies is to say that any social service agency that shields or diverts youngsters from the juvenile justice system is, at least at that time, a part of the child welfare system.

What Services Do These Agencies Provide?

The Child Welfare League of America defines services which "are designed specifically to ensure the child's right to care and protection" as child welfare services. This means generally "providing or seeing that a child has whatever is considered essential for him to develop fully and to function effectively in society; . . . it also means fulfilling the child's rights to these requirements." This applies to anyone "from birth through youth who is considered dependent on the care and protection of parents and society."[47] More specifically, the services include:

> a) Services to support and reinforce parental care including social work service for children in their own homes, child protective service for neglected, abused and exploited children, and services to unmarried parents.
> b) Services to supplement parental care or compensate for its inadequacies, including homemaker service, day care (group and family), and

services for children with special needs (emotionally disturbed and handicapped).

c) Services to substitute in part or in whole for parental care including foster family care service, group home care service, institutional care service, residential treatment service and adoption service.

d) Preventive services including early case finding and intervention to protect children at risk and to avert unnecessary separation from parents and social action to ensure conditions and services that will promote wholesome child development, strengthen family life and preserve the child's own home and reduce the incidence of circumstances that deprive children of the requirements for their optimal development.[48]

Clearly not all children who receive such services would otherwise end up in the "formal processes of the juvenile justice system." Nevertheless, the fact that such agencies consider it their task to work with children and youth in trouble makes it highly likely that much more delinquency is known about than is reported to the police.[49] Moreover, knowledge by schools, the police, and other agencies that a particular agency is working with a particular child may discourage encapsulating responses to delinquent behavior.

The Extent of Diversion by Social Service Agencies

The National Center for Social Statistics of the Federal Department of Health, Education and Welfare reported in 1970 that about three million children receive such services annually. Table 5.5 shows the location of children while receiving service; most were living at home.

TABLE 5.5. Children Receiving Social Services from State and Local Public and Voluntary Welfare Agencies (March 1970)[50]

Location of Service	State and Local Public Agencies	Voluntary Agencies and Institutions
Served while in "the home"	2,397,000	44,000
Independent living arrangements	10,500	4,800
Foster Family Homes	243,000	41,300
Group Homes	3,500	2,500
Institutional Care	63,100	63,300
Adoptive Homes	42,700	37,900
Elsewhere	8,000	21,000

(The unduplicated total is 2,909,000.)

Youngsters who become involved in this alternate system for dealing with troubled youngsters are "diverted" from the juvenile justice system; they are nevertheless encapsulated into another system. Often the ways in which youth are handled are not much different from system to system (although the label is different). Consider the following data on institutionalization which were assembled from a variety of sources by Alfred J. Kahn:

> A relatively complete institutional census conducted in 1966 showed the following: 60,500 children in 955 institutions for the dependent and neglected (children without families or in danger from their families); 55,000 in 414 institutions meant for the adjudicated or adjudicable delinquent; 13,900 in 307 institutions for the emotionally disturbed; 8,000 in 145 psychiatric inpatient units; 6,000 in 201 maternity homes; 1,800 in 54 temporary shelters awaiting planes or facilities; 10,900 in 242 more secure (detention) facilities awaiting court dispositions or facilities.
>
> Left out of the census because of jurisdictional issues were 701 facilities for mentally retarded children and 373 for the physically handicapped. The child total was about 165,000 - 170,000 for the institutions studied and approximately 100,000 for the others; the 1972 grand total estimate for institutionalized children is 250,000. [600,000 children were psychiatric outpatients as well.][51]

While the degree to which these statistics reflects diversion is unclear, and the characteristics of the children selected for such diversion are relatively unknown, patterns similar to those observed in the schools (poor and minority children have a higher *probability* of being left to the courts and the police) seem to apply here as well. For example, state officials in Pennsylvania have noted that the Cornwells Heights Youth Development Center (reform school) in Philadelphia is overwhelmingly populated by black youth while the Eastern State School and Hospital (for mentally disabled youngsters) across the street is predominantly white. The dynamics of how this phenomenon comes about are obscure for the juvenile court makes the decisions only about Cornwells Heights; the referrals to Eastern State School are from a variety of other sources. Nevertheless, this phenomenon raises the question of whether white youngsters who are "acting out" end up in the less stigmatizing institution, and if so, how? The dynamics of such a process (if it exists) would be extremely diffuse, requiring the cooperation of a wide range of agencies and institutions in the community, extending, therefore, considerably beyond the components of the juvenile justice system. Consider, however, the facts that:

Kahn reports that, "not at all atypically, one Massachusetts mental hospital found only 17 percent of the children in its wards to be psychotic." Indeed, Szasz has charged that the label "mentally ill" is frequently assigned to those who are troublemakers. Psychiatrists thus serve as "policemen of the unconscious" as well as therapists of the mentally ill.[52]

Consideration of some of the pressures on community agencies which lead them to seek to trim caseloads and divert the more "difficult" cases to other institutions (like the schools and the juvenile justice system) provides some insight into how some youngsters end up in court, rather than in a social service office.

Social Agencies' Failure to Divert

Community service agencies fail to divert by not being available when needed. Again, hard data on the dynamics of this process are scanty, although it can be inferred from court, probation, and police social service data that community agencies have failed to divert a large number of youngsters. Kahn reports that "between 150,000 - 200,000 cases of dependent and neglected children may have some exposure to *court* social services."[53]

Furthermore, several hundred thousand have exposure to social services of various degrees of intensity and competence rendered by probation officers and court intake departments. Smaller numbers are helped by trained juvenile police in special juvenile aid bureaus. Many are held in jail or detention with no service at all.[54]

One need only talk to police juvenile specialists or probation officers to find anger and frustration at social service agencies for being unavailable at crucial times. Normal operating hours of nine to five, Monday through Friday, mean that services are not available during the periods of 7 p.m. to 2 a.m. and on weekends — the hours when most juveniles are picked up by the police. Hospital emergency rooms, which will not deal with drunken kids or youngsters on a "bad trip," often leave no alternative but jail. Complaints that child welfare supervisors keep unlisted telephone numbers or leave their phones off the hook on weekends and holidays are not infrequent. Mental health workers have been heard to tell youngsters diverted to them by the police, "You don't have to be here, you know. You have your rights. If you don't want to come back, you don't have to." Such professionals are perceived by police and probation officers as not really open to referrals. Agencies that fail to develop ties to court intake officers so as to achieve more complete and professional social investigation reports also constitute a failure among diversionary agents.

> At present, because of expediency or lack of diagnostic data, children are often committed without regard to how well their needs will be met by the selected institutions. . . . Furthermore, many of the committed children may not be best served by institutionalization but are committed due to lack of meaningful, diagnostic data upon which an alternative, community-based treatment plan might be structured.[55]

The correctness of these contentions is supported by a large body of literature which cites the lack of "linkages" between the various human service subsystems of the community;[56] there are also widespread efforts to create "umbrella" agencies, multiservice centers, and access and advocacy programs.[57]

Indictments from within the welfare system and calls for reform add to the case against community agencies. The argument goes that at the street level, many organizations effectively displace their original goals and reorient their missions because they need to appear successful. They select the "best" clients, the ones most likely to respond quickly and make the agency look good, and tend to avoid minority and lower-class people who may be harder to work with.[58]

> Thus, public welfare systems try to keep their budgets down and their rolls low by failing to inform people of the rights available to them; by intimidating and shaming them to the degree that they are reluctant either to apply or to press claims and by arbitrarily denying benefits to those who are eligible.[59]

These agencies are under a vast pressure imposed by inadequate resources, high caseloads, conflicting political, public, and professional pressures, bureaucratization, and a white middle-class orientation.

> The poor, especially the families from ethnic groups within the lower class, who according to the ideal norms of these agencies should receive the greatest amount of attention, are quietly shunted aside.[60]

Another confounding phenomenon is a tendency for inexperienced or less competent people to end up in the more problematic neighborhoods. Sjoberg, Brymer, and Farris note that when agencies serve all classes of people — as do schools and social service agencies — the poorly qualified staff drift into lower-class neighborhoods or beginning staff are placed in "hardship" districts, "and then the most capable move up into upper-status . . . districts where higher salaries and superior working conditions usually prevail. Thus, the advancement of lower-class children is impeded not only because of their cultural background, but because of the poor quality of their [staff]."[61]

In summary, it appears that social service agencies observe considerable amounts of delinquency which they choose to ignore or not to report. Furthermore, they divert many youngsters from the juvenile justice system (by drawing them into the child welfare system). This occurs as a function of services provided, by being a source of referrals, and by affording labels other than "delinquent" to troubled youngsters. It is also the case that, like schools and families, these agencies seem to fail most consistently with certain types of youngsters.

Summary

Perhaps the two most salient facts to emerge from these discussions of identification and diversion in the family, schools, and social welfare agencies are: (1) the dynamics of causation, identification, and diversion within and between these societal subsystems and the formal juvenile justice subsystem are extremely complex *and* consequential for young people, and (2) there is very little information on how, why, when, and whom these agencies decide to divert or refer to the courts or police.

All in all, the evidence presented in this section paints a picture of society as highly tolerant of "delinquent" and "criminal" behavior — devoting considerable effort and resources to keeping young people from the very institutions it has established supposedly to deal with delinquent behavior. Among those not diverted from the formal processes of juvenile justice, there appear to be certain categories of individuals that receive disproportionate attention. Furthermore, the self-report studies discussed earlier suggest that most youngsters are involved from time to time in illegal behavior. Current research also suggests that ties to family, school, social agencies, or peers (or lack of such ties) are more predictive of *official* delinquency than are poverty and social class per se.[62] It is the failure of societal institutions to provide support, cognitive skills, socialization, and guidance for youngsters which leads to encapsulating experiences.

Thus, as pointed out by Matza, youngsters who lack the effective support of the major societal institutions are put under severe strain.[63]

In particular, youngsters who are cut off from secure family ties and rewarding school experiences, whether they be rich or poor, have nowhere to turn but to peers — most of whom are themselves in the throes of the adolescent search for identity.[64] What ensues is a tendency for such youngsters to succumb to peer pressures, which often lead to identifiable delinquent behavior — mischief, truancy, defying adults, alcohol and drug abuse, poor grades, etc. Lacking the effective institutional supports of school, family, or social agencies, the child has trouble breaking out of a "vicious circle" of delinquency. Many youngsters just "drift" in a cumulative labeling cycle in which acts that may serve as cries for help (acting out behavior) are met by negative sanctions from societal institutions and the stigma of official delinquency. A delinquent career is born.

> The absence of satisfying relationships with parents and school produces strain, strain in turn feeds back and further worsens already tenuous, institutional ties. The result is a circular, and ever-worsening problem, which explains, we believe, the reason that both poor institutional ties and strain have an extremely high and direct relationship to delinquency, rather than always being mediated by the intervening variable of peer identification.
>
> . . . This progressive deterioration leads, in turn, to an increasing association with other boys having similar problems. But while this association may be quite innocent in terms of the way the boys see it — they are in search, primarily, of companionship — it leads to increasing condemnation by people in authority. When that condemnation results in official sanctioning, suspension from school or, worse still, official adjudication as delinquent, then the problem, at least for many boys, is compounded. . . . Unless broken institutional fences can be mended, the stigma of official sanctioning only compounds the strain, strengthens ties to delinquent peers, and leads to a repetition of the whole pattern.[65]

Thus it seems reasonable to conclude that when a family, school, or social agency refers a youngster to the court or to the police, they are pushing their failures onto another agent of the community — the juvenile justice system. In considering the next chapter on the police as identifier and as referral agent, it is important to bear in mind that it is not "the average delinquent" who tends to come to the attention of the juvenile justice system, but rather the delinquent with whom others have been insufficiently concerned.

The following are recommendations of the National Advisory Commission on Criminal Justice Standards and Goals.

Priority: Preventing Juvenile Delinquency *

The highest attention must be given to preventing juvenile delinquency, to minimizing the involvement of young offenders in the juvenile and criminal justice system, and to reintegrating delinquents and young offenders into the community. By 1983 the rate of delinquency cases coming before courts that would be crimes if committed by adults should be cut to half the 1973 rate.

Street crime is a young man's game. More than half the persons arrested for violent crime in 1971 were under 24 years of age, with one-fifth under 18. For burglary, over half of the 1971 arrests involved youths under 18.[a]

There is strong evidence that the bulk of ordinary crime against person and property is committed by youths and adults who have had previous contact with the criminal justice or juvenile justice system. Recent evidence in support of this assumption is a study of delinquency in all males born in 1945 who lived in Philadelphia from their 10th to their 18th birthdays. Specifically the study concluded that the more involvement a juvenile had with the police and juvenile justice authorities, the more likely he would be to be further involved.[b] Of the 9,945 subjects, 3,475 (35 percent) came in contact with police at least once. Of this delinquent group, about 54 percent had more than one contact with police. This 54 percent was responsible for 84 percent of all police contacts in the group. Eighteen percent of those having repeated contact with the police had five or more contacts and were responsible for 52 percent of all police contacts in the delinquent group.

Increased efforts must be made to break this cycle of recidivism at the earliest possible point. One approach is to

*SOURCE: National Advisory Commission on Criminal Justice Standards and Goals, *A National Strategy to Reduce Crime*, Washington, D.C.: U.S. Government Printing Office, (1973), p. 23 and 25.

a *UCR — 1971*, p. 121.

b Wolfgang, Figlio, and Sellin, *Delinquency in a Birth Cohort*, chs. 6, 14.

minimize the involvement of the offender in the criminal justice system. Minimized involvement is not a fancy phrase for "coddling criminals." It means simply that society should use that means of controlling and supervising the young offender which will best serve to keep him out of the recidivism cycle and at the same time protect the community. It is based on an easily justified assumption: the further an offender penetrates into the criminal justice process, the more difficult it becomes to divert him from a criminal career.

People tend to learn from those closest to them. It is small wonder that prisons and jails crowded with juveniles, first offenders, and hardened criminals have been labeled "schools of crime."

People also tend to become what they are told they are. The stigma of involvement with the criminal justice system, even if only in the informal processes of juvenile justice, isolates persons from lawful society and may make further training or employment difficult. A recent survey conducted for the Department of Labor revealed that an arrest record was an absolute bar to employment in almost 20 percent of the State and local agencies surveyed and was a definite consideration for not hiring in most of the remaining agencies.[c]

For many youths, as noted above, incarceration is not an effective tool of correction. Society will be better protected if certain individuals, particularly youths and first offenders, are diverted prior to formal conviction either to the care of families or relatives or to employment, mental health, and other social service programs. Thus a formal arrest is inappropriate if the person may be referred to the charge of a responsible parent, guardian, or agency. Formal adjudication may not be necessary if an offender can be safely diverted elsewhere, as to a youth services bureau for counseling or a drug abuse program for treatment. Offenders properly selected for pretrial diversion experience less recidivism than those with similar histories and social backgrounds who are formally adjudicated.

c Herbert S. Miller, *The Closed Door: The Effect of a Criminal Record on Employment with State and Local Public Agencies*, report prepared for the U.S. Department of Labor (February 1972), p. 100.

To assure progress toward the goal of minimizing the involvement of juveniles in the juvenile justice system, the Commission proposes that the 1973 rate of delinquency cases disposed of by juvenile or family courts for offenses that would be crimes if committed by adults be cut in half by 1983.

The Department of Health, Education, and Welfare, which collects information on juvenile courts, estimates that a little less than 40 percent of cases disposed of by courts are cases of running away, truancy, and other offenses that would not be crimes if committed by an adult.[d] These are the so-called juvenile status offenses.

The remaining 60-odd percent of cases estimated to be disposed of by juvenile or family courts are nonstatus crimes, those that would be crimes if committed by adults. It is the rate of these cases which the Commission would propose to cut in half.

Meeting the goal, the Commission believes, should result in significant decreases in crime through preventing recidivism and might also prove to be far less costly than dealing with delinquents under present methods. To process a youth through the juvenile justice system and keep him in a training school for a year costs almost $6,000.[e] There is no reason to believe that the cost of a diversionary program would exceed this figure, since most such programs are not residential. Indeed, diversion might prove to provide significant savings.

One final note should be added. Minimizing a youth's involvement with the criminal justice system does not mean abandoning the use of confinement for certain individuals. Until more effective means of treatment are found, chronic and dangerous delinquents and offenders should be incarcerated to protect society. But the juvenile justice system must search for the optimum programs outside institutions for juveniles who do not need confinement.

d Estimates from U.S. Department of Health, Education, and Welfare.

e Derived from "Youth Service System: Diverting Youth from the Juvenile Justice System," paper prepared by the U.S. Department of Health, Education, and Welfare.

Priority: Improving Delivery of Social Services

Public agencies should improve the delivery of all social services to citizens, particularly to those groups that contribute higher than average proportions of their numbers to crime statistics.

There is abundant evidence that crime occurs with greater frequency where there are poverty, illiteracy, and unemployment, and where medical, recreational, and mental health resources are inadequate. When unemployment rates among youths in poverty areas of central cities are almost 40 percent and crime is prevalent, it is impossible not to draw conclusions about the relationship between jobs and crime. The Commission believes that effective and responsive delivery of public services that promote individual and economic well-being will contribute to a reduction in crime. The rationale for the value of a variety of services is well expressed in the Commission's *Report on Community Crime Prevention.* Having called for citizen action on such priorities as employment, education, and recreation, the report points out:

This is not to say that if everyone were better educated or more fully employed that crime would be eliminated or even sharply reduced. What is meant is that unemployment, substandard education, and so on, form a complex, and admittedly little understood amalgam of social conditions that cements, or at least predisposes, many individuals to criminal activity.

Thus a job, for example, is just one wedge to break this amalgam. Increased recreational opportunities represent another. Though one wedge may not have much effect on an individual's lifestyle, two or three might.

The Commission is aware that improvement of social services to a degree necessary to have an impact on crime will take time. Building career education programs into elementary and secondary school curriculums, for example, cannot be accomplished in the next 2 or 3 years. But it must begin now if society is to realize benefits at the end of 10 years and beyond.

The Commission particularly wishes to call attention to the provision of drug and alcohol abuse treatment. Communities must recognize the diversity of drug abuse and alcohol problems and the need for a number of alternative treatment approaches. Citizens must be willing to make the investment that such treatment requires, not merely because it will reduce crime but because adequate treatment is essential to deal with an increasingly serious national health problem.

References

1. Donald J. Black and Albert J. Reiss, Jr., "Police Control of Juveniles," *American Sociological Review* 35, no. 1 (February 1970): 63 - 77.

2. Victimization studies indicate that a large proportion of offended parties do not report to the police. See, for example, Philip Ennis, *Criminal Victimization in the U.S.: A Report of a National Survey* (Washington, D.C.: U.S. Government Printing Office, 1967). Also, Sophia Robinson, *Can Delinquency Be Measured?* (New York: Columbia University Press, 1936) has a discussion of delinquency known to social service agencies, but not reported to the police or juvenile court.

3. See Paul F. Secord and Carl Backman, *Social Psychology* (New York: McGraw-Hill, 1964), pp. 9 - 92.

4. For a discussion of the importance of social typing, see Earl Rubington and Martin Weinberg, *Deviance: The Interactionist Perspective* (New York: Macmillan, 1968), pp. 13 - 29, 67 - 87.

5. Legislative Reference Service, Library of Congress, *Profile of Youth — 1966* (Washington, D.C.: U.S. Library of Congress, 1966), pp. 166 - 99. This report contains "A Study of the Problems, Attitudes and Aspirations of Rural Youth," by Elmo Roper and Associates; analysis of the study by Dr. William Osborne.

6. Ibid., p. 184.

7. Ibid.

8. Ibid., p. 185.

9. Ibid.

10. Excellent reviews of the literature pertaining to correlations between attitudes and behavior are contained in Allan W. Wickers, "Attitudes Versus Actions: The Relationship of Verbal and Overt Behavioral Responses to Attitude Objects," *Journal of Social Issues* 25 (Autumn 1969): 41 - 78; and Allen E. Liska, "Emergent Issues in the Attitude-Behavior Consistency Controversy," *American Sociological Review* 39, no. 2 (April 1974): 261 - 72.

11. Darrell J. Steffensmeier and Robert M. Terry, "Deviance and Respectability: An Observational Study of Reactions to Shoplifting," *Social Forces* 51, no. 4 (June 1973): 417 - 26.

12. *Ibid.*, p. 423.

13. See for example Philip Ennis, *Criminal Victimization in the United States* (Washington, D.C.: U.S. Government Printing Office, 1967).

14. There are other problems with victimization studies, such as possible response biases through faulty memory and intentional exaggeration or concealment of offenses. But, while these are important, they do not merit repetition here. See Philip H. Ennis, *Criminal Victimization in the United States,* (Washington, D.C.: U.S. Government Printing Office, 1967).

15. Both the N.O.R.C. study and the Dayton - San Jose study support this contention.

16. Ennis, *Criminal Victimization,* p. 44.

17. The Dayton - San Jose data indicate that only about five percent believe that the police would not do anything; this low level may indicate that in Dayton - San Jose the public have a more positive view of the police than is true nationally. However, the difference appears to be a consequence of measurement and reporting differences.

18. Theodore Lowi, *The End of Liberalism,* (New York: W. W. Norton, 1969).

19. Alain Touraine, *The Post-Industrial Society: Tomorrow's Social History: Classes, Conflict and Culture in the Programmed Society,* trans. L.F.X. Mayhew (New York: Random House, 1971).

20. White House Conference on Children (1970), *Report to the President* (Washington, D.C.: U.S. Government Printing Office, 1970), p. 228.

21. Ibid., pp. 228 - 9; The Report lists fourteen different forms of family, including the nuclear family, the dual-work family, second-career family,

commune family, unmarried-parent-and-child family, and the homosexual-couple-and-child-family. It states: "With increasing frequency children move from one family form to another before they reach puberty. The infant of a newly married couple may enter the "single-parent form" if the marriage breaks up. When the single parent remarries, the child moves into a "remarried form" and may be adopted by the new parent, gaining either step- or half-brothers or -sisters. In addition, the mother may need or desire to work, placing the child in a dual-work family form.

22. E.g., Betty Ford, the wife of the President, recently indicated publicly that she knows her children have tried marijuana.

23. E.g., Nazi Germany and Red China.

24. Valuable reviews of this literature are contained in the section on "Family and Delinquency" in the *Task Force Report: Juvenile Delinquency and Youth Crime* of the President's Commission on Law Enforcement and Administration of Justice (Washington, D.C.: U.S. Government Printing Office, 1967), pp. 195 - 205; and in Lamar T. Emprey and Steven G. Lubeck, U.S. Department of Health, Education and Welfare (SRS-153-1970) *Delinquency Prevention Strategies* (Washington, D.C.: U.S. Government Printing Office, 1970).

25. Albert J. Reiss, Jr., "Sex Offenses: The Marginal Status of the Adolescent," *Law and Contemporary Problems* 25 (Spring 1960): 309 - 33; and Ira Reiss, *The Social Content of Premarital Sexual Permissiveness* (New York: Holt, Rinehart & Winston, 1967). In John Goldmeier and Robert D. Dean, "The Runaway: Person, Problem or Situation?" *Crime and Delinquency* (October 1973), pp. 539 - 44, it was found that "while 75 percent of the runaways in the study said that they seldom or never felt at ease in their homes, only 6 percent of the non-runaways expressed such a high degree of discomfort about their home situations."

26. Drew Hyman, Daniel Katkin, and John Kramer, *"Love 'Em or Leave 'Em,"* (Paper delivered at the 1973 Conference of the American Society of Criminology, New York, N.Y., November 1973).

27. Edwin M. Lemert, *Instead of Court: Diversion in Juvenile Justice*, National Institute for Mental Health, Center for Studies of Crime and Delinquency, DHEW Publication No. (HSM) 72-9093 (Washington, D.C.: U.S. Government Printing Office, 1971), Chap. 2, "The School Model," pp. 19 - 34.

28. *Philadelphia Inquirer* 291, no. 154 (December 1, 1974). p. 1A - 2A.

29. Task Force on Juvenile Delinquency, The President's Commission on Law Enforcement and Administration of Justice, *Task Force Report: Juvenile Delinquency and Youth Crime* (Washington, D.C.: U.S. Government Printing Office, 1967), pp. 222 - 304.

30. See, for example, Paul H. Bowman, "Effects of a Revised School Program on Potential Delinquents," *Annals of the American Academy of Political and Social Science* 322 (1959): 53 - 61; and Edward H. Stalken, "Chicago's Special Schools for Social Adjustment," *Federal Probation* 20 (1956): 31 - 6.

31. Lemert, *Instead of Court*, p. 28.

32. White House Conference on Children (1970), *Report to the President*, p. 374.

33. Bertram M. Beck and Deborah B. Beck, "Recreation and Delinquency," *Task Force Report*, pp. 331 - 42.

34. White House Conference on Children (1970) *Report to the President*, pp. 374 - 5.

35. Walter E. Schafer and Kenneth Polk, "Delinquency and the Schools," *Task Force Report*, pp. 222 - 77.

36. James S. Coleman et al., *Equality of Educational Opportunity* (Washington, D.C.: U.S. Government Printing Office, 1966).

37. Robert D. Vinter and Rosemary C. Sarri, "Malperformance in the Public School," *Social Work* 10 (January 1965): 3 - 13.

38. Richard A. Cloward and James A. Jones, "Social Class: Educational Attitudes and Participation," in *Education in Depressed Areas*, ed. A. H. Prasow (New York: Teachers College Press, 1963); and Ralph Turner, *The Social Context of Ambition* (San Francisco: Chandler, 1964).

39. *Task Force Report*, p. 230.

40. Vinter and Sarri, "Malperformance," p. 9.

41. *Task Force Report*, p. 230. See also Office of Education, U.S. Department of Health, Education and Welfare, "Delinquency and the Schools," in *Task Force Report*, pp. 278 - 304.

42. *Task Force Report*, p. 229; Shafer found differences of this type in two Michigan high schools. For example, he reported that 35 percent of working-class students were in the bottom quartile of their graduating class in academic achievement, while the comparable middle-class figure was 15 percent. In addition, middle-class students dropped out only one-fourth as often as working-class students. Differences in reading test scores were just as striking. Finally, Reiss found that in his Nashville sample over twice as many low-status students received a D or E in English; but in an Oregon study of high school students, Polk and Halferty found that over five times as many blue-collar as white-collar boys received a modal grade of D or F. Hollingshead, Abrahamson, Havighurst and many others have reported similar findings for many different types of schools and communities.

43. David Gottlieb and Bruce Bullington, *Welfare and Educational Policies and Procedures with Regard to Student Drug Abuse and Rehabilitation*, Report No. 32, (University Park, Pa.: The Center for Human Services Development, Pennsylvania State University, July 30, 1973).

44. Drew Hyman and Daniel Katkin, *A Fundamental Dilemma of American Society*, a report prepared for the American Public Welfare Association (March 1973). See also William M. Evan, The Organization-Set: Toward a Theory of Interorganizational Relations," in *Approaches to Organizational Design*, ed. James D. Thompson, (Pittsburgh: University of Pittsburgh Press, 1966), pp. 173 - 91; Rita Braito, Steve Paulson, and Gerald Klonglon, "Domain Consensus: A Key Variable in Interorganizational Analysis," in Merlin B. Brinkerhoff and Philip R. Kunz, *Complex Organizations and their Environments* (Dubuque, Iowa: Wm. C. Brown Company, 1972), pp. 176 - 92; F. E. Emery and E. L. Trist, "The Causal Texture of Organizational Environments," in Brinkerhoff and Kunz, *Complex Organizations and Their Environments*, pp. 268 - 81.

45. Lemert, *Instead of Court*, speaks of three "models" of juvenile justice.

46. National Center for Social Statistics, *Children Served by Public Welfare Agencies and Voluntary Child Welfare Agencies and Institutions,* Department of Health, Education and Welfare (March 1970), Report E-9.

47. Child Welfare League of America, *A National Program for Comprehensive Child Welfare Services* (New York: Child Welfare League of America, 1971).

48. Ibid. Most of this material is direct quotation, although some additional liberties have been taken to make the style conform to the present text. See also, Alfred J. Kahn, *Social Policy and Social Services* (New York: Random House, 1973), esp. Chaps. 1 and 2; and Charles L. Schulze, et al., *Setting National Priorities: The 1973 Budget* (Washington, D.C.: The Brookings Institution, 1972), section on "Child Care," pp. 252 - 90. In addition, Robert Morris, "Welfare Reform 1973: The Social Services Dimension," *Science* 181, no. 4099 (10 August 1973): 515 - 22 discusses types of social services and attempts of the federal government to rationalize resource allocation and delivery. He proposes a functional typology of services rather than the categorical approach currently used to organize services; and J. Bloedorn et al., *Designing Social Service Systems* (Chicago: American Public Welfare Association, 1970) discusses services and describes the systems model of APWA which has been implemented in several localities and is being tested in several others.

49. Robinson, *Can Delinquency Be Measured?*

50. The table is included in Kahn, *Social Policy and Social Services,* p. 46. The ultimate source of data is The National Center for Social Statistics, Department of Health, Education and Welfare, Report E-9, (March 1970).

51. Kahn, *Social Policy and Social Services,* p. 44 - 5.

52. Martin Rhein, "Institutional Change: A Priority in Welfare Planning," *Child Welfare* 45, no. 5 (May 1966): 259 - 68.

53. Kahn, *Social Policy and Social Services,* p. 45.

54. Commonwealth of Pennsylvania, Department of Public Welfare, *Annual Public Welfare Report* (1970 - 71).

55. Bloedorn, et al., *Designing Social Service Systems;* Morris, "Welfare Reform 1973"; and Kahn, *Social Policy and Social Services.*

56. Ibid.; also Eric Nordlinger, *Decentralizing the City,* (Cambridge, Mass.: The MIT Press, 1972); and George J. Washnis, *Municipal Decentralization and Neighborhood Resources* (New York: Praeger Special Studies in U.S. Economic and Social Development, 1972).

57. Richard Cloward and Frances Fox Piven, "Poverty, Injustice, and the Welfare State," *The Nation* (28 February 1966), pp. 230 - 5.

58. Gideon Sjoberg, Richard A. Brymer, and Buford Farris, "Bureaucracy and the Lower Class," *Sociology and Social Research* (April 1966), pp. 325 - 37. See also Robert K. Merton, *Social Theory and Social Structure,* (New York: Free Press 1957), pp. 195 - 206; and Robert Presthus, *The Organizational Society* (New York: Vintage Books, 1965).

59. Martin Rhein, "The Strange Case of Public Dependency," *Transaction,* (March - April 1965), pp. 16 - 23.

60. Sjoberg, Brymer, and Farris, "Bureaucracy and the Lower Class."

61. Ernest W. Burgess, "The Economic Factor in Juvenile Delinquency," *Journal of Criminal Law, Criminology and Police Science* 43 (May -

June 1952): 29 - 42; Joseph W. Eaton and Kenneth Polk, *Measuring Delinquency* (Pittsburgh: University of Pittsburgh Press, 1961); F. Ivan Nye, James F. Short, Jr., and V. J. Olsen, "Socio-Economic Status and Delinquent Behavior," *American Journal of Sociology* 63 (January 1958): 318 - 29; Albert J. Reiss and Albert L. Rhodes, "The Distribution of Juvenile Delinquency in the Social Class Structure," *American Sociological Review* 26 (October 1961): 730 - 2; LaMar T. Empey and Maynard L. Erickson, "Hidden Delinquency and Social Status," *Social Forces* 44, (June 1966): 546 - 54; LaMar T. Empey, "Delinquency Theory and Recent Research," *Journal of Research in Crime and Delinquency* 4 (January 1967): 28 - 42; Martin Gold, "Undetected Delinquent Behavior," *Journal of Research in Crime and Delinquency* 3 (January 1966): 27 - 46; and LaMar T. Empey and Steven G. Lubeck, *The Silverlake Experiment* (Chicago: Aldine, 1970).

62. David Matza, *Delinquency and Drift,* (New York: John Wiley & Sons, 1964); James F. Short, Jr., and Fred Strodtbeck, *Group Process and Gang Delinquency* (Chicago: University of Chicago Press, 1965).This observation was made over three decades ago in Frank Tannenbaum, *Crime and the Community*, (New York: Columbia University Press, 1938).

63. Matza, *Delinquency and Drift.*

64. LaMar T. Empey, and Steven G. Lubec, *Delinquency Prevention Strategies*, U.S. Department of Health, Education and Welfare, Youth Development and Delinquency Prevention Administration (Washington, D.C.: U.S. Government Printing Office, 1971), pp. 5 - 6.

65. Ibid.

6

The Police: Gatekeeper of the Juvenile Justice System

Let gentleness my strong enforcement be.

*—Shakespeare (*As You Like It*)*

A policeman's lot is not so hot.

— Clayton Rawson

In the last chapter, attention focused on the individuals and institutions in the community which may bring children to the attention of the police or the courts. At this point, the focus shifts to the police themselves as an institution responsible both for receiving referrals from other community actors and for seeking actively to identify delinquent behavior. This chapter discusses the police as the primary "gatekeeper" into the juvenile justice system.

The Dual Role of the Police

The police play a dual role in the process of diversion from and entrance into the juvenile justice system. On the one hand, they serve as an agency to which parents, schools, community agencies, and the public refer misbehaving youngsters. When parents and members of the public wish to report youthful misconduct, the police are the most accessible resource available.[1] Social agencies and schools frequently call on the police to deal with misbehaving youngsters — although they may sometimes contact the court directly. The police also serve

as identifiers through routine patrols in the community and investigations of reported crimes by victims. Thus the police, either through referrals from other community actors or through their own initiative, act as the single major decision maker regarding the diversion or encapsulation of youngsters.

It has been shown that youngsters whom other community institutions do not wish to divert are perhaps the most frequent contact of the police; nevertheless, diversion continues to be as frequent as encapsulation, even at this point in the process of the juvenile justice system. Consider the following report of research by Norval Morris and Gordon Hawkins in Chicago.[2]

> We find that of every hundred youth arrested, only forty reach the court intake process. Of those forty, only twenty actually reach the court. Those figures are accurate; the next figure is a guess, but we think it is a reasonably informed guess. We believe, and the police in the area share this view, that the hundred they arrest represent five hundred "probable cause" arrest situations.
>
> So five hundred arrest situations on the streets are reduced to one hundred arrests, reduced to forty court intakes, reduced to twenty in court and then of those twenty a very few will find themselves in the

correctional system. Thus the police are deciding more largely than the judges whether the criminal justice system should be invoked. Of the five hundred arrest situations, police and court intake personnel exercise judicial discretions and prosecutorial discretions in relation to twenty. To analyze our system of criminal justice under the mythology that the police make an arrest when they see what they think is a properly arrestable criminal and that they then pass him on to others in the system to handle is wild nonsense.

Police encounters with youngsters result from notification by agencies or the public,[3] or from direct observation by police officers of delinquent behavior.[4] Often the intent of those who make referrals is that the youngsters be encapsulated. Consideration of the police responses to referrals, and to observed delinquent behavior will be discussed in the next two sections.

Community Actors as Identifiers: Referrals to the Police

The police often become a dumping ground for the community's problem youths. Schools, social welfare agencies, parents, and other individuals frequently respond to antisocial behavior by threatening to call the police. When such threats fail to achieve their purpose, police intervention is solicited. The police are used by these community actors to represent the full force of the punitive authority of the community. These factors place police officers in a position which requires them to perform a variety of expected, often conflicting roles in the community.

> Democracy's ideological conflict between the norms governing the work of maintaining order and the principle of accountability to the rule of law pervades the justification for various demands upon the policeman. He may be expected to be rule enforcer, father, friend, social servant, moralist, streetfighter, marksman, and the officer of the law.[5]

Thus the pervasive pressures and conflicting values of the juvenile justice system are perhaps manifest most directly in police decisions about what to do with youngsters suspected of having committed delinquent acts.

It must be noted that the police may sometimes be circumvented, and referrals of troubled youngsters made directly to court rather than to the police. But with increasing numbers of officers on duty in schools (for both protective and public relations functions), it is likely that schools are referring to the police more frequently than in the past. Parents and members of the public probably contact the police first in most cases, simply because they are accessible twenty-four hours a day.

Referrals to the police about problem children initiate complex decision-making processes. The police have available a broad range of responses from which they can choose. They can ignore the request; but that is unlikely because it might antagonize the public or representatives of public agencies upon whom the police are frequently dependent for information and support. Thus, it is likely that some response will be made. It may be that an officer will merely talk to the youngster; but it should be remembered that the authority of the police is such that the youngster may perceive a casual chat as ominous and threatening. That perception may have "corrective" effects; but it may begin a cumulative self-identification and labeling cycle as well.

Frequently the police are constrained, because of the attitude of the agency making the referral, to "do something serious." Generally the police are not called until other agencies have attempted to deal with the problem themselves. A call to the police means that the agency's tolerance has been broken and removal of the youngster is desired. Thus, pressure is exerted on the police officer to assume responsibility for the child. Even if the police do not perceive the problem as a serious one, the fact that the individual or agency making the referral is unable or unwilling to cope with the youngster normally restricts the options of the police officer. It is generally inappropriate, and sometimes impossible, to leave the youngster in a situation which has become intolerable to parents, school officials, or social agencies (and perhaps even for the youngster).

Although the exercise of "political" pressure and the unwillingness of community actors to provide services may restrict the options available to the police, it is nevertheless always within the power of the police officer to veto attempted referrals. The officer may attempt to convince the complainant that formal intervention would be inappropriate. He may respond to a teacher's complaint about a youngster's use of marijuana, for example, by suggesting that the local drug abuse program be contacted. Or in a truancy situation, he might find that going with the child to his home is more effective in getting the parents involved than taking him to the police station. The fact that police typically seek to precipitate such diversionary responses is reflected in the statistics cited earlier.

It follows then that police officers are constantly involved in negotiations with parents, members of the public, school personnel, and social service agencies. In some cases, the police feel that referrals are motivated by a desire to get rid of problem youngsters. In other cases, they may feel that referrals are made too late — after the youngster has become entrenched in a systematic pattern of delinquency. The police (and the juvenile court as well) want to be made aware of problems, but they do not want to be the dumping grounds for the "tough cases" of other agencies, nor do they want to be the last informed. While the police want to be helpful, they do not want merely to help agencies solve their own failures. They want to be involved in consultation, not merely called in to do the dirty work. In short, the referral process is not always amicable. The police are frequently in conflict with other community agencies about the appropriate nature of police work. Too often they feel, perhaps correctly, they have been relegated to the role of "toughs."

The Effects of Offense and Offender Characteristics on Police Decisions

The police role in identifying delinquency is greatly complicated by ambiguity about the meaning of the term "delinquent." Offenses such as burglary, robbery, and auto theft are clearly delinquent acts and present little choice to the police officer about whether to arrest youngsters. Less serious offenses, such as curfew violation, skipping school, buying cigarettes, present the officer with a situation for the exercise of discretion. Surely not all minor offenses need (or deserve) official processing. Consider whether the police officer in the following cases handled these situations appropriately.

1. Bob F., a twelve-year-old with no previous legal problems, was observed in his own neighborhood at 10:45 p.m. This was forty-five minutes after curfew. Officer Bradley stopped him, inquired if everything was all right, and watched to be sure he got home safely.

2. Fred H., also a twelve-year-old, who had been observed roaming the streets after curfew on several previous occasions, was observed hanging around downtown at 10:45 p.m. Officer Bradley stopped him, asked where he lived, and took him home in the squad car. Fred's parents were informed about his behavior and were warned that continued curfew violations would bring Fred into contact with a "bad element" and could result in official processing.

3. Bruce B., a twelve-year-old, who had already been in several scrapes with the law for theft, and whose family had previously failed to respond to requests for supervision, was observed downtown after curfew. In this case, Officer Bradley arrested the youngster, and took him to the police station where a referral was made to juvenile court; the youngster was placed in shelter care pending disposition.

Bob F. apparently presents little threat either to himself or to others at this time. Fred H. may appear to be heading for trouble. Bruce B. is, from the perspective of Officer Bradley, both threatened by parental unconcern and a potential threat to the public. While these three cases do not enumerate the full range of curfew-violation situations, they do demonstrate: (1) the wide range of discretion available to police officers, (2) the variability of circumstances under which the same offense may take place and consequently, the ways it may be viewed by the police, and (3) the options available and how the availability of these options is affected by the social circumstances of the offender.

The cases of Bob, Fred, and Bruce illustrate the role of the police in disposing of relatively nonserious offenses (especially status offenses). Typical responses are to send the youngster home, to make a direct contact with parents, or to make a referral to school authorities or social agencies. Obviously, these options would have been less appropriate had the youngsters been observed stealing a car, breaking into a vending machine, shooting out streetlights with a zip gun, or sexually assaulting a young woman. In these latter cases the police officer would be expected to deal with the violations much more severely.

Studies by Piliavin and Briar[6] and Goldman[7] suggest that (1) the likelihood of arrest is related to the seriousness of the offense; (2) in cases involving less serious offenses, police discretion is considerable;

and (3) that the exercise of such discretion involves considerations about the personal and social characteristics of the offender.[8]

> *In smaller communities, it is much more likely that the police officer will "know" problem youngsters through either reputation or personal contact. Thus, it may well be the case that prior police contacts are much more difficult to "live down" in smaller communities.*

Piliavin and Briar noted that police officers in the field have access to very little information about youngsters — such as past offense record, school performance, family situation, or personal adjustment.[9] Thus, decisions made in the field, and even those made at the station, are based on superficial information (cues) resulting from the immediate interaction of the police officer and the youngster(s) observed.

These cues included the youth's group affiliations, age, race, grooming, dress, and demeanor. Older juveniles, members of known delinquent gangs, Negroes, youths with well-oiled hair, black jackets, and soiled denims or jeans (the presumed uniform of "tough" boys), and boys who in their interactions with officers did not manifest what were appropriate signs of respect tended to receive the more severe disposition.[10]

Aside from previous record and seriousness of present offense, the most important decision factor indentified in the research was the *demeanor* of the youngster.

The cues used by police to assess demeanor were fairly simple. Juveniles who were contrite about their infractions, respectful to officers, and fearful of the sanctions that might be employed against them tended to be viewed by patrolmen as basically law-abiding or at least "salvageable." For these youths it was usually assumed that informal or formal reprimand would suffice to guarantee their future conformity. In contrast, youthful offenders who were fractious, obdurate, or who appeared nonchalant in their encounters with patrolmen were likely to be viewed as "would-be tough guys" or "punks" who fully deserve the most severe sanction: arrest.[11]

These findings are complemented by a study of police-citizen interactions in Boston, Chicago, and Washington, D.C. Donald Black

and Albert Reiss, Jr.[12] found that when a youngster was either "very deferential" or "antagonistic" he was more likely to be arrested than when he behaved in a "civil manner" (neither deferential nor antagonistic). Seriousness of the offense, prior record, *and* the demeanor of the youth are the most important variables in police-youth interactions.

Other factors such as race and sex, may also enter into police decisions — especially where less serious offenses are involved. Ours is a society which is solicitous about females; thus, it might be expected that police would ignore or tolerate much more misbehavior among females than among males — except perhaps where sexual offenses are concerned, such as illegitimacy or prostitution. Delinquent acts by females tend to be noticed by or reported to the police less frequently. Available research does suggest, however, that when girls do come to the attention of the police (especially where serious offenses are involved) sex is *not* a significant variable in determining whether an arrest will occur.[13]

There has been considerable mention of race and social class as factors in police decisions. Available research shows that black juveniles are more likely than whites to be stopped.[14] Black youths have higher arrest rates than whites.[15] Lower-class, and especially minority youngsters are more frequently referred to the police by families, schools, and community agencies than are youngsters from the total population of whites. It has also been suggested that blacks are dealt with more severely than whites by police officers and by the remainder of the justice system.

> Negroes are more likely to be suspected of crime than are whites. They are also more likely to be arrested. If the perpetrator of a crime is known to be a Negro, the police may arrest all Negroes who were near the scene — a procedure they would rarely dare to follow with whites. After arrest, Negroes are less likely to secure bail, and so are more liable to be counted in jail statistics. They are more liable than whites to be indicted and less likely to have their cases *nol prossed* or otherwise dismissed. If tried, Negroes are more likely to be convicted. If convicted, they are less likely to be given probation. For this reason they are more likely to be included in the count of prisoners. Negroes are also more liable than whites to be kept in prison for the full term of their commitments and correspondingly less likely to be paroled.[16]

Furthermore, police surveillance practices may be a factor leading to the more frequent contact between police officers and black youngsters, thus increasing the probability that identification and arrest may occur. The National Advisory Commission on Civil Disorders, for example, has stated:[17]

> Some conduct — breaking up of street groups, indiscriminate stops and searches — is frequently directed at youths, creating special tensions in the ghetto where the average age is generally under 21. Ghetto youths, often without work and with homes that may be nearly uninhabitable, particularly in the summer, commonly spend much time on the street. Characteristically, they are not only hostile to police, but eager to demonstrate their own masculinity and courage. The police, therefore, are often subject to taunts and provocations, testing their self-control and, probably, for some, reinforcing their hostility to Negroes in general. Because youths commit a large and increasing proportion of crime, police are under growing pressure from their supervisors — and from the community — to deal with them forcefully. "Harassment of youths" may therefore be viewed by some police departments — and members even of the Negro community — as a proper crime prevention technique.

Several studies tend to suggest, however, that the higher

incidence of processing of black youths into the juvenile justice system is *not* the result of police discrimination *per se*.[18] For example, Robert Terry studied 9023 offenses known to the police in one city from 1958 to 1962.[19] In examining the decisions made in these cases, he found only 755 referrals to the probation department and only 246 of these received court hearings. Attempting to determine the factors which affected police decision on these cases, he concluded that while race was certainly a factor in eventual statistics, police decisions were dependent primarily on the seriousness of the offense and the prior record.

> . . . Mexican-Americans, Negroes, and lower-status offenders are over-represented in . . . police records. . . . [T]his over-representation does not, on the basis of the evidence examined in this study, appear to be a *direct* result of these characteristics. The over-representation of these individuals is not the result of discrimination by control agencies.[20]

Additionally, the image of the police as highly discriminatory in their arrests and referral decisions is not supported by other available studies.

> Apparently the police are more impressed by the nature and seriousness of offenses than by any other factors. The major route to the juvenile court appears to be heavily traveled by those juveniles who are most persistently involved in lawbreaking. The four investigations certainly do not provide much factual underpinning for claims that the principal determinants of police action center about such things as economic status or racial characterisitcs.[21]

The apparent contradiction between public beliefs about the police, arrest statistics, and the findings of these studies cannot be resolved here. Available evidence suggests, however, that at the point of arrest, the police use legalistic criteria such as offense and prior record. It also suggests that factors such as race, sex, age, and social class enter in as a function of referrals from other community actors, policy on patrol practices, and the demeanor of youngsters who come into contact with police officers. In addition, it seems that the increased frequency of contact between certain types of youngsters and the police, in combination with the immediate interaction variable of demeanor (rather than police discrimination at the point of arrest) is responsible for higher incidence of referrals from certain types of groups.

Recruitment and Socialization of Police as Factors Which Affect Police Decision Making

The importance of the police in identifying and encapsulating young people suggests the need to inquire more deeply into the factors which affect their decision-making processes. The previous section focused on the impact of characterisitcs of individuals and their behavior on the decisions of police officers. This section discusses the impact on police decisions of several factors: recruitment; training; and socialization into the police role; professional development; and interorganizational relations.

Recruitment and Socialization into the Police Role

The manifest goal of the police is to maintain order through the enforcement of law. This does not imply that the ultimate goal is to enforce the law in *all* cases of violations; it has been shown that diversion is the rule with the police as well as with other community actors. Consider the public outcry, (and the overload on the system), which would result, for example, if the police actually processed all traffic offenses or all youngsters who skipped school or all curfew violators. It is unlikely that the community would accept such a level of enforcement. Thus the police must decide when to ignore, when to refer to another agency, and when to refer on into the formal processes of juvenile justice. This is not an easy decision. In addition to the offender characteristics we considered in the preceding section, variables in the recruitment, the training, and the socialization by other officers are salient factors affecting police decisions.

Throughout this discussion it is important to bear in mind that these variables, and others discussed herein, interact differentially, often cumulatively, in encounters between police officers and youngsters.

The individual who enters police work is often pictured as a punitive, authoritarian individual who desires the power and control that reside in the role of the policeman. Decisions made by such officers would be expected to be primarily punitive — arrest and referral to court. As pointed out above, however, police officers' decisions are much more lenient than beliefs would suggest. In addition, data from available studies suggest that police officers are *not as punitive* and authoritarian as some popular images might convey. John H. McNamara's study of police recruits in New York City, for example, found that the recruits reflected less of a punitiveness orientation than did *community leaders*.[22] He did find that police measured slightly higher on authoritarianism than the general public, but within the limits expected for people from a lower-middle-class background (from which the officers were recruited).[23] This study lends support to a more "normal" view of the police officer — as the kind of person who diverts a sizable proportion of misbehaving youngsters and who makes decisions to arrest on "legalistic" criteria.

The socialization of police officers into their role, however, leads them to observe certain types of behavior more readily and to perceive certain acts as threatening to the community. Jerome Skolnick has noted that police " . . . as a result of combined features of their social situation, tend to develop ways of looking at the world distinctive to themselves, cognitive lenses through which to see situations and events."[24] These "cognitive lenses" provide police with a working definition of the world around them. They enable officers to decide what circumstances are suspicious, who acts and looks like a youngster in need of arrest, who should get a court referral, and who should be detained or sent home.

> Consider the rookie patrolman who, in addition to responding to his own conceptions of the police role, must accommodate to the demands placed upon him by:
>
>> 1. fellow officers in the station house, who teach him how to get along and try to "correct" the teachings of his police academy instructors;
>> 2. his immediate superiors, who may strive for efficiency at the expense of current practices;
>> 3. police executives, who communicate expectations contradictory to station-house mores; and
>> 4. the general public, which in American cities today is likely to be divided along both class and racial lines in its expectations of police practices and behavior.
>
> . . . it is a common feature of organizational behavior that individuals in an organization need to develop simplifications, or some kinds of

"shorthand," by which they can make decisions quickly and expeditiously. A policeman develops simplifications which suggest to him that crimes are in the process of being committed.[25]

The fact that police operate within a community environment which is often (perhaps correctly) perceived as hostile, leads them to gravitate toward other officers as a source of support, values, and behavior. Police officers "tend to live inside the police world, and have less contact with people in other occupations than do most other groups in society."[26] This social isolation is not entirely self-selected by police but is in part an outgrowth of the stereotyping (labeling) of the police by community actors.[27] By the same token, the peculiarities of police work — danger, constant contact with hostile suspects, victims hostile because of their loss — all support the development of a "fraternity of the wearers of the badge."[28]

> A significant portion of the police and other agency personnel manage to curtail interaction in official matters and therefore mutually isolate each other within the social control system. This phenomenon is particularly noticeable between the police and social workers which may reflect the presence of conflicting operating ideologies, lack of professional respect and ignorance of the others' operations.[29]

The development of a "shorthand to decision" which provides a cognitive screen through which observed or reported delinquency must pass is an outgrowth of a police subculture, a code among police officers. This code provides a rationalizing basis for self-respect and decision making independent of conflicting external pressures. The elements of strong social cohesion, constant threat of danger and challenge in the community, and extensive legal authority "generates distinctive cognitive and behavioral responses in police"[30] which affect the manner in which the broad discretionary powers of police officers are applied. Suspicious circumstances — particularly those signifying danger, disruption of community routine, or threats to police authority — will certainly influence the response of an officer to an offender.

Professionalism and Specialization of Juvenile Police

The increasing professionalization of police and the development of special police juvenile officers also affect police decisions. Police have not traditionally been recognized as "professionals" in the same sense as doctors or lawyers. Skolnick suggests, rather, that the police have evolved, along with their subculture, a particular "craftsmanship" ethos:[31]

> The policeman views criminal procedure with the administrative bias of the craftsman, a prejudice contradictory to due process of law. That is, the policeman tends to emphasize his own expertness and specialized abilities to make judgments about the measures to be applied to apprehend "criminals," as well as the ability to estimate accurately the guilt or innocence of suspects.

The appointment of some policemen as "juvenile specialists" (often with little or no special training or resocialization) tends to inject this "law enforcement" ethos more prominently into police relationships with young people. What occurs is that specialists have a direct mandate to devote their energies full time to young people — how to handle them, whom to identify, whom to keep records on, etc.; in short, juveniles are taken more seriously than before.[32]

> A juvenile officer develops a special sense of perception attuned to persons, places and events affecting the behavior of young people. He becomes well read and accomplished in the special laws concerning juvenile cases. He is sensitive to the needs and laws concerning juvenile cases. He is sensitive to the needs and problems of the community's young people and can often match up community resources with them to head off trouble. He is an important police department link with the schools, recreational facilities, employment agencies and youth-serving organizations. And above all, his special training and insight make it possible to keep many cases out of court by working with the child and his parents — an outcome which is highly beneficial not only to the child but to the whole community.[33]

The most obvious effect of establishment of such a role in police departments is the diversion of youngsters from juvenile court to alternative resources.[34] Moreover, there is a stated objective that the police juvenile specialist actively participate in a juvenile justice system, the stated goal of which is to act "in the best interests of the child." Thus it might be expected that police juvenile officers would divert large numbers of children from the formal processes of juvenile justice; on the other hand, the pressures to show arrests and results, which are part of the traditional police role, do work on the juvenile officers as well, and create measures for encapsulating actions toward juveniles.

Thus, the police juvenile officer is "betwixt and between"

traditional police responsibilities and behaviors and those which might be more characteristic of social work. For instance, investigation of cases is consistent with the traditional law enforcement function; but the responsibility to meet the "appropriate needs" of the child is not such a function. Kobetz lists six options for police juvenile officers:

1. Release.
2. Release accompanied by an official report describing the encounter with the juvenile.
3. Release to parent or guardian accompanied by an official reprimand.
4. Referral to social agencies for further rehabilitation.
5. Referral to the juvenile court without detention.
6. Referral to the juvenile court with detention.[35]

The juvenile officer, whose job includes many social work functions, takes on responsibilities not only different from but antithetical to the traditional police role. One study of police juvenile officers, for example, found that forty percent of their regular police colleagues defined the juvenile officer's job as "so-so important," or "not important at all."[36] Interestingly enough, the juvenile officers perceived that juvenile court judges and probation officers thought their duties to be much more important than their colleagues did. This information suggests that police juvenile specialists are under an additional strain which comes from a necessity to decide whether to be part of the regular police subculture. Furthermore, it seems they often choose to develop more of an affiliation with social work personnel, for reinforcement in this direction comes from probation officers, child welfare workers, judges, and others.

The refinement of the use of such police juvenile officers may mean that dispositions of police juvenile officers will reflect greater use of diversionary resources in the community; referral to court will be used only as a last resort. There is both opportunity and threat in such developments. If officers make greater use of nonlegal consideration, then the important aspect of police decisions will be not the legal issues involved, but the prevailing perspective on the definition of delinquency and its causes. For example, if broken homes or standing on street corners or being poor are believed to be a factor related to the genesis of delinquency, then youngsters who exhibit such characteristics will be identified more frequently for encapsulation by the police (and others). Such a phenomenon clearly contains the seeds of injustice.

Interorganizational Factors and the Police

We have seen that the majority of delinquent acts observed by families, schools, peers, social agencies, the public, and the police remain "hidden" or are handled informally in the community. When any of these community actors decides neither to tolerate youthful misbehavior nor to handle delinquents informally, the police are the agency most frequently called upon. Thus, police contacts represent a hightly skewed distribution of what are, perhaps, the most troubled and difficult-to-handle youngsters in the community. Despite these facts, the police divert well over half the youngsters with whom they have contact.

The idea that the police process a larger proportion of lower-class and minority groups than exist in the population at large is correct. The assertion that this is a result of police decisions alone may well be incorrect. There is evidence which suggests, rather, that the combination of a large number of variables (of which the police are but one) accounts for this phenomenon. Nevertheless, it is through the police "gate" that most young people enter the juvenile justice system. In this way, the police, to a great extent, control the input to the remainder of the juvenile justice system — detention, adjudication, and disposition — and the police control the diversion of reported delinquents back into the community. Thus police decision-making processes have special significance because they are the last stage at which complete diversion can be achieved. A child sent on for further processing may yet be diverted, but he will not emerge unscathed. The centrality of the police derives from the fact that they are the gatekeeper for all the other agencies and institutions of the formal juvenile justice system.

References

1. Donald Black and Albert Reiss, Jr., "Police Control of Juveniles," *American Sociological Review* 35, no. 1 (February 1970): 63 - 77.
2. Norvil Morris and Gordon Hawkins, *An Honest Politician's guide to Crime Control* (Chicago: University of Chicago Press, 1970).
3. Black and Reiss, "Police Control," p. 66.
4. Jesse Raymond James and George H. Shepard, "Police Work with Children" in *Municipal Police Administration*, ed. George D. Eastman and

Esther M. Eastman (Washington, D.C.: International City Management Association, 1971), p. 148.

5. Jerome Skolnick, *Justice Without Trial* (New York: John Wiley & Sons, 1966), p. 17.

6. Irving Piliavin and Scott Briar, "Police Encounters with Juveniles," *American Journal of Sociology* 70 (September 1964): 206 - 14.

7. Nathan Goldman, *The Differential Selection of Juvenile Offenders for Court Appearance* (New York: National Council on Crime and Delinquency, 1963).

8. See also Black and Reiss, "Police Control."

9. Piliavin and Briar, "Police Encounters," p. 159.

10. Ibid.

11. Ibid., p. 210.

12. Black and Reiss, "Police Control."

13. Albert J. Reiss, Jr., "Sex offenses: The Marginal Status of the Adolescent," *Law and Contemporary Problems* 25 (Spring 1960): 309 - 33; and Ira L. Reiss, *The Social Content of Premarital Sexual Permissiveness* (New York: Holt, Rinehart & Winston, 1967).

14. Piliavin and Briar, "Police Encounters."

15. Edward Green, "Race, Social Status and Criminal Arrest," *American Sociological Review* 35, no. 3 (June 1970): 476 - 90.

16. Jessica Mitford, *Kind and Usual Punishment* (New York: Alfred A. Knopf, 1973), pp. 54 - 5.

17. National Advisory Commission on Civil Disorder, *Report* (New York: New York Times Press, 1968), p. 303.

18. Green, "Race, Social Status and Criminal Arrest;" Black and Reiss, "Police Control."

19. Robert M. Terry, "Discrimination in the Handling of Juvenile Offenders by Social Control Agencies," *Journal of Research in Crime and Delinquency* 4 (July 1967): 218 - 30.

20. Ibid.

21. Donald Gibbons, *Delinquent Behavior* (Englewood Cliffs, N.J.: Prentice-Hall, 1970), p. 39.

22. John H. McNamara, "Uncertainties in Police Work: the Relevance of Police Recruits' Background and Training" in *The Police*, ed. David J. Bordua (New York: John Wiley & Sons, 1967).

23. Ibid., p. 195 - 6.

24. Skolnick, *Justice Without Trial*.

25. Michael Lipsky, "Street-Level Bureaucracy and the Analysis of Urban Reform," in *Blacks and Bureaucracy: Readings in the Problems and Politics of Change* (New York: Thomas Y. Crowell, 1972), pp. 171 - 84.

26. Paul Jacobs, *Prelude to Violence* (New York: Random House, 1966), p. 48.

27. Skolnick, *Justice Without Trial*.

28. Elmer Johnson, *Crime, Correction and Society* (Homewood, Ill.: Dorsey Press, 1970).

29. John P. Clark, "Isolation of the Police," *Journal of Criminal Law, Criminology and Police Science* (September 1956), p. 313.

30. Skolnick, *Justice Without Trial*. p. 42.

31. Ibid., p. 159.

32. James Q. Wilson, *Varieties of Police Behavior* (Cambridge, Mass.: Harvard University Press, 1968), p. 72.

33. Richard J. Kobetz, *Police Work with Juveniles* (1972), p. 176.

34. Wilson, *Varieties of Police Behavior*.

35. Kobetz, *Police Work with Juveniles*, p. 13

36. Fred Hussey and John Kramer, *A Research and Development Program for Enhancing the Performance of Juvenile Police Specialists* (University Park, Pa.: Institute for Human Development, 1974), pp. 16 - 42.

7 Detention

> *"Were you ever punished?"*
> *"Only for faults," said Alice.*
> *"And you were all the better for it, I know!"*
> *the Queen said triumphantly.*
> *"Yes, but then I had done the things I*
> *was punished for," said Alice: "that makes all*
> *the difference."*
> *"But if you* **hadn't** *done them," the Queen said,*
> *"that would have been better still, better and*
> *better, and better!"*
>
> — *Lewis Carroll*

If a child charged with delinquency is released into the custody of his parents while awaiting trial, his first encounter with the formal processes of juvenile justice will take place at a probation officer's desk, or perhaps in a judge's chambers or in a courtroom. That encounter may scare the child, but it is not likely to terrify or brutalize him. If, however, a child is perceived as needing treatment or custody while awaiting his day in court, he will be placed in a detention facility and may well become terrified; it is possible, though unlikely, that he may be brutalized. It is almost certain that he will be exposed to conditions that are inappropriate for children.

This chapter has three main sections. The first describes the conditions throughout the United States under which young people are held in detention. The second addresses interactions within the system which contribute to the inadequacy of detention facilities and to their excessive utilization. The final section explores alternatives to existing patterns of detention.

The Inadequacy of Juvenile Detention Facilities

Ninety-three percent of the nation's juvenile court jurisdictions, serving 44.3 percent of the population in about 2800 different counties and cities, have no place of detention other than the county jail;[1] and county jails are generally "the most backward and neglected of all detention, correctional and penal institutions."[2] Fewer than 20 percent of the jails in which *allegedly* delinquent youngsters are held while awaiting trial are of sufficiently high quality that the federal government would house convicted adult felons in them.[3]

Only five states (Arizona, California, Connecticut, Idaho, and Maryland) prohibit the detention of juveniles in jail;[4] in thirteen additional states (Alaska, Arkansas, Georgia, Kansas, Massachusetts, Montana, Nevada, New Mexico, North Carolina, South Carolina, Tennessee, Texas, and Wyoming), juveniles detained in jails must be kept in separate sections apart from adult prisoners.[5] The separate section requirement, however, is often interpreted to mean only a separate cell.[6]

> Thus, although the placement of juveniles in jail is commonly deplored, it is not surprising that more than 100,000 are held annually in these facilities. The statutory prohibitions are relatively weak, and, furthermore, there is no penalty for an official who places a youth in jail. Given the frequent lack of alternative facilities, police and others have to resort to placing very young children, or even infants, in jail upon occasion.[7]

Jails are sometimes described as so depressing as to be able to drive children to attempts at suicide. They are often so poorly supervised that children can become the objects of physical, sexual, and even murderous assault.[8] Consider some of the stories that are told about the Cook County Jail in Chicago, an antiquated facility designed to hold 1500 inmates, which regularly holds 3000, of whom about 300 are juveniles awaiting trial.

Charles Siragusa, executive director (in 1968) of the Illinois Crime Investigating Commission, said of the jail, "You'd have to go back to the Spanish Inquisition to find anything as bad." Joseph R. Rowan, executive director of the John Howard Association, calls the Cook County Jail "a jungle — the most terrible I've come across in twenty-six years of correctional work."[9]

Bill Davidson wrote a magazine article, "The Worst Jail I've Ever Seen," in which he described this five-story building as:

> ". . . a grey stone fortress . . . unlike modern prisons, which are airy and well-lighted, this one is a Bastille-like warren of dark cells. The smell of dirt and decay is overpowering. There are solid steel doors where there should be windows. The corridors are filthy with bits of dropped food and spittle."[10]

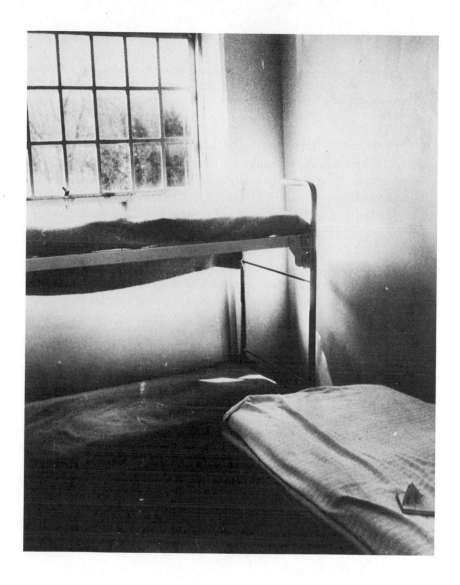

Davidson described atrocities which he and other investigators found commonplace, such as this one involving a juvenile:

". . . a 14-year-old boy arrested on disorderly-conduct charges (later dismissed) was thrown into a Cook County Jail cell-block with accused murderers, thieves and homosexuals. His first night on the tier, the boy was taken in a cell and repeatedly raped anally by an inmate known as Big Red. The guards are required to lock their cells at night, but all cells were open. Although the boy's cries were clearly audible to the guards, none of them dared to enter the cell tier during the attack."[11]

After "Big Red" was transferred to another tier the next day,

> ". . . four inmates seized the boy and shaved off his blond hair with a dry razor. They so lacerated his scalp with the filthy razor, that when he showed up in court the next week his head was covered with infected sores."

Unfortunately, atrocities occur in places other than just Cook County. In Arizona, for example, four teenage boys, jailed in January 1965 on *suspicion* of having stolen beer, died of asphyxiation from a defective gas heater when they were left without supervision for eleven hours.[12] In Indiana a thirteen-year-old boy held in a jail while awaiting a hearing on auto theft hanged himself from one of the bars of his cell.[13] The 1971 N.B.C. television documentary speaks with incredible candor about incidents in which children detained in jails in all parts of the country have been beaten, punched, and kicked by guards and inmates, or strapped to their beds for days on end, or placed for long periods in solitary confinement, or tortured by the excruciatingly painful injection of drugs.

Even were it not for the omnipresent possibility of brutalization, jails would appear to be dreadfully inadequate places for the detention of children — or other human beings.

> A typical jail is a series of small barred cells, resembling cages in a zoo, at best equipped with a narrow cot, . . . a flush toilet, and a wash bowl with running water; although the wash bowl is often lacking, and one toilet may serve a number of cells. Exercise space is usually lacking, as are activities of any kind. Prisoners, even before their guilt is proven, often simply sit or stand in the cell day after day. Some jails have a day room in which prisoners may mill around, with the stronger ones sometimes abusing the weaker and smaller ones. The jail may be kept well painted and clean, or not, depending upon the local situation. Many jails are so old that even an attempt at cleanliness and sanitation is only partly successful.[14]

There are fewer reports of brutalization in specialized juvenile detention facilities; and most such institutions are newer and more comfortable than jails. There is reason to fear, however, that such institutions may not really be much of an improvement.

Detention "homes" are frequently best described as "jail-like." Living spaces are generally locked or barred. Youngsters are searched, stripped, showered, and reclothed. The daily routines are strictly enforced, and the general regimen is similar to that of total-adult institutions.[15] At their best, detention centers are dull and boring places; at their worst they are nightmarish.

> . . . Jesse Elmore alleges that he is being held in a "terrible jail." He states that he is being kept under lock and key, behind bars, and in occasional solitary confinement; that this "jail" lacks doctors or psychiatrists, and does not afford even a minimal program of guidance or instruction; that he is "suffering from irremediable harm every moment of detention." Jesse Elmore is thirteen years old. The "terrible jail" is the Juvenile Receiving Home [in the District of Columbia].[16]

Philadelphia's house of detention, the Youth Study Center, is one of the newest and most attractive in the country; but it appears to be far from adequate. The center is on the Benjamin Franklin Parkway, an imposing, tree-lined avenue, modeled on the Champs Elysees in Paris. The Parkway boasts stunning fountains, carefully tended flower beds, and elegant museums of art and science. The detention center itself is magnificiently landscaped; and its grounds are ornamented with statuary that cost the city $100,000. Unfortunately the grounds are barely visible through the tiny windows of the cells in which children are kept. In 1968 Judge Lisa Aversa Richette of the Philadelphia Juvenile Court described the Youth Study Center in this way:[17]

> The planners forgot to include an outdoor play area in the blueprint: it has never been added. Boys and girls are kept in separate wings that are connected by moatlike ramps and tunnels. Every door — opened as a person goes in or out, bolted after he passes through. The gymnasium has served a dual function almost from the very first day the Center opened: by day an *indoor* recreation area; emergency sleeping quarters at night. The overflow is such that, at this writing, between fifty and sixty children have to sleep on thin mattresses which have been placed on the floor, only a few feet of space between each.

Judge Richette went on to refer to a newspaper interview with Robert F. Perkins, the Center's second executive director:[18]

> (The Center) is a storage bin for hundreds of children who have no other place to go . . . ninety-three percent (93%) of the counties in the United States provide only jail or jail-like facilities for youth detention; Philadelphia's juvenile jail has a fancier title and better statuary.

In the summer and fall of 1974 the Youth Study Center was propelled into the middle of a heated controversy. On July 16, State

Representative David Richardson led a six-man team on a 7½-hour surprise inspection of the facility. He emerged calling it "filthy, degrading, and dehumanizing."[19] The Rev. Henry Nichols declared that it is "cruel and unusual punishment to be sent to such a place."[20] Within a week of the tour, Representative Richardson was demanding that the center be closed and was alleging that "Mayor Rizzo keeps his (police) dogs and horses in better pens than they have down there (at the center)."[21]

Eugene Montone, the current executive director of the Center, responded by saying that Richardson was trying to make a "political football" of the Center, as "part of a move afoot to close all [correctional] institutions."[22]

Given that Representative Richardson is a black liberal Democrat from Philadelphia, and that the closing of correctional institutions is probably fairly popular amongst his constituency, Montone's response is probably not altogether unrealistic.

"I'll buy some of the filth," said Montone. "I don't deny that. But it's not as bad as he's making it. I know the sheets aren't as clean as they should be, but they're not filthy. Look at the clientele. You have to force them to take a shower. Sure, after two days, the sheets are going to be dirty.

"I might be putting my foot in my mouth and saying things nobody wants to hear. . . . but if Mr. Richardson wants to talk about filth, let him go to the neighborhoods they came from."

As to the charges of homosexuality, Montone said he's heard of two incidents in his four years as director, and neither could be substantiated. Montone said there have been times when a supervisor might have used "unnecessary force" on one of the youths, "but I wouldn't label it as brutality."[23]

We do not mean to suggest that all detention facilities for juveniles are brutalizing or dehumanizing or even just filthy. Clean, decent institutions that provide reasonable food, acceptable sleeping facilities, adequate medical and hygienic services, recreation, and even counseling exist in many jurisdictions. The authors of this book have observed some such facilities in Minnesota, New York, Massachusetts, California, and Pennsylvania. No doubt there are many others. It is certainly possible to conceptualize in the abstract what a "good" detention facility would be like. The National Probation and Parole Association has listed eight services that ought to be found in all detention centers:[24]

1. Administrative — including secretarial, bookkeeping, and telephone services, community relationships, and staff development and supervision.
2. Health services providing medical and dental examinations and treatment.
3. Casework services with the children, with reports to the probation office and court on each child's needs and potentialities.
4. Clinical services — including psychological testing, psychiatric diagnoses as needed, and assistance to the staff in handling children.
5. Group work services, such as recreational and creative activities and daily living activities.
6. School — since many children are of school attendance age, and also to help structure the child's day. The Board of Education typically supplies teachers, who must adjust their teaching to each child's customary placement in school so that he or she may return to school when released.
7. Religious activities.
8. Institutional services, such as housekeeping, laundry, food services, and maintenance of buildings and grounds.

The unfortunate reality, however, appears to be that most youngsters held in detention are not treated as well as they ought to be. There appear to be several reasons for this, not the least of which is that the youngsters, particularly the disadvantaged youngsters who are the primary residents of detention centers, are a politically powerless group. There are, however, many additional explanations. These are explored in the next section.

Systemic Interactions That Contribute to the Inadequacy and Overutilization of Detention Facilities

The inadequacy of detention throughout the nation is related in part to the actual structure and governance of detention centers; it is also related to external pressures which affect the operation of these facilities. Each of these propositions requires consideration.

The Structure and Governance
of Detention Centers

Perhaps the most striking characteristic of detention in the United States is that it is a function of county and city governments which are generally underfinanced and always looking for ways to save money. Most counties, particularly the smaller ones, have chosen not to construct special juvenile detention facilities; that explains why so many young people have their first experience with "justice" in county jails. Only ten states (Arizona, California, Idaho, Louisiana, New Mexico, Ohio, Pennsylvania, South Carolina, Utah, and Washington)[25] require that all counties provide separate, specialized detention facilities for juveniles.

In at least one of those states, Pennsylvania, a majority of counties are not in compliance with the law. Only 22 of the state's 67 counties actually have detention centers other than jails. Twenty-six counties do not even have access to facilities in neighboring counties.[26]

Three states (Connecticut, Delaware, and Rhode Island) have state-operated juvenile facilities which serve all counties.[27] Legislation in eight states (Colorado, Kentucky, Missouri, Nevada, Oregon, South Dakota, Virginia, and Wisconsin) mandates that large counties (those with populations of more than 100,000) provide juvenile detention facilities.[28] In the remaining twenty-nine states there are laws permitting, but not requiring, the existence of specialized detention centers for youngsters.[29]

Most small communities simply do not have dentention centers; those that do rarely have the resources to operate well-equipped institutions, nor to employ well-trained staff.[30] In fact, few facilities outside of urban areas have any professional staff at all, other than custodial.[31] Even in urban settings, professional resources are spread thin because of institutional overcrowding. Furthermore, the individuals who work in detention centers are generally not the best available. This is so for several reasons. First, the nature of the work, which involves very short-term involvement with youngsters (11 days is the national average length of stay in detention),[32] probably disenchants many professional educators and social workers whose motivation to help often requires long-term involvement. Beyond that, the fact that detention workers generally work in inadequate facilities and with inadequate resources often causes them to be perceived by probation officers and other helping professionals as glorified babysitters, or worse, as guards.[33] In addition, the scarcity of funds for detention programs means that detention work usually pays less than probation or other types of social work; and the opportunities for promotion and self-improvement of the worker are generally more limited.

External Pressures

Detention centers do not do their own intake. Policemen, judges, and others decide who shall be detained and for how long. The mix of attitudes among these decision makers is such that children wind up being detained for reasons so different and conflicting that it is almost impossible to imagine any institution processing *all* detainees effectively. Furthermore, the different intake reasons can result in unpredictably excessive numbers of youngsters detained while awaiting trial, thus creating severe crowding in the facilities.

Let us consider, in turn, (1) how decisions to detain are made, by officials over whom the centers have no control; (2) the extent to which these decisions are based on differing and sometimes conflicting justifications; and (3) the extent to which detention services are influenced by the pressure of the external (and inconsistent) public officials who determine when detention facilities are to be used.

How and By Whom Detention Decisions Are Made

In most states the initial decision about whether to detain a child is made by a police officer, although he may not be legally empowered to make the decision.[34] Often arresting officers make the decision themselves; sometimes they turn cases over to their supervisors or to special juvenile officers.[35] In some jurisdictions decisions to detain are made by probation officers.[36]

Thirty-five states and the District of Columbia require judicial review of the decision to detain within some set period of time (usually 48 or 96 hours; in Idaho and Washington, D.C., the review must take place within 24 hours, in Illinois within 36, in California, Georgia, and Ohio within 72).[37] Of these 35 states only 18 (Alaska, California,

Colorado, Georgia, Idaho, Illinois, Indiana, Maine, Maryland, Michigan, New York, North Dakota, Ohio, Oregon, South Dakota, Tennessee, Utah, and Vermont — plus the District of Columbia) require that the judge's review of the detention decision involve an actual hearing with the juvenile or his attorney appearing before the court.[38] In sixteen other states (Delaware, Florida, Hawaii, Iowa, Kentucky, Minnesota, Missouri, Nebraska, Nevada, New Mexico, Rhode Island, South Carolina, Texas, Virginia, Wisconsin, and Washington) judicial review means only that an administrator justifies and seeks approval of the detention decision at a proceeding at which the child is neither present nor represented.[39] In the fifteen states not already accounted for there is no involvement of judges at all in reviewing decisions to detain.

Several options are available to the public officials who make and review detention decisions. The most obvious possibility is to release a child in the custody of his parents while he awaits trial. This is done in all states, although some require that the parents sign a statement promising to bring the child to court on the appearance date.[40] Three states (California, Minnesota, and Nebraska) allow the child to be released on his own signature.[41] If a child is to be detained, it may be in jail or in a detention facility. It can also be in a group home or foster home, but such facilities exist in only a very small number of jurisdictions; so the choice is generally between release or detention in an institution. Sometimes the choice is limited by parents who refuse to allow the child to come back home.

Given the knowledge that detention centers are generally not very nice places, it might be expected that most youngsters would be sent home to await a hearing on their innocence or guilt. That, however, is not the case. It has been reported, for example, that more than 400,000 juveniles, approximately two-thirds of all those apprehended by the police, were held in detention centers or county jails in 1965.[42] It is appropriate to wonder what justifications there are — or what justifications there are supposed to be — for treating so many young people so harshly.

The Different and Conflicting
Justifications for Detention

Three clusters of justifications for detention associated with the three models of juvenile justice systems developed in Chapter 3 (due process, crime control, and rehabilitative) can be identified.

The only justification for holding a person in detention that is compatible with *due process* values is to assure that he will not abscond from the jurisdiction before trial. Bail has generally been considered a reasonable way to ensure that a person accused of an offense will not abscond. Many jurisdictions, however, allow a person to go free without posting bail if he seems likely to show up at the trial.[43] The position that a person (adult or child) should be held in detention only when there is a high probability that he will abscond or be absconded from the jurisdiction implies that most people will be released.

> [T]he decision to detain should be based on demonstrated behavior, not subjective opinion. . . . To assume that a child will abscond, there should be a history of absconding. To assume that he will not appear in court he should first be given the opportunity to appear.[44]

Nevertheless, some number of youngsters are certainly detained every year because some policeman, or judge, or probation officer is of the opinion that only detention can ensure continued presence in the jurisdiction. There is no way of telling how often that belief underlies a decision to detain, nor how often the belief is valid.

Remember that 400,000 youngsters are held in detention during the course of a year. How many of them do you suppose would run away from home in order to avoid a juvenile court hearing? Where would they go? How would they get there? What would they do for food and money? Do you suppose that most alleged delinquents have so little attachment to home and friends, and are so competent and secure that they could just pack up and go off on their own?

It is likely that a *much* larger number of children are held in detention because of the desire of public officials to *control crime*. The fear that a child will commit offenses while awaiting trial is often used to justify detention. The prestigious Uniform Juvenile Court Act, for example, provides that detention may be used when it

> . . . is required to protect the persons or property of others or of the child. . . .[45]

Many state statutes include similar provisions. In Colorado, for example, the law requires that a child be released

> . . . unless . . . the protection of the community requires that he be detained.[46]

In one reported case a juvenile court judge responded to a defense attorney's request that a child be released while awaiting trial by saying

> No. . . . Are you going to put up surety against his actions? If you will draw me a contract or your agency will draw me a contract assuring me that anyone who is harmed or anything is damaged by this boy that they will pay all damages, I would consider it. (sic)[47]

This attitude towards detention involves a presumption of guilt. Officials are not likely to be fearful of a child's future offenses unless they are fairly well convinced (in advance of the trial, remember) that he has committed some in the past.

In cases in which policemen, judges, and probation officers are convinced in advance of a youngster's guilt, they may have other reasons for favoring the use of detention. One is to assure continued easy access to the youngster while the case against him is being prepared.[48] Another is to throw a good fright into the youngster in order to keep him on the straight-and-narrow in the future.[49] Yet another is to assure that the child gets some punishment even if he winds up winning his case in court or receiving a "lenient" deposition.[50]

That these justifications may not seem appropriate in a nation that claims to exist "under laws," nor in a juvenile justice system that purports to be primarily concerned with helping children in trouble does not mean that they do not frequently underlie the decision to detain. There is no way to know for sure how often a presumption of guilt is in the mind of a decision maker who opts for detention. The huge numbers of children held in detention facilities (most of whom would almost certainly not abscond if released) suggests that such motivation may not be infrequent.

The *rehabilitative* orientation of the juvenile justice system may provide yet another set of justifications for the use of detention. A child may be held in detention not because he is likely to abscond, nor because he seems dangerous, but because he is considered to be in need of treatment or other services. The presumption of "need" may, in a sense, be parallel to the presumption of guilt.

> Instead of being merely a waiting period, detention should begin the process of rehabilitation and lay the groundwork for later treatment . . . Although the detention home is not a training school, staff attitudes can and should begin the training process. . . .[51]

It is important to note that the same legislation that authorizes the detention of children if they seem to present a threat to the community also authorizes detention for the purposes of providing needed care, treatment, and custody. The Uniform Juvenile Court Act, for example, authorizes detention when it

> . . . is required to protect . . . the child or because . . . he has no parent, guardian, or custodian or other person able to provide supervision and care for him. . . .[52]

Another example is provided by legislation in Colorado which mandates a child's release

> . . . unless his immediate welfare . . . requires that he be detained.[53]

Some observers believe that rehabilitative concerns underlie many, perhaps most, decisions to detain.[54] Data indicating that youngsters charged with status offenses are detained more often than youngsters charged with serious offenses[55] suggest that the child's condition rather than his dangerousness may indeed be the determinant in many instances in which detention is used.

What do you make of the fact that therapeutic concerns appear to underlie a considerable number of decisions to detain even though detention centers appear to do so little that is therapeutic?

It is not possible to determine how frequently decisions to detain are based on due process concerns, or on crime control concerns, or on rehabilitative concerns. It is clear, however, that children are detained for very different reasons by decision makers over whom the facilities have virtually no control, and that those decision makers generate different and conflicting expectations about what detention facilities ought to be doing.

The Impact of External Pressures on Detention Services

The fact that youngsters are sent to detention for so many different reasons makes it impossible for facilities (especially, given their limited resources) to provide specialized services. The presence of dangerous youngsters, for example, requires security measures which pull resources away from treatment programs. And, in fact, it simply may not be possible to establish the trusting relationship necessary for treatment in the context of a secure institution which keeps youngsters under lock and key.[56]

Furthermore, the plethora of justifications for detention contributes to the overcrowding of facilities. If there were fewer justifications for detention, there would be fewer cases in which a justification could be found. The National Council on Crime and Delinquency estimates that more than three times as many youngsters experience detention as ought to.[57] Overcrowding makes the facilities more oppressive, contributes to stretching resources too thin, and adds to staff demoralization by worsening the conditions of work. Consequently, external pressures — the numerous justifications for detention — exacerbate the problems of attempting to operate the facilities optimally.

Additionally, the highly discretionary nature of decision making may contribute systematic bias in the selection process. Public officials making decisions to detain in the absence of clear guidelines may be inclined to see middle- and upper-class families as better able to treat, discipline, or ensure the presence at trial of their children.[58] Lower-class and minority-group children, aware that they form a significant majority of children detained, may (accurately?) perceive themselves as objects of discrimination and bias. Their anger and resentment at unfair decision making may exacerbate all the problems and constant tensions which characterize detention facilities in general.

Alternatives to Existing
Patterns of Detention Use

It is compellingly important that communities develop strategies to minimize the use of detention facilities — especially of institutional detention facilities. This viewpoint is based on the observation, documented in the first part of this chapter, that many detention centers are positively oppressive places. Hypotheses derived from the labeling perspective reinforce the argument by suggesting that detention, even in a decent facility, may be harmful to children.

> Locking up children charged with or suspected of offenses, before adjudication, probably does more to contribute to the army of habitual criminals than any other procedure in what is called the juvenile justice system. It is difficult for an adult who has not been through the experience to realize the terror that engulfs a youngster the first time he loses his liberty and has to spend the night or several days or weeks in a cold, impersonal cell or room away from home or family. . . . the speed with which relatively innocent youngsters succumb to the infectious miasma of "Juvy" and its practices, attitudes, and language . . . is not surprising. The experience tells the youngster that he is "no good" and that society has rejected him. So he responds to society's expectation, sees himself as a delinquent, and acts like one.[59]

Reductions in the utilization of detention facilities could be achieved in at least four ways:

1. Through an outright prohibition on the placement of dependent and neglected children (persons in need of supervision) in secure detention facilities. Such a rule would reduce institutionalized populations in juvenile facilities by at least one-half.[60] Such an approach is actually contemplated by the newly enacted Federal Juvenile Justice and Delinquency Prevention Act of 1974.

2. Through the development of programs of "home detention." Under home detention the child remains in his own home, but is placed under the close supervision of an indigenous worker who has had a ten-day period of orientation and job training. The worker's job is to keep the youngster out of trouble and to make sure he appears in court. Each worker is responsible for five children and is expected to see each child at least once every day. Home detention workers should be paid at least as much as child care workers in institutional detention facilities (in St. Louis they are paid approximately $1,000 more).

Preliminary evaluations of existing home detention programs around the country indicate that they are effective both in limiting new offenses during the pretrial period and in guaranteeing a youngster's presence at trial. The cost of home detention programs, incidentally, is about one-quarter that of regular detention.[61] It is believed that many allegedly dependent-neglected children, and many youngsters charged with delinquency, could be maintained at home with good, close supervision.

3. Through the development of programs of shelter and foster care. Shelter care means the temporary care of children in physically unrestricting facilities pending court disposition. Typically a small-group home or a foster home for an individual child might be used. Recently the use of foster-group homes (placing more than one child in an existing family unit) has been encouraged. Traditionally foster parents have received minimal remuneration, intended only to defray the expenses of maintaining the child. The prevailing logic has had it that a family should take children in because they love them, not because they want to make a profit. It ought to be recognized, however, that caring for children — particularly children in trouble — is hard work, and that the payment of a decent wage for such work will encourage larger numbers of competent parents to make their homes available to foster children. In Minnesota and Wisconsin, the foster parents of small-group homes receive approximately $200 per child per month. That cost is approximately one-third the cost of maintaining a youngster in an institution.[62] It is plausible to expect that many of the allegedly dependent-neglected youngsters now detained in jails and specialized juvenile facilities might benefit immeasurably from this type of treatment. Similarly it is reasonable to expect that good foster homes would be sufficiently secure to hold most alleged delinquents in the jurisdiction until their hearings.

4. By assuring that qualified personnel are available to make detention decisions twenty-four hours a day, seven days a week. Many youngsters, particularly in jurisdictions where a decision to detain a child must be made by a police supervisor or a police juvenile specialist, or a probation officer, rather than by an arresting officer, are held in a police lockup or other detention facility until the decision maker is available. A child arrested in the late afternoon may be held overnight until the juvenile officer comes to work in the morning. A child arrested on a Friday afternoon may not be seen until some time on Monday. Thus, large numbers of youngsters for whom detention is absolutely unnecessary may be held in dingy and oppressive facilities for hours or even days.[63] The cost of maintaining extra personnel would be offset at least in part by the savings that would accrue from minimizing the costs of institutionalization; and the service provided would be of immense value to the many children currently held in detention because no one is available to decide that they can go home.

Even if some jurisdiction succeeded in establishing extensive programs of the type described above, it is likely that secure facilities would still be necessary to keep some youngsters from absconding, others from victimizing the community, and still others from themselves becoming victims. In any event, it is unlikely that any jurisdiction will succeed in establishing so complete a set of alternatives to detention in the immediate future; and it is unimaginable that all jurisdictions will make such progress. Therefore it is necessary that we consider ways in which detention facilities might be improved.

1. *Detention decision making should be standardized.* The development of guidelines for the use of detention would help reduce the breadth of the range of cases that get sent to detention; and facilities dealing with fewer types of problems might be better able to cope. Intake officers authorized to send youngsters to detention ought to receive special training and ought to be selected from among the ranks of experienced personnel.[64] This might contribute to greater rationality in decision making and would facilitate the implementation of guidelines.

2. *Regionalization should be encouraged to help small counties develop adequate facilities.* Counties that currently detain youngsters in jails could be encouraged to pool resources to establish a centrally located facility that would be adequate to meet the needs of children. State legislatures could facilitate regionalization by making funds available to help in the construction of such facilities.[65]

3. *The quality of staff and the adequacy of program aids must be improved.* The salaries of detention workers ought to be at least comparable to those of professionals involved with other agencies. Good supervision for staff should be available in detention centers; and promotion into supervisory jobs ought to be facilitated as a way of recruiting career-oriented professionals. Good people can be employed only if they are paid a competitive wage and given adequate opportunities for advancement. The recruitment of good staff members will be facilitated if they are provided adequate tools with which to do the jobs expected of them. Programs (that is, recreational opportunities,

workshops, special classes, arts and crafts projects and such) are the tools of professional group workers. Detention facilities must have the resources that make it possible for concerned employees to interact effectively and helpfully with the children for whom they are responsible.[66] A detention center without an educational program and with no recreational facilities other than a television set and some comic books will bore children and good staff members alike. Both will wish to move on.

Concluding Thoughts

Detention facilities throughout the United States are inadequate and oppressive. The children who experience them must surely perceive them as punitive. Punishment, however, is generally conceptualized as following a trial; in this case it precedes it. A significant number of youngsters held in detention are never adjudicated delinquent; they are diverted out of the system before their hearings, or simply win their cases. Perhaps those youngsters are especially bitter; perhaps not, though, because for them the experience can at least fade to a memory.

References

1. Robert Winslow, ed., *Juvenile Delinquency in a Free Society* (Encino, Calif.: Dickenson, 1973), p. 158.
2. Ruth S. Cavan, *Juvenile Delinquency: Development, Treatment and Control* (New York: J. B. Lippincott, 1969), p. 389.
3. Report of the Attorney General's Committee on Poverty and the Administration of Criminal Justice (Washington, D.C.: U.S. Government Printing Office, 1964), p. 69.
4. Mark M. Levin and Rosemary C. Sarri, *Juvenile Delinquency: A Comparative Analysis of Legal Codes in the United States* (Ann Arbor, Mich.: National Assessment of Juvenile Corrections, 1974), p. 32
5. Ibid., p. 34.
6. Ibid.
7. Ibid.
8. Winslow, *Juvenile Delinquency in a Free Society,* p. 158.
9. Quoted in Bill Davidson, "The Worst Jail I've Ever Seen," *Saturday Evening Post* (July 13, 1968), p. 17.
10. Ibid.
11. Ibid.
12. Winslow, *Juvenile Delinquency in a Free Society,* p. 158.

13. Ibid., p. 158.

14. Cavan, *Juvenile Delinquency: Development, Treatment and Control,* p. 389.

15. Margaret K. Rosenheim, "Detention Facilities and Temporary Shelters," in *Child Caring: Social Policy and the Institution,* eds. Donnell M. Pappenfort, Dee M. Kilpatrick, and Robert W. Roberts (Chicago: Aldine, 1973), p. 260.

16. Jonathan Weiss, "The Poor Kid," 9 *Duquesne L. Rev.* 590, 597 (1971).

17. Lisa A. Richette, *The Throwaway Children* (New York: J. B. Lippincott, 1969), p. 19.

18. Ibid., p. 20.

19. Elmer Smith, in *Philadelphia Evening Bulletin* (August 3, 1974), p. 20.

20. Ibid.

21. Zackary Stalbert, in *Philadelphia Daily News* (August 2, 1974), p. 12.

22. Smith, in *Philadelphia Evening Bulletin,* p. 20.

23. Joe Clark, in *Philadelphia Daily News* (July 31, 1974), p. 13.

24. Standards and Guides for the Detention of Children and Youth (New York: National Probation and Parole Associates, 1958), pp. 34 - 5.

25. Levin and Sarri, *Juvenile Delinquency: A Comparative Analysis of Legal Codes,* p. 34.

26. Pennsylvania Advisory Council on Juvenile Delinquency Planning, *Report,* (Harrisburg: Pennsylvania Department of Public Welfare, 1971), p. 32.

27. Levin and Sarri, *Juvenile Delinquency: A Comparative Analysis of Legal Codes,* p. 34.

28. Ibid., p. 35.

29. Ibid.

30. Thomas H. Hughes, "Humanizing the Detention Setting," 35 *Federal Probation* 21, 25 (September 1971).

31. Margaret K. Rosenheim, "Detention Facilities," p. 263.

32. Law Enforcement Assistance Administration, *Children in Custody: A Report on the Juvenile Detention and Correctional Facility Census of 1971* (Washington, D.C.: National Criminal Justice Information and Statistics Service, 1974), p. 4.

33. Winslow, *Juvenile Delinquency in a Free Society,* p. 162.

34. Monrad G. Paulsen, "The Changing World of Juvenile Law: New Horizons for Juvenile Court Legislation," 40 *Pennsylvania Bar Association Quarterly* 34, 35; also see, Helen Sumner, "Intake into the Juvenile Justice System," *Crime and Delinquency* 160.

35. See, for example, Richard H. Chused, "The Juvenile Court Process: A Study of Three New Jersey Counties," 26 *Rutgers Law Review* 488 (1973).

36. Levin and Sarri, *Juvenile Delinquency: A Comparative Analysis of Legal Codes,* p. 29.

37. Ibid., p. 30.

38. Ibid.

39. Ibid.

40. Ibid., p. 29.

41. Ibid.

42. Sanford J. Fox, *The Law of Juvenile Courts in a Nutshell,* (St. Paul: West Publishing, 1971), p. 107.

43. See, for example, Herbert Sturz, "An Alternative to the Bail System, *Federal Probation* 23 (December 1970): 12 - 17.

44. Richard M. Ariesshn and Fredrisk I. Closson, "Alternatives to Juvenile Deention," 24 *Youth Authority Quarterly* 20, 21 (Winter 1971).

45. Uniform Juvenile Court Act, § 14.

46. Colorado Children's Code, § 22-2-2(2).

47. Cited in Fox, *Law of Juvenile Courts,* p. 106.

48. Rosenheim, "Detention Facilities," p. 268.

49. Thomas Wood, "Detention Provisions of the New Juvenile Act of 1972," 30 *Quarterly of the Pennsylvania Association of Probation, Parole, and Corrections* 19 (Autumn 1973).

50. Cavan, *Juvenile Delinquency: Development, Treatment and Control,* p. 397; see also Alfred J. Kahn, *Planning Community Services for Children in Trouble* (New York: Columbia University Press, 1963), p. 278.

51. Rosenheim, "Detention Facilities," pp. 259 - 60.

52. Uniform Juvenile Court Act, § 14.

53. Colorado Children's Code, § 22-2-2(2).

54. Hughes, "Humanizing the Detention Setting," p. 21; also see Kahn, *Planning Community Services,* p. 277ff.

55. Larry Schultz, "The Problems of Problem Children," *Nation* (October 1973), p. 426.

56. See Daniel Katkin, "Presentence Investigation Reports: An Analysis of Uses, Limitations and Civil Liberties Issues," 55 *Minn. L. Rev.* 15 (1970).

57. For a discussion of this estimate, see Kahn, *Planning Community Services,* p. 284.

58. See, for example, J. R. Ferster and R. Courtless, "The Intake Process in Affluent City," 22 *Hastings Law Journal* 1127 (1971).

59. This proposition was cited approvingly by Justice Tobriner of the Supreme Court of California in *In Re M.,* 89 Cal. Rptr. 33, 473 P. 2d 737, 37 Cal. 3d 16 (1970).

60. Schultz, "Problems of Problem Children," p. 426.

61. John Howard Association, *Juvenile Detention and Alternatives in Florida* (Jacksonville: Divison of Youth Services, 1973), pp. 19 - 20.

62. Ibid., pp. 20 - 21.

63. See, for example, Drew Hyman, Daniel Katkin and John Kramer, *The Role of the Department of Public Welfare in the Youth Service System of Pennsylvania: A Stance for Cooperation* (Harrisburg: Department of Public Welfare, 1974), pp. 35 - 7.

64. John Howard Association, *Juvenile Detention,* p. 48; see also *Standards and Guides for the Detention of Children and Youth* (Hackensack, N.J.: National Council on Crime and Delinquency, 1961) p. 26.

65. There is a national trend in this direction. See Levin and Sarri, *Juvenile Delinquency: A Comparative Analysis of Legal Codes,* p. 35; also see Kahn, *Planning Community Services,* p. 291.

66. Kahn, *Planning Community Services,* p. 288.

8 Juvenile Court Philosophy

And I think that saving a little child,
And fotching him to his own,
Is a derned sight better business
Than loafing around the Throne

— John Milton Hay

The juvenile court is not merely an additional component of the juvenile justice system; it is the very hub of that system. It is the embodiment of legitimate authority and the locus of power. It is the epicenter from which the principles and philosophies that guide the entire system radiate outward.

The centrality and importance of the juvenile court are such that it requires extensive discussion in this chapter and the next. This chapter focuses on philosophical distinctions between juvenile courts and their counterparts in the adult criminal justice system; its purpose is to explicate the values and characteristics that make juvenile courts unique. Chapter nine describes the procedural operation of juvenile courts from intake through disposition.

The Conceptual Difference Between Criminal and Juvenile Courts

Juvenile courts were created by nineteenth-century reformers who wanted troubled children to be dealt with in a forum not dominated by the traditional punitive orientation of criminal courts.[1] These reformers were (and their program continues to be) deeply influenced by the belief that traditional penological measures were inappropriate for children. Initially the point must be made that this belief is usually predicated on assumptions about the nature of children rather than assumptions about the nature of criminal punishment. Indeed, there are several fairly compelling justifications for the proposition that adults who offend against the law ought to be punished. In the next section of this chapter we will review those justifications, and then see if we can determine why it is so widely believed that the misbehavior of children ought not to be responded to punitively. In subsequent sections the nonpunitive philosophy of juvenile courts will be re-examined in the light of recent Supreme Court decisions that seem to make juvenile courts conform more closely to the traditional standards of adult justice.

Most of the examples in the next section involve adult rather than juvenile offenders. That is because the immediate purpose is to describe the philosophy that dominates criminal justice systems, so that the special philosophy of juvenile justice may be contrasted to it in the rest of the chapter.

The Traditional Justifications for Criminal Punishment

Few modern penologists feel that the imposition of criminal sanctions (punishments) is inherently desirable. The whole range of sanctions, from suspended sentences and probation on the one hand to incarceration and execution on the other, involves humiliation, restrictions on liberty, and the imposition of psychological and physical pain. Modern penology tends to view such treatment of individuals by the societies to which they are a part as unfortunate and lamentable — but necessary.[2] The necessity, it is argued, derives from the fact that criminals, were their behaviors permitted to go unchecked, would inflict still graver harms on innocent members of society. Civilized states, this position has it, should seek to minimize the total amount of pain to be experienced by individuals; the inflicting of harm on some persons is justifiable only if it serves to minimize the total amount of pain that will be experienced by the general population. This position, called utilitarianism (because punishment is seen as having purpose, or utility), was developed by the great English philosopher, Jeremy Bentham.[3]

The utilitarian justifications for punishment are that it deters people from committing offenses, and incapacitates those who will not be deterred. There is an additional nonutilitarian justification which has historically exerted great influence over the development of justice systems and which still exerts great influence today (despite a fading out of vogue in some circles): it is retribution — the belief that it is right for the wicked to be punished. Each of the utilitarian justifications as well as the retributive ideal deserves elaborate consideration here, before we move on a consideration of why they may not be appropriate in the special case of juvenile offenders.

Deterrence

The goal of deterrence is to use the threat of punishment as a device to induce people to refrain from committing crimes. It is not so much that we want a person who hurts us to be punished as that we want him to decide not to commit the harmful act in the first place. Consider the following language from the Old Testament:

> When a malicious witness comes forward to give false evidence against a man, and the two disputants stand before the LORD, before the priests and the judges then in office, if, after careful examination by the judges, he be proved to be a false witness giving false evidence against his fellow, you shall treat him as he intended to treat his fellow, and thus rid yourselves of this wickedness. *The rest of the people when they hear of it will be afraid: never again will anything as wicked as this be done among you.* You shall show no mercy: . . .(emphasis added).

Deterrence is generally thought to be of two types: specific and general.[5] Specific deterrence refers to the inhibiting influence of punishment on the future behavior of people who actually experienced it. General deterrence refers to the inhibiting (or intimidating) effect that the punishment of one individual may have on the rest of the community. If you are stopped for speeding, brought to a magistrate, fined, and subsequently decide to drive within the limit, specific deterrence has taken place. If, on the other hand, a friend observes your misfortune and decides that he too had better drive within the limit, general deterrence has taken place. The difference between specific and general deterrence is the difference between learning from one's own experiences and learning from someone else's.

It is sometimes suggested that deterrence, however nice the theory, just doesn't work. But the criticisms of this utilitarian approach are not altogether convincing.

. . . it is sometimes said that a high rate of repeated offenses, or recidivism as it is technically known, among persons who have already been once subjected to criminal punishment shows that deterrence does not work. The fact of recidivism may throw some doubt on the efficacy of *special* deterrence, but a moment's reflection will show that it says nothing about the effect of *general* deterrence. An even more preposterous argument is sometimes heard to the effect that the very existence of crime or (more moderately but equally fallaciously) the increase in crime rates is evidence that deterrence does not work. Unless we know what the crime rate would be if we did not punish criminals, the conclusion is unfounded.[6]

Your own personal experiences quite probably generate some evidence in support of the proposition that deterrence actually works — that is, that some people can be deterred from committing some crimes. When driving on super highways, for example, why do you tend to stay at or near the speed limit? Is it because you have a deep moral sense that speeding is wrong and dangerous, or is it because you are reluctant to be fined, or frightened about the possibility of losing your license? When considering the possibility of using a friend's identification (to drink while underage, or to fly youth-fare while overage, for example), do you tend to be more concerned with the ethics of the behavior or with the probabilities of getting away with it? You may have noticed that lots of people cheat on their income taxes, but that they generally don't cheat very much; do you suppose such cheating is limited by a moral sense about how much tax evasion is acceptable, or is it fear of the consequences that induces people not to stray too far from the straight and narrow? On reflection it seems fairly clear that there are many behaviors from which many people may be deterred.

On the other hand, however, it is also quite likely that there are many crimes that are not deterrable. Impulsive crimes of passion, for example, may be motivated by forces so far beneath the level of consciousness that rational thoughts about consequences may never enter the picture. The deterrence model assumes that man is a rational animal who seeks to minimize pain and maximize pleasure, and thus that the threat of punishment will cause him to avoid behaviors. Psychologists are quite likely correct in suggesting that men are not always very rational,[7] and that assessment, of course, suggest that people can not always be deterred. Nevertheless, the fact that some acts (or some actors) may not be deterrable does not mean that deterrence is not a potent force in securing obedience to legal standards in the everyday lives of most people.[8]

In sentencing adults who have been convicted of crimes, it certainly seems reasonable that courts ought to examine the issue of whether some form of punishment may have the effect of dissuading the offender from continuing in his wrongful ways (specific deterrence); in addition, the possibility that the punishment of an offender may serve to make him an example to others in the community, and thus help to reduce the incidence of crime, ought also to be considered. A story may help dramatize this point.

At three o'clock on the morning of Thursday, August 8, 1963, the most incredibly daring and successful armed robbery in the history of Great Britain took place. The robbers relieved the Royal Mail train from Glasgow to London of banknotes worth $7,282,600.00. It was, by all accounts, the greatest train robbery in history. Overnight the robbers became not archvillians, but heroes, in the public eye.

> The cool daring of the raid and the enormous sum of money involved was like a tonic, a badly-needed fillip to offset the misery of a sunless summer. Only the most serious-minded railed against the fact that in the end it would be the public's money that made good the loss. In an age of free vouchers, trading stamps and dreams of quick riches via the football pools there were chuckles in place of condemnation and the toast in pubs and clubs throughout the land was "the best of British luck to them."[9]

The general admiration for the cunning, competence, and courage of the train robbers even came to be reflected in advertisements. The American branch of Landrover launched an advertising campaign which boasted in the following manner that their vehicles had been used in the caper:

> We are strictly on the side of law and order. But can you blame us for feeling a certain warm glow when we read that the perpetrators of England's greatest robbery also chose a Landrover to do the job?
> The Armed Services of twenty-six countries used the Landrover, the police forces of thirty-seven, legions of country squires, desert chieftains, titled people and oil prospectors. Not to mention sportsmen and all sorts of nice families who use them for skiing.
> But what a marvellously splendid proof of the pudding it is that the chaps who pulled off the Great Train Robbery were equally discerning.[10]

When finally the robbers were caught and convicted, the fact that they had become cultural heroes influenced the sentencing judge's decision. Heroes or not, these men had committed a serious crime in which they had threatened and endangered human life. In the process they had beaten and severely injured the conductor of the train. But the excitement engendered by the enormity of their loot made them popular, and even made it seem likely that others might try to replicate their behavior. Judge Davies was strongly of the opinion that the sentences had to be so severe that infatuated hero worshippers would think twice before embarking on similar courses of behavior. In meting out twenty- and thirty-year sentences, the judge said:

> You . . . have been convicted . . . of a crime which in its impudence and enormity is the first of its kind in this country.
> I propose to do all in my power to ensure that it will also be the last of its kind. Your outrageous conduct constitutes an intolerable menace to the well-being of society. Let us clear out of the way any romantic notions of dare deviltry. This is nothing less than a sordid crime of violence inspired by vast greed. All who have seen the nerve-shattered engine driver can have no doubt of the terrifying effect on the law-abiding citizen of a concerted assault by armed robbers. To deal with this crime leniently would be a positively evil thing to do.
> When a grave crime is committed it calls for grave punishment, not for the purpose of mere retribution but that others similarly tempted will be brought to the realization that crime does not pay, and the game is not worth even the most alluring candle. Potential criminals who might be dazzled by the enormity of the prize must be taught that the punishment they risk must be proportionately greater.[11]

You may be inclined to believe that Judge Davies was too harsh on these people, but his position was certainly based on rational and logical premises. Faced with the prospect that others — perhaps youthful amateurs — might try similar capers and that the result might be a spate of armed robberies and even murders throughout the land, the judge fell back on classic penological theory.

A purpose of justice systems has traditionally been to ensure that the fruits of crime will be bitter so as to dissuade everyone from harvesting them. That is what deterrence is all about.

Incapacitation

In addition to specific and general deterrence, some forms of punishment, such as imprisonment and execution, may also be aimed at reducing the offender's capacity to commit further crimes. In the case of imprisonment, this incapacity lasts for the duration of the sentence; in the case of capital punishment, the incapacity obviously lasts forever.[12] While it is true that convicts may rob from one another and may even assault one another, it is also true that being in prison reduces one's opportunities to perpetrate crimes on the public.[13] Thus, incapacitation — the isolation of dangerous offenders from the mainstream of society — is traditionally justified as a way of protecting the public. Most inmates in American prisons, however, have never committed such serious crimes that their incarceration can realistically be said to be necessary for the public welfare. Yet in some cases, incapacitation may be seen to be the primary thing a society might hope to achieve through punishment.

Consider, for example, the case of Charles Manson — a thief turned spiritual leader turned murderer.[14] Manson, who had spent many years in reform schools and prisons, on a variety of charges, was the messianic, spiritual leader of a commune of young "groupies" (hero worshippers) who lived on a ranch near Los Angeles in the late 1960s. Many of Manson's followers were between the ages of thirteen and fifteen; most were girls. They were deeply involved in a religious cult whose main precept was obedience to Charles Manson. The group's main economic activity for many years was stealing Volkswagens, stripping them, and selling them as dune buggies.

Manson, whose control over the group was virtually hypnotic, began planning the ritual murders of people he felt did not understand his religious movement. The most famous of his victims was the Hollywood actress Sharon Tate. Miss Tate and several of her friends were bound, hand and foot, and then cut to death in a bizarre and gruesome manner. Manson's young groupies, male and female, participated in the murders with fervor and enthusiasm. Members of the commune who hadn't participated in the murders remained loyal to Manson for quite some time afterwards; indeed, throughout his trial there were loyal followers picketing outside the Los Angeles courthouse.

There is no reason to believe that punishing Manson will achieve either specific or general deterrence. Were he to be released from prison, it is quite likely that he would return to some bizarre and sinister life style. And it is not likely that other individuals with similar messianic visions and charismatic powers will be frightened by Manson's punishment. People who are crazy enough to do such things are crazy enough to believe that they'll get away with it.

It might be hoped that Manson, while institutionalized, could be rehabilitated; but the psychiatric arts are not so well developed that a "cure" is really likely. In any event, while it may be charitable to advocate rehabilitation, most of us would probably concede that the most important objective in dealing with so dangerous an offender is the protection of the public. Men like Charles Manson, and there are very few such men, need to be isolated from society in order to ensure that innocent people are not injured. Even the staunchest proponents of rehabilitation programs are likely to agree that appropriate security measures must be taken to protect the average citizen from truly frightening offenders. In this regard they are somewhat like the persecuted Russian rabbi who responded to the question: "Is there a proper blessing for the Czar?" by saying, "Yes, my son! may God bless and keep the Czar — far away from us."

Incapacitation is the social policy of keeping dangerous offenders "far away from us."

Retribution

Retribution is almost certainly the most controversial of the traditional justifications for the imposition of punishment. On the one hand it is argued that awful acts deserve awful denunciations, and that societies remain civilized only through the moral condemnation of immoral behavior.[15] On the other hand it is argued that societies, by stooping to vengence, imitate the worst in men and thus lose the ethical leadership that might exhort men to higher standards of humanity and civilization.[16]

Deterrence and incapacitation are rationales for punishment derived from *ideas* about how human behavior may best be regulated; retribution is derived from *feelings* about the appropriateness and justness of criminals paying a price for their wrongful behavior. When deterrence motivates the imposition of a penalty it is because it is *thought* that fear of the penalty may stop potential offenders; when retribution motivates the imposition of a penalty it is because it is *felt* that the offender deserves to have something happen to him. The classic statement of this attitude that the punishment ought to fit the crime is found in the Old Testament:[17]

> When one man strikes another and kills him, he shall be put to death. Whoever strikes a beast and kills it shall make restitution, life for life. When one man injures and disfigures his fellow-countryman, it shall be done to him as he has done; fracture for fracture, eye for eye, tooth for tooth; the injury and disfigurement that he has inflicted upon another shall in turn be inflicted upon him.

The critics of retribution have developed arguments that are both insightful and humane. Oliver Wendell Holmes commented on the argument sometimes made in favor of retribution — that the fitness of punishment following crime is axiomatic and is instinctively recognized by unperverted minds; Holmes said:

> . . . I think it will be seen, on self-inspection, that this feeling of fitness is absolute and unconditional only in the case of our neighbors. It does not seem to me that any one who has satisfied himself that an act of his was wrong, and that he will never do it again, would feel the least need or propriety, as between himself and an earthly punishing power alone, of his being made to suffer for what he had done, although, when third persons were introduced, he might, as a philosopher, admit the necessity of hurting him to frighten others. But when our neighbors do wrong, we sometimes feel the fitness of making them smart for it, whether they have repented or not. The feeling of fitness seems to me to be only vengeance in disguise.[18]

Clarence Darrow, in arguing against the imposition of the death penalty on behalf of two college students who had viciously murdered a fourteen-year-old boy for the thrill of it, asserted that the imposition of violent penalties tends to debase the community and make men less humane:

> They say we come here with a preposterous plea for mercy. When did any plea for mercy become preposterous in any tribunal in all the universe? Mr. Savage (the prosecutor) tell this court that if these boys are hanged there will be no more boys like these. Mr. Savage is an optimist. If these two boys die on the scaffold, which I can never bring myself to imagine, if they do die on the scaffold the details of this will be spread over the world. Every newspaper in the United States will carry a full account. Every newspaper of Chicago will be filled with the gruesome details. It will enter every home and every family. Will it make men better or make men worse? How many will be colder and crueler for it? How many will enjoy the details? And you can not enjoy human suffering without being affected for the worse. What influence will it have upon the millions of men who read it? What influence will it have upon the millions of women who read it, more sensitive, more impressionable, than men? What influence will it have upon the infinite number of children who will devour its details as Dickie Loeb (one of the defendants) has enjoyed reading detective stories?[19]

Central to these antiretributive views is the belief that societies should not treat individuals — not even the most dangerous and depraved individuals — in cruel and inhuman ways. Is it clear, however, that retribution has to be vengeful and vicious? Obviously Darrow thought so. Consider another of his comments in the final summary from the Loeb-Leopold murder case:

> When the public is interested and demands a punishment it thinks of only one punishment, and that is death; when the public speaks as one man it thinks only of killing. I have heard in the last six weeks nothing but the cry for blood. I have heard from the office of the state's attorney only ugly hate.[20]

But the fact that the demand for retribution is often a call for blood does not mean that retribution must be bloody. In the Loeb and Leopold case, one might agree with Darrow's position abhoring the death penalty and still feel that some punishment was necessary because it is fair and just that murderers be punished. It is even possible to imagine a case in which the imposition of *any* punishment (no matter how mild) would be justified only on retributive grounds, and in which the imposition of some punishment would be both fair and appropriate. The case of Adolph Eichmann is illustrative. You should know at the outset that Eichmann was executed for his crimes; but the point being made here is that *any* punishment that might have been imposed would have been justified solely on the basis of retribution.

Eichmann was one of the prime organizers of Germany's "final solution to the Jewish problem." He was instrumental in the development of concentration camps and mobile slaughterhouses in which six million European Jews were massacred.[21] While many of these murders took place in the comparatively antiseptic environment of gas chambers and ovens, many others involved the cruelest possible forms of torture. Parents who watched their children dig graves, stand in them and get shot, then had to cover the graves and dig their own. Eichmann, the planner, was fully responsible for the maintenance of these operations; he was also fully aware of what they actually looked like in the real world. He was a frequent visitor to the sites of the destruction he had organized. Fifteen years after the fact, he commented that he could still see "a woman with a child. She was shot and then the baby in her arms. His brains splattered all around, also over my leather coat."[22]

At the end of the war Eichmann, while professing himself ready "to jump with joy into my grave in the knowledge that I drag with me millions of jews,"[23] nevertheless took many precautions befitting a prudent man who was hoping to live. He destroyed all documents referring to the existence of his office and managed to make an escape to Argentina. There he lived, inconspicuously, harming no one, until in May of 1960 he was captured and abducted by Israeli agents.

As might be expected, there was a mighty clamor for his execution, and he did in fact become the only individual ever executed in Israel, where capital punishment exists only for the crime of genocide. Let us, however, put aside the issue of how severe a punishment would be appropriate and ask instead what possible justifications there might be for any punishment at all.

Deterrence seems hardly to be an issue. It is unreasonable to justify a punishment for Eichmann on the grounds that it might dissuade some future Eichmann or Hitler from aspiring to power. Men who would wage war are not likely to be deterred by the thought that if they lose they might be punished; presumably the possibility of losing is the thing that might deter them.

Similarly, incapacitation seems hardly to be an issue. However dangerous and hateful Eichmann might have been during the years of Nazi power in Germany, he had not during the fifteen years between the war's end and his capture hurt a single soul. He was no longer a menace or threat of any type. Whatever justification there might be for punishing Eichmann, surely it was not that he was too dangerous to be out on the streets.

Still putting aside the question of whether he ought to have been executed, let us consider whether he ought to have been left alone. If neither deterrence nor incapacitation require the imposition of punishment, then punishment is either unjustifiable or appropriate solely on the grounds that men who have offended in so cruel and vicious a manner deserve to have something happen to them. The death sentence was retributive; but a prison sentence would also have been based on retribution. Indeed, even if Eichmann had been required to work in hospitals aiding the aged and infirm victims of his concentration camps, the sentence would have been derived not from utilitarian principles of penology, but from the feeling that so vicious a crime requires that some price be exacted.

The argument being made here is not that retribution ought to be a major element in the sentencing of all offenders, but only that it may be an appropriate consideration in some cases. Even in a civilized and humane society, people may sometimes feel the appropriateness of doing something — not necessarily something bloody or cruel, but something — to individuals who have offended in particularly vicious and unacceptable ways. Thus, it may be said that deterrence, incapacitation, and retribution are all part of the traditional justification for imposing criminal sanctions.

There is an additional justification for the imposition of criminal sanctions: to provide rehabilitative services. The rehabilitative ideal has influenced the development of adult criminal justice systems, but it has particularly significant impact in the world of juvenile justice.

Juvenile Justice and the Case for Rehabilitation

It is widely believed that with hard work and good intentions the criminal can be transformed into a better man.[24] Everyone is supposed to gain in the process: the offender is helped, and his reformation serves to protect society against future offenses. Appealing though it is, the rehabilitative ideal is subject to some very serious criticisms. For a start, it is not clear that anyone actually knows how to rehabilitate offenders.[25] Beyond that, there is the danger that therapeutic jargon may be used to hide traditional punitive behaviors. Dean Francis Allen of the University of Michigan Law School commented on this many years ago:

> Too often the vocabulary of therapy has been exploited to serve a public-relations function. Recently, I visited an institution devoted to the diagnosis and treatment of disturbed children. The institution had been established with high hopes and, for once, with the enthusiastic support of the state legislature. Nevertheless, fifty minutes of an hour's lecture, delivered by a supervising psychiatrist before we toured the building, were devoted to custodial problems. This fixation on problems of custody was reflected in the institutional arrangements which included, under a properly euphemistic label, a cell for solitary confinement. Even more disturbing was the tendency of the staff to justify these custodial measures in therapeutic terms. Perhaps on occasion the requirements of institutional security and treatment coincide. But the inducements to self-deception in such situations are strong and all too apparent. In short, the language of therapy has frequently provided a formidable obstacle to a realistic analysis of the conditions that confront us. And realism in considering these problems is the one quality we require above all others.[26]

Nevertheless, it is clear that rehabilitation is generally regarded as a humane alternative to punishment, and that in the forseeable future correctional programs will seek to justify themselves in terms of their capacity to help rather than their potential to punish. It may be wondered why this concern for rehabilitation has only recently begun to develop (a century, after all, is a short time in the history of criminal law). The answer appears to be more complex than simply that men are becoming more civilized and humane (a questionable proposition at best); the emergence of the rehabilitative ideal had to await the development of a body of social scientific theory that would cause men to think about the possibility of actually achieving therapeutic reform in individuals. Think back to Chapter 2; all the explantations of delinquency discussed there were products of the post-Darwin world.

The reformers who began the movement to replace punishment with treatment in the last years of the nineteenth century were not merely humanitarians; they were also positivists. The impact of scientific positivism on the generation that "discovered" it was tremendous; they believed that new scientific knowledge would make it possible to restructure and improve the world. The generation before them had believed the universe to be mysterious and incomprehensible. The generation after them was to believe the universe to be rational, an entity whose mysteries must be subject to unraveling. The transition took place during their lives with such events as the discovery of the atom, the promulgation of the theory of evolution, and the emergence of the social sciences. The reformers who introduced considerations of treatment into the law marched beneath the banner of scientific positivism, buoyed by the belief that human behavior is the product of antecedent causes, and that knowledge of the causes permits planned intervention to facilitate behavioral change. Enthusiastic, zealous, and firm in the belief that their new understanding of human behavior gave them the power to change it, the reformers argued for the creation of institutions based on the rehabilitative ideal.

The fact that the reform movement focused on the establishment of special courts for children rather than on radical modifications of the techniques used to process adult offenders was no mere accident. The juvenile court was born in this age of reform[27] because the reformers were not only positivists, they were also child savers. Their argument that juvenile offenders should be treated with special care was derived from two main considerations: (1) that children are not altogether responsible for their behavior; and (2) that the state has an affirmative duty to help "socialize" children.

Childhood and Responsibility

The criminal law has always recognized that it is inappropriate to punish people who are not responsible for their behavior. Punishment is appropriate only for those who are culpable and blameworthy. The label "criminal" is not affixed to all those who harm others, but only to those whose harmful acts are purposeful. Thus it is that accidents are not crimes,[28] that insanity is a defense to a criminal accusation,[29] and that the criminal prosecution of children under the age of seven has never been permitted.[30] The reformers, knowing that children do not magically become mature or responsible at seven, merely argued for an extension.

Their argument was strengthened by the developing body of social scientific theory that holds that patterns of human behavior are molded in childhood by environmental conditions. In this view, the delinquency of the child is primarily evidence of parental failure. A

child in trouble with the law does not deserve punishment and will not benefit from it. Rather, he deserves (as all children deserve) firm but solicitous care and custody. If a child's parents are unable or unwilling to provide such care and custody, then the state must intervene *on his behalf.*

The State as Parent

To the reformers, the manner in which a society responds to youthful misconduct was not primarily an issue of penology, or of criminal law; it was part of the broader problem of creating a utopian social order.

> If education could be converted from the "sterile" dissemination of a certain body of information to a means of adjusting men "in a healthful relation to nature and their fellow men," so the system of justice, at least as applied to children, could also be made to serve the same end.[31]

Thus the State, acting through its juvenile courts, was not to intervene in order to further such traditional penological values as deterrence, incapacitation, and retribution; rather, it was to undertake the general tutelage of a child in much the same way that "wise" parents would. Judge Julian Mack, one of the first and finest juvenile court judges, summarized this position as follows:

> There is a . . . (fine and noble) legal conception hidden away in our history that . . . (should be) invoked for the purpose of dealing with the youngster that has gone wrong. That is the conception that the State is the higher parent; that it has an obligation, not merely a right, but an obligation, toward its children; and that is a specific obligation to step in when the natural parent, either through viciousness or inability, fails so to deal with the child that it no longer goes along the right path that leads to good, sound, adult citizenship.[32]

This "noble" conception, generally referred to as the *parens patriae* doctrine, was the major assumption around which the juvenile justice system was constructed. Under the influence of this doctrine the juvenile courts became less concerned with the specific nature of the offense the child was alleged to have committed than with the child's *condition.* The notion that the punishment should fit the crime was replaced by the notion that the treatment plan should fit the offender. Thus, the issues that the juvenile court reformers wanted addressed in case hearings were very different from the issues traditionally addressed in criminal cases. Instead of focusing on the issue of factual innocence or guilt, it was suggested that the most important information for the court to obtain was as follows:[33]

1. Cause of the complaint.
2. The child's developmental history, habits, and conduct — including previous delinquency.
3. Home conditions:
   a. composition of the family.
   b. type of dwelling; and living and sleeping arrangements.
   c. conditions in the home which may have a special relation to the child's conduct.
   d. constructive possibilities in the home.
4. The child and his school:
   a. present standing with reference to academic progress and conduct.
   b. school history.
5. The child's working history (if he has been employed).
6. The child's recreational activities and connections with churches, clubs, and social agencies.

The Juvenile Court's job was to determine *why* a child misbehaved and to help him change his ways. This emphasis on helping children is obviously very attractive. It represents an attempt to introduce humanitarian and scientific principles into the law. In historical perspective, however, it can be seen that the desire to replace the traditional values — deterrence, incapacitation, and retribution — with a new emphasis on rehabilitation was responsible for the diminution of the procedural rights of children — a change that in recent years has become a very important issue. The right to resist intervention has traditionally been more readily available to adults whom the state wished to punish than to children whom the state wished to help.

The Rehabilitative Ideal and the Rights of Children

The justification for the procedural rights afforded an adult in a criminal case is that, if the accused is convicted, something valuable is to be taken away from him — his liberty. Children, it was argued, are not entitled to liberty, but to warm, loving, solicitous care and custody. Should a child be adjudicated delinquent, the state must make such custody available. Consistent with the *parens patriae* doctrine, the nation's juvenile courts conceptualized themselves as seeking to provide children in trouble with the type of care they might receive at the hands of "wise" parents; the reformers held that the relationship between a parent and child — even an erring child — can not be regulated by the same rules that apply in felony prosecutions involving adults. The reformers were convinced not only that the usual rules of criminal procedure were unnecessary, but also that many of those rules would interfere with the attempt to provide regenerative therapeutic treatment. Throughout the nation, appellate courts accepted this logic and ruled that the nonpunitive intentions of the juvenile court made its proceedings noncriminal in nature.

> The natural parent needs no (due) process (of law) to temporarily deprive his child of its liberty by confining it in its own home, to save it and to shield it from the consequences of persistence in a career of waywardness, nor is the state, when compelled, as *parens patriae*, to take the place of the father for the same purpose required to adopt any process as a means of placing its hands upon the child to lead it into one of its courts.[34]

Such decisions freed the juvenile courts from the traditional due process restraints that are at the core of American criminal procedure.

Defense attorneys became, at best, infrequent participants in juvenile courts. The proceedings were conceptualized as neither criminal nor adversary,[35] therefore the participation of an attorney did not seem to the reformers to be necessary. Indeed, such a presence might even detract from the desired informal and therapeutic relationship between the child and the court.

Similarly, the privilege against self-incrimination (guaranteed in criminal prosecutions by the fifth and fourteenth amendments) did not have much force in the juvenile courts. No doubt the reformers felt that the right to remain silent would undermine the very nature of the juvenile courts. After all, the judge was viewed primarily as a clinician; and successful therapy is impossible with a child whose response to questions is: "I plead the fifth."

For similar reasons, jury trials were not permitted in juvenile court. The reformers' aim was to allow no agent — neither lawyer, nor the fifth amendment, nor even a jury — to stand between the child and the court. It was feared that the presence of a jury would make informality impossible and might even undermine the confidentiality of the proceedings. Furthermore, the *parens patriae* doctrine lent itself to an argument against the use of juries: as one court put it, "whether the child deserves to be saved by the state is no more a question for a jury than whether the father, if able to save it, ought to save it."[36]

Similar propositions were invoked to permit a relaxation of the usual rule that convictions be based on *proof beyond a reasonable doubt*. Juveniles could be adjudicated delinquent on less sufficient evidence. Judge Ben Lindsey of the Denver Juvenile Court justified this procedure as follows:

> The whole proceeding is in the interest of the child and not to degrade him or even to punish him. We do not protect the child by discharging him because there is no legal evidence to convict, as would be done in a criminal case when we know that he has committed the offense. This is to do him a great injury, for he is simply encouraged in the prevalent opinion among city children . . . that it is all right to lie all they can, to cheat all they can, to steal all they can, so long as they "do not get caught" or that you have "no proof."[37]

It is important to note that the erosion of the rights of children was neither gradual nor malicious. Due process of law simply was not compatible with the humanitarian zeal of the founders of the juvenile justice system. Thus, in pursuit of the rehabilitative ideal, the ideal of justice came to be largely canceled out.

The Re-Introduction of Due Process Values

In recent years the therapeutic model of justice has come under serious attack. The argument that children, regardless of their factual innocence or guilt, deserve to receive appropriate rehabilitative services has increasingly often been countered with the argument that children, like everyone else, deserve to be left alone unless the state can prove their guilt beyond a reasonable doubt in a fundamentally fair hearing. In addition, the argument has increasingly often been made that rehabilitation is not actually being achieved by institutions in the juvenile justice system.[38] Doubts about the fairness of juvenile court hearings and uncertainty about the extent to which rehabilitation has actually been realized have fueled the fires of a new reform movement. This movement for the reintroduction of constitutional rights has been based on two types of criticism of the juvenile courts. One challenges the appropriateness of the *parens patriae* doctrine in a democracy: the other, while not actually critical of the state-as-parent concept, suggests that the juvenile courts have failed to fulfill the responsibilities to children which that doctrine imposes upon them. Both positions lead toward the conclusion that continued procedural informality is unacceptable.

Criticism of Parens Patriae

Proponents of the *parens patriae* doctrine maintain that the juvenile courts cannot be considered punitive because they are merely providing the decent custodial care and firm limits that children in trouble with the law are presumably lacking at home. The essence of the *parens patriae* position is that due process safeguards are not required in juvenile court cases because the entire proceeding is in the child's interests: children are entitled not necessarily to liberty, but to constructive care.

Critics of the *parens patriae* doctrine argue that the classification of any group of people as not entitled to liberty in their dealings with governmental agencies tends to undermine the delicate balance between individual freedom and state power which a democratic government must seek to maintain.

> 'The mere deprivation of liberty, however benign the administration of the place of confinement, is undeniably punishment.' This proposition may be rephrased as follows: Measures which subject individuals to the substantial and involuntary deprivation of their liberty are essentially punitive in character, and this reality is not altered by the facts that the motivations that prompt incarceration are to provide therapy or otherwise contribute to the person's well-being or reform. As such, these measures must be closely scrutinized to insure that power is being applied consistently with those values of the community that justify interferences with liberty for only the most clear and compelling reasons.[39]

The inference to be drawn from this position is quite clear: courts should deal only with individuals whose behavior is so intolerable as to threaten the societal fabric, and even then only when the individual's guilt has been satisfactorily proven through a procedural system that has safeguards against erroneous accusations. The value of the rehabilitative ideal is seen as something less than the value of justice. These critics feel that juvenile courts must be conceptualized not primarily as helping agencies, but as courts of law.

> A child brought before the court has a right to demand, not only the benevolent concern of the tribunal, but justice. And one may rightly wonder as to the value of therapy purchased at the expense of justice. The essential point is that the issues of treatment and therapy be kept clearly distinct from the question of whether the person committed the acts which authorize the intervention of state power in the first instance.[40]

Criticism of the Juvenile Justice System's Functioning as Parens Patriae

The second position does not challenge the propriety of the *parens patriae* doctrine per se, but rather questions the ability of the juvenile courts to fulfill the responsibilities of surrogate parents.[41] This line of argument has it that the history of the juvenile courts is a history of unfulfilled promises to children; having broken these promises, the courts have forfeited their legal and moral justifications for procedural informality.

One such promise has always been that findings of delinquency are to carry neither legal nor social stigma. But the police records of youngsters are often kept on the same open "blotters" as those of adults, and confidentiality of court records is so often breached that there is no real protection from the stigma that accompanies public knowledge that one has committed a wrongful act.[42]

The promise that juvenile court hearings are to be easily understood, fair, and consonant with the treatment process has gone unfulfilled, in large measure because judges have been unable to do the job required of them. According to the original paradigm, children's court judges were to have not only legal training, but also a "thorough knowledge of psychology, mental hygiene, sociology and anthropology, at least those branches of anthropology that deal with criminology, cultural history of the race and racial traits. . . ."[43] In practice, judges throughout the nation have been hampered by a lack of training, by overloaded calendars, and by time-consuming administrative responsibilities.[44]

In a sense the most basic promise of the juvenile court movement has been that children will receive from the court treatment of the same nature as might be received from parents, and that where institutionalization is required, the conditions will be healthful.[45] Here, too, there appears to have been more honor in the breach of the court's obligations than in the observance. The conditions under which children are sometimes institutionalized are nothing less than shameful. There are "reform schools" throughout the country in which it is common for children to be beaten with straps,[46] slapped and punched by guards,[47] tied to their beds for days on end,[48] and held for prolonged periods of time in solitary confinement.[49] As recently as 1969 Howard James, writing in *The Christian Science Monitor,* reported what he saw:

> It is hard to believe that in the late twentieth century the American people would sanction such brutal treatment of children. Perhaps the human race is not far removed from those animals that attack their young.
>
> One can safely compare what happens in some reform schools with the process used in converting virile Africans into shuffling slaves in the early days of our nation. One sees this same head-hanging shuffling in certain juvenile prisons in North and South Carolina, in Ohio and Indiana and Illinois, or in Washington and Oregon — and at points between.
>
> Testimony of members of the Pueblo's crew (American seamen who had been held captive and tortured by North Koreans) indicates they were treated little worse by their North Korean captors than are some inmates in the Indiana Boys' School, the Indiana Reformatory in Pendleton, the Arkansas prison system, the John C. Richards School in South Carolina, the Florida School for Boys, and other institutions across the United States.[50]

Even aside from such atrocities, it can be argued that the most decent and humane institutions for children offer a standard of care that is less than the original promised by the juvenile court reformers. Institutional programs are often so underdeveloped and understaffed that one cannot speak of them in any sense as the equivalent of parental care and protection. Low salary levels make it very difficult for institutions to recruit and retain competent professional staff; and paraprofessional salaries are often so low that it is unlikely that people can be found who will adequately fill the role of surrogate parents.[51] The most pernicious consequence of these staffing problems is that institutional programs are often inadequate to keep children active, happy, and mentally healthy. Once again Howard Jame's observations are illustrative:

> One of the worst weaknesses of institutions is lack of activity for active children. The night I visited the Ferris School in Delaware one staff member was absent and two cottages were combined with only one man to supervise. Boys were crowded into two noisy rooms with little to do.
>
> In South Carolina boys went to their crowded dormitories and sat on their beds in their underwear after supper.
>
> In Indiana teenage boys were put to bed at 8 p.m. because of lack of staff. There is an inoperative swimming pool on the grounds and a gym. Staff members take boys out to play for short periods after supper "when they are in the mood." For some guards this means once every week at best.
>
> I was urged not to visit the Indiana Boys' School on Good Friday because the employees get the day off and the institution is "shut down." That means a skeleton crew and no program.
>
> Even at Maple Lane in Washington, one of the nation's finest reform schools, there is little activity on a Sunday afternoon. The Sunday I visited Maple Lane I found girls deeply depressed because they had no visitors.[52]

All this evidence that the state has failed to keep its promises to treat children with the loving care and solicitousness of a "good" parent supports the argument that the responsibilities of the *parens patriae* doctrine have gone unfulfilled and that the juvenile courts have lost their claim to procedural informality. When the state truly acts to protect the health and well-being of children, a grant of far-reaching power may be acceptable; when, however, the claim is a mere sham, belied by even the most casual observations, the due process proponents insist that "there is neither legal nor moral justification for the circumvention of constitutional protections or the assertion of state control in the name of *parens patriae.*"[53]

Both of these positions — that *parens patriae* is an inappropriate concept in a democracy and that, appropriate or not, the responsibilities imposed by the doctrine have never been adequately fulfilled — underlie the recent revisions in juvenile court procedure imposed by the United States Supreme Court; all new developments in the nation's juvenile justice systems must be evaluated in the light of these revisions. It is appropriate at this point to review briefly the major elements of the recent constitutional history of the juvenile court.

Legal Revisionism

In *Kent* v. *United States*[54] the Supreme Court had occasion for the first time to review the operation of a juvenile court. The case raised only very narrow issues, but the decision put the legal community on notice that the Supreme Court was not altogether satisfied with the operation of the juvenile justice system.

On September 2, 1961, sixteen-year-old Morris Kent entered an apartment in Washington, D.C. He raped the woman who lived there and stole her wallet. Because he left fingerprints in the apartment, Kent was easily traced by the police, who took him into custody on the afternoon of September 5, 1961. The following afternoon Kent's mother retained a lawyer, who promptly conferred with the Social Service Director of the Juvenile Court. They discussed the possibility that the Juvenile Court might waive jurisdiction. (Waiver, you will recall, is the process by which a juvenile court declines to take a case which it has the legal power to try, and sends the accused child to an adult criminal court for trial. Generally, waiver is contemplated only for older juveniles alleged to have committed serious crimes.) The consequences of a decision to waive jurisdiction had the potential to be very important for Kent: if the juvenile court retained jurisdiction and adjudicated him delinquent, the maximum sentence could have been treatment in a reform school until reaching the age of twenty-one; a criminal court, on the other hand, could have sentenced Kent to death. As might be expected, Kent's lawyer made it clear that he opposed waiver of jurisdiction. Nevertheless, a short time later the Juvenile Court judge entered an order waiving jurisdiction to the United States District Court for the District of Columbia. No hearing on the issue of waiver was ever held. Presumably the judge read Morris Kent's social service file and reached his decision on the basis of evidence contained in it. He did not provide the lawyer with a copy of the file, nor with an opportunity to discuss its content.

The case reached the Supreme Court in 1966. *The question was whether Kent, who had been convicted in the District and sentenced to a term of 30 to 90 years in prison, had been unfairly denied the protection of the juvenile court.* The Juvenile Court Act of the District of Columbia provided that the Juvenile Court could waive jurisdiction in serious cases, but only after conducting "a full investigation." The Supreme Court decided that a "full investigation" had not taken place, for such an investigation would have permitted Kent an opportunity to state his side of the case.

We do not consider whether, on the merits, Kent should have been transferred; but there is no place in our system of law for reaching a result of such tremendous consequences without ceremony — without hearing, without effective assistance of counsel, without a statement of reasons. It is unconceivable that a court of justice dealing with adults, with respect to a similar issue, would proceed in this manner. It would be extraordinary if society's special concern for children, as reflected in the District of Columbia's Juvenile Court Act permitted this procedure. We hold it does not.[55]

Strictly speaking *Kent* was not a constitutional case. The Supreme Court decided it by interpreting the statutory requirement of a "full investigation" to mean that the Juvenile Court judge had exceeded his authority by making the waiver decision without a hearing at which Kent and his lawyer could have presented evidence to support their contention that the case should have stayed in juvenile court. The Supreme Court reached its interpretation, however, by reading the statute "in the context of constitutional principles relating to due process and the assistance of counsel."[56] In essence, the Supreme Court said that the legislature that wrote the statute must have intended for there to be waiver hearings, otherwise the statute would not have been constitutional. *Thus,* Kent *became the first case in which the Supreme Court ever suggested that "constitutional principles" might be applicable to juvenile court procedures. The particular procedures involved in that case were related to the process of waiving jurisdiction; but the Court dropped several broad hints that if an appropriate case came before it, it would be willing to consider whether other juvenile court procedures were consistent with the Constitution.* Indeed, the Court almost seemed to be inviting a future challenge on broader and more basic issues.

There is much evidence that some juvenile courts, including that of the District of Columbia, lack the personnel, facilities and techniques to perform adequately as representatives of the State in a *parens patriae* capacity, at least with respect to children charged with law violation. There is evidence, in fact, that there may be grounds for concern that the child receives the worst of both worlds: that he gets neither the protections afforded adults nor the solicitous care and regenerative treatment postulated for children.[57]

Shortly thereafter the case of Gerald Francis Gault[58] provided the Supreme Court with the opportunity for which it had seemed to be looking.

Fifteen-year-old Gerald Gault was adjudicated delinquent in an Arizona juvenile court because he allegedly made an obscene telephone call.[59] His trial took place without any notice of the specific charges against him ever having been given either to him or to his parents (it is very hard, perhaps impossible, to prepare an adequate defense if you do not know in advance of the actual hearing what it is you are being charged with having done; imagine how you would feel if you were arrested this afternoon, told it was because you'd "done something wrong" and that a trial was scheduled for tomorrow morning). The family was never advised of a right to counsel. In addition, the woman who claimed to have received the obscene call was not present at the hearing and thus could not be cross-examined. Furthermore, Gault was questioned by the judge without having been advised of the privilege against self-incrimination. An adult guilty of the same offense could receive a maximum punishment of two months' imprisonment or a fine between five and fifty dollars after adjudication; however, young Gault was committed for treatment to the State Industrial School for a period of time to extend until he was "cured" or until his twenty-first birthday, whichever came first.

Gault's family attacked the constitutionality of the adjudication in the Supreme Court of Arizona; but they were unsuccessful. That court stood four-square on traditional juvenile court philosophy. Prior notice of the exact charge was said to be unnecessary because "the policy of the juvenile law is to hide youthful errors from the full gaze of the public and bury them in the graveyard of the forgotten past." The absence of counsel was said to be inconsequential because "the parent and the probation officer may be relied upon to protect the infant's interest." And the denial of the privilege against self-incrimination was found to be proper because "the necessary flexibility for individualized treatment" would be enhanced by it.[60]

On all three points the Arizona court was reversed by the Supreme Court. *In re Gault* stands for the proposition that juveniles must be accorded "the essentials of due process and fair treatment."[61] Specifically, the Court held the following.

> 1. The child and his parents are entitled to a written notice of the charges which must "set forth the alleged misconduct with particularity," and which allows sufficient time for the preparation of a defense.[62]
> 2. The due process clause of the Fourteenth Amendment to the United States Constitution requires that in cases in which commitment

of a juvenile to an institution is possible "the child and his parent must be notified of the child's right to be represented by counsel retained by them, or if they are unable to afford counsel, that counsel will be appointed to represent the child."[63]

3. The Fifth Amendment right to remain silent is as "applicable in the case of juveniles, as it is with respect to adults."[64]

4. "We now hold that absent a valid confession, a determination of delinquency and an order of commitment to a state institution cannot be sustained in the absence of sworn testimony subjected to the opportunity for *cross-examination* in accordance with our law and constitutional requirements (emphasis added)."[65]

The logic underlying the Supreme Court's opinion is of particular importance. In large measure the decision seems to be based on the view that the juvenile justice system had not satisfactorily fulfilled the responsibilities imposed on it by the *parens patriae* doctrine. The court pointed out that the claim of confidentiality has been "more rhetoric than reality;"[66] it maintained that the adjudicatory process has been confusing and antitherapeutic.[67] Perhaps most important, the court found that the institutions to which juveniles are remanded fall far short of the standards suggested by the rehabilitative ideal.

> Ultimately . . . we confront the reality of that portion of the juvenile court process with which we deal in this case. A boy is charged with misconduct. The boy is committed to an institution where he may be restrained of liberty for years. It is of no constitutional consequence — and of limited practical meaning — that the institution to which he is committed is called an Industrial School. The fact of the matter is that, however euphemistic the title, a "receiving home" or an "industrial school" for juveniles is an institution of confinement in which the child is incarcerated for a greater or lesser time. His world becomes "a building with white-washed walls, regimented routine and institutional laws. . . . Instead of mother and father and sisters and brothers and friends and classmates, his world is peopled by guards, custodians, state employees, and "delinquents" confined with him for anything from waywardness to rape and homicide.[68]

All of this implies that, had the juvenile justice system been truer to its mission, the results in *Gault* might never have obtained. In essence, the Supreme Court declared that the informal procedures used by the juvenile courts were no longer permissible because the bedrock to which they were anchored — the notion that the state was functioning as a parent — was illusory rather than real. Due process rights were extended to children only when it became undeniably clear that the humanitarian ideals of the juvenile courts reformers had not been realized.

In the years since *Gault* (which was decided in 1967) two other very important juvenile court cases have reached the Supreme Court. One extended the rights of juveniles; the other indicated that children's rights need not be as extensive as the rights afforded adults accused of crime.

In *In re Winship*[69] (in 1970) the Supreme Court was called upon to decide how much proof is necessary to sustain a finding of delinquency. Adults can not be convicted of crimes unless the proof establishes *guilt beyond a reasonable doubt.* Traditionally children, however, have been adjudicated delinquent if a *preponderance of the evidence* suggested they had committed a prohibited act. In other words, a man could be found criminal only if there was no doubt he had committed the act in question, while a boy could be found delinquent if it seemed likely that he had committed the act in question. The guilt-beyond-a reasonable-doubt standard has always been considered basic in American law. Consider the following language from a 1952 dissenting opinion by Mr. Justice Felix Frankfurter, which was cited approvingly in the *Winship* decision:

> [I]t is the duty of the Government to establish . . . guilt beyond a reasonable doubt. This notion — basic in our law and rightly one of the boasts of a free society — is a requirement and a safeguard of due process of law. . . .[70]

This important due process right had never been viewed as applicable in juvenile court because of its inconsistency with the *parens patriae* doctrine. A troubled child, it was traditionally argued, should not be denied the help of the juvenile court merely because some doubt existed as to whether he committed a specific delinquent act:

> [A] child's best interest is not necessarily, or even probably, promoted if he wins in the particular inquiry which may bring him to the juvenile court.[71]

In *Winship,* as in *Gault,* the Supreme Court found the traditional juvenile court philosphy to be unconvincing. The fact that a delinquency proceeding can result in an extensive period of incarceration in a reformatory was again viewed as decisive; the Court was of the opinion that a child should not have to face the possibility of "institutional confinement on proof insufficient to convict him were he an adult."[72]

> We therefore hold . . . that, where a . . . child is charged with an act . . . which renders him liable to confinement for . . . years, then, as a matter of due process . . . the case against him must be proved beyond a reasonable doubt.[73]

After *Winship* was decided it appeared that the Supreme Court was fast moving toward the position that delinquency proceedings for children would have to be heard in the exact same way as criminal trials involving adults. Then, in 1971, in *McKeiver* v. *Pennsylvania,* the Court found a constitutional right of adults accused of crimes which is not also a right of children charged with delinquency: the right to a trial by jury. In asserting that juvenile courts do not have to provide jury trials, the Court took the position that even after *Kent, Gault,* and *Winship,* it was prepared to allow some procedural informality to remain in the juvenile justice system in order to facilitate the goal of providing helpful, regenerative care and treatment.

> 1. Some of the constitutional requirements attendant upon the state criminal trial have equal application to . . . state juvenile proceeding(s). . . . Among these are the rights to appropriate notice, to counsel, to confrontation and to cross-examination, and the privilege against self-incrimination. Included, also, is the standard of proof beyond a reasonable doubt.
> 2. The Court, however, has not yet said that *all* rights constitutionally assured to an adult accused of crime also are to be enforced or made available to the juvenile in his delinquency proceeding. Indeed, the Court specifically has refrained from going that far. (Quoting language from the *Kent* decision, which had also been cited approvingly in *In re Gault,* the Court said):
> "We do not mean by this to indicate that the hearing to be held must conform with all of the requirements of a criminal trial. . . ; but we do hold that the hearing must measure up to the essentials of due process and fair treatment."[74]

Thus, almost a decade after all the litigation began, it is possible to make a list of new procedural rights of children; but it is not possible to synthesize a clear, lucid, unified theory about the impact of constitutional requirements that children processed through juvenile courts be guaranteed a *fundamentally fair hearing.* Apparently such a hearing will be very similar in nature to a criminal trial; but the fact that the juvenile justice system aspires to help rather than punish children (even though there are serious doubts about how helpful it actually is) still justifies the use of procedural informalities that would not be accepted in a criminal court. These hybrid procedures are the subject of extended analysis in Chapter 9.

References

1. See, for example, Lowell J. Carr, *Delinquency Control* (New York: Harper & Brothers, 1940), p. 148; Henry H. Goddard, *Juvenile Delinquency* (New York: Dodd, Mead, 1921), pp. 1 - 3.

2. See, for example, Richard Wasserstrom, "Why Punish the Guilty?" *University* (Spring 1964), p. 14.

3. See, for example, Jeremy Bentham, *An Introduction to the Principles of Morals and Legislation,* ed. J. H. Burns and H. L. A. Hart (London: Athlone Press, 1970) pp. 11 - 33, 156 - 90; Mary P. Mack, ed., *A Bentham Reader* (New York: Pegasus, 1969).

4. *Deuteronomy* 19:16 - 22.

5. See, for example, Herbert Packer, *The Limits of the Criminal Sanction* (Stanford, Calif.: Stanford University Press, 1968), p. 39.

6. Ibid.

7. See, for example, Gerard Lauzon, *Sigmund Freud: The Man and His Theories,* trans. Patrick Evans (New York: Paul S. Eriksson, 1965), pp. 143 - 4; Franz Alexander, *The Scope of Psychoanalysis* 1921 - 1961 (New York: Basic Books, 1961). pp. 484 - 8.

8. For an excellent discussion of the types of offenses which are most likely to be deterred, and the situations in which deterrence is likely to take place, see William Chambliss, *Types of Deviance and the Effectiveness of Legal Sanctions,* 1967 Wis. L. Rev. 703. Chambliss distinguishes between goal-oriented "instrumental" crimes such as theft, and emotional "expressive" crimes such as murders which are committed for their own sake rather than as means to achieve some other goal; he suggests that "expressive" crimes are not easily deterrable, and that the deterrence of "instrumental" crimes depends not only on the severity of the punishment, but on the probability of being caught.

9. John Gosling and Dennis Craig, *The Great Train Robbery* (Indianapolis: Bobbs-Merrill, 1965), p. x.

10. Ibid., pp. 46 - 47.

11. Ibid., pp. 94 - 95.

12. Packer, *Limits of the Criminal Sanction,* pp. 48 - 50.

13. For an excellent discussion of this issue, see John Kaplan, *Criminal Justice: Introductory Cases and Materials* (Mineola, N.Y.: Foundation Press, 1973), p. 26.

14. See, "Trials: Helter Skelter," *Newsweek* 76 (August 10, 1970); 21 -

2; Steven V. Roberts, "Charlie Manson: One Man's Family," *New York Times Magazine* (Jan. 4, 1970), pp. 10 - 14.

15. See Patrick Devlin, *The Enforcement of Morals* (London: Oxford University Press, 1965) pp. 6 - 7.

16. See Ledger Wood, "Responsibility and Punishment," *Journal of Criminal Law and Criminality 28* (Jan.-Feb. 1938): 635 - 6; Meyer Levin; *Compulsion* (New York: Simon & Schuster, 1956), pp. 424 - 54.

17. *Leviticus* 25:17 - 22.

18. Oliver Wendell Holmes, *The Common Law,* ed. M. Howe, 1 (Cambridge, Mass.: Belknap Press of Harvard University Press, 1963), p. 39.

19. Irving Stone, *Clarence Darrow for the Defense,* (Garden City, N.Y.: Doubleday, Doran, 1941), pp. 414 - 15.

20. Ibid., p. 414.

21. For an excellent discussion of this case, see Gideon Hausner, *Justice in Jerusalem* (New York: Harper & Row, 1966).

22. Ibid., p. 75.

23. Ibid., p. 267.

24. See, for example, President's Commission on Law Enforcement and Administration of Justice, *Task Force Report: Corrections* (Washington, D.C.: U.S. Government Printing Office, 1967), pp. 2 - 4 especially.

25. See Packer, *Limits of the Criminal Sanction,* p. 55; American Friends Service Society, *Struggle for Justice* (New York: Hill & Wang, 1971).

26. Francis A. Allen, "Criminal Justice, Legal Values, and the Rehabilitative Ideal." Reprinted by special permission of the Journal of Criminal Law. Criminology & Police Science, Copyright © 1959 by Northwestern University School of Law, Vol. 50, No. 3.

27. The first Juvenile Court was created in Chicago in 1899; see W. V. Stapleton and L. E. Teitelbaum, *In Defense of Youth* (New York: Russel Sage Foundation, 1972), p. 130.

28. See, for example, *Fain* v. *Commonwealth* 78 Ky. 183, 39 Am. Rep. 213 (1879).

29. See Abraham Goldstein, *The Insanity Defense* (New Haven: Yale University Press, 1967).

30. Stapleton and Teitelbaum, *In Defense of Youth,* p. 1.

31. Ibid., p. 15.

32. Julian Mack, "The Chancery Procedures in the Juvenile Court," in *The Child, The Clinic, and the Court,* ed. J. Addams (New York: New Republic, 1927), pp. 311 - 12.

33. Herbert Lou, *Juvenile Courts in the United States* (Chapel Hill: University of North Carolina Press, 1927).

34. *Commonwealth* v. *Fisher,* 213 Pa. 48, 53, 62 At. 198, 200 (1905).

35. Stapleton and Teitelbaum, *In Defense of Youth,* p. 31.

36. *Commonwealth* v. *Fisher.*

37. Ben Lindsey, "The Juvenile Court of Denver," in *Children's Court in the United States,* ed. S. Barrows (Washington, D.C.: U.S. Government Printing Office, 1904), p. 107.

38. See, for example, Howard James, *Children In Trouble: A National*

Scandal (New York: D. McKay, 1970).

39. Allen, "Criminal Justice, Legal Values" pp. 226, 229.

40. Ibid., p. 230.

41. Oman Ketcham, "The Unfulfilled Promise of the American Juvenile Court," in *Justice for the Child,* ed. M. Rosenheim, (New York: Free Press, 1962).

42. Ibid., pp. 28 - 30.

43. Ibid., p. 22.

44. Ibid., p. 31.

45. Ibid., p. 27 - 28.

46. See James, *Children In Trouble,* p. 88.

47. Ibid., pp. 90 - 93.

48. See, for example, the 1971 National Broadcasting Corporation television special, *This Child is Rated X.*

49. The N.B.C. documentary *This Child is Rated X* is illustrative of this point too. Also see James, *Children in Trouble,* p. 88, also p. 94:
   "I found hundreds of boys and girls around the nation locked in solitary-confinement cells for days, weeks, even months."

50. James, *Children In Trouble,* p. 88.

51. See, for example, Pennsylvania Advisory Council on Juvenile Delinquency Planning, *1971 Comprehensive Juvenile Delinquency Prevention and Control Plan for Pennsylvania,* p. 39.

52. James, *Children In Trouble,* pp. 99 - 100.

53. Ketcham, "The Unfulfilled Promise of the American Juvenile Court," p. 27.

54. 383 U.S. 541.

55. Ibid., p. 545.

56. Ibid.

57. Ibid., pp. 555 - 6.

58. *In Re Gault* 387 U.S. 1 (1967). Note that the terminology used in juvenile courts cases reflects the rehabilitation orientation of the juvenile courts. Children are taken into custody, not arrested; the hearings are not *People* v. *Gault,* but *In Re Gault,* because the whole matter is considered in the child's interest, not against him.

59. The remarks which the woman who received the phone call claimed to have heard took the form of three questions: "Do you give any?" "Are your cherries ripe today?" "Do you have big bombers?" Nicholas N. Kittrie, *The Right to Be Different: Deviance and Enforced Therapy* (Baltimore: Johns Hopkins Press, 1971), p. 122.

60. Application of Gault, 99 Ariz. 181, 407 P. 2d 760 (1960).

61. 387 U.S. 1, at 30 (1967).

62. Ibid., p. 33.

63. Ibid., p. 41.

64. Ibid., p. 55.

65. Ibid., p. 57.

66. Ibid., p. 24.

67. Ibid., p. 26.

68. Ibid., p. 27 (emphasis added).
69. 397 U.S. 358 (1970).
70. Ibid., p. 362.
71. From the decision of the Court of Appeals of New York State in *In Re Winship* 24 N.Y. 2d at 199, 299 N.Y.S. 2d, at 417, 247 N.E. 2d at 255.
72. *In Re Winship,* 397 U.S. 358, p. 367 (1970).
73. Ibid., p. 368.
74. *McKeiver* v. *Pennsylvania,* 403 U.S. 528, 535 (1971).

9 Juvenile Court Process

Truth happens to be an idea. It becomes true, is made true by events. Its verity is in fact an event, a process: the process namely of its verifying itself, its veri-fication. Its validity is the process of its valid-ation.

— *William James*

Other agencies may divert youngsters or initiate the process of encapsulation; only the juvenile court can formally determine that a child is delinquent. The immediate consequences of a finding of delinquency may be as severe as commitment to a state institution until the child shall reach the age of twenty-one. The stigma attached to such treatment may haunt a child well into adult life.

It might be anticipated that decision making in the juvenile courts would be characterized by form and ceremony designed to guarantee careful weighing of evidence and thoughtful deliberation about the child's innocence or guilt. The ideal model of a juvenile court might well be expected to resemble the ideal model of a court that metes out justice to adults.

Adults charged with crimes are tried in criminal courts which are (or are supposed to be) characterized by conflict. The interests of the individual (who wishes to preserve his liberty and maintain his reputation) are conceived as antithetical to those of the state (which seeks to prove his guilt and restrict his freedom). The representatives of each party have a strong personal stake in making their cases as persuasive as possible; defense attorneys and prosecutors alike build their reputations and careers on the ability to win cases. A criminal trial with all the trappings of adversarial procedure may be analogized to a deadly earnest sporting event.

Not only are most sporting events zero-sum games in which one player must lose and the other win; even more fundamental is the condition that each player try to win. . . . Within the ethic of the institution, it is understood that each fighter will attempt to throw his best punches, that each will strain to achieve victory. Otherwise the fight will not be considered genuine. *Procedure is as important as outcome.*[1]

Most criminal trials, it is true, do not actually have all the trappings of adversarial procedure. Prosecutors and defense attorneys often arrange "deals" which give a partial victory to each.[2] Nevertheless, the possibility of conflict is ever present; and the institutions and norms of the criminal justice system are compatible with and accepting of that possibility.

In the juvenile court, as was pointed out in the last chapter, the conflict mores of the adult court were never adopted. The court's goal was to provide troubled children with needed care, custody, and treatment; and in the pursuit of those objectives, conflict was seen as inappropriate and impermissible.

> . . . There was almost a change in *mores* when the Juvenile Court was established. The child was brought before the judge with no one to prosecute him and none to defend him — the judge and all concerned were merely trying to find out what could be done on his behalf. The element of conflict was absolutely eliminated.[3]

The first juvenile courts replaced the formal processes of the criminal justice system with informalities intended both to spare the child from psychological trauma and to facilitate a new focus on the child's *condition* rather than on his guilt. The participation of lawyers in children's courts was perceived as unnecessary and undesirable because it might interfere with the relationship between the judge and the troubled child he sought to help. "The accoutrements of due process . . . — public trials, shields against self-incrimination, adversary inquiry into the single event which brought the child to court — seem (ed) irrelevent."[4] Thus, the juvenile court evolved into a tribunal unique in the history of American jurisprudence.

All that began to change, however, in 1967. The decision of the Supreme Court in *In re Gault*[5] and other cases discussed in the last chapter mandated the nation's juvenile courts to accommodate to basic elements of due process of law. Children were afforded the right to remain silent and were assured of representation by counsel. Presumably children's courts were to be restructured — made more compatible with the conflict orientation they had sought for so long to avoid.

It is folly to believe that complex social organizations can be transformed overnight. At best, social reality *approximates* the constitutional interpretations of the Supreme Court. Just as public schools did not immediately integrate, even though the High Court found that the Constitution required it, neither did juvenile courts immediately embrace due process standards even though the Court found that the Constitution mandated it. The 1970s have been a period of accommodation and compromise in the history of the juvenile court movement. If children's courts are not yet in conformity with the expectations of the Supreme Court, neither are they any longer in conformity with the intentions of the reformers who created them.

The purpose of this chapter is to examine the operation of modern juvenile courts. Although there are important differences from jurisdiction to jurisdiction, four major stages in the operation of all juvenile courts may be identified: (1) intake; (2) determination of jurisdiction; (3) adjudication; and (4) disposition. In the remainder of this chapter we shall look at each of these stages, focusing attention on the interaction between legalistic forces which are striving to refashion the juvenile court into a major component of a conflict-tolerant justice system, and the traditional forces which are seeking to maintain the ethic of cooperation which has been the court's legacy.

Intake

Diversion from the formal processes of adjudication continues to be a major characteristic of the juvenile justice system right to the doors of the courthouse. Approximately half of all youngsters taken into custody by the police are never required to walk through those doors because their cases are informally "adjusted" at intake.[6]

There is evidence that youngsters held in detention are less likely to benefit from an informal adjustment than are youngsters who are not detained during the pretrial period. Only 43 percent of detained youngsters are released at intake as compared to 64 percent of nondetained youngsters.[7] These data are subject to two possible interpretations: (1) that detention decision makers are reasonably effective in identifying guilty, dangerous, or troubled youngsters; or (2) that non detained youngsters, by being well-behaved during the pretrial period, are able to cultivate the appearance of decency and mental health.

Juvenile courts are unique among trial courts in exercising control over the cases which will be brought to their attention. Control of this type has existed in the juvenile courts since their inception, and has been justified as essential to maximize the effective use of scarce resources available for treatment. One early observer described intake procedures as follows:

> One of the most important features of the juvenile-court procedure is the elimination of cases that do not require formal court action or prolonged treatment and the informal or unofficial adjustment of problems involved in these cases. Prior to the filing of a petition, children are often given treatment and placed under supervision by common consent of all parties concerned when judges or probation officers deem that no formal judicial treatment or official determination of the child's status is necessary.[8]

Traditionally intake decisions have been the product of informal deliberations involving the child, his family, and a probation officer working for the court. Even in the post-*Gault* era, the supporting cast usual in criminal dramas has been conspicuously absent from intake hearings:[9] defense attorneys do not generally appear, and when present they are rarely active participants. There appear to be three reasons for that: the first is that many lawyers are co-opted into the therapeutic ideology of the juvenile court and believe it would be wrong to interfere in an informal process designed to make help available to a troubled youngster; the second is that many delinquency cases are assigned to public defenders whose caseloads are so excessive that they can not possibly give adequate attention to all their cases; the third is that most attorneys recognize that the discretion of a probation officer at intake is virtually unlimited and that a lawyer who is "too feisty" might be "punished" by the probation officer's refusing to agree to an informal adjustment for the accused.[10]

Juvenile court personnel have generally regarded the intake process as a last chance to give the child a break. They have seen their role as dispensing "diversion" to half the youngsters who come to court, rather than as denying it to the other half. This benevolent self-perception has caused them to expect cooperation from all those involved with the defense; lawyers, because they have shared that perception, or because they've been overworked, or because they've decided that antagonizing the probation officer is a bad tactic, have generally adopted a nonadversarial posture.

It is reasonable to expect, however, that intake hearings may involve more adversarial conflict in the future. There is a growing body of literature that suggests that lawyers are increasingly *unimpressed* by the rehabilitative rhetoric of the juvenile court;[11] and there is pressure mounting for a reduction of public defender caseloads which would leave attorneys more time for involvement in each case. In addition, there are two strategic reasons why defense attorneys might want to fight harder at the intake hearing: one is that informal adjustments generally involve a referral to probation or to some community-based helping agency;[12] a lawyer with a good case might prefer to avoid intake altogether in an attempt to win his client's unconditional release at a trial. The second reason is to avoid making information available to the probation officer which might prove detrimental at subsequent stages of the judicial process. If a probation officer decides *not* to "adjust" a case informally, and a finding of delinquency is entered at the hearing, incriminating statements made at intake may be used to help determine disposition.[13] A lawyer's refusal to cooperate at intake (by advising his client to remain silent, for example) may actually protect a child eventually adjudicated delinquent against the imposition of a harsh sentence.

Determination of Jurisdiction

The term jurisdiction refers merely to the *power* of a court to hear a case. A court in California, for example, is without power to hear a case involving a New York resident alleged to have committed an offense in New York. Jurisdictional issues are related to more than just geography. For example, a juvenile court cannot hear cases involving offenses allegedly committed by adults. The age at which a person is said to be an adult is determined by statutes. In most states, juvenile courts have jurisdiction only over persons who are younger than seventeen years old.[14]

Until recently juvenile court jurisdiction over girls extended for a longer time than jurisdiction over boys. In Illinois, for example, a boy had to be under sixteen to be dealt with as a juvenile rather than as an adult offender, but girls were not considered adult until seventeen.[15] *In a liberated age this practice seems to be disappearing. Only Illinois, Oklahoma, and Texas still maintain such a distinction on the statute books, and state courts held those statutes to be unconstitutional.*[16]

Juvenile courts do not have jurisdiction over *all* youngsters within a given geographic area — only over children who have committed acts that would be considered crimes if committed by adults, over children who have committed status offenses, and over dependent-neglected children.

In thirty-eight states and the District of Columbia, children who have committed criminal acts are called "delinquent." Twelve states (Alaska, California, Hawaii, Idaho, Kentucky, Maine, Michigan, Missouri, Nevada, Oregon, Utah, and Virginia) use less stigmatizing terms such as "wards of the courts."[17] *All fifty states and the District of Columbia have statutes that bring status offenses such as "incorrigibility," "immorality," "waywardness," "idling," "beyond reasonable control of parents," "unruliness," and "in need of supervision" within juvenile court jurisdiction.*[18] *In twenty-five states and the District of Columbia, such children are identified as delinquent; in the other states less stigmatizing labels such as "child in need of supervision" are used.*[19]

Issues of geography, age, and nature of the offense are seldom of such complexity that separate jurisdictional hearings are necessary to determine whether a juvenile court can or should have a formal hearing to determine a child's innocence or guilt. Consequently jurisdictional hearings occur only rarely. In some cases, however, they are very important. A court may sometimes decide that a child's condition is such that it does not have jurisdiction over him — and may therefore order his unconditional release. In other cases a juvenile court that clearly has jurisdiction may decide to *waive* it, allowing the child to be tried and sentenced in an adult criminal court.

The Relevance of the Child's Condition

New York State has pioneered a new jurisdictional prerequisite for juvenile courts. In that state a child can not be adjudicated delinquent or found to be in need of supervision unless he "requires supervision, treatment, or (in the case of a delinquent) confinement."[20] The Uniform Juvenile Court Act has adopted a similar approach and suggests that juvenile courts have jurisdiction only over children "in need of treatment or rehabilitation."[21] The newly developed Juvenile Act in Pennsylvania has incorporated similar language.[22]

The importance of such provisions is that they allow a defense attorney to challenge the court's jurisdiction by maintaining that his client (while he may have committed the act in question) is not in need of treatment or other services. Let us briefly review the case of *Edwin M.* discussed in Chapter 4; it is a good illustration of the way in which a case can be removed from a court's jurisdiction if the alleged offender appears not to need the services the court traditionally supplies to those adjudicated delinquent:[23]

Five youngsters were involved in the case. They were charged with having fatally stabbed another youngster, an act that, if performed by an adult, would constitute the crime of murder. A series of pretrial motions, raised primarily by the defense, caused the hearing to be put off for two years. When the trial finally began, the youngsters' attorney moved to dismiss the petition on the ground that the boys were no longer in need of any rehabilitative treatment that the juvenile court might be able to provide. Social workers, teachers, and psychiatrists testified that the boys had made a good adjustment during the intervening years. It was not argued that they had become model citizens, only that they were making reasonable progress toward that goal. The court took the position that its power to adjudicate children delinquent is dependent not only on the commission of some delinquent act but also on their need for "supervision, treatment, or confinement."[24] As these youngsters no longer seemed to have such need, the court granted the motion to dismiss the petition.

Such a result in a criminal court dealing with adult offenders would be unimaginable. Criminal courts are primarily concerned not with the welfare of the offender but with such traditional penological values as deterrence, social protection, and retribution, each of which demands that individuals who commit murder receive some sort of punishment. In explaining his decision on Edwin M.'s disposition, Judge Guerreiro spoke of the special proportions of the rehabilitative ideal in juvenile courts:[25]

> The Family Court is not a Criminal Court with punitive objectives. The purpose of this court is to rehabilitate children and to make services available to them, not to vindicate private wrongs.

The importance of the decision in Edwin M.'s case derives not from the power of the court that decided it (for decisions of the Family Court of New York City have no binding precedential effect in any other court) but from the logic of the opinion. Surely the result in this case will encourage child advocates in states with similar statutory restrictions on juvenile court jurisdiction to make more frequent use of jurisdictional hearings. As more and more states follow New York's lead and the recommendations of the Uniform Juvenile Court Act, it is quite likely that jurisdictional hearings will begin to take on new importance.

Waiver of Jurisdiction

In all states except New York and Vermont, juvenile court judges are empowered, at least in some cases, to waive jurisdiction over a minor and order his transfer to the criminal court.[26] In thirty-five states and the District of Columbia there are minimum ages beneath which a child may not be transferred out of the juvenile justice system. The minimum age varies, however, from thirteen in Mississippi and Illinois to sixteen in several other states including California, Hawaii, New Jersey, Rhode Island, and Wisconsin.[27] In many states the alleged offense looms as the major determinant of whether a child may be transferred to the criminal justice system. In Pennsylvania and Massachusetts, for example, a child of any age may be sent to trial in a criminal court if he is alleged to have committed murder.[28] In Tennessee jurisdiction may be waived if the child is older than fifteen and is alleged to have committed murder, rape, armed robbery, or kidnapping; jurisdiction may be waived in other cases only if the child is older than sixteen.[29]

Until fairly recently, waiver decisions were made in an altogether informal manner. Probation officers presented reports to the judge about a child's background and character. If the child appeared to be a bad risk for rehabilitation (a persistent offender, for example) or a danger to the community, the judge might waive jurisdiction. Generally no hearing was held on the issue, and the child had no opportunity to examine or respond to the information contained in the probation officer's report. That has changed.

The procedures by which juvenile courts reach decisions about waiver of jurisdiction came to the critical attention of the United States Supreme Court in 1966 in the case of *Kent* v. *United States.*[30] A quick review of that case, which was fully described in the last chapter, will point out the problems inherent in the informal approach to a waiver hearing. Morris Kent was arrested at age sixteen in connection with charges of housebreaking, robbery, and rape. He was subject to the exclusive jurisdiction of the District of Columbia's juvenile court, unless that court after a "full investigation" decided to waive jurisdiction and remit him for trial to the United States District Court.[31] After an "investigation" by the juvenile court probation officer, jurisdiction was waived. Morris Kent was never given a hearing of any sort. The Supreme Court held the waiver invalid. Terming the waiver decision critically important, the Court held that a hearing was required and that Kent's lawyer was entitled to copies of probation records and similar reports. The juvenile court was said to have abused its discretion by failing to act with "procedural regularity sufficient in the particular circumstances to satisfy the basic requirements of due process and fairness."[32] The Court noted that a juvenile court could have sent Kent to a reform school until he reached the age of twenty-one, but that the criminal court to which the case was waived could conceivably have imposed a sentence of death. Thus, a decision to waive jurisdiction is a decision of such great significance, the Court maintained, that it must be reached by regular procedures that ensure fairness.

Waiver decisions frequently involve very serious consequences for the child involved. In one Alabama case a fourteen-year-old was transferred to criminal court, where a life sentence (which could not have been imposed by a juvenile court) was ordered.[33] *In one Missouri case a fifteen-year-old child waived to criminal court was sentenced to forty years in prison.*[34]

The trend in jurisdictional hearings is clearly away from the traditional informality that used to characterize all juvenile court proceedings. There is now a firm expectation that lawyers will be present and that they will be given access to the information they need in order to represent their clients' interests effectively. Frequently, however, these proceedings are less adversarial in nature than we might now expect them to be. Good lawyers know that a too-vigorous defense may antagonize the judge — particularly an older judge who has been on the juvenile bench for a long time, who has a firm commitment to the doctrine of *parens patriae,* and who is not yet accustomed to the presence of lawyers in his courtroom. Frequently a good attorney can do no more than present an image of his client as a decent youngster who ought to have another chance. If that is not the type of due process safeguard the Supreme Court envisioned when it mandated the participation of lawyers in waiver decisions, it is at least something more than children have traditionally been afforded.

Adjudication

The comparatively small number of youngsters (about 300,000 per year in the entire United States) who are not diverted at intake (or at some earlier decision-making stage) move on to the formal process of adjudication. Until recently even this most formal component of the juvenile justice system was altogether lacking in due process safeguards. The juvenile court judge was conceptualized by the reformers as a loving grandfatherly sort of fellow who would conduct an informal, non-adversarial inquiry into the nature of a child's problems. In one early case the procedural informality of children's courts was justified as follows:

> The desideratum is to obtain, by the use of kindness and sympathy, the confidence of the child and of its parents if possible, to convince them that the judge and probation officer are friends and not the avengers of offended law. Good results are far more likely to be obtained in this way by the use of informal methods than by bringing them into a court conducted with the form and ceremony attendant upon trials for crime, where all the proceedings suggest that the law is about to be invoked to inflict punishment upon hardened malefactors.[35]

The use of kindness and sympathy was thought to preclude the use of legalisms commonly found in adult criminal courts. The participation of attorneys was discouraged as an undesirable interference in the relationship between the child and the court.[36] Juries were seen as altogether unnecessary; as one judge put it: "Whether the child deserves to be saved by the state is no more a question for a jury than whether the father, if able to save it, ought to save it."[37] The Fifth Amendment privilege against self-incrimination was rejected in the juvenile courts because of its incompatability with the necessity of learning about the child in order to provide therapeutic services.[38] Similarly, the prevailing standard about the quality and sufficiency of proof necessary to sustain a conviction (proof beyond a reasonable doubt) was abandoned in favor of a much more casual standard (a preponderance of the evidence). As recently as 1964 an appelate court in the District of Columbia was able to write that it would be unnecessary and improper "to inject into a juvenile delinquency proceeding the strictly criminal concept of guilt beyond a reasonable doubt.[39]

Traditionally, then, juvenile court hearings have borne little resemblance to trials in criminal courts. The juvenile and his family would appear, unrepresented, before a judge in chambers, or in some other informal setting. The public was excluded. Often witnesses were not called. A dialogue would ensue on the basis of which decisions would be made about what seemed "best" for the youngster. The entering of findings and the formal statement of disposition were almost incidental. Presumably that has been altered considerably in the wake of a series of Supreme Court decisions, discussed in the last chapter, which have significantly expanded the rights of juveniles.

Consider again the specific holdings of the decision in *In re Gault:*[40]

> 1. The child and his parents are entitled to notice of the charges which they are called upon to answer, and such notice must be written, it must "set forth the alleged misconduct with particularity," and it must be timely given. "Due process of law requires notice of the sort . . . which would be deemed constitutionally adequate in a civil or criminal proceeding.
> 2. "(T)he Due Process Clause of the Fourteenth Amendment requires that in respect of proceedings to determine delinquency which may result in committment to an institution in which the juvenile's freedom is curtailed, the child and his parent must be notified of the child's right to be represented by counsel retained by them, or if they are unable to afford counsel, that counsel will be appointed to represent the child."
> 3. The respondent in a delinquency proceeding is entitled to the

privilege against self-incrimination, and it is "applicable in the case of juveniles, as it is with respect to adults."

4. "(A)bsent a valid confession, a determination of delinquency and an order of commitment to a state institution cannot be sustained in the absence of sworn testimony subjected to the opportunity for cross-examination in accordance with our law and constitutional requirements."

Three years later, in *In re Winship*,[41] the Court extended *Gault* by holding that findings of delinquency could be based only on proof beyond a reasonable doubt. In 1971, however, the Supreme Court made it clear that it did not intend to force juvenile courts into an altogether adversarial model. In *McKeiver* v. *Pennsylvania*,[42] the Court held that juveniles do not have a constitutional right to a jury trial. The decision was guided by the Court's anxiety that

> . . . the jury trial, if required as a matter of constitutional precept, will remake the juvenile proceeding into a fully adversary process and will put an effective end to what has been the idealistic prospect of an intimate, informal protective proceeding.[43]

In deciding *McKeiver* the Supreme Court went to great lengths to document that it had never intended to transform juvenile courts completely. Consider the following excerpts from that decision.[44]

> . . . The Court . . . has not yet said that *all* rights constitutionally assured to an adult accused of crime also are to be enforced or made available to the juvenile in his delinquency proceeding. Indeed, the Court specifically has refrained from going that far:
> "We do not mean by this to indicate that the hearing to be held must conform with all of the requirements of a criminal trial or even of the usual administrative hearing; but we do hold that the hearing must measure up to the essentials of due process and fair treatment." *Kent,* 383 U.S., at 562. . . .
> . . . The Court, although recognizing the high hopes and aspirations of Judge Julian Mack, the leaders of the Jane Addams School and other supporters of the juvenile court concept, has also noted the disappointments of the system's performance and experience and the resulting widespread disaffection. . . . There have been, at one and the same time, both an appreciation for the juvenile court judge who is devoted, sympathetic, and conscientious, and a disturbed concern about the judge who is untrained and less than fully imbued with an understanding approach to the complex problems of childhood and adolescence. There has been praise for the system and its purposes, and there has been alarm over its defects.

. . . The Court has insisted that these successive decisions do not spell the doom of the juvenile court system or even deprive it of its "informality, flexibility, or speed." *Winship*, 397 U.S., at 366. . . .

In short, the constitutional restraints upon the adjudicatory processes of the juvenile court are not yet altogether clear. There must be sufficient formality to assure the juvenile "the essentials of due process and fair treatment"; but there is, apparently, still room for informality in the pursuit of "noble" goals. The traditional ethic of cooperation is still to be encouraged, but it must be made compatible with at least some of the conflict mores which dominate criminal trials.

The consequence of all this ambiguity is that juvenile courts are still unique institutions in American jurisprudence. They are different from adult criminal courts in very fundamental ways; often they are also different from one another in very fundamental ways. Some juvenile courts are open to the public; most are closed. Some courts make a maximum effort to assure the child a fair due process hearing; others view due process concerns as a hindrance to the real business of helping troubled children. In some courts defense attorneys are shown every possible consideration in order to facilitate their preparation of the best possible case (through the liberal granting of continuances, for example, to make adequate time available); in other courts active and effective participation of lawyers is greatly discouraged.

These variables in the functioning of the modern juvenile court can best be explicated by examining a few of the important components of the adjudicatory stage of the judicial process. We shall look, in turn at: (1) the role of the prosecutor; (2) the defense attorney's relationship with his client; and (3) the potential influence of the court on the behavior of attorneys.

Prosecution in Juvenile Courts

The traditional juvenile court process did not include a legally trained prosecutor. The function of collecting evidence and calling witnesses was performed by the complainant against the child, or by the court's probation officer, or by the judge himself. The presence of an attorney "prosecuting" the case against a juvenile was perceived as altogether inappropriate in proceedings conceptualized as "on behalf" of the child.[45] Indeed the mere presence of a prosecutor would have suggested that the state had some interest other than just child saving. Surely a judge and probation officer were all the professional staff necessary to determine how best to meet the troubled youngster's needs.

Before the *Gault* decisions, complainants in juvenile court had little need for legal representation. They told their story to the judge, answered what questions he might have, and left without ever having to worry about the legal sufficiency of the evidence they'd presented, and without ever having to face rigorous cross-examination.[46] The *Gault* decision, however, opened the courthouse doors to defense attorneys; and that seems to have generated a need for prosecutors.

> The provision of (defense counsel) has inevitably introduced adversary proceedings into the Juvenile . . . court. There is no question that the presence of (defense attorneys) is desirable to protect the rights of children . . . (and to invoke) the legal procedures to which defendants in the Criminal Courts are entitled, the preparation of witnesses, cross-examination of the petitioners and complaining witnesses, and the preparation of briefs on questions of law.
>
> In contrast, where a citizen files a petition alleging that an offense has been committed against him or his child, there is no one to interview the petitioner or complaining witnesses prior to the trial, no one to conduct the direct examination other than the Judge, no one to cross-examine the respondent and his witnesses other than the Judge, and no one to prepare a brief on questions of law.
>
> . . . . .
>
> Thus, the present law results in a paradoxical situation. . . . The Family Court . . . provides counsel for defendants and no personnel or machinery to assure the adequate presentation of cases against minors even when they are charged with acts which would constitute a felony if committed by an adult.
>
> . . . . .
>
> Unless legislation is enacted to correct the present imbalance in legal services . . . there is grave danger that cases will be dismissed for lack of proper presentation, that citizens will be discouraged from seeking redress in the court, and that legal questions will not be given adequate consideration. The present situation inevitably results in injuries to citizens, to delinquent children, and to the entire community.[47]

Concerns of this type have clearly prompted a movement towards the increased use of prosecuting attorneys in juvenile court. Three recently promulgated model juvenile court statutes have recommended the presence of a prosecutor in court proceedings.[48]

Eight states (Illinois, Minnesota, New Jersey, New Mexico, Tennessee, Texas, Vermont, and Wyoming) and the District of Columbia have enacted such requirements,[49] at least in certain types of cases.[50] In many other states juvenile courts are empowered to request the participation of a prosecutor.[51]

Despite the increasing use of prosecuting attorneys, there does not appear to be consensus about their roles. Many judges are concerned that a "hard-nosed" district-attorney type will undermine the informality and therapeutic goals of the juvenile court. To avoid such an outcome, many states have placed the prosecuting function in the hands of lawyers who are not involved in the handling of adult criminal cases.[52]

> In a further effort to moderate the prosecutorial stance of attorneys assigned to the juvenile court, statutes generally eschew the term "prosecution" and instead define the attorneys' role with such phrases as "assist in the ascertaining and presentation of evidence," "perform any duties in connection with the court proceedings as the judge may request," "present the case in support of the petition and assist in all stages of the proceedings, including appeals." Some statutes mandate the attorney's presence and are silent about his functions.[53]

Missouri went so far as to legislate a *parens patriae* relationship between the alleged delinquent and the prosecutor by combining the functions of juvenile officer and prosecutor in one person. The Appellate Court struck down that statute:

> The *parens patriae* relationship does not exist between prosecutor and child but between court and child. Prosecutors are in the business of prosecuting transgressions against the welfare of society and the conviction of those responsible therefor. They are not engaged in the rehabilitation of the child and the treatment of his emotional and family problems. . . .[54]

Some experts, and probably a fair number of legislators in Missouri, are of the opinion that the Appellate Court went too far — that a prosecutor in juvenile court *can* be less than single-mindedly devoted to securing the conviction of offenders;[55] obviously, however, there is considerable disagreement about the nature of prosecution in juvenile courts. It is likely that the trend towards the increased use of prosecuting attorneys will expand considerably before consensus begins to emerge about the prosecutor's role. In the meantime we can anticipate that there will be considerable variation from jurisdiction to jurisdiction, and that the attitudes and experiences of individual prosecutors and judges will be the primary determinants of the manner in which the function will be fulfilled. Many prosecutors are likely to be co-opted into the ethic of cooperation which is dominant in courts with strong commitment to the *parens patriae* doctrine. Many others, no doubt, will strive to engage in the type of conflict that characterizes criminal trials; and in some courts that adversarial stance will probably be warmly welcomed.

Defense in the Juvenile Courts

Despite the decision of the Supreme Court in *In re Gault*, defense attorneys as well as prosecutors are still not present at some juvenile court hearings. A significant percentage of youngsters charged with delinquency opt to waive the right to representation by counsel. Often that decision reflects a thoughtful consideration by the child or his parents, based perhaps on a desire to resolve the matter as quickly as possible, or perhaps on a desire to pay the consequences of indiscretion and misbehavior. Sometimes, however, elements of coercion are clearly present. Probation officers, for example, have been known to suggest that the participation of a defense attorney (which might be expensive) may not make a significant difference in the resolution of a case. A judge in New York once went so far as to advise a father: "Mr. Celli, you may get a lawyer if you wish, but I will tell you frankly that a lawyer will not change my mind. When I find out about the case I will make my own decision."[56]

Those youngsters who do not waive the right to counsel are very frequently represented by public defenders; a significant percentage of the juvenile court's clientele is, after all, quite poor. Public defenders are so often overworked that they are incapable of giving adequate attention to most of their cases. Private attorneys retained by other youngsters often make their livelihoods by handling large numbers of cases at low fees. Those lawyers, too, give inadequate attention to many of their cases. In almost all cases, then, the quality of the lawyer-client relationship in juvenile court is likely to be something less than the ideal characterized in Perry Mason.

> [A] busy defense counsel come(s) to rely on police, court clinic, and probation officials to provide him with information about his client which he needs in order to speak for the child. . . , but which he has

neither time nor training to investigate for himself. In such circumstances it becomes difficult to oppose the views of law enforcement and court personnel with the zealous and single-minded devotion to the child's interests which is often taken for granted as the automatic consequence of decreeing a right to counsel.[57]

In addition there seems to be considerable disagreement within the legal profession about the proper nature of the lawyer-client relationship in juvenile court. An interesting study done in a southern California county in 1970 identified three distinct orientations among lawyers.[58]

Some lawyers believe they should represent juveniles with the same vigor with which they represent adults. As one attorney said:

> There is no substantial difference between the position of a defendant in juvenile court from that of a defendant in adult court as far as I'm concerned. I know there is all this talk about rehabilitation, but in practice, if you look at what happens after a case is over and the kid is in CYA (California Youth Authority), it's just like a jail. . . . I fight for whatever the kid wants. Of course I have to be reasonable . . . but I try to get the best deal for a kid, just like I do in my defenses in adult court.[59]

Another group of lawyers seem to feel that the rehabilitative orientation of the juvenile court justifies a departure from the traditional adversarial stance.

> The juvenile court is a non-adversary system designed to rehabilitate these minors. . . . I don't want these kids to get the idea that they are beating the rap. When they do something wrong, they ought to face it. . . . I treat them like they are my own kids.[60]

The single largest group of attorneys, however, saw the appropriate relationship to juvenile clients as something between these two extremes. In their view the lawyer's job is to advocate, but with something less than the single-minded zealousness appropriate to adult criminal cases. Most lawyers, in short, are ambivalent about their relationships to juvenile clients. On the one hand, professional ethics indicate that a vigorous defense is always in order; on the other hand, personal ethics suggest that helping a factually guilty child to beat a rap in juvenile court may not be in anyone's best interests — not even the child's. It is unrealistic to expect that such ambivalence will always be resolved in favor of a vigorous insistence on the exercise of all constitutional rights.[61]

The Court's Influence on
Attorney Behavior

Even defense attorneys and prosecutors who intend to perform in a firm, adversarial manner may sometimes find themselves forced into roles more compatible with the traditional juvenile court ethic of cooperation. Juvenile court judges have considerable influence over the behavior of attorneys who practice before them. Mechanisms both of co-optation and of coercion are employed by judges who support the doctrine of *parens patriae* in order to secure compliance to their expectation that juvenile court hearings will be nonadversarial inquiries into the child's best interests.

Lawyers who practice in the juvenile courts, because they are often young and inexperienced, may be particularly susceptible to judicial influence. Legal aid offices frequently assign their newest staff member to practice in the low-pressure environment of juvenile court. "The court's relative informality is abused to mask the usual ineptitude and inexperience of new attorneys."[62] It is hardly surprising that such attorneys should look to the judge before whom they practice for guidance or that they should be responsive to his expectations.

Even experienced attorneys who practice repeatedly in the juvenile courts may find themselves co-opted into the institutional ethic of cooperation.

> Whenever an individual works with the same people over a period of time, relationships, either friendly or antagonistic, necessarily develop. Because the attorney has to deal with these people on a day-to-day basis, he needs their continuing cooperation. He needs friends who can bend the rules. If he asserts his client's legal rights, he is made to feel "unreasonable," an obstacle in the system's attempt to "help" the juvenile and family. Sometimes the court attempts to coopt defense attorneys into its treatment efforts by giving him access to probation records and generally by making him feel that he is part of the court team. When the court asks him to make a contribution to its efforts, the lawyer is pressured to make "constructive" suggestions which go along with the system.[63]

Pressures towards compliance are not always co-optive in nature; sometimes they are downright coercive. Judges committed to the *parens patriae* model of justice can succeed in making effective adversarial practice impossible in their courtrooms. A judge's refusal to grant a continuance in a case, for example, may seriously limit the available time in which a defense attorney can locate witnesses and identify technicalities upon which the case could be won. Refusals of that type are common in some jurisdictions.[64]

The most extreme manner in which a judge may discourage adversarial practice in his court is by letting it be known that the clients of conflict-oriented, "uncooperative" attorneys will be dealt with harshly. One such lawyer in New York City tells of the day an irate judge looked down at him from the bench and said: "Counselor, why do you make so many procedural motions; surely you know that it is the decision to grant or deny probation that brings home the bacon." The most ominous possible interpretation of that remark is that vigorously represented juveniles, if adjudicated delinquent, may be denied lenient dispositions.

There is evidence that that actually happens with regularity in some jurisdictions. A carefully controlled experiment in a moderately large northeastern city (identified only as Gotham) found that vigorously represented youngsters were more likely than unrepresented youngsters to be adjudicated delinquent (even with factors such as severity of the offense, prior record, and quality of home life kept constant). Furthermore, after adjudication, represented youngsters were less likely than unrepresented youngsters to receive probation, and were more likely to be committed to a correctional institution.[65]

Consider the dilemma of a well-trained, experienced advocate who appears in juvenile court before a judge who resents adversarial practice. If he persists in handling the case vigorously and in exploiting all possible legal maneuvers, he may actually injure his client. A lawyer's commitment, after all, ought to be to his client, not to his theory of legal practice. Thus, conforming to the court's expectations may become an essential component of a competent defense or prosecution. It is hardly surprising, then, that many lawyers refrain from entering procedural motions in juvenile court cases,[66] or that they willingly participate in informal conferences in the judges' chambers, during which all claims to due process safeguards are effectively waived.[67]

Disposition

It is a central premise of the juvenile justice system that a delinquent child ought not be punished in accordance with his crime, but ought rather to be treated in accordance with his needs. Thus, at the dispositional stage, attention is supposed to focus on how best to provide services to the child rather than on how best to protect the community. In theory the nature of the child's offense should not be of any great relevance; treatment strategies should be determined by his psychological and social condition rather than by the specific content of his antisocial behavior. Thus, while a criminal court is normally expected to sentence an armed robber more severely than a shoplifter, a juvenile court could determine that the comparatively minor offense had been committed by a more seriously disturbed youngster, who should be committed for treatment; the same judge might place the serious offender on probation if he felt that child's condition merited it.

Of course it is quite likely that serious acting-out behavior will be considered evidence of the child's troubled psychosocial condition. It is, nevertheless, quite common for youngsters who have offended seriously to be treated leniently, and for youngsters who have not behaved too badly but who are perceived as deeply troubled to be sent away from home for treatment.

The therapeutic model of justice assumes that courts will have sophisticated diagnostic resources available to them and that they will be able to employ a broad range of treatment methods in the pursuit of each child's best interests. The reality, however, is considerably less attractive.

[D]ispositional decisions are severely restricted by such practical factors as the lack of adequate diagnostic and dispositional facilities. In reality, the dispositional decision may be nothing more than a Hobson's choice, an attempt to make do with inadequate and inappropriate facilities.[68]

Dispositional Options

In theory, at least, juvenile courts are supposed to have an extensive range of dispositional alternatives available with which to "individualize" justice according to the needs of each child. The options ought to include the following:

1. *Dismissal* — the unconditional relinquishment of jurisdiction over a juvenile or family. Obviously, a case must be dismissed where the allegations have not been proven; but a case may also be dismissed when the judge believes the child is not in need of treatment and that an extended involvement in the life of the child will not be in his or the community's best interests.[69] Judges may also dismiss a case if they believe that the allegations, even if proven, are not sufficiently serious to warrant judicial intervention (e.g., profanity,[70] or rock throwing[71]).

2. *Suspended judgment* — a refusal to enter a finding of delinquency or a formal order of disposition, on the condition that the child

modify his behavior during a specified period of time.[72] Sometimes a referral to a community agency may be part of the arrangement.[73]

3. *Order of Protection* — generally a command to the parent that he or she refrain from acts which are believed to make the home an improper place for a child, to refrain from abusing or neglecting the child.[74]

4. *Probation* — the conditional release of a child under the formal supervision of an officer of the court or of a related agency.[75] The child may be required, in addition to meeting regularly with a probation officer, to fulfill such other reasonable conditions as the judge imposes. These may include getting a job, undergoing psychiatric treatment, avoiding known criminals, going to school, refraining from the use of alcohol or drugs, obeying curfew, or (more bluntly but somewhat more vaguely) just staying out of trouble.[76] Probation is the most frequently used disposition throughout the United States.[77]

5. *Placement in a foster home* — a dispositional alternative used in all American jurisdictions to remove a child from an environment that is seen as harmful without imposing institutional regimentation.[78]

6. *Fines or restitution to the victim* — may be imposed by the juvenile courts with or without an accompanying commitment to probation in twenty-one states (Arkansas, California, Colorado, Delaware, Kentucky, Maine, Maryland, Massachusetts, Minnesota, Nebraska, New Mexico, New York, Ohio, Oregon, Pennsylvania, South Dakota, Tennessee, Utah, Virginia, Wisconsin, Wyoming) and the District of Columbia.[79]

7. *Commitment to a private institution* — a dispositional option in all jurisdictions except for Alaska and Arizona.[80] Generally such institutions may be within *or* outside the child's home state. The optimum use of such institutions would be to meet the specialized needs of a unique child. In Massachusetts, for example, it is possible for the Division of Youth Services to send a disturbed delinquent child to incredibly expensive (upward of $40,000 per year per child) psychiatric hospitals.[81]

8. *Commitment to a public institution* — possible in all jurisdictions.[82] In some states the juvenile court may commit a child to any public institution it chooses. In many states, however, the child is committed to the care of an agency which determines where the child goes; in some cases the agency may actually refuse to place the child in any facility.[83] In almost all states the institution to which a child has been committed may determine the date of his release.[84]

Despite this impressive range of possibilities, most juvenile court judges in the United States find that they do not really have much to choose from. Most of the eight options listed above are not readily available in most communities. Generally judges are forced to choose among outright dismissal, probation entailing inadequate and infrequent supervision, or commitment to a state reformatory.

> The reasons for this narrow and largely ineffectual range of dispositional alternatives are complex. The long-standing inability of the juvenile justice system to obtain more than financial starvation from state legislatures accounts for much of this dismal picture. . . . But other factors are also at play. The failure of psychiatry to meet the unrealistic expectation that it could "cure" delinquency produced both a reluctance to provide funds for carrying on psychotherapy with delinquents, and an unwillingness on the part of psychiatric professionals to enter a field that has few visible satisfactions of success. The emphasis by social scientists on the social causes of delinquency . . . has also made it less attractive to build up resources for dealing with individual psychology. This same emphasis has produced the focus of much current reform effort aimed at keeping children out of the juvenile court in the first place.[85]

Dispositional Decision Making

Choosing among dispositional alternatives is a matter largely within the discretion of judges; juvenile court judges, however, are vested with more discretionary power of this type than are most others. In criminal courts, for example, statutes generally limit the sentencing powers of judges. An adult petty offender, no matter how nasty or disturbed he appears to be, can not (except under extraordinary circumstances)[86] be sent off to prison. In juvenile court, on the other hand, judges are empowered to make whatever disposition seems to them to be best, up to and including commitment to an institution until the child shall reach the age of twenty-one, without regard to the seriousness of the offense.

> Individualized justice is *the* basic precept in the philosophy of the juvenile court. More generally, it is commended to all officials who deal with juveniles. We should, it is suggested by enlightened professionals, gear our official dispositions to suit the individual needs of the accused rather than respond in automatic fashion to the offense he has allegedly committed. The relating of disposition to the individual instead of to the offense is a central aspect of the modern *treatment* viewpoint.[87]

Individualized justice requires information about the offender and his environment. Social investigation reports are intended to uncover the necessary facts. These reports, which are prepared by probation officers, and which generally contain recommendations for disposition, are often quite broad in scope.

Almost all juvenile courts have yet another device available for obtaining information about a child's psychosocial condition: a court clinic. The clinic can be as formal as a center to which a child can be committed for observation, or as informal as a working arrangement with an individual psychologist or psychiatrist. Its purpose is always to provide the judge with diagnostic information and with recommendations for the disposition of cases.[88]

There is reason to fear that the evaluations and recommendations contained in clinic and social investigation reports are not frequently helpful. Social workers, psychologists, and psychiatrists involved in the process may depend on the judge for employment, and may therefore be very concerned with writing reports that will prove compatible with pre-existing judicial biases. Additionally, they may be very concerned about the future misbehavior of a child identified as a good risk; that fear results in a considerable tendency toward diagnostic caution. Furthermore, delinquent youngsters may perceive probation officers and others involved in the process as hostile and untrustworthy; they may therefore choose to behave in a disrespectful and uncooperative manner. Robert Emerson has described the potential impact of such behavior on the staff of a clinic:

> The delinquent may define the clinic as part of the authoritarian court setting and respond evasively or hostilely to the clinic's efforts to "help" him. If he maintains this stance, the clinic will evaluate him as unfeeling, secretive, and anti-social. Moreover, clinic personnel will ascertain neither his inner feelings nor his subjective accounts for his behavior. This ruins the psychiatric assessment of his character and leads to unfavorable recommendations to the court. In this way, the suspicious and uncooperative delinquent helps destroy his "last chance" to escape incarceration and hence possible permanent stigmatization at the hands of the court.[89]

Even if the helping professionals involved in this diagnostic process develop an accurate and insightful image of a particular child, they may be unable to provide the judge with really helpful recommendations. They are, after all, constrained by the reality that far too few high quality programs are available for the care and treatment of troubled youngsters. One exceptionally talented judge has observed:

> The value of diagnostic studies and recommendations is too often reduced to a paper recommendation. In shopping for placement, probation officers are forced to lower their sights from what they know a child needs to what they can secure. Their sense of professional responsibility is steadily eroded. The judge, in turn, becomes the ceremonial official who in many cases approves a disposition which he knows is only a dead end for the child.[90]

The nature of the "ceremony" at which the judge finally determines the fate of a child who has been adjudicated delinquent has changed considerably in recent years. Prior to *Gault*, few juvenile courts had separate hearings for the determination of disposition. Social investigation reports were generally prepared for the judge before the adjudicatory hearing, so that he could be familiar with the background and character of the child whose alleged delinquency was under consideration. The court's purpose, it will be remembered, was to determine whether the child's *condition* was such that he could appropriately be dealt with as a delinquent. It was seen as desirable that all available information be considered at the adjudicatory stage. Today, however, hearings are bifurcated. That means that the issue of innocence or guilt is resolved at a separate hearing before the issue of disposition is considered. Use of information contained in a social investigation report before the conclusion of the adjudicatory stage is no longer permitted.[91] It is thought possible that information appropriate at the dispositional stage (about the child's character, for example) might bias the judge at the earlier adjudicatory hearing and deny the juvenile a fair hearing. This practice of separating the dispositional decision from the decision about innocence or guilt is in conformity with the practice of criminal courts.[92]

Of the two parts of the now-bifurcated juvenile court hearing, the dispositional hearing is far less formal. It is generally agreed that the juvenile has a right to be represented by counsel at the dispositional stage.[93] The rules of evidence, however, are considerably relaxed; the judge is free to consider almost any type of evidence that may be brought to his attention, including material that would clearly be inadmissible at the adjudicatory hearing.[94]

It is not likely that the presence of lawyers will have much impact on the processes by which dispositional decisions are made.[95] Most lawyers, feeling perhaps that they don't know enough about social work and psychotherapy to intervene effectively, tend to be inactive at this final stage of the judicial process. Many defense attorneys believe that their job is to try to win a case; having lost it, there is little left for them to do. Even were that not the case, few defense attorneys have resources available to them with which to develop an independent psychosocial diagnosis of the child. Probation officers present the material they have gathered, and lawyers are able to do little but listen to it. In a few large cities, legal aid offices have employed social workers to develop defense-oriented social investigations and recommendations; but that is not common practice.

Even if they have adequate resources available to them, defense attorneys have to be cautious about how they proceed at a dispositional hearing. This is so because the discretion of the judge is virtually unlimited, and antagonizing him will do no good. Even a too-rigorous cross-examination of the probation officer, who may be well liked and respected by the judge, is potentially dangerous. The best a good defense attorney can do is to approach the bench respectfully and present an image of his client as seen in the best possible light. A recently published guide for lawyers on advocacy in the juvenile courts suggests that every possible attempt ought to be made to keep a child from being institutionalized, however:

> While aggressively pursuing these goals, it is important to avoid antagonizing the judge or probation officer. Defense counsel should not assume an unnecessarily argumentative or adversarial stance during the dispositional decision-making process. Regardless of his own personal opinion about the nature of juvenile court proceedings and his opinion of his client's real need for treatment, defense counsel is best advised to approach the judge and probation officer in a spirit of cooperation toward fashioning the best possible "treatment plan."[96]

Concluding Thoughts

The characteristic of judicial processes in the juvenile courts which has emerged most clearly from this discussion is that they continue, in large measure, to be informal in nature. The Supreme Court's mandate to include due process safeguards has influenced juvenile courts, but has not brought about a complete (or even a very considerable) departure from the traditional ethic of cooperation. Juvenile court judges and probation officers continue to exercise a vast amount of discretionary power. Therefore, concluding thoughts in this chapter ought to be about them and their qualifications to execute their powers effectively.

The juvenile court movement once had great expectations for judges. The characteristics of "ideal" juvenile court judges would place them among the great men of their generation. The reality has been disappointing. Too often judges are untrained either in law or in the behavioral sciences.

> A recent study of juvenile court judges . . . revealed that half had not received undergraduate degrees; a fifth had received no college education at all; a fifth were not members of the bar.[97]

These factors are both a cause and consequence of the low status of juvenile court judges in the legal profession. Many talented lawyers aspire to the judiciary, but most would not want to serve on the bench of a children's court. Consequently, where special juvenile courts exist, they sometimes have trouble getting the type of professional staff that is hoped for.

Some jurisdictions do not have that problem because they do not have special juvenile courts; juvenile cases come up at special sessions of some other court and are heard before a judge who spends most of his time on other matters. Three-quarters of all juvenile court judges spend most of their time on cases involving criminal and civil law problems of adults.[98] While those jurisdictions may have an easier time recruiting judges, they have other problems: part-time juvenile court judges may never have an opportunity to develop expertise and sophistication about the legal and developmental problems of children.

Inadequacies in the training of judges, and the part-time quality of much of their involvement propel probation officers into a potentially powerful situation in the court. Many judges are dependent on their probation officers for clinical and social insights into the problems of the children who come before them. In many jurisdictions, however, probation officers are poorly equipped for such responsibility. Often they do not have formal training in the behavioral sciences. Most states do not even have minimal educational requirements for probation jobs.[99] The pay and status of probation officers are low in comparison to that enjoyed by psychotherapists and psychiatric caseworkers. Consequently, job turnover is high, with the best and most highly trained workers moving on to better jobs most quickly.

The dependency relationship between judges and probation officers cuts both ways. While many judges do not know enough about juvenile delinquency to do their jobs unassisted, many probation officers could not hold their jobs at all without a judge's support. In the vast majority of jurisidictions, probation officers are not unionized and are not protected by civil service.[100] They work for the local government and can be fired at will. A dissatisfied judge would merely have to request that the county commissioners get him a new officer, and the old one would be looking for work. That means that probation officers, even the best of them, must be thoughtful about the opinions and preferences of the judges for whom they work. It would not be politic to recommend leniency too often in cases where the judge was inclined to be harsh, for example. Thus, the power of probation officers to influence judges is nullified, at least in part, by the necessity that the probation officer appear to have attitudes and values compatible with those of the judge.

American communities have failed to make sufficient resources available to secure a cadre of the best possible professionals for the juvenile court.[101] The failure of the juvenile justice system to achieve its lofty goals of justice and special treatment for children may not be due to that inadequacy alone; but it is at least arguable that better salaries and higher status would attract to the juvenile courts judges and probation officers who might better cope with the problems of problem children.

References

1. Jerome Skolnick, "Social Control in the Adversary Process," 11 *Journal of Conflict Resolution* 52 (1967).

2. See Sandford Kadish and Monrad Paulsen, *Criminal Law and Its Processes* (New York: Little, Brown, 1969), pp. 1125 - 50.

3. Jane Addams, *My Friend, Julia Lathrop* (New York: Macmillan, 1935), p. 137.

4. W. Vaughan Stapleton and Lee E. Teitelbaum, *In Defense of Youth* (New York: Russel Sage Foundation, 1972), p. 103.

5. 387 U.S. 1 (1967).

6. See Chapter 4 of this book.

7. See The Vera Foundation, *Bail in the United States, 1964,* A Report to the National Conference on Bail and Criminal Justice (Washington, D.C.: The Foundation, 1964).

8. Frank Miller et al., *The Juvenile Justice Process* (Mineola, N.Y.: Foundation Press, 1971), p. 1286.

9. Ibid., p. 1287; also see Robert Winslow, ed., *Juvenile Delinquency in a Free Society* (Encinoma, Calif.: Dickenson, 1973), p. 144; and Sanford Fox, *The Law of Juvenile Courts in a Nutshell* (St. Paul, Minn.: West Publishing, 1971), pp. 147 - 9.

10. See, generally, Stapleton and Teitelbaum, *In Defense of Youth.*

11. See Douglas J. Besharov, *Juvenile Justice Advocacy: Practice in a Unique Court* (New York: Practising Law Institute, 1974), pp. 45 - 53.

12. Fox, *Law of Juvenile Courts,* pp. 147 - 8.

13. Ibid., p. 149.

14. Mark M. Levin and Rosemary C. Sarri, *Juvenile Delinquency: A Comparative Analysis of Legal Codes in the United States* (Ann Arbor, Mich.: National Assessment of Juvenile Corrections, 1974), p. 13.

15. Ill. Juv. Ct. Act 702 - 2.

16. Levin and Sarri, *Juvenile Delinquency: A Comparative Analysis of Legal Codes in the United States,* p. 13.

17. Ibid., p. 11.

18. Ibid., pp. 11 - 12.

19. Ibid., p. 12.

20. McKinney's New York Family Court Act, § 731(c), 732(c), 751.

21. Uniform Juvenile Court Act § 2(3), (4)(iv).

22. Pa. Juv. Act of 1972, § 2.

23. *In re Edwin R.,* 323 N.Y.S. 2d 911 (1971). In Chapter 4 the case was discussed under the name of Edwin M. Both youngsters were involved in the case (along with several others). The official report of the case was given Edwin R.'s name, but he didn't actually benefit from the decisions because he'd gotten into further trouble while the case was pending and wound up being transferred to criminal court.

24. Ibid.

25. Ibid.

26. Levin and Sarri, *Juvenile Delinquency: A Comparative Analysis of Legal Codes in the United States,* p. 19.

27. Ibid., p. 20.

28. Ibid.

29. Ibid.

30. 383 U.S. 541 (1966).

31. The requirement of a "full investigation" was imposed, but not defined by statutes of the District of Columbia. This is important because some legal scholars maintain that the Supreme Court's decision in *Kent* involved an interpretation of the statutory language rather than of the Constitution. If that is true, the implications of the decision would be somewhat limited. See Daniel Katkin, 'Presentence Reports: An Analysis of Uses, Limitations and Civil Liberties Issues," 55 Minn. L. Rev. 15, 26 - 30 (1970).

32. *Kent* v. *United States,* 383 U.S. 541, 553 (1966).

33. *Hall* v. *State,* 284 Ala. 569, 226 So. 2d 630 (1969).

34. *Jefferson* v. *State,* 442 S.W. 2d 6 (Mo., 1969).

35. *State* v. *Scholl,* 167 Wisc. 504, 509, 167 N.W. 830, 832 (1918).

36. See Chapter 3 in this book.

37. *Commonwealth* v. *Fisher,* 213 Pa. 48, 54, 62 Atl. 198, 200 (1905).

38. See Stapleton and Teitelbaum, *In Defense of Youth,* p. 19.

39. See *In re Bigesby,* 202 A. 2d 785, 786 (D.C. Mun. Ct. App., 1964).

40. *In re Gault,* 387 U.S. 1, 33 (1967) as quoted in W. Vaughan Stapleton and Lee E. Teitelbaum, *In Defense of Youth* (New York: Russell Sage Foundation, 1972), pp. 29 - 30.

41. 397 U.S. 358 (1970).

42. 403 U.S. 528 (1971).

43. Ibid.

44. Ibid.

45. M. Marvin Finelstein et al., *Prosecution in the Juvenile Courts* (Washington, D.C.: U.S. Government Printing Office, 1973), p.9; also see Besharov, *Juvenile Justice Advocacy,* pp. 39, 43.

46. Besharov, *Juvenile Justice Advocacy,* p. 39.

47. *In re Lang,* 44 Misc. 2d 900, 905 - 906, 255 N.Y.S. 2d 987, 992 (Family Ct., N.Y. Co., 1965).

48. National Council on Crime and Delinquency, *Model Rules,* Rule 24 (1969); U.S. Department of Health, Education, and Welfare, *Children's Bureau Legislative Guide,* 15 (1969). *Uniform Juvenile Court Act,* §24 (b).

49. Finkelstein et al., *Prosecution,* p. 12.

50. In New Jersey, for example, the participation of a prosecutor is mandatory only "where the complaint charges the juvenile with causing death." New Jersey Juvenile and Domestic Relations Court Rules, Rule 5: 9 - 1 (d) (1972).

51. Finkelstein et al., *Prosecution,* p. 12.

52. Besharov, *Juvenile Justice Advocacy,* p. 44.

53. Ibid.

54. *In re F- C-,* 484 S.W. 2d 21, 25 (Mo. App. Ct., 1972).

55. See, for example, Besharov, *Juvenile Justice Advocacy,* pp. 44 - 5.

56. *In the Matter of Celli,* 27 A.D. 2d 702, 276 N.Y.S. 2d 967 (1967). On appeal, the father's waiver of the right to counsel was found to have been unconstitutionally coerced.

57. Fox, *Law of Juvenile Courts,* p. 160.

58. Charles E. Clayton, "The Relationship of the Probation Officer and the Defense Attorney after Gault," 34 *Federal Probation* 9 (March 1970).

59. Ibid., p. 12; also see Thomas Welch, "Delinquency Proceedings — Fundamental Fairness for the Accused in a Quasi-Criminal Forum," 50 *Minn. L. Rev.* 655 (1966).

60. Clayton, "Probation Officer and Defense Attorney," p. 12. Consider the following statement: "You might represent a guilty client against whom the state has very little evidence or only a tainted confession. On the other hand, the child might have very real emotional problems, caused by his parents, that may become acute and lead to more serious criminal behavior unless intercepted. Needless, to say, each situation must be settled on its facts." Patrick T. Murphy, "Defending a Juvenile Court Proceeding," 15 *Practical Lawyer* 33 (1969).

61. Clayton, "Probation Officer and Defense Attorney" p. 13; also see Fox, *Law of Juvenile Courts,* p. 161.

62. Besharov, *Juvenile Justice Advocacy,* p. 47.
63. Ibid.
64. See Stapleton and Teitelbaum, *In Defense of Youth,* pp. 111 - 34.
65. Ibid., pp. 63 - 94. These findings were just short of statistical significance at the .05 level. That means that statisticians maintain that the findings of this study would occur through the operation of chance no more than five times if the research were repeated one hundred times.
66. Ibid.
67. For a dramatic documentation of the use of informal conferences, see the Frederick Wiseman film, *Juvenile Court.*
68. Besharov, *Juvenile Justice Advocacy,* p. 374.
69. Ibid., pp. 375 - 6.
70. See *Young* v. *State,* 120 Ga. App. 605, 171 S.E. 2d 756 (1969).
71. See *Jones* v. *Commonwealth,* 185 Va. 335, 38 S.E. 2d 444 (1946).
72. See *In re M.C.F.,* 293 A. 2d 874, (D.C. Cir., 1972).
73. Besharov, *Juvenile Justice Advocacy,* p. 377.
74. Ibid., 378 - 9.
75. Ibid., p. 379.
76. Ibid., pp. 380 - 1.
77. Levin and Sarri, *Juvenile Delinquency: A Comparative Analysis of Legal Codes,* p. 53.
78. Ibid., p. 54.
79. Ibid.
80. Ibid.
81. This information was obtained in an interview with Dr. Jerome Miller, former Director of the Mass. Department of Youth Services.
82. Levin and Sarri, *Juvenile Delinquency: A Comparative Analysis of Legal Codes,* pp. 55 - 6.
83. This is the case in Massachusetts, for example.
84. Levin and Sarri, *Juvenile Delinquency: A Comparative Analysis of Legal Codes,* p. 56.
85. Fox, *Law of Juvenile Courts,* p. 204.
86. Katkin, "Habitual Offender Laws: A Reconsideration," 21 *Buffalo L. Rev.* 99.
87. David Matza, *Delinquency and Drift* (New York: John Wiley & Sons, 1964).
88. For an excellent discussion of this point, see Besharov, *Juvenile Justice Advocacy,* pp. 395 - 8.
89. See Robert Emerson, *Judging Delinquents: Context and Process in Juvenile Court,* (Chicago: Aldine, 1969), pp. 266 - 7.
90. Justine W. Polier, *A View From the Bench,* (New York: National Council on Crime and Delinquency, 1964), p. 30.
91. See, for example, *In re Gladys R.,* 1 Cal. 3d 855, 464 P. 2d 127, 83 Cal. Rptr. 671 (1970); also see McKinney's New York Family Court Act §746 (b) (1973).
92. See Daniel Katkin, *55 Minn. L. Rev.* 17 (1970).
93. Fox, *Law of Juvenile Courts,* pp. 197 - 8.

94.   Ibid., pp. 198 - 202.

95.   For an excellent discussion of attorney participation at the dispositional stage, see Besharov, *Juvenile Justice Advocacy,* pp. 412 - 36.

96.   Ibid., p. 413.

97.   President's Commission on Law Enforcement and Administration of Justice, *Task Force Report: Juvenile Delinquency and Youth Crime* (Washington, D.C.: U.S. Government Printing Office, 1967), p. 7.

98.   Ibid.

99.   Levin and Sarri, *Juvenile Delinquency: A Comparative Analysis of Legal Codes,* p. 47.

100.   Ibid.

101.   President's Commission, *Task Force Report,* p. 7.

An Interview with Judge Maurice Cohill, National Association of Juvenile Court Judges

Judge Cohill is the senior judge of the juvenile court in Allegheny County (Pittsburgh), Pennsylvania. He has served as an officer of the National Council of Juvenile Court Judges and was instrumental in the creation of a research institute called the National Center for Juvenile Justice. Judge Cohill is a scholarly and articulate spokesman; needless to say, however, his comments reflect his own attitudes and beliefs, not those of *all* juvenile court judges.

On Status Offenses, Courts, and Community Agencies

Katkin: Let's begin with the jurisdiction of the court. There is a considerable amount of conflict about whether juvenile status offenders, such as truants and runaways, ought to come to the attention of the juvenile courts. Many people contend that such problems should be the responsibility of parents, schools, religious institutions, and social agencies, and, in turn, that the justice system ought to have jurisdiction only over individuals who have committed acts which would be crimes if committed by adults. What do you think about the jurisdiction of the juvenile court?

Judge: I am one of those people who disagrees with that position and I feel very strongly about it. I am all for diversion of status offenders, but I do have some concerns. First of all I'm always concerned about whether the child's rights are being protected — often informal handling by noncourt agencies leads to infringements on basic rights. Secondly, there are cases where the force of the court is needed to keep youngsters in line.

To illustrate the first situation, let's say that we set up a youth service bureau to handle truant kids. Johnny goes to school and they say, "Johnny you missed 120 days of school this year, so you will have to go to the youth service bureau." So Johnny goes to the youth service bureau and sees the social worker at the intake office who says, "Johnny, you missed 120 days of school this year." Johnny says, "Yes, I was sick." O.K., now if he was sick and was legally absent from school, maybe he needs some help — maybe he needs some tutoring and so forth and so on — but he should not be under any legal compunction to have to get it. If that case came into court, the charge of truancy would be dismissed. I doubt that it would be [dismissed] if processed by a youth service bureau; they would say, "O.K., either you do what we tell you to do, or go to court." He would in fact be forced to do their bidding without due process of law — that's an infringement on his constitutional rights.

There's another reason why I believe status offense cases belong in court. In some cases the power and the force of the court can have a beneficial influence. Yesterday I heard a case in court about five girls running around hitchhiking. Two of them were raped at gunpoint by a guy who picked them up. After that was over, they hitchhiked some more. I think somebody has to step into such situations to help the kids, and I think it has to be done with the force of the court. We don't have all the answers. But just the fact that they are in court makes the difference in some cases. What I'm saying is that certain kinds of kids need that kind of force to get them to shape up.

Yes, I think that status offenses belong in court; and in Pennsylvania most school officials, certainly some of the ones around here, are very sorry that truancy has been taken out of the delinquent side of the ledger [by a 1972 law]. All the school people I talk to think that child welfare here is doing a lousy job with the truants; child welfare is not geared up to do a good job for them.

Katkin: Do you think child welfare services could be beefed up — made more adequate?

Judge: Child welfare services could be beefed up, but I think again they don't have the force of the courts. You know what I mean. I am not out to just stick kids with delinquent labels. I am not out to commit kids. But child welfare institutions do not have the authority which delinquency institutions have.

I would like to talk a little bit more about status offenses. Maybe I said this to you yesterday. I have said it a lot of times. I think that society has to worry more about kids who go out drinking every night than about a kid who on impulse steals a car and joy-rides. The one that is out drinking every night is the one that is guilty of a status offense, while the one that steals a car is guilty of a felony. Yet I contend that the problem drinker needs a lot more treatment than the kid who did a stupid, foolish and immature thing. But only with the court order will he take treatment.

Katkin: That's probably true, I suppose. The other kind of case we chatted about yesterday is the notion that to remove status offenses from the law we don't have any clear mandate to deal with any kid who is doing some destructive stuff. An 8-year-old kid who runs away from home and lives on a beach hasn't done anything to hurt anyone else or society, but damage to persons or property by youngsters is increasing every year.

Judge: Yes, that's right and I'm really concerned about it. But again I think that most knowledgeable judges are going to say, "Well, O.K., we won't call it incorrigibility any more. We are going to call it exactly what it is. If his mother said he was smoking pot then he'll be charged with possession of marijuana. And if he banged his mother up, instead of calling it incorrigibility we'll call it assault and battery." But, I'll bet not one percent of the cases that I've ever heard involving so-called "incorrigibility" involved what, by themselves, were truly delinquent acts. I mean legally delinquent acts. It's just a question of labeling and a question of the degree of the offense. We have, of course, many kids who commit delinquent acts that we find "deprived" because we feel that they can be helped in a "deprived" or "dependent and neglected" type of program rather than a program for delinquents. We hang the label on them which we think will get the most help, and I think that's true of most of the judges that I know.

Katkin: One of the things that interests me is that self-report deliquency studies indicate that upwards of 80 percent and in fact one in York, Pennsylvania found upwards of 92 percent of the kids, who were randomly selected at schools, self-reported that they commit acts which could result in an adjudication of delinquent.

Judge: And the other eight percent are liars! Ha. Ha. At least, if I look back at my own childhood with any degree of honesty, I can't imagine anybody living past the age of six who hadn't committed delinquent acts.

Katkin: My three-year-old assaulted a little girl down the street the other day; I suppose that's his first delinquency.

Judge: I think it's a part of life. Frankly, I have kids standing in front of me in court for things not nearly as serious as I did. But I just didn't get caught.

Katkin: As a judge, how do you deal with such facts?

Judge: I try to be understanding about it. I try, if I can, to avoid hanging a label on them. Sometimes, obviously, I need help of one sort or another. Here in Allegheny County we do have this practice of often continuing cases and then dismissing — which the law permits you to do. And of course, under the new act, we have the device of the 6 months or year consent decree, which we use in many cases. Under this procedure there is no formal hearing, and if they successfully complete the period of probation provided in the consent decree, the petition is dismissed.

Quixotic Encapsulation

Katkin: Now let's talk about who gets encapsulated into the system. Consider the self-report data in the York [Pa.] study. I estimate that the 92 percent figure means that there are 1.4 million kids who commit delinquent acts out of the 1.6 million in the state. In 1973, 92,000 youngsters were apprehended. Forty-five thousand were sent by the police on to the courts. And of those 45 thousand that actually got to the courts, some number probably were diverted during the intake process. I don't have a clear fix on that.

Judge: Here it would normally be about 50 percent.

Katkin: And by the time you get to the far end of the system, there were during that year only about 3000 kids who were institutionalized in the entire state. Are you confident that the kids who get to court are in some significant way different from the others who were diverted earlier?

Judge: That's a difficult question to answer because I understand that various judges around the state handle cases differently. Intake varies from one court to the next, and if the intake varies, obviously in different counties there will be different classes of kids going into court.
    So much depends on the police too. You know we've got 129 different municipalities here in Allegheny County — Pittsburgh being one, and 128 others. We have 115 different police departments. There are something like 42 school districts and from that maze there is no telling how they decide who to send in. You can have a police chief in one community that as soon as somebody ignores a "keep off the grass" sign, he sends him in. In another community they will wait until they commit 5 burglaries before sending them in; you know they put them on an "unofficial probation" or something in their own community. Then, of course, they send them in here and want me to hang them on a first appearance. However, I never go for that; I don't like to commit kids on

their first appearance. The police say, "He's done this," and, "He's done that." I say, "Yes, but we have never had a chance to work with him." So I think it's a very difficult question to answer. Each court, each community, and each agency will handle kids differently.

Katkin: That's one of the things that really concerns me, particularly with the nonviolent juvenile offenders. When I sit in the court watching, I keep wondering to myself how many other kids there are who did the same thing. The incorrigibility cases triggered the thought in my mind — what these kids were accused of could probably be found for almost any kid in the state . . .

Judge: Right.

Katkin: . . . and to what extent is it just this kid's bad luck that brings him to court?

Judge: Yes, but I'm saying that the judges will find for incorrigibility if they find that the kid needs help and are not confident that the help will come from the Youth Service Bureau, or what have you.

Katkin: I'm sure that one of the things that kids who come through the juvenile court must think is that they are being treated unfairly — because they know hundreds of other kids who have done the same thing.

Judge: Sure, and some of the parents feel that way too.

Detention

Katkin: O.K., let's move to another topic. How do you see the function of pretrial detention? What are the purposes for which you would have a kid held in a detention center?

Judge: Well, we try to go by the three classic purposes: (1) if he is a threat to run away, (2) if he's a threat to himself, or (3) a threat to others. There's also a fourth one in practice: in many cases the reason we detain a child is because the parents refuse to take him home. I found out a long time ago that in such situations he's safer or she is safer in the detention house, than on the street.

Katkin: What percentage in detention do you feel are here for that reason?

Judge: Oh, I would hesitate to guess at the percentage. My guess would be maybe 30 percent of the girls. The girls seem to be more a victim of this kind of thing. Parents are more scared about girls than they are about boys.

Katkin: Why do you think that is?

Judge: I think it's just the sexuality. The danger of getting pregnant. The danger of getting raped. I think most of these parents are truly concerned about these girls but unfortunately they don't know how to cope with them. They just say, "Here, you do it, Judge, I don't want her. I don't want to take a chance." So they insist that we keep them.
Community facilities aren't always the answer either. We've got a very good one here in Pittsburgh called Amicus House. Amicus House is just a crash pad for teenagers on the run. They can take up to about 15 down there. We support them. Sometimes in the middle of night we'll get awakened: Amicus House has a youngster, and her parents are trying to take her out. We always give them a restraining order so they can keep the child till the next morning when we have a hearing on it. But then some of these kids run away from Amicus House too. Some kids are just runners. You've got to treat them that way and try to get them some place to get that out of their system.

Due Process in Juvenile Court

Katkin: I'm a little concerned about taking up a lot of your time. I have been interested in looking at courts around the states and some of the procedural differences. One of my observations is that in your court the elements of due process are very clear. It seems to me that it's better if the procedural regularity is protected. I'm not sure if "better" is the word I want, but it's visible in your court. One of the arguments that has sometimes been made, particularly before Gault, is that the procedural requirements in juvenile court interfere with rehabilitative purposes — that due process would make it harder to relate to kids — that you couldn't have the relationship of the fatherly judge being helpful to the kids. How do you reconcile the due process requirements with the informal ideal of the juvenile court?

Judge: Well, only one thing bothers me. And it still does — actually. We basically give them all the rights of adults. We had all those rights present in our hearings even before Gault except for one: that is, the right for the child to remain silent. That's one I still disagree with, but since the Supreme Court says you've got to do it, we do it. It still gravels me that a 12- or 13-year-old youngster is able to take the Fifth Amendment. I guess I'll never reconcile that in my own mind and I told that to Justice Fortas. He was here in Pittsburgh speaking and I was with one of the delegations of the Bar Association that went out to meet him at the airport. I rode in the back seat of the car with him on the way to town and told him, with all due respect, that I disagree with that particular aspect of the decision. I just think that children should be open. I know a lot of judges would disagree with me on this issue.

As for the other things, we did not announce at the outset of the hearing [a youngster] could have an attorney: "You may have an attorney and if you can't afford one, one will be appointed for you and so forth." But in cases where the parents might [want legal representation], we used to say, "You know you can bring an attorney into court." We didn't say, "If you can't afford one, we'll appoint one." But sometimes if the parent would volunteer, "I'd like a lawyer but I can't afford one," we did have a cadre of lawyers at the bar association who were willing to come out and represent kids. Thus, we did provide free legal service but we didn't advertise it. Now we have three full-time public defenders out here.

Katkin: Have you found the participation of attorneys to be problematic?

Judge: No. I've found it's fine. I think in most cases the lawyers share my philosophy about kids and very rarely do we have one electing to [have his client] remain silent. Naturally, I don't pressure lawyers or anything like that, but I think most of them share my concern. We have very few . . . "tigers" that come out here to represent their clients; once in awhile you have one, and it's funny. Sometimes a public defender that's been down around the criminal courts for a long time — perhaps someone brand new — will come out here. The first week he'll act like a tiger for awhile and then he'll realize finally that we're not trying to hang everybody that walks in the door. And I think they begin to share our philosophy that we're trying to help the kids. Not that they won't fight if they think they've got a basic and valid legal point. I think the attitude of the lawyers — both public defenders and private lawyers — has been very good out here.

Katkin: They don't perceive juvenile court as a criminal court out here?

Judge: Once in awhile somebody does, but very rarely.

Katkin: How about the presentence investigation reports at the end of the hearing? Do you find them useful at all?

Judge: Oh, I think as far as I'm concerned, we are only as good as our probation officers — and rely on them completely. I would estimate that I follow my probation officer's recommendation somewhere between 90 and 95 percent of the time.

Katkin:　What sort of information is the most important?

Judge:　To me this is strictly a personal thing. The home situation is important. So is the kind of concern the parents express or show. The other thing is the school record.

Katkin:　Is that reflected primarily in grades or behavior?

Judge:　No, I don't expect every kid to be a genius. If I see a kid with a 100 I.Q., I expect him to be a C student with a few Bs thrown in. If I see he's got 120, I expect him to be mostly Bs with some As. If I see he's flunking everything, then I know something's haywire. I don't expect miracles. I expect kids to live up to their abilities as best as they're able. The other things I look at are truancy and discipline problems — particularly class cutting and that kind of thing.

Dispositional Options

Katkin:　Suppose that a child is adjudicated delinquent and found to be in need of supervision — something like incorrigibility — what dispositional options are available to you?

Judge:　Well, first of all if we feel the child needs some sort of treatment, I rarely dismiss [his case] out of hand; that is, unless I find a child is absolutely not guilty and there is no way we can find him guilty based on what I've heard. For example, I may find that he has done something but he's never been known to us before. Or he might have been known to us before in a minor kind of a way (on an intake adjustment basis or that kind of thing). In such cases I will often continue the case for a period of time. During this period he is under sort of loose supervision of a probation officer; this is not the same degree of supervision as formal probation, but the judge can specifically tell him to make it pretty tight.

Katkin:　You were talking of the range of the dispositions available.

Judge: Yes, so the first choice, for a mild once-over, is a
continuation. Sometimes we use the continuation to decide
whether there should be a commitment or a probation.
Normally we either put them on probation or dismiss the case
— depending on how they behave. I usually say to the
youngster, "I am going to let you be the judge in this case,"
and explain to them what my alternatives are. Of course, I
usually imply they are going to go to the gas chamber if they
don't shape up. But anyway, I say, "Now at the end of three
months I'm going to review this case, and what happens to you
three months from now is going to be entirely up to you, not
me." I think it's pretty effective. It's particularly good with
school truancy cases. I also try to use that philosophy with the
cases that come in by the child welfare services route, but it is
not as easy.

Katkin: Do you ever have a kid that suggests a more serious
alternative than the one you have in mind?

Judge: Oh, I have had some kids who think they ought to go
away. Usually they are the ones who are in a miserable home
situation and want to get out. But this does not happen very
often.

  Then, of course, the next option is probation. We've
become quite sophisticated in probation here in Allegheny
County in the last seven years. In 1968, I secured a grant of
$100,000 in conjunction with our Health and Welfare
Association from the Edgar Kaufman Charitable Foundation
in Pittsburgh. We hired four people from the Youth
Development Center at Warrendale who were trained in
guided group interaction techniques. We wanted to try two
things: first we wanted to see if guided group interaction
would work for kids who were at home, not in a cocoon like you
have at a Youth Development Center. In the community, they
are with their group for an hour or two, and then with their
peers for 2 or 3 days, and then back with the group (which

usually meets twice a week). We felt that the technique had been working pretty well at the Youth Development Center and wanted to determine whether it would work on the street where the kids get polluted by rubbing shoulders with their delinquent peers as soon as they walk out the door of your office.

Secondly, we wanted to see how the community setting would work. We tried it for two years, and I felt it was very successful. We did it in as sophisticated a way as we could. We had a control group and an experimental group. We had four fellows in the office: a supervisor and three probation officers. Each team had an experimental group and a control group of kids and we compared our arrest rates.

The experimental group got the full treatment. They had extramural sports, all kinds of things. The kids in the control group were given just the usual probation services — see the guy once a month and crisis intervention if he got arrested. We found the arrest rates among the experimental groups were significantly lower than in the control group; and the office was right in Northview Heights, which is one of our very toughest projects.

Katkin: How were the kids selected for the project?

Judge: Randomly. At random. They were all from Northview Heights. No, as a matter of fact, there was one group from down in Manchester which is even tougher than Northview Heights.

Katkin: Were these kids you might normally have sent to an institution?

Judge: No.

Katkin: Kids you would place on probation?

Judge: Right. So anyway we were very satisfied. We were then able to secure Governor's Justice Commission funds to continue the project. We established one office on the north side and one on the south side, and then just this past year, 1974, in the fall, we went into full community-based probation. Now we have five programs in the city and four in the county. They are all based on that model that we started back in 1968, and now nearly all of our probation officers receive training in guided group interaction.

We are also trying to establish an active volunteer program. We have even appointed one of our probation officers as the volunteer coordinator. And we have a program where volunteer college students tutor kids in the probation centers, and this kind of thing. So we are reaching out in lots of different directions. It all costs money, that's the trouble. But I'm generally satisfied the way probation seems to be coming along.

Katkin: Then you're using probation more, and with success.

Judge: Yes.
    Then of course, the fourth alternative is institutionalization. I think between 10 and 12 percent of the cases that we hear result in commitments. If you look at our statistics for 1974, of the total number of cases heard, 10 to 12 percent went to institutions.

Katkin: I have a couple of questions on institutions, but first one about the probation programs you described. The guided group interaction program (GGI) is essentially a group therapy modality. But when you go back to the fact that the vast majority of kids commit delinquent acts, why are we to assume that because a kid is caught he needs therapeutic invervention? If so many kids commit delinquent acts — especially for lesser and status offenses — then isn't that normal behavior? And if its normal behavior why is a therapeutic modality indicated?

Judge: Good question. I'll answer it with an anecdote. One day I had a kid in court who was charged with automobile theft. It occurred because he and his buddy were out of money and they wanted to get some cash by donating some blood to the blood bank out in Oakland. They went to the blood bank and it was closed. They were walking along the street and saw a VW with keys in it, so they took the VW and drove it downtown and went to the blood bank downtown. They were caught and brought before me for disposition. Of course, they admitted doing it. I made a finding that they'd stolen a car, and that this was a delinquent act. Then the probation officer started giving me all the reasons why they had stolen a car, including the fact the parents were separated and the fact that they hadn't been doing well in school and all the rest. I said, "You know, I think they took the car because they wanted a ride downtown and didn't have bus fare." So I agree that many kids don't need therapy. But I also think most of the kids we see do need some help — although I certainly don't believe for an instant that these two jokers who took the VW should be put in a GGI group. I might continue their case or, if they had been known to us before, put them on probation for awhile to teach them that they shouldn't steal cars. But I don't think that every kid is ideal for GGI. I think it could be harmful to some. I think we have to be very careful about the ones we assign to the guided group interaction.

Katkin: You say that some of the kids that come before you need some sort of help. Do you think that most of the kids who need some kind of help finally get here, or are there huge numbers of kids in this community who could use some help and never get here at all?

Judge: Well, I would suspect that in this community, Allegheny County, a higher percentage of kids who need help come to our attention than in many communities. I often think of the words of William Rey, one of our outstanding city citizens. When he was president of the Pittsburgh Board of Education, he said that Allegheny County is "big enough to be interesting but small enough to be manageable." I think he is right. It is an amazing potpourri of nationalities and groups. It's interesting — I think that these things add up to the kind of community where people keep their eyes on each other. In the big city, the policemen are impersonal; when the policeman doesn't know you and when you're committing a delinquent act, he is much more apt to arrest you and take you to juvenile court. If he knows you, as in a smaller town, he'll take you home to mama. And we do have these 128 other municipalities besides Pittsburgh and most of them have their own police force. I think all this adds up to people keeping an eye on things a lot better than in a huge impersonal metropolis.

Katkin: How about social class distinctions? Presumably there is a considerable percentage of upper-class and middle-class kids who also have psychological problems. Yet my hunch is that most of those kids don't end up in juvenile court.

Judge: I'm sure you're right. I think that's probably true across the U.S. Many laymen say it's because the parents are buying the policemen off and so forth. I don't buy that. As I just said, in many cases the policeman knows the kid and will take him home if it's an upper-class community. He's going to take him home rather than out to the detention home. The reason [these citizens] are financially successful is because they have had a pretty good education, and if they've had a pretty good education, they are going to recognize when junior gets into trouble that he may need help of one kind or another — whether it be sending him off to a private school or buying the services of a pyschologist or a psychiatrist, or whatever it is. I think generally it's the degree of education that the parents have which enables them to provide the services which we in the court try to provide for the kids from the ghetto.

Katkin: Do you think the services you provide the poor kids are equivalent to services that fairly affluent suburban folks can buy for their kids?

Judge: I would say not "we" as the court, but I think "we" as the community are doing a pretty adequate job. For example, think of the services provided under the Mental Health and Mental Retardation Act: we have 8 or 9 "catchment areas" in the county; each one has a "base service unit," where counseling is provided, psychological and psychiatric testing is available, and all the rest. Now I am not sure that a psychologist who's on a contract with one of these places is necessarily going to be as good as the guy who's been in private practice for 20 years. . . .

Katkin: Yes, sure, at fifty bucks an hour.

Judge: Yes, but many of them are; and many of the guys who get fifty bucks an hour from a private client are volunteering. Also, we have an excellent staff — what I call our mental health team — here at the court. These are all highly competent and skilled psychologists and psychiatrists. They all have their own private practices, but I think many work for us 50 percent of the time. These are people who just like the work and feel they are doing a service by working for us. They sure could make more money than we pay them by the hour.

Katkin: If one believes that psychological intervention is necessary to deal with delinquents, there's a presumption that the causes of delinquency are psychological in nature. Are you fairly comfortable with that assumption?

Judge: When you say "psychological," I don't think in terms of emotional imbalance or emotional disturbance. "Psychological" help is offered by people who can help others deal with their problem, by people trained to help others. I know an awful lot of people who I don't think are crazy that go to a psychologist or psychiatrist. I have much faith in their system.

When I order a psychological test, I've heard enough of these cases that I can tell you what the guy is going to say in his evaluation. I can tell you that the thing at the end he's going to say is, "It's an adolescent reaction and prognosis is guarded." But I also know that's only the first step; and once you get that, then you can go to a psychologist or a psychiatrist or even a skilled social worker or psychiatric social worker to help the child deal with the shortcomings he's got at home, or to learn how to react when Dad comes home drunk, without going out and stealing a car. You know I have great faith in the thing, and I don't say the problems are psychological in nature in a sense that it represents imbalance on the part of the child — to me it just represents a way to help this kid.

Katkin: I was referring to the roots of delinquency. Some people tend to see it in very psychological terms and others see it as caused by poverty-related problems. And, in fact, the group of people who see delinquency as an outgrowth of poverty and limited opportunity and things of that nature will probably not be inclined to think that psychological intervention is necessarily the most appropriate. I suppose that one of the cornerstones of the juvenile court system is that working with the individual and his problems is at least a reasonably effective way.

Judge: Yes, you teach them it's a tough old world and very few get out alive.

Katkin: Ha. Ha. Do you know any? O.K., you had started talking about the 10 or 12 percent of kids sent on to institutional programs. How many institutions are there available to you?

Institutions and Kids

Judge: Well, let's see, offhand I can think of about seven which we generally use for the delinquent children. There are four that are offered by the State Department of Welfare. There's the Youth Development Center by Waynesburg which is for girls of all ages. It's the only girls' institution in the state, but I suspect we're probably responsible for about 60 percent of the population at Waynesburg. Then there is the Youth Development Center at Warrendale for boys 15½ and under. The Youth Development Center at Newcastle is for boys 15½ and over. The Youth Forestry Camp down at Raccoon State Park in Beaver County is for boys 15 and up.

Now Raccoon Forestry Camp is a relatively small institution. They have room for about 50 boys: right now there are 65 in the institution. They live down in the state recreational park. Many of the boys have jobs in the city of Beaver and many others work in the park. We send kids down there that are not apt to be violent, and they usually aren't real bright. They're just kids that need to be removed from their home for one reason or another and they try to teach them good work habits — that's what the emphasis is there. Newcastle, on the other hand, boasts of vocational and educational academic training. Warrendale is more academic because of the age of the kids. At Waynesburg it's a combination — I think they have a very good school program at Waynesburg and in addition have many vocational outlets for these kids: cosmetology, home economics, and some of the girls work in the town of Waynesburg. So these are the four provided by the State Department of Welfare.

We also use Gilmary School and Gamendale which are girls schools. Gilmary's in Coreopolis here in Allegheny County and Gamendale's in Erie. There's also Harbor Creek School in Erie. Those three, Gamendale, Gilmary, and Harbor Creek, are all Catholic institutions but they are nondenominational as far as the kids they take are concerned. In Gamendale, the kids go to public school; at Harbor Creek and Gilmary the kids go to school on campus. Then there's Pennsylvania George Jr. Republic at Ferro City which is for boys — a small percentage of boys there go to Grove City Public school (the ones that are doing well academically); most of the rest of them go to school on the campus. I think that's basically it for our delinquent institutions.

Then we have the two semiadult institutions: The State

Correctional Institution at Camp Hill for boys, and Muncy for women. We use them as a last resort with kids that are usually violence prone, or have been through other spects of our program and are still committing acts of violence, or are what I would consider to be a threat to the community.

Katkin: The kid who gets sent to an institution — do you have any idea how long he generally stays?

Judge: Well, we have the string on them. We can pull them back anytime but we send them on indefinite commitments. Usually it varies, but what I'm giving you right now is guesswork. (You could verify my guesses with the institutions because I'm sure they have these figures at their fingertips.) But I will guess and say the average length of stay for a girl at Waynesburg, Gilmary, or Gamendale is around 9 months. At Gilmary you know if you sent them in September and they seem to be doing all right they will be recommended for release the following June. My guess is at Warrendale it's probably 7 or 8 months, and my guess is at Newcastle it's around 6 months.

Katkin: Now, do you think these places like Newcastle and Warrendale are really able to make a significant contribution to a kid's development in 6 months?

Judge: I like to think they are, but I'm not sure. I think the programs are good there. I think that sometimes they're under tremendous pressure these days because they're overcrowded. Warrendale's got a capacity for 145 or 150 and the last I heard they had 160. At Raccoon Forestry Camp, the capacity is supposed to be 50 and they have around 65. Newcastle is supposed to be 230 and they have 250.

Katkin: How do you think they can deal with the overcrowding problem?

Judge: Well, they complain bitterly, but I refuse to keep a kid here. I tell them that as soon as possible after we order a commitment, they will be delivered to the institution. I do this because when I came to work here in 1965 we had kids in our detention home for as long as 4 months after they had been committed. The state said they didn't have room for them in their institutions, so I got on the TV and radio and newspaper and made a speech one day. It was a speech but I let all the people know what I was going to say. We had had a couple of girls in the detention house who had been there so long that they ate some ground glass so they could go to the hospital and get a change of scenery. About a week after that hit the news media, all of a sudden these institutions had room for our kids. Since then every once in awhile — within the last month I've got a communication from Newcastle — they say, "Please hold off sending boys here; we're too crowded." And I say, "Not on your life." They've got a cottage out there that they hadn't opened because they didn't have staff for it. I said, "You get the staff. Don't complain to me, you've got room for them." And I just refuse to keep kids. Of course, now we've got a relatively decent detention home, but that's no reason to detain them any longer than when we had the old decrepit one.

Katkin: Do you think the state ought to be putting more institutional facilities in?

Judge: Well, they've got to make greater provisions for kids being removed from their own homes. I hope it would be community-based facilities. But I am also aware of the fact that 2 years ago the state started a community-based facility for kids from Warrendale; and at present they've got about three kids I think. They've also got one so-called facility in the north of Pittsburgh but they've only had one boy in it the last I heard.

Katkin: How does that happen, or is it as much a mystery to you?

Judge: Well, it's bureaucracy and people I think. They have the wrong people running the one on the north side, and with the state requirement you don't have 24-hour house parents. There are people working on shifts and I don't see how you can be a substitute parent if you are working on an 8-hour shift.

Katkin: Particularly the midnight to 8 a.m. shift.

Judge: Certainly.

Katkin: Do you think if there were an adequate number of community-based programs serving Allegheny County that the institution population might fall officially?

Judge: I would suspect so. Particularly the younger boys, the ones at Warrendale; maybe 30 or 40 percent of them could make it if they were in foster homes or group homes within the community. But it is very difficult to find the people, the right people to run these things.

Katkin: How come you only use two adult institutions? Why would you not send a kid to Rockview, for example?

Judge: I don't think we can. I think it's illegal. I think the only two adult institutions (when I say adult institutions, two institutions operated by the Dept. of Justice) that we can legally send young people to are Muncy and Camp Hill.

Katkin: Now presumably when you send a kid to one of those institutions they stay for a longer period of time.

Judge: I'll guess Camp Hill is probably around 15 months, and (I don't have any women at Muncy right now) at Muncy it's, I'd guess, 15 months to two years.

Katkin: Do you think that when kids come back from Camp Hill or Muncy they are better? By better I don't necessarily mean that they were sick and now they're better.

Judge: I think a few might be better. For the majority of kids sent to Camp Hill, we have found that everything else we have been able to throw at them has not rehabilitated them. Usually when I send somebody to Camp Hill, the community needs to be protected from him.

Katkin: But is 15 months enough protection?

Judge: I don't know that, most of them are over 18 when they come out.

Katkin: I guess the thing I was wondering about was the frustration. If the purpose is protection, we are buying only a very short period of protection.

Judge: Well, with young people, I think there's a lot to be said for maturation. There's a lot more difference between a 15-year-old and an 18-year-old than there is between a 25- and 28-year-old. I think just recently Judge Tomilly was telling me (I haven't seen the study myself, but he was telling me) there is a recent study that indicates that about half the people in prison have gotten into trouble before they were 18 and about half the people in prison have never gotten into any trouble till after they were 18. This is sort of interesting you know. It would indicate to me that a significant percentage of the population who got into trouble before they were 18 grew out of it.

Katkin: True. Do you think that the institutional setting facilitates or debilitates that maturation process? One of my concerns in this area is that adolescence is largely a time for learning how to cope with the pressures of the community, to learn how to live one's life, to handle freedom, to deal with the opposite sex; and another concern is that if kids are going to outgrow their delinquency by getting mature, then institutions are not going to help that process.

Judge: Well, I like to think (and again I'm not speaking for Camp Hill or Muncy — I really can't because I just don't think they necessarily rehabilitate) they give a person a chance to grow up and not hurt anybody else. But maybe in the process . . . I really have a question about what good it does to cage somebody up, as far as helping him is concerned . . . but as far as the other institutions go, I look at them as providing, I hope, a helpful program.

10 Dispositions

The Mikado's ideal of justice is compatible with the traditional goals of criminal justice systems. The seriousness of the offense may reasonably be thought to dictate the appropriate severity of sanctions if the purpose of punishment is: (1) to deter future offenses; (2) to protect the community by incapacitating dangerous offenders; or (3) to exact retribution. Presumably, the Mikado was unconcerned with rehabilitation. The rehabilitative ideal requires that justice be individualized; that is, that treatment strategies be tailored to meet the needs rather than the deeds, of offenders.

The nature of a youngster's offense provides some information about his character, his personality, and perhaps even about his problems; but it is a gross oversimplification to believe that all youngsters who offend in similar ways will benefit from similar treatment strategies. Rich and poor children who shoplift, for example, are probably motivated by different concerns. Truants with prior records of good scholarship are probably different in many ways from truants who have always had trouble with school. Indeed, even seemingly similar youngsters are likely, upon careful examination, to show differences. The rehabilitative ideal of the juvenile justice system can be achieved only if attention focuses on the child as a unique individual, and if a broad range of dispositional possibilities exists.

In theory the dispositional power of juvenile courts is extensive and open ended.[1] Douglas Besharov, a district attorney with considerable experience in New York City's juvenile courts, suggests:

> The list of dispositional alternatives is never complete. The only real limitation on the type of dispositions that can be fashioned is the im-

agination of counsel or probation officer in making a dispositional proposal and the receptivity of the judge in accepting it.[2]

Dispositional possibilities may be loosely clustered into three main types. The first of these, entailing outright dismissal and suspended judgments, is comparatively diversionary (or at least it is comparatively nonencapsulating). These dispositions free a child from restraints upon his liberty and are comparatively nonstigmatizing; but coming as they do after extensive involvement with many agencies and officials in the formal system, they cannot be said to leave the child untouched. The second cluster of dispositions entails only minimal elements of care, supervision, or treatment, with the child remaining in his home or in a similar community setting; these community-based correctional modalities include orders of protection, probation, foster homes, and group homes. The third cluster of dispositions involves comparatively major restrictions of liberty and the removal of the child from his community into a public or private institution.

These clusters are sufficiently broad so that one might reasonably expect that treatment would be individualized for children in trouble. However, the promise of individualized justice has gone largely unfulfilled. Most juvenile courts actually have very few dispositional choices available to them, and those are often inadequate. The options available in most juvenile court cases are limited to:

> . . . outright dismissal, probation entailing loose and infrequent supervision, or commitment to a state reform school.[3]

In the remainder of this chapter attention will focus, in turn, on each of the three clusters of dispositions just identified. The potentially expansive scope and actual limitations of each cluster will be explicated, and reasons for the gap between the ideal and the real states of juvenile corrections will be explored.

The Least Encapsulating Dispositions

The definition of delinquency is so broad that many youngsters who are adjudicated delinquent may never have offended seriously and may not be particularly troubled.

> Much juvenile misbehavior is a symptom of adolescent immaturity which will disappear by itself and is not a sign of serious social or psy-

chological pathology requiring the intervention of society. Such distinctions can not be articulated successfully in statutory provisions.[4]

In disposing of such cases, judges may be disinclined to order any form of supervision. Indeed the child may have been sent to the court by officials who anticipated that no supervision would be ordered, but who thought that the formalism of the courtroom ceremony would impress the child with the seriousness of his behavior and of the possible sanctions. The threat of future court-ordered supervision, possibly even in an institutional setting, may serve to impress the youth with his responsibility to protect himself from sanctions, if not of his responsibility to the community. Two dispositions are available in these cases: (1) dismissal; and (2) suspended judgment.

Remember that the issue of innocence or guilt has already been decided at this point, and concern focuses only on the disposition of those found delinquent.

Dismissal

Dismissal of a case involves the "unconditional rejection or relinquishment of jurisdiction over a juvenile or a family."[5] Aside from cases in which a child is found to be factually innocent and cases in which waiver to a criminal court seems appropriate, delinquency petitions are dismissed only when absolutely no form of supervision, care, or custody is required.

In such cases dismissal may reflect a judge's rational strategy of nonintervention. The court hearing alone may be deemed adequate to shock a youngster into conforming behavior. The threat of sanctions in the future, the judge's effectiveness at the art of moral suasion, and his ability to alarm and perhaps even embarrass parents may combine to exert a "correcting" influence.

Very little is known about judicial use of dismissals in cases in which the facts would substantiate a finding of delinquency. A study of juvenile courts in New York City found that 18 percent of all cases are dismissed.[6] Within the city the percentage varies considerably, from a low of 5.7 percent in Brooklyn to a high of 41.6 percent in Staten Island. In Pennsylvania data indicate that 38 percent of all cases are dismissed;[7] and the Children's Bureau indicates that for fifteen states the figure is 45 percent.[8] It is not known what proportion of these cases were dismissed because of unsubstantiated complaints and what proportion were dismissed despite the substantiation of a complaint because of a strategy of nonintervention. Some judges indicate, however, that as many as 75 percent of all cases they dismiss involve factually guilty youngsters.

Suspended Judgment

The other minimally encapsulating disposition — suspended judgments — involves refraining "from entering a formal order of disposition on the condition that the juvenile or family conform to certain conditions regulating their behavior for a fixed period of time."[9] While dismissal of a case leads to its closure, a suspended judgment holds the case in abeyance pending some adjustment on the part of the youth or his family. Advocates of this procedure argue that

> . . . in some instances a formal appearance in court is sufficient "treatment," and giving the child a record as an adjudicated delinquent may, in these cases, do more harm than good.[10]

While a suspended judgment is diversionary by virtue of the fact that it prevents further penetration into the system at the time of disposition, it is encapsulating to the extent that the case is held open for a period of time to see if the youth will get into any further trouble. State law usually limits the length of time that a case may be suspended to six months or one year.[11]

Community-Based Dispositions

A decision to dismiss or suspend judgment reflects a judge's perception that a particular delinquent youngster does not need supervision, care, or custody available through agencies or institutions associated with the juvenile justice system. In cases in which such leniency does not seem appropriate, judges are generally constrained to choose between institutionalization and probation. Probation is the classic (and in many jurisdictions the only) community-based way of intervening in the youth's life; in some jurisdictions, however, a considerably greater range of dispositional possiblities exist in the community.

> *Community-based correction refers to treatment that takes place in a community environment and which permits the offender to participate in the day-to-day activities of community life.*

Recent efforts to generate extensive community-based correctional programs are related in large measure to frustration about the inability of institutional programs either to fulfill the rehabilitative function or to provide humanitarian care.

> Institutions tend to isolate offenders from society, both physically and psychologically, cutting them off from schools, jobs, families, and other supportive influences and increasing the probability that the label of criminal will be indelibly impressed upon them.[12]

This statement by the President's Commission on Law Enforcement and the Administration of Justice suggests the acceptance of a labeling perspective (see the discussion in Chapter 2). Isolating an offender from his normal social environment may encourage the development of a delinquent orientation and thus of further delinquent behavior. The issues raised by the Commission indicate a need to integrate rather than isolate the offender, to reduce rather than simplify the delinquent label. Community-based correctional programs such as probation, foster homes, and group homes represent attempts to respond to these issues by normalizing social contacts, reducing the stigma attached to being institutionalized, and providing opportunities for jobs and schooling.

Court dispositions are often compromises between the incompatible pressures to secure deterrence, incapacitation, retribution, and rehabilitation. Community-based programs do not permit the freedom of dismissal or of suspended judgments, but neither do they isolate offenders from the community as institutions do. Community programs are sometimes perceived as being easy on the youngster, and thus as not providing sufficient punishment or supervision to insure deterrence, incapacitation, and retribution. On the other hand, commitment to such programs represents a considerable degree of restriction and punishment when compared to dismissal, suspended judgment or informal processing out of the system at an early stage. An extensive look at probation, the most commonly used form of community program, and a brief overview of other programs will provide insight into the operation of community-based dispositional options.

Probation

"Probation is the conditional release of a juvenile under formal supervision of the juvenile court's probation service or other court related agency."[13] Probationary dispositions usually involve the continuation of the youngster in the community setting, but with the imposition of restrictions on his behavior. The range of restrictions that the court may impose on a youngster placed on probation is relatively open in most states. In California, for example:

> The court may impose and require any and all reasonable conditions that it may determine fitting and proper to the end that justice may be done and the reformation and rehabilitation of the ward enhanced.[14]

Statutes in other states specify that several particular conditions of probation may be imposed, including: paying restitution, getting a job, going to school, obeying parents, undergoing special treatment (such as for narcotic addiction or psychiatric problem, etc.).[15] Courts generally have sufficient latitude so that individualization to the perceived needs of the youth placed on probation is at least theoretically possible.

In keeping with the notion of the juvenile court's conception of "individualized" justice, the conditions of probation should reflect an extensive investigation into the youth's behavior and the potential causal forces for his delinquency. Consider, for example, the case of a youngster arrested as part of a group in a stolen car. Suppose this youth had never been in trouble before but the other youths had extensive histories of delinquency. It might well be that this youngster's problem was that he became involved with the wrong crowd; probation with the restriction that he not keep any further company with this crowd might be the most reasonable disposition. A suspended judgment would not provide supervision to ensure that the condition of probation was accomplished, and an institutional disposition would be overly restrictive for his offense and prior record. Thus, probation provides the court a peculiar opportunity to meet the individual's needs while securing at least some control over his future behavior.

The Probation Officer and the Community

The probation officer has traditionally been responsible for two key functions: personally providing counseling to the probationed youth and serving as a link to other community services. While his

counseling skills used to be viewed as his most significant contribution to his client, of late the counseling role has given way to a "broker" role, in which the probation officer organizes community services for his probationers; he links these youths to the available resources — such as vocational rehabilitation centers, vocational schools, mental health centers, employment bureaus, church groups, and even the boy scouts. Although broad utilization of community resources is probably helpful in most cases, it does have inherent risks: linking a youngster with one or more of these groups may actually amplify a small problem into a much larger one; overattendance to the youngster and his "problem" may turn the "problem" into an attention-getting device or may reinforce the youngster's, or the community's, perception that the problem is serious. In either case, further delinquency may ensue.

There are two main reasons for the trend among probation officers to conceptualize themselves as social brokers rather than as providers of direct counseling service. One is that probation officers simply do not have the training, skills, and abilities to provide their clients with all the different types of assistance they might require. The other is time: even if probation officers possessed the superhuman skills necessary to do psychotherapy, vocational training, employment counseling, etc. with diverse types of children, their workloads are such that they would not have the time. Excessive workloads, in fact, are probably the single greatest pressure away from the direct-service model of probation work.

It is generally recommended that a probation officer's caseload should be 50 work units.[15] Each presentence investigation (P.S.I.) is counted as five units. A P.S.I. is weighed so heavily because of the amount of time required to adequately complete such an investigation. In fact one study found that probation officers were putting thirteen times as much effort on one presentence report as on one supervision case.[16] Daniel Glaser suggests that the presentence report produces a tangible product which supervisors use to evaluate the officer's performance.[17] The evaluation by superiors prompts the officer to spend an inordinate amount of time on this aspect of his job to the neglect of less supervised functions. In larger metropolitan areas, this conflict is prevented by having officers specialize in intake, presentence investigations, and supervision; however, specialization is not possible in most smaller departments.

We are primarily interested in the probation officer as he is involved in the disposition of a case; but we must keep in mind that this one person frequently also serves the court as an intake officer and as an investigator of a juvenile's background for disposition too.

Figure 10.1 presents the percentage of juveniles being supervised by officers with workloads of 50 or fewer cases, 51 - 70 cases, 71 - 100 cases, and over 100 cases. A majority of juveniles on probation are seen by officers with caseloads exceeding 70, and that workload does not include the officer's P.S.I.s and intake work.[18] Even without reference to P.S.I.s and intake work, the probation officers' loads far exceed the recommended level. What this means is that the officer either gives superficial attention to his total caseload or gives intensive supervision to a small proportion while paying scant attention to the rest.

Effectiveness of Probation

Criminal justice is not known for its diligence in adequately testing the impact of its many programs. The ability of probation to reform or at least to reduce a youngster's misbehavior has been studied

FIGURE 10.1 Percentage of Juveniles Supervised by Officers with Various Caseload Sizes

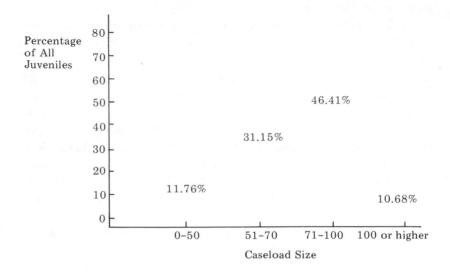

as thoroughly as any area of justice, but there are still many unanswered questions. For example, few attempts have been made to compare probation to an institutional disposition.

Roger Hood and Richard Sparks,[19] in their excellent review of research into probation, make this assertion:

> For many offenders, probation is likely to be at least as effective in preventing recidivism as an institutional sentence.

Most attempts to evaluate probation have focused on the proportion of youths *successfully completing their probationary period*. In general these studies indicate that between 15 and 30 percent of those placed on probation successfully complete their probation without having a formal complaint made against them.[20] However, this is a rather vague finding, because it fails to specify (1) the success rate after release from probation; (2) the percentage apprehended for an offense but not dropped from probation; and (3) the relative effectiveness of probation compared to other dispositions.

Studies following up youths after their discharge from probation indicate that from 16 to 42 percent commit new offenses for which they are convicted.[21] One study of Allegheny County, Pennsylvania (Pittsburgh), in 1940 followed the criminal careers of youths for ten years after their release from probation.[22] It found that 16 percent were convicted of other offenses, but only 5 percent were convicted for felonies. A 1937 study by Jay Rumney and Joseph P. Murphy[23] in New Jersey followed 131 juveniles for eleven years after they were on probation: 42 percent had committed major offenses during that period.

Caseload Size and Probation Effectiveness

Attempts to compare probation to alternative dispositions suffer because the youngsters receiving different dispositions may not be comparable. Research examining the effect of caseload size on probation effectiveness has not been so handicapped, and thus more valid information is available.

It has generally been assumed that smaller caseloads will result in more time for counseling and supervision by the probation officer, and thus that smaller caseloads will result in greater effectiveness.

Results of experiments testing this assumption have not always been supportive. Lohman et al.[24] compared the effectiveness of four types of probation workloads: intensive caseloads (25 offenders with an average of 6.71 contacts per month), ideal caseloads, normal caseloads, and minimum-supervision caseloads (125 offenders averaging .48 contacts a month); the researchers found no differences in terms of new major violations by probationers. There is, in short, little reason to be confident that probation actually accomplishes very much, and even less reason to believe that excessive caseloads are the source of all problems.

Other Community-Based Programs

Foster Homes.   In many instances the juvenile court simply does not have an appropriate disposition for a youngster who is not seriously delinquent and who does not need the control exercised in an institution, but whose home situation is not appropriate for regular probation or suspended judgment or dismissal. If the home does not provide the appropriate supervision and care thought to be necessary to deter further violations, then the court may look for other options; frequently there may be only one — institutionalization. One option that has been used for many years but which is difficult to develop for youths appearing before the juvenile court is foster homes. Foster home placement involves the removal of a youth from his own home and placement in a private home.

Even though there is generally some remuneration for taking foster children, it is difficult to find families willing to take an older child, especially one having trouble with the law. Development of such foster home placements requires good cooperation between welfare departments (which typically investigate and approve those wishing to be foster parents) and the juvenile court. Unfortunately this cooperation rarely exists, so foster home placement is infrequently used for delinquents. When it is used, it is frequently combined with probation supervision.

Group Homes. Group homes are community homes which are normally licensed by the state and designed to house six to ten youngsters, under the supervision of professional childcare workers. Like foster homes, they provide an alternative to institutionalization for youngsters who are not wanted at home or who seem to require more care and supervision than they can get at home. Group homes generally provide some form of psychological treatment. The usual foster home basically provides a place for the youth to reside, and the only "treatment" is that the youth is living in a normal, hopefully happy, home. A group home, on the other hand, attempts to provide a more therapeutic milieu. Professional counselors are often involved in the program, perhaps providing both group and individual counseling.

Institutions

Institutional commitment is presumably the last resort for a youngster whose behavior has been so serious or persistent as to render inappropriate a suspended judgment, a probation, or any other community placement. Institutions vary, however, in terms of the type of treatment offered, the security-control emphasis in the institution, the quality of the physical facilities, the quality of staff, and the types and seriousness of the crimes of the youngsters housed there. Indeed, institutions are for children so dissimilar from one another that we must be very cautious in assessing them as places to live, be punished in, or be rehabilitated in.

The child who ends up incarcerated is not necessarily (or even usually) a serious delinquent; often children are institutionalized because of the failure of the community (and in particular, of parents) to present options to the court. The decision to incarcerate a youngster may reflect his behavior, but just as importantly it reflects his limited opportunities. In this section we will explore institutional placement as a disposition and will discuss its ability to fulfill the justice system's responsibility to deter, punish, and rehabilitate.

Power of the Juvenile Court

In most states the juvenile court has few, if any, restrictions on its ability to place youngsters in an institution. It is not uncommon, however, for state law to specify that a youth may be placed in a training school only if he is adjudicated delinquent, as opposed to dependent or neglected. The Pennsylvania Juvenile Court Act of 1972, for example, states that:

(a) If the child is found to be a deprived child the court may make any of the following orders of disposition best suited to the protection and physical, mental, and moral welfare of the child:

    (1) Permit the child to remain with his parents, guardian, or other custodian, subject to conditions and limitations as the court prescribes, including supervision as directed by the court for the protection of the child.

    (2) Subject to conditions and limitations as the court prescribes transfer temporary legal custody to any of the following: (i) any individual in or outside Pennsylvania who, after study by the probation officer or other person or agency designated by the court, is found by the court to be qualified to receive and care for the child; (ii) an agency or other private organization licensed or otherwise authorized by law to receive and provide care for the child or (iii) a public agency authorized by law to receive and provide care for the child. . . .

(b) Unless a child found to be deprived is found also to be delinquent he shall not be committed to or confined in an institution or other facility designed or operated for the benefit of delinquent children.[25]

Contrast the orientation of this section of the law with the following section that details the dispositional options for youths adjudicated delinquent by the court:

If a child is found to be a delinquent child the court may make any of the following orders of disposition best suited to his treatment, supervision, rehabilitation, and welfare:

(1) Any order authorized by section 24 for the disposition of a deprived child.

(2) Placing the child on probation under supervision of the probation officer of the court or the court of another state as provided in section 34, under conditions and limitations the court prescribes.

(3) Committing the child to an institution, youth development center, camp or other facility for delinquent children operated under the direction or supervision of the court or other public authority and approved by the Department of Public Welfare.

(4) Committing the child to an institution operated by the Department of Public Welfare or special facility for children operated by the Department of Justice.[26]

The basis for separating delinquent and dependent-neglected youngsters is that all too often a child's only offense is that he has been a victim of parental neglect and of the failure of the community to provide services; this child might be placed in an institution with malicious youths who prey upon such "deprived" youths and sometimes socialize them into serious misbehaviors.

Obviously, however, the caricature of a delinquent as "brutal" is an oversimplification. Howard James notes after extensive investigations into juvenile justice across the country that ". . . there is a very fine line — often blurred — between the neglected child and one accused of being delinquent."[27] Consider the following case cited by Howard James.

> Bill, who is small for his age, has not seen his father, an ex-convict, for several years. His mother, brother, and sister are on welfare, as is his grandmother. His family moves frequently, and there is town gossip about his mother — although she is also reported to have serious eye trouble and a heart condition.[28]

Bill was first placed in a foster home but was later placed in the state reform school. Howard James quotes the judge that Bill was accused of

> breaking the limb of a neighbor's cherry tree; taking empty pop bottles off a truck; fighting; shoplifting; stealing toys; running through a

vegetable garden; pulling up vegetables; entering a dairy and taking small change; stealing a purse from a woman at a laundry; spraying water around a gas station, followed by cussing; getting caught with his hands in a barbershop cash register; getting caught with his hands in a cash register in a laundry; vandalism at a neighbor's; climbing a peach tree, and sassing the woman who told him to stop picking green fruit; and hanging around the railroad station, climbing aboard trains (among other things).[29]

Bill could as easily be adjudicated "deprived"as "delinquent." As a consequence of the judge's discretionary decision to attach the more serious label, Bill's institutional experience may be significantly more rigorous than it might have been. In any event, the "delinquent" label certainly does not imply that the youngster is necessarily malicious nor that he is not deprived or neglected.

In some states the formal title of the disposition makes little difference because the judge can place the youth in any juvenile institution that he desires. Other states such as Pennsylvania limit the judge to sending the delinquent children to delinquent-serving institutions and deprived youths to institutions for only deprived youngsters. Yet other states have a system wherein the judge can find the youth either "delinquent" or "neglected," then send him to a state system, such as the Department of Youth Services, which has power to place the child in any particular institution or to place him in a community-based program.

Statutory Limitations on Length of Institutional Stay

In keeping with the rehabilitative ideal of the juvenile justice system, it has been customary to send children to institutions until they were "cured" or reached majority (which is 18 in some states and 21 in others).[30] In this fashion a child could be kept until he was "right" for release or he had accomplished all that he could in the institution and it was time for him to try his wings in the "real" world. This assumes, of course, that institutions can and do rehabilitate youngsters and that the professional staff can and do recognize when the child is prepared for his entrance back into the society. Clearly, neither of these assumptions is true. Institutions simply have not demonstrated capacity to rehabilitate offenders, even if a majority of youths do not recidivate, this success can not necessarily be attributed to the institution.

> *Remember that in the first chapter we pointed out*
> *that almost everyone commits a delinquent act*
> *and that only a few fall into systematic deviance*
> *(i.e., most drop out with no "treatment" in an*
> *institution). Consider this statement by the*
> *National Advisory Commission concerning*
> *institutions for both younger and older offenders:*
> *The failure of major institutions to reduce*
> *crime is incontestable. Recidivism rates are*
> *notoriously high. Institutions do succeed in*
> *punishing, but they do not deter. They protect*
> *the community, but that protection is only*
> *temporary. They relieve the community of*
> *responsibility by removing the offender, but*
> *they make successful reintegration into the*
> *community unlikely. They change the*
> *committed offender, but the change is more*
> *likely to be negative than positive.*[31]

Training schools have not only been unable to fulfill the re-habilitative goal held out for them; they have actually served to inflict extra "treatment" or "punishment" upon youngsters because of their youth. For example, children can be institutionalized for minor violations that are not even offenses for adults, and they can be held for more extensive periods of time than can adults convicted of the same offense. As the incongruities of our inability to rehabilitate and of our inflicting of this "treatment" for extensive periods of time has become more apparent, there has developed a trend for states to limit the length of time a child can serve, such as a three-year maximum[32] (unless sent to an adult court) and to restrict the length of time that a youth could serve to no longer than would be the case if he were an adult. Such laws restrict the discretion of the institution to retain a youth because of institutional misbehavior or because of his "failure" to participate in a constructive way (from the perception of the staff) in the life of the institution — whether it be in treatment programs or whether in marching in a straight line from cell to dining hall.

Institutional Care

On June 30, 1971 there were 35,931 children in training schools; 5666 in ranches, forestry camps, and farms; and 1045 in halfway houses and group homes.[33] Moreover, with the average length of stay being 8.7 months in training schools, 6.6 months in ranches and forestry camps, and 7.2 months in halfway houses and group homes,[34] we know that many more youngsters are in institutions each year than were there on any one particular day; in fact estimates usually approach 100,000 children a year.[35] Such statistics, however, fail to adequately represent the qualitative aspects of institutionalization and the impact of institutional deprivation on children.

Children are commonly sent *to* institutions not because of the care and help they will receive there, but to get them out of the community. Considering this orientation, we should not be surprised to find that the community knows little about what goes on inside institutions; but such ignorance extends even to the judges who place children there. The impact of this lack of concern is to relegate almost completely to the institution the kind of care that the youngsters receive.

> . . . the public focuses upon its short-range, immediate protection rather than being concerned about the additional hostility and hatred being engendered within these youths as they are subjected to brutalization to keep them confined.[36]

Physical isolation from "normal" society is "brutal" in and of itself. But institutions do more than passively isolate youths. They attempt to regiment them into a way of life not similar to "normal" living; and they use physical and psychological coercion to pressure them into conformity with the demands of a socially, psychologically, and sexually perverted existence.

Documentation of the use of physical brutality is provided by Howard James.

> Audie E. Langston, an employee of the Florida Division of Youth Services, witnessed past floggings at the Florida School for Boys in Marianna. He describes them as "sickening."
> 'A young boy (was) taken into a stark, bare, dimly lit room where he was compelled to lie on a small cot and receive licks with a heavy leather strap. At the time the strap was being wielded by a man who was at least six feet, three inches and weighed well over two hundred pounds. . . . The child quivers and writhes. . . .'[39]

Physical brutality is not limited to one institution or even one state; James found that training schools in Indiana, Maryland, North

Carolina, New York, Delaware, Tennessee, Montana, and several other states either covertly or explicitly use physical brutality to control youths.[38]

Psychological and social coercion is much more subtle, but just as debilitating to a youngster. Children are removed from family and friends, placed in sterile institutional environments (even if the walls are a "homey" pastel color) and demanded to demonstrate subserviance to institutional rules in order to secure timely release. What does it indicate about a youngster's rehabilitation that he walks quietly to meals, says "yes, sir," and "no, sir" instead of running away? Institutions reward those who conform, and punish those who misbehave (i.e., disrupt the smooth functioning of the institution). It is possible, however, that those who adapt to institutional living become unfit for noninstitutional living, and those that rebel against institutional controls are maintaining their own, perhaps more appropriate, identity.

Our society rewards aggressiveness in business, but aggressive youngsters in institutions are a nemesis and are pressured to subjugate themselves to the institutional norms. Stifling of initiative and agressiveness is likely to result. Children who have been unfortunate enough to be institutionalized are unlikely to benefit from the experience. At best they are no worse for the experience; but at worst they are an unredeemable resource for our society, one that grows more hostile with each encounter with our justice system.

Deinstitutionalization and Normalization

Dissatisfaction with institutional programs has existed for two reasons: (1) because such programs are sometimes brutalizing, and (2) because they always necessitate an unnatural environment for children. Consider, for example, Justice Fortas's observation in the *Gault* decision:

> The boy is committed to an institution where he may be restrained of liberty for years. It is of no constitutional consequence — and of limited practical meaning — that the institution to which he is committed is called an Industrial school. The fact of the matter is that, however euphemistic the title, a "receiving home" or an "industrial school" for juveniles is an institution of confinement in which the child is incarcerated for a greater or lesser time. His world becomes "a building

with whitewashed walls, regimented routine and institutional hours. . . ."[39]

In recent years a national movement of some magnitude has begun to demand that large, secure institutions for juveniles be closed.[40] Massachusetts has already gone out of the reform school business and there are indications that other states may follow. Milton Luger, former director of the National Association of State Juvenile Delinquency Program Administrators, maintains:

> With the exception of a relatively few youths it (would be) better for all concerned if young delinquents were not detected, apprehended, or institutionalized. Too many of them get worse in our care.[41]

Proponents of deinstitutionalization maintain that children are best off in their own communities and that communities are best protected when children are helped to accommodate to the demands of social life. Aside from the actual closing of institutions, there are two main strategies for developing community services for troubled children: diversion and normalization. Effective programs of diversion at the early stages of processing in the juvenile justice system will reduce the number of children adjudicated delinquent, or dependent-neglected. Presumably, that will allow more intensive community-based supervision for the dwindling numbers of children that do need to be brought into the system.

Normalization is a term for the belief that the resources of the justice system should be aimed at providing nondiverted youngsters with experiences that approximate as nearly as possible those of normal community life. The money currently expended on maintaining children in institutions, it is argued, could be better spent on providing services to families. If a child's family is unable to provide appropriate care and supervision, then resources ought to be invested in providing a "nearly normal" experience, perhaps at a foster home or foster-group home. Life in group homes is considerably different from typical family life, but it is also much less regimented than life in institutions.

Scholars and practitioners alike are increasingly concerned with the development of community-based treatment programs. While it is premature to maintain that the heyday of institutions is passed, it is at least clear that there is growing sympathy for the notion that troubled children can not be trained for freedom in captivity.

Concluding Thoughts

At present, judges have comparatively few dispositional alternatives. Too frequently they are compelled to select institutional programs because there are no others. The inadequacy of reform schools, however, is becoming more apparent; and the national movement to close them is accompanied by attempts to create a broad range of new community-based programs. It is at least reasonable to hope that conditions may be significantly improved in the near future. In Massachusetts, more than three hundred innovative, experimental community-based programs for children in trouble have come to life since the closing of state training schools. If that trend holds true in other states, we may soon witness a day when communities really will be able to provide each child with services that every parent might wish for his own child.

References

1. Douglas R. Besharov, *Juvenile Justice Advocacy* (New York: Practising Law Institute, 1975).
2. Ibid., p. 375.
3. Sanford J. Fox, *The Law of Juvenile Courts in a Nutshell* (St. Paul: West Publishing, 1971), p. 203.
4. Besharov, *Juvenile Justice Advocacy,* p. 377.
5. Ibid., p. 375.
6. Office of Children's Services, *Juvenile Injustice,* Judicial Conference of the State of New York, 1973 (New York: The Office, 1973).
7. Pennsylvania Department of Justice, *Pennsylvania Juvenile Court Dispositions, 1972* (Harrisburg: Bureau of Criminal Justice Statistics, 1972), p. 15.
8. Juvenile Court Statistics, 1957, Childrens Bureau Statistical Series, No. 52 (Washington, D.C.: Children's Bureau, 1959), p. 7.
9. Besharov, *Juvenile Justice Advocacy,* p. 377.
10. Fox, *Law of Juvenile Courts,* p. 210.
11. Ibid.
12. President's Commission on Law Enforcement and the Administration of Justice, *The Challenge of Crime in a Free Society* (Washington, D.C.: U.S. Government Printing Office, 1967).
13. Besharov, *Juvenile Justice Advocacy,* p. 379.
14. California Welfare and Institutions Code 730 (West 1972).
15. The President's Task Force Report: *Corrections* (Washington, D.C.: U.S. Government Printing Office, 1967) p. 29.
16. Daniel Glaser, "Corrections of Adult Offenders in the Community" in *Prisoners in America,* ed. Lloyd E. Ohlin (Englewood Cliffs, N.J.: Prentice-Hall, 1973), p. 103.

17. Ibid.

18. President's Commission, *Challenge of Crime,* pp. 98 - 9.

19. Roger Hood and Richard Sparks, *Key Issues in Criminology* (New York: McGraw - Hill, 1970), p. 186.

20. See Ruth S. Cavan, *Juvenile Delinquency* (Philadelphia: J.B. Lippincott, 1969), p. 449.

21. Ibid. pp. 449 - 50.

22. Lewis Diana, "Is Casework in Probation Necessary?" *Focus* 34 (January 1955), pp. 41 - 52.

23. Jay Rumney and Joseph P. Murphy, *Probation and Social Adjustment* (New Brunswick, N.J.: Rutgers University Pres, 1952), pp. 162 - 3.

24. J. D. Lohman, A. Wahl, and R. M. Carter, *The San Francisco Project, Research Report No. 11,* (Berkeley, Calif.: School of Criminology, University of California, 1967).

25. Pennsylvania Juvenile Act of 1972.

26. Ibid., p. 22.

27. Howard James, *Children in Trouble* (New York: David McKay Co., 1969), p. 26.

28. Ibid., p. 25.

29. Ibid., p. 26.

30. Fox, *Law of Juvenile Courts,* p. 219.

31. National Advisory Commission on Criminal Justice Standards and Goals, *Corrections* (Washington, D.C.: U.S. Government Printing Office), p. 1.

32. Pennsylvania Juvenile Act of 1972.

33. U.S. Department of Justice, *Children in Custody,* (Washington, D.C.: National Criminal Justice Information and Statistics Service, 1974).

34. Ibid.

35. Besharov, *Juvenile Justice Advocacy,* p. 385.

36. James, *Children in Trouble,* p. 90.

37. Ibid., p. 89.

38. Ibid., pp. 88 - 102.

39. *In Re Gault* 387 U.S. 1. (1967).

40. James, *Children in Trouble,* p. 82.

41. Milton Luger in James, *Children in Trouble,* p. 108.

An Interview with Dr. Jerome Miller: A Radical Perspective on Juvenile Corrections

Dr. Miller came to national prominence in the late 1960s and early 1970s when, as Director of the Massachusetts Department of Youth Services, he closed that state's training schools. Dr. Miller is committed to the view that most youngsters who are labeled "delinquent" ought never to have been brought into the justice system at all, and to the belief that the comparatively small number of young people who are genuinely in need of rehabilitation could best be served in small, community-based programs.

Dr. Miller believes that community corrections programs cannot be adequately developed while large institutions still exist. The institutions make it comparatively easy to deal with a problem child by sending him away; and they syphon off a tremendous percentage of the resources available for correctional programs.

In recent years Dr. Miller has worked as the head of Child Welfare in Illinois and as Commissioner of Children and Youth in Pennsylvania. He is perhaps the nation's most outspoken, and most visible, advocate of closing the institutions. Our interview with him took place in a small classroom at the Pennsylvania State University, with about twenty students and faculty members present.

Institutions Are Made To Be Closed

Katkin: Perhaps you could start off by telling us about some of the reforms in juvenile corrections that you initiated when you were Director of the Division of Youth Services in Massachusetts.

Miller: Sure. What we did in Massachusetts was to move entirely out of training schools or (what do they call them) reform schools — large institutions for delinquent youth. We closed them all down. . . . As a matter of fact, the ideal institution, I feel, is one with no inmates. They do very well. The staff come and go on time, lawns are well kept, the cafeteria runs well, and they don't do much harm to anyone.

I think the same is true of state mental hospitals, large institutions for the retarded, certainly of correctional institutions — simply don't exist to serve their clientele; they exist for other reasons. They exist because of economic conditions in local areas. They exist because of political patronage positions in state government. They exist because of certain historical traditions over the last hundred years that provide people a lot of reassurance, albeit false, but they have very little to do with their stated purpose of helping inmates. And of course as an administrator of an agency that has such institutions you're never held accountable for their stated purpose. There's a dichotomy (if you put it in Robert Merton's terms) between latent and manifest goals — between what is preached manifestly about these institutions and what really their latent purpose is, which has very little to do with the manifest statement.

You can survive forever as a career administrator in state government if you do a few things: keep your staff happy, stay within your budget, and avoid incidents that overflow into the community. Basically if you do those three things you'll be viewed as a very successful career-bound state administrator and can build up quite a reputation without any reference to whether or not what you're doing does any good or harm to the people that are your clientele. It would be kind of akin to running, let's say, a medical hospital in a city or a county on the basis that the doctors and nurses are reasonably comfortable, everybody's staying within their budget, and very few patients are jumping out the window; despite the fact that someone notices, by the by, that 60 to 80 percent (as would be true in corrections) of the patients get more ill or die while they are in your care.

Kramer: Did you take the job in Massachusetts intending to close the state's reform schools?

Miller: No, not really. When I first went to Massachusetts I told the search committee that asked me to come and I told the Governor that I planned to move into a lot of community-based programs, but I also harbored the hope of making our training schools therapeutic communities and of making them decent humane treatment facilities. I think we learned fairly soon that that was kind of a false hope, not for clinical or professional reasons but for political reasons. I think if you look at it historically you will see that the problem is not one of developing decent treatment programs in large institutions. The problem is the political one of sustaining them. Inevitably they go down the drain after a year or two or three.

If you look at the history of corrections you will find that. You will find every 5 or 10 years an incident, a riot, a killing, a series of escapes, a suicide, a something or other that calls the outside world's attention to what's going on. There will be a call for reform. You'll have an infusion of funds, new programs, maybe a few new staff if it's not a politically entrenched system. Then if you look at it 5 years later, it's about where it was before, only the staff have either left or are socialized to the old system. Then you have to have another incident and another call for more reform, but not much happens.

It was my hope that we could make the places humane, but I think fairly soon that my staff I brought with me and I pretty well agreed that it was going to be 4 years of swimming up river just to get the programs to be reasonably decent. And at the end of the 4 years we'd have no guarantee at all that when we left things wouldn't slip back.

For instance, the essence of a therapeutic community in an institution is that it's based on very fragile staff-client relationships. The subtle sorts of interactions that have to go on in a decent and caring institutional setting are difficult to create. It requires a lot of staff training, a lot of staff confronting of their own problems and feelings. It involves all sorts of issues that are fairly delicate to keep in balance. And what you generally find is that such programs develop around a charismatic leader, a charismatic superintendent, or director of program services, or something. Conversely, however, one can undo the finest therapeutic community that might have taken 3 or 4 years to build — one can undo it in 3 or 4 days. Because, unlike building such a place, you can unbuild it or tear it down with a few rules: a few regulations on the bulletin board can undo the finest therapeutic community. Just a couple of pages long, or maybe five or six proper rules such as: people go to bed at a certain time, social workers only talk to certain people, visiting hours are restricted as of such and such, and a few other things, and the whole thing is down the drain.

Unfortunately you can't put rules up that say staff will as of tomorrow relate decently to clientele and will do such and such. It doesn't work that way. I think characteristically that's what happens.

Our first year there . . . I was just trying really to survive the first year. We didn't have adequate budget for new programs. I had all patronage staff. Of about 1000 employees, about 800 were political appointees without benefit of any civil service. The legislature in their wisdom gave them all civil service coverage before I arrived so that they were unfirable and untransferable. No new positions were funded, including my own. I had to freeze a couple of vacant other salaries to pay my own salary. I couldn't hire any of the assistant commissioner's positions that were created in the new legislation because none of them were funded for almost a year after I arrived. So the first year was more or less survival and trying to humanize places as best we could.

I tried to open the institutions up to the public by bringing people in and by loosening up a bit. That caused a great deal of upset, both within the institutions and in the community.

The Governor's Wife Gets an Eyeful

Hyman: How did you finally get into a position to begin the process of closing the training schools?

Miller: The first chance we had to make a break in the institutions came about a year after I arrived. When I took the Governor's wife out to one of the institutions (I had taken her around kind of to see places) she had an interest in this area. I took her around without telling anyone it was the Governor's wife and without any particular to-do. We always went unannounced; even if she told me a week or so before she was coming, I never told anyone else.

So we went out to Bridgewater, which was our maximum security unit. I don't know if you've even seen "Titticut Follies," the movie. You ought to if you haven't, because it's still an accurate assessment, an accurate portrayal of what goes on in hospitals for the criminally insane in Massachusetts. It's just as accurate today as it was when it was made in the middle-late sixties.

We had the juvenile version of that, our juvenile Bridgewater, with identical kinds of buildings about a quarter of a mile from the adult facility. That was for our supposed "most vicious, most dangerous" kids. I took her out that evening along with her . . . she had kind of a bodyguard that went with her, and with one of the older employees in the department who had been around a long time. When we arrived at this walled institution a fellow let us in at the gate, but there was no one around in the administration building. It was very depressing. It was in the early evening, dusk, and it was that time of year when it wasn't very pretty out.

The place was very, very dirty. We walked up the hall with urine on the floors, and the place stank. And it had an awful feel to it. This is a place built in the late 1800s, a big marble and stone facility.

There were no kids around. They were out in the yard. They had a walled yard in the back. We went out into the yard, and as we came into the yard there was a mass escape attempt. As we walked in, the kids started running for all the walls and the staff started running to pull them off. So then she was able to observe firsthand a situation of kids being pulled, being pummelled, and handcuffed, and tossed on the ground, and sworn at, and carried off. The kids were then marched into the gymnasium where they proceeded to have a riot, stomping on the floors and punching out the windows and chanting. No one went out of the way to be very nice to Mrs. Sargent because they didn't know it was the Governor's wife, and certainly didn't go out of their way to be very nice to me because I was not well liked in the agency. I had been there about a year and was viewed as overly permissive, etc. I thought she had a chance to view things pretty well as they are . . . as they were.

The kids were then put in their individual rooms. During that time we went around together and chatted with the kids in their rooms. They call them rooms. They were like cells. We chatted at some length and she got to know a number of kids by name and we discussed some of the situations that were going on.

The upshot of it was that she got to see what one usually does not get to see in tours of institutions. As the word spread later in the evening that this was the Governor's wife, as we went back through the areas that had been terrible on our way in, they were terribly clean on our way out. Everything began to kind of shape up behind her. I took for granted that she would have something to whisper in the Governor's ear that night about her day's experiences. In chatting with my staff I suggested that we now had an opportunity to do some new things.

On Closing Institutions

So we decided that maybe this would be our chance to close that place. We decided (and I don't remember the exact date; this was something like a Monday). I think on a Wednesday we met and decided we might want to close it, and within a week, maybe ten days at the most, it was closed. We sent out a team of not so sophisticated clinicians, because the department didn't have any sophisticated clinicians, along with some old-line staff who kind of knew the kids historically. And we screened through the population. We paroled the majority home. We developed a closed cottage on the grounds of one of the other institutions for about a dozen kids, 12 or 15 kids, who were there on serious sorts of crimes of murder, rape, and that sort of thing. And we closed it.

We found that we were able to do that easily. There was no great uproar. The staff didn't really even have time to have a union meeting around it before it was closed. We invited out the media so they could film the door closing, which they did very nicely. They came out, said this is the end of Bridgewater, the door slammed, and the guy wrapped it up so that it became a fact. Once it's on television it's a fact. And we got out of there and there was virtually no upset. There was no upset in the legislature. There was no upset anywhere. The reason was that no one really had a chance to form up around it. We didn't broadcast it until it was done and we were out of there.

We should have learned from that, but we didn't. And when it came to closing a couple of the other places, we did it the traditional way. We announced, for instance, that the Shirley Industrial School for Boys, which was for the older boys, was to be phased out over a 9- to 15-month period — that we would slowly lower the number of inmates. Well, we learned that the minute you announce that you're going to lower the number of kids in an institution you can expect it to go up. That's exactly what began to happen. And then we had no end of trouble within the institutions.

Hyman: Be more specific, O.K.? What sorts of trouble?

Miller: There were riots, fires, racial confrontations, escapes, runaways. In one group we almost had more escapes in one month than we had kids in the school. We had only about 125 kids. I think we had in excess of 100 runaways in that one month. They would pass each other in groups of 15 and 20 leaving. Most of it related to dysfunction within the social system of the institution itself. And most of it very honestly was staff stimulated: escape map posted on the bulletin board in the administration building — things like that, very unconscious sabotage — flag put upside down as a signal of distress from the central office. A lot of things like that occurred, and it was just hell for a number of months.

It stimulated a couple of major legislative investigations of the department, petitions being circulated through every bar in the community, demands from the townspeople to meet the Governor, his meeting with them, pickets at the statehouse. It was on and on and on. It was kind of incident after incident. There were never more than 3 or 4 days that went by without some sort of minor or major incident at that place.

We finally did get out of it, but I think we learned that it would have been better had we kept our mouths shut and just done what we were going to do — planned it and then done it. We were able to ride out the political upset with the legislature primarily because I'd cultivated a relationship with the head of the committee that investigated us and he kept them in line. Most of them were legislators from the local area who were really most concerned about their patronage people at the institution. As long as we could keep that calm, they didn't rake away too much at us.

So, we closed a number of them. We closed the Boys' School for Little Boys. We had one for 80 to 100 little boys, 12 and under, all adjudicated delinquent — a very modern new motel-like place. That place had all the little kids with crew cuts and little striped t-shirts and chino pants and tennis shoes. Everybody looked alike and acted alike. It was kind of a crazy place — the kind of place that would reassure most folks walking in about how well fed and taken care of these little kids are. But they'd been totally institutionalized — almost mechanized.

We closed the girls' facility, the oldest girls' training school in the nation, the Lancaster Girls' Industrial School. That was slower to close than all of them for a couple of reasons. One is that for my first 2 to 3 years in the State, it was run by a matriarch lady who had been there for years, and in no way would I take her on publicly. There's no way you could win it beating an old lady. Although it was probably among the most repressive institutions in the state, it stayed in business for a while. . . .

Its kind of interesting as a sidelight, I think, to note that in corrections generally the sickest and worst institutions are the women's institutions. Even though they have a facade of treatment and nonbrutality, they are much more difficult and sort of weird.

The last place we closed was the Lyman School for Boys, which at one time had about 300 kids in it.

I just had a sort of irrelevant thought, but I want to mention it — it's about taking advantage of mistakes.

Katkin: You're the boss . . . shoot.

Mistakes — Threat and Opportunity

Miller: When I first arrived I had quite a reputation, you know; I was going to be permissive and let things slide and be a very loose administrator, etc. A couple of judges called very angrily saying that the kids that they had committed were appearing on the street within a few days of their commitment. I'd given authority to the local institutional clinical and cottage committees to parole kids, which in Massachusetts, within the law, I could do. The law never said that I should do it that way, but I could do it that way and not go to jail. So I set it up that way.

And a couple of cottages were in fact paroling kids right away. A couple of psychologists in one of the cottages were doing this. I think in a couple of instances that it was a matter of setting me up a bit, and setting the administration up, because some kids were paroled immediately who were clearly dangerous kids on the street.

So I sent out a little memo, really a PTA memo (a protect-thy-ass memo) that said that every kid should stay a minimum of 3 months. The tradition in Massachusetts when I arrived was 9 to 18 months: Bridgewater was always 18 months; the others ran about 9 months. So I said they should stay a minimum of 3 months, and it was really just to avoid a hassle with all the courts till I got my feet on the ground.

Maybe my own unconscious came out because I haven't reread the memo since, but that was interpreted at the institutions as a maximum of 3 months — that every kid could only be with us 3 months and had to be paroled. I didn't catch on that that was happening until it had become a practice. And the reason I didn't catch on was that no one said anything about it.

I got a couple of calls from judges on individual cases. I looked into it and tried to justify the move. But it had gone on for a number of months before I realized what was happening, that is, that no one was doing more than 3 months, everybody was being paroled in under 3 months. To our surprise, that had gone on quite some time and there was no great upset, either in the state or in the courts. So we said let's keep our mouths shut, which we did.

Immediately our population began to fall dramatically. If you had [a youth sentenced to] 9 months, you could cut it by two-thirds. So that whereas we had hundreds of kids in training schools in the first year, then it started to drop dramatically, which made it a lot easier when [we started to close down] those places.

When it came time to get out of that last place, the Lyman School for Boys, we'd really learned our lesson about how to do it. So we told the superintendent: only one week. He told the staff on a Friday, and I don't think the staff believed him. And I'm not really sure he believed us. And then on a Monday morning we brought in about 100 university students, and they each took a kid and left. It was closed, . . . just like that. There was virtually no uproar. We got out of there without any major incidents. They went up to the University of Massachusetts during the winter break and lived in dormitories with students, one-to-one, boys and girls; and we developed out of the University a placement procedure in collaboration with the Department of Human Relations there. The kids were there anywhere from 2 to 6 weeks depending on the kid and his advocate. We paid the students for being advocates.

It was fairly well planned, but because there had been so many problems as to whether we were going to close that school or not — whether we could get by with it legally — that it was almost the day before we decided to do it that we really knew we could do it. Even though we had told the superintendent we could do it, we really weren't sure. So it wasn't the best planned program on earth. We didn't have enough advocates.

The Case for Deinstitutionalization

I can remember when we arrived at the University of Massachusetts, a number of people going up and down the hallways of the University soliciting students, asking if they'd like to be an advocate, because we had some extra kids. But I think it showed us one thing: that is that perhaps we overestimated the need for specific planning in each of these cases. And we overestimate the need for services for every kid that's caught up in the juvenile system. As a matter of fact, Lloyd Ohlin's group at Harvard did a nice study on this, and it was their impression that by and large those kids did better after the fact than had we taken the normal slow route out of the institution.

And, of course, that fits very well with some recent things that you may be aware of. For instance, when Lester Maddox was governor of Georgia, kind of on impulse, he went into one of the prisons and released a number of the prisoners that he felt sorry for. They had told him a sad story, and he just sent them home. Some bright sociologist took the time to follow them up. I forget how many; I think 25 or 30. And he found they did better by and large than the control group that went out under normal parole or a group that finished the sentence.

Following one of the Supreme Court decisions, the state of Florida had to release somewhere over 300 prisoners because of violations of their right to counsel. There was no question at all that the majority of these prisoners were guilty of the crimes for which they were incarcerated. But because of the decision, they had to be released or given a retrial. Someone, on the basis of the Georgia experience, did the same research. Some sociologists followed them up. And of course what they found is that the group did significantly better than those that finished their sentence or the ones that went out on normal parole.

Katkin: Presumably, then, you do not merely think that new programs ought to be created which will be improvements over the old institutional programs; you think that anything would be better, even that nothing would be better than that which currently exists in most states?

Miller: Yes, I believe that. And that belief colored much of my action in Massachusetts. We were being so harmful in that system that if we just closed the places, with no alternatives, . . . a few kids would still have been better off. I don't think one can publicly say we shouldn't create alternatives. We should. But the present system is so bad that even without alternatives we would do well to close institutions. The institution with no alternatives is a political risk. It has nothing to do with public safety or with the need for rehabilitation. What we have in most states is not only not rehabilitating, for the most part it's actively harmful.

If there was one overriding finding of President Johnson's commission on law enforcement it is that the best service we can do any juvenile offender is to divert him from the system we've set up to treat him. The more of our treatment he has, the more likely he is to get in difficulty when he gets out. The deeper he gets in that system, the more hard-core he gets. And that's been borne out again in an indirect way by Wolfgang and Selin's famous cohort study with Philadelphia kids. At least one can say that there's no evidence in that study that the juvenile justice system at all inhibits the criminal career, and probably there's evidence that it contributes to it. But certainly, at least, as I say, it doesn't inhibit it.

So we got out of all those places and then we developed our alternatives. We had alternatives initially for a few kids but I inherited basically a state system of institutions with no purchase-of-care money. Out of an eight- or ten-million-dollar budget, I may have had $100,000 for purchase of care for different kinds of service — outside of institutions.

With LEAA (Federal Law Enforcement Assistance Administration) help, we were able to obtain a couple of million dollars for buying alternatives. As you know, with LEAA, it's slow getting money. In retrospect, it could have been a tragedy if we had gone the normal route of saying we won't get out until the LEAA money is here and we set up our group homes with it. We kept talking about 18 group homes. I can recall talking about 18 group homes for two and a half years waiting to get that damn money from LEAA that they had approved but got got caught in the state bureaucracy and federal bureaucracy. So that we were actually still talking about it when we closed the institutions. I don't think more than 2 or 3 of the places were actually going.

Diverse Options for Diverse Youth

Katkin: What did you do with those kids who were released before the money came in with which to create new programs?

Miller: We decided it would be so long getting those group homes under state auspices that we'd just put some of that money . . . in a pot and pay for purchase of services from a private agency. We felt that the private agencies would respond if the money were there. And in fact they did, not necessarily the traditional private agencies. I don't think the traditional agencies responded very much. After a while they did. But they waited to make sure we were winning. The nontraditional ones, I think, came through first.

A wide range of options then, in a sense, created themselves. When we left Lyman School, which was the last training school, we didn't have enough options to cover ourselves for more than a months or so. We had made some contracts. We had set up some informal foster homes. We had decided on a longer term thing at the University of Massachusetts whereby some kids would live in dorms with students — very, very makeshift sorts of options for the most part. We contacted prep schools who were willing to take one or two delinquent kids among their more affluent populations. We did some unusual things, like we arranged for a contact with a sailing ship, a marine biologist's ship that was chasing humpback whales. You can do anything you can think of if you have the money.

Think of all the flexibility that you'd want if you had a brother or sister or son or daughter who was in trouble and the state gave you $8 to $10 thousand a year to solve the problem. Chances are that you'd think of something more unusual and interesting than a state training school. (And remember, a year in reform school costs a hell of a lot more than $10,000.) So we thought up a lot of options. Some of them are very crazy but we made use of them for the moment, while we could, knowing they probably wouldn't survive. Others survived into more traditional agencies. We had proposals for Zen Buddhists and macrobiotic group homes; and we had proposals for black Muslim group homes. We had proposals from travel services to put kids on 3-month tours of the United States on Greyhound buses — everything in mind you could think of. We were taking about anything that seemed reasonably humane and decent and noncoercive. If it had a professional program behind it, great! If it didn't and it looked like no one would be hurt, we might even give it a whirl. Out of that all sorts of things began to develop.

What's It Like Now in Massachusetts?

. . . Whereas we had, I would say, at most a half dozen community programs when we started, this year they have kids from the department probably in two or three hundred programs around the state; things like, there was a consortium in Boston of artists, sculptors and painters who would meet regularly. We did a contract with them to take a number of kids. They were delinquent kids in the day program. We did a number of contracts with college students, private nonprofit consortiums of college students, to develop advocacy programs where we pay them to spend 15, 20, or 25 hours a week with the kid in the evenings. You have to realize we were coming out of a system where we paid $200 to $300 dollars a week to keep a kid in a training school. The advocacy program developed into some nonprofit business run by the students and kids together: ice cream parlors, a couple of pizza-sub shops, all sorts of things developed. They sent some kids to Norway for mountain climbing. It was much cheaper than institutionalization and a lot more interesting. Outward Bound Programs, British survival training programs, military school. . . . If a kid wants to go to military school, I have no misgivings about it. I guess the big things is if they wanted to do it, and a lot of kids did; so we contracted with some of the more posh military schools. [We had] kids hiking the Applachian trail from Connecticut to Vermont — all sorts of interesting things.

Kramer: How were decisions made about which kids got into which programs?

Miller: To a considerable extent we allowed our kids the options to shop. Now I hesitate to hope, really, that that will continue, knowing state bureaucracies. I think it will be less and less the case as time goes by and that will be the undoing of the new system ultimately. The fact that the choice will be taken away: it won't be taken away by hard-hats or Joe Sixpack or law-and-order freaks. It will be taken away by professional social workers and psychologists and psychiatrists who have always had a tradition of taking such choices away from the poor. They never would take it away from upper middle class. Otherwise they'd go out of business. But with the poor, and the state paying the bill, they'll always have a business. Certainly, they want to be the "experts" and decide — choice for the client doesn't enter the process. In fact, it challenges it. And I think if what we did in Massachusetts is to be undone, it'll be undone by our liberal professional peers, not by any rightwing backlash.
    We allowed kids, for instance, to manipulate. I think it's a fine healthy middle-class value. We never insisted that a kid

stay in a group home if he didn't like it. We might insist that he couldn't go back to his own community if there was some sort of thing going on there. But we'd offer him the option of going somewhere else, which would upset the group homes no end. A kid could aways come down to the central office and say, "I don't like that place." We'd call them and say, "What's going on?" And they'd say, "Disregard him and send him back. He's just manipulating." We'd say, "Well O.K., you go back and talk with them, but if you don't like it, you can try this one."

That sounds like you're being had by kids. But in a sense what I was trying to develop was a system, as I say, that would allow to our kids what has always been allowed to disturbed or troubled upper middle-class kids. Certainly they are never told to stay in a place because it's good for them, . . . unless their parents are fairly pushy. But there is that ability, at least for the family, if not for the kid, to manipulate the system and to move from place to place, to ask hard questions like: "When's he gonna get better?" And if they don't like it, they take their money and go elsewhere. Certainly one gets that impression looking at the back pages of the *New York Times* Magazine — that there's a great deal of room for manipulation in the private sector for private care of affluent kids.

Katkin: We've been talking for quite a long time. Our readers will have plenty to think about. Thanks for your time.

Miller: Thanks for your interest.

11 An Ounce of Prevention

The child is father of the man.
— *William Wordsworth*

Clearly it is with young people that prevention efforts are most needed and hold the greatest promise. It is simply more critical that young people be kept from crime, for they are the Nation's future, and their conduct will affect society for a long time to come.

— *President's Commission on Law Enforcement and the Administration of Justice: Task Force on Juvenile Delinquency*

The most clearly articulated, manifest goal of all juvenile justice systems is the prevention of *crime*. From intake through treatment and aftercare, the efforts of juvenile police specialists, teachers, social workers, juvenile court judges, probation officers, correctional officers, and others are intended to turn young people from lives of crime. Juvenile justice systems would be undeniably successful (even if delinquency rates remained high) if they were able to prevent delinquents from growing into adult offenders.

The juvenile court was created by reformers who sought to reduce crime by protecting and rehabilitating children in trouble. The reformers were certain that children, because they are not altogether responsible for their behavior, and because of their great capacity for change and growth, should never be seen as *confirmed* criminals (no matter how serious or frequent their offenses), but rather as *potential* criminals. The intervention of the juvenile justice system, with its emphasis on rehabilitation and the best interests of the child, was

designed to turn the child from waywardness toward the "path that leads to good, sound, adult citizenship."[1] Just as the spread of cancer may be prevented by early diagnosis and treatment, so, it was hoped, the spread of crime might be prevented by the early diagnosis and treatment of delinquency. Intervention after a problem has been identified but before it has become serious is called *secondary prevention.*

The vast majority of the resources of juvenile justice systems are expended on programs of secondary prevention; and most of the rest of this book is about those programs. This chapter, however, is about *primary prevention* — the attempt to forestall children from becoming delinquent in the first place. The difference between the two types of prevention may, perhaps, be best illustrated through an analogy to medicine. Isolating people who carry typhoid fever in order to stop the spread of that disease constitutes secondary prevention. Determining the conditions under which the typhoid bacillus thrives and altering those conditions (as by improving sewage and sanitary facilities) constitutes primary prevention. Antibiotics which keep bacterial infections from being serious are a form of secondary prevention. Immunization, which protects people from ever being susceptible to a disorder, is a form of primary prevention. *In criminology, secondary prevention means the reformation of young offenders, primary prevention means changing the conditions that lead to delinquency.*

Obviously, the prevention of delinquency is an even more desirable social goal than the successful treatment of delinquents. It is better both for the child involved and for society that the child be kept from crime than that he be "cured" of it. Yet programs of primary prevention are extremely uncommon, and the resources committed to them are scarce indeed. This is so, at least in part, because other goals (such as deterrence, retribution, and incapacitation) are thought by many in the system to be more important and more deserving of scarce resources; but it is true also because prevention requires knowledge about causes, and there is very little solid, well-confirmed knowledge about the causes of delinquency.[2] However desirable the goal may seem, we simply do not know how to go about achieving it.

While the absence of agreed-upon "facts" about the causes of delinquency is lamentable, it does *not* necessarily mean that efforts to achieve delinquency prevention are impossible. Theories about the causes of delinquency exist, and those theories suggest ways to develop prevention programs. It is arguable, in fact, that the best way to through experimentation develop knowledge about delinquency is through experimentation with activist programs intended to prevent it.

> We are on our way toward learning what does and what does not prevent delinquency, but we still have far to go. Progress toward that objective will call for close cooperation between practice and research, with both parties looking hopefully to theory and to experience for ideas about the direction in which to move next. Practice can not and should not wait upon research, nor should research be delayed until practice is well established. We shall be most likely to discover how to prevent delinquency if research is undertaken coordinately with the development of new measures and the refinement of old ones, if research and practice are conceived as inseparable parts of a single process.[3]

By both "doing" and "evaluating" we may learn what works and what does not; in the process we may also learn why some things work. The point has already been made that very little has actually been done in the area of delinquency prevention; now it must be added that there has been even less "evaluating" than "doing." Most delinquency prevention programs come into the world, run their course, and depart — leaving no permanent, objective record of their success, nor of their failures.[4] Thus, past experience provides very little guidance in planning for the future.

In thinking about how to prevent delinquency, then, we have little to go on except theories about causation. Positivists are inclined to believe that individuals must be changed. Community-oriented theoreticians are concerned with modifying societal processes. Interactionists believe that prevention means reducing the chances that individuals will be labeled delinquent. In the remaining sections of this chapter each of these orientations will be explicated, and such research findings as exist will be discussed.

Prevention Programs Derived from the Individual-Oriented Perspective

The basic elements of postitivist criminology are (1) that delinquents are meaningfully different from nondelinquents, (2) that the differences are *determined* by factors which are beyond individual control, and (3) that these differences are the causes of delinquency.[5] The crucial differences among individual-oriented theories relate to perceptions about what types of factors actually determine delinquency. Lombrosians, with their emphasis on inherited physical traits, are, in a sense, the "purest" positivists; not only do they see delinquents as fundamentally different from the rest of us, they also see the differences as residing entirely within the individual. Sociological and social-psychological positivists, while concerned about individual differences, seek the determinants of human behavior in the social environment. Between these poles of individual-oriented models are the psychological approaches which seek the explanations of individual differences both in the individuals themselves and in their environments.

Biogenetic Approaches

Lombrosian criminology provides no practicable leads to the prevention of delinquency. If delinquency is an inherited, biological characteristic, it can be prevented only through the compulsory sterilization of people who are deemed likely to produce delinquent progeny; and that is not about to happen. There have been occasional laws in some American jurisdictions which have permitted the sterilization of "defective" people, notably congenital idiots; and there are certainly individuals in most communities who favor programs of eugenics planning to limit the procreation of "inadequate" people. Nevertheless, programs designed to sterilize all people who might have delinquent children would be frightening to the vast majority of the population, and would be opposed on principle by such diverse groups as the Catholic Church (which opposes contraception generally), the American Civil Liberties Union (which opposes government infringement on individual freedom), and the Black Panthers (which sees such programs as discriminatory and genocidal). Widespread use of eugenics planning programs has never been attempted in the United States or most other places (Nazi Germany being an exception), and in the face of widespread opposition it is inconceivable that such an approach will be attempted in the foreseeable future.

Clinical Psychological Approaches

Other individual-oriented approaches, however, have had tremendous influence in the conceptualization and implementation of delinquency prevention programs. Clinical psychologists, psychiatrists, and social workers have had the most impact.

> The popularity of the psychological approach rests on the fact that it offers a direct and simple method of dealing with the person who is a problem. It offers an opportunity for parents to take children with problems to a specialist, just as a television set is taken to another kind of specialist for repair. In contrast, the sociological point of view, with its emphasis on social process, offers no comparably simple course of action. Its programs are not so neat or so readily applied.[6]

Committed to the view that delinquency is the product of unhealthy psychological processes, clinical prevention programs, if they are to be effective, must operate on youngsters who possess the psychological characteristics associated with delinquency. Identifying those characteristics has not yet proven possible. While we know that some social factors (such as being poor or coming from a broken home) correlate highly with the probability of becoming delinquent, we do not know which individual personality and behavioral characteristics also correlate highly.[7] Clinicians, when they have been pushed to identify such characteristics, have tended to be expansive; they describe so many factors that there is hardly anyone of whom it can be said: "He is not at all like that."

This tendency of psychiatrists, psychologists, and social workers to identify almost all forms of youthful behavior with potential delinquency was clearly illustrated in the experience of the St. Paul "Community Service" project. The project centered around a child guidance clinic which solicited referrals of potentially delinquent youngsters from schools, police departments, churches, juvenile court, social welfare and health agencies. The clinic suggested to all its referral agencies that the following types of behavior might be considered symptomatic of delinquency:[8]

Bashfulness	Gate-crashing	Stealing
Boastfulness	Hitching rides	Stubborness
Boisterousness	Ill-mannered	Sullenness
Bossiness	behavior	Tardiness
Bullying	Impudence	Tattling
Cheating	Inattentiveness	Teasing
Cruelty	Indolence	Temper displays
Crying	Masturbation	Thumb-sucking
Daydreaming	Nail-biting	Tics
Deceit	Negativism	Timidity
Defiance	Obscenity	Truancy from home
Dependence	Overactivity	Truancy from school
Destructiveness	Overmasculine	Uncleanliness
Disobedience	behavior	Uncouth personality
Disorderliness	(of girls)	Underactivity
Drinking	Profanity	Undersirable
Eating	Quarreling	companions
disturbances	Roughness	Undesirable
Effeminate	Selfishness	recreation
behavior	Sex perversion	Unsportsmanship
(of boys)	Sex play	Untidiness
Enuresis	Sexual activity	Violation of
Fabrications	Shifting activities	street-trade
Failure to perform	Show-off behavior	regulations
assigned tasks	Silliness	Violations of
Fighting	Sleep disturbances	traffic
Finicalness	Smoking	regulations
Gambling	Speech disturbances	

Thus far one potent form of criticism has been leveled at the clinical programs: they have been unable to effectively define the characteristics of the population with which they must work. There is an additional and more important criticism to be made: clinically oriented programs, when subjected to rigorous evaluation, have not been demonstrably effective in preventing delinquency.

Most clinical programs have been undertaken without any evaluation component at all. And in others research has meant only that the therapists involved in a project were asked whether they thought their clients had made progress (hardly surprisingly, the answer is usually affirmative).[9] Very infrequently rigorous scientific evaluation of the effectiveness of clinical intervention has been undertaken. The results are disheartening. The Cambridge-Somerville Youth Study, perhaps the most famous piece of action research ever undertaken, indicated that counseling does not prevent youngsters from becoming delinquent.[10] The methodology used in the project was impeccable: 650 boys under twelve years of age were selected for the project from a list of approximately 1900 names submitted by teachers, probation officers, social agencies, and police officers. Some of the boys were thought to be likely candidates to become delinquent, others were not. Information about the boys was obtained from the records of schools and social agencies, from interviews with parents and from psychological examinations of the boys themselves. Then each of the boys was "matched" with the boy in the group who was most similar to him on a composite of about 100 factors, such as age, religion, intelligence, educational performance, personality, neighborhood, and social adjustment. Thus, two nearly identical subgroups of 325 boys each were constructed out of the original 650 (See Table 11.1). It was reasonable to expect that the rates of delinquency in each of these groups would be about the same over time. If psychotherapy is effective as a means of preventing delinquency, then providing counseling services to the boys in one group should have resulted in a lower rate of delinquency in that group than in the other group. That is exactly what was attempted in the Cambridge-Somerville project.

TABLE 11.1. Results of the Cambridge-Somerville Youth Study

Type of Group \ Type of Offense	Serious or Minor	Serious Only
Treatment 325 boys (100%)	90 boys (27.7%)	76 boys (23.4%)
Control 325 boys (100%)	85 boys (26.1%)	67 boys (20.6%)

One subgroup of the matched pairs was randomly selected as a treatment group, and the youngsters in that group received special services. The other group of "diagnostic twins" became a control group, receiving no services.

The experiment lasted ten years, at the end of which time it was found that boys in the *control* group had appeared in court *less* often, for both serious and minor offenses. The *treatment* group had apparently committed *more* crimes, and more crimes of a serious nature.

The differences between the groups were not very great; so it certainly can not be concluded that the provision of counseling services actually *increases* the probability of delinquency. But neither, obviously, can it be concluded that psychotherapy is a valuable tool with which to achieve delinquency prevention.

A similar project was undertaken about twenty years later at a vocational high school for girls in New York City.[11] Four hundred potentially delinquent girls were randomly divided into an experimental group and a control group (the girls were not actually matched as in the Cambridge-Somerville project, but random selection provides a pretty good likelihood that the groups would be very similar to one another). The experimental group members received individual casework services and group therapy. Teachers, social workers, psychologists, and sociologists combined their skills and insights in a concerted effort to prevent the delinquency of members of the treatment group. The combined services were *not* effective in abating delinquency patterns.

The argument being made here is not that programs of psychotherapy are useless. It is altogether possible that youngsters in the treatment groups in both of these studies were helped to resolve personal problems; and it is undeniable that the resolution of problems, and the reduction of anxiety, and the modification of undesirable character traits are all valuable both to the individual and to society. That a youngster may have been "helped," however, does not necessarily mean that he or she will refrain from law-violating behavior. Psychotherapy, whatever its merits, does not appear to be an effective technique of primary prevention.

Social-Psychological Approaches

Sociologists and social psychologists in the individual-oriented school see delinquents as fundamentally different from nondelinquents. Unlike Lombrosians, who find the determinants of delinquency in genetic inheritance, and the Freudians, who find them in intra-psychic conflict, these theoreticians maintain that delinquency is "determined" by attitudes and values which are a product of environmental influences, such as peer pressure. Delinquency can be prevented only if the attitudes and values of individual potential delinquents are changed, but such changes can be achieved only by modifying environmental conditions. Thus, programs consistent with this orientation seek to change the immediate environment of potentially delinquent youngsters in order to inculcate and nurture law-abiding sentiments.

Programs in the Schools

After family, school is perhaps the most important part of a child's environment. Children between the ages of six and sixteen spend more waking hours at school than at any other place. Thus, theoreticians concerned with changing the attitudes and values of potential delinquents have long thought of the public schools as an appropriate point for intervention.

Sociologists and social psychologists who see delinquency as a "healthy," learned pattern of behavior tend to see schools as particularly important in programs of delinquency prevention, because the schools have contact with children for long enough periods of time to teach new attitudes and values. Professor Walter Miller, for example, takes the position that delinquency is a natural outgrowth of lower-class values, which emphasize the importance of "toughness, smartness, excitement, fate, and autonomy."[12] If children are to be prevented from delinquency, they must be exposed to, and convinced by, the standards and values of the dominant culture — which, presumably, emphasizes hard-work, diligence, responsibility, and good behavior. Two examples of experimental programs tried in New York City may illustrate the way in which attempts are made to inculcate middle-class values through the schools.[13]

The Higher Horizons programs[14] provide special guidance and small-group counseling, "inspirational" talks from business leaders and professional people, trips to places of interest, information about occupations and pre-vocational instruction, conferences with parents, and efforts to enlarge the cultural experiences of the students. Students in these programs have contact not only with teachers, but with college students, various types of professionals, and a range of volunteers. Thus school becomes not merely a place of learning, but a place in which to meet different types of people. There is some evidence that students enrolled in Higher Horizons programs do achieve higher reading levels and better grades than might otherwise be expected. There is no evidence, however, that their patterns of involvement in delinquent acts is altered. As with counseling programs, it is probably true that there are benefits both for the individual involved and for society, but reduced delinquency does not appear to be one of these benefits.

All-Day Neighborhood School programs are another attempt to compensate for the "cultural deficiencies" of youngsters from deprived homes.[15] Such schools, established in a few of New York's deteriorated neighborhoods, provide special tutoring during the regular school day. In addition, the schools provide supervised play between three and five in the afternoon, when the children of working parents would otherwise be at home, unsupervised. Psychologists are on hand during the play sessions to assist teachers in looking for signs of emotional disturbance. In the evenings the schools are open for community meetings and for conferences with interested parents. The impact of these programs on delinquency rates has not been assessed. It seems plausible that keeping kids off the streets for a few additional hours every day may reduce involvement in delinquent acts just by leaving

them with less time in which to break the law (although it is important to remember that children can and do break the law even while at school).[16]

In short, there is not much reason to believe that schools, at least as they currently exist, can be effective in changing the attitudes and values of potential delinquents. And we must realize, too, that the hardest-to-reach, most resistant youngsters are likely to be the most difficult to work with in a classroom situation, which requires structure and attentiveness.

Recreation Programs

There is strong sentiment, but little evidence, in support of the proposition that participation in organized leisure-time activities builds character and helps children grow into mature and responsible adulthood.[17]

> A number of character-building and recreational organizations secure public or voluntary funds on the assumption that their presence is necessary to combat crime and delinquency.[18]

Little Leagues, it is argued, do not merely provide fun; they provide an opportunity to learn sportsmanship and fair play. Scouting teaches reverence, charity, service, and honor. The Fresh Air Fund sends children to camp not merely because camping is fun, but because it is believed that organized play in a country setting helps to impart basic American values. In the nation's cities, the community centers, schoolyard programs, boys' clubs, police athletic leagues, and a myriad of other organizations seek support from the public on the grounds that they teach decency and help turn youngsters away from crime and delinquency.

Behind these claims there is one of two beliefs — (1) that effective participation in organized play requires the formation of attitudes which favor cooperation and sharing and which inhibit the tendency towards delinquency (in the language of differential association theory, that participation in a positive group will increase the total number of meaningful associations which favor law-abiding behavior and minimize the total number of meaningful associations which favor delinquency); or (2) that youngsters turn to crime because they have nothing better to do in their spare time. The second of these views is particularly naive, as it overlooks the potential significance of all biological, psychological, and social factors — other than the adequacy of recreational facilities — in the genesis of delinquent behavior.

The most frequently offered evidence in support of the utility of recreation programs is that "children who take part in organized lesiure-time activity are less often delinquents."[19] Sheldon and Eleanor Glueck, for example, compared the life histories of 500 adjudicated delinquents and 500 youngsters without official police records who were from the same types of neighborhoods in Massachusetts. The nondelinquent youngsters had been involved significantly more often in organized recreational and character-building activities.[20] It is unclear, however, whether the data prove that recreation programs prevent delinquency or just that youngsters who are less likely to become delinquent are more likely to seek out programs of organized play. Some theories view delinquents as the most alienated, rebellious youngsters in society; adherents of such theories argue that potential delinquents would never gravitate to the boys' clubs or police athletic leagues, and that such groups attract only youngsters who aren't likely to become delinquent in the first place. This criticism is reinforced by the findings of a survey of group-work agencies which found that most such agencies are not "identified closely with the underprivileged and insecure elements in our population, nor with the age groups among which delinquency is most prevalent."[21]

Several studies have attempted to assess the effectiveness of recreational programs by measuring delinquency rates in a community before and after the introduction of a boys' club or similar organization. In addition, delinquency rates in communities in which such programs have been introduced have been compared with rates in similar neighborhoods in which there are no equivalent programs. The results indicate that the formation of recreational organizations *does* help prevent delinquency.[22] It can not be concluded, however, that these activities actually build character and develop law-abiding attitudes and values. It may simply be that boys who play basketball for a couple of hours a day have less time left in which to engage in criminal acts.

In short, the sum total of existing knowledge fails to prove conclusively either that organized recreational activities have value in preventing delinquency or that they have no value. The most reasonable conclusion seems to be that recreation is good for children, that it certainly does not harm them, and that it *might* be of some value in preventing delinquency.[23]

Street Worker Services

Street worker programs represent the most significant effort to make recreation a means of preventing delinquency. Recreation in these programs, however, doesn't mean organized play; it means whatever kids do in their leisure time.

> The common assumption that the problem of . . . delinquency will be solved by the multiplication of playgrounds and social centers in gang areas is entirely erroneous. The physical layout of gangland provides a realm of adventure with which no playground can compete. The lack is not of this sort. The real problem is one of developing in these areas or introducing into them leaders who can organize the play of boys, direct it into wholesome channels and give it social significance. . . .[24]

Street workers (sometimes called detached workers, because they work outside of, or detached from, the agencies that employ them) do not wait for young people to come to them; they locate groups of delinquents or near-delinquents and seek to redirect antisocial tendencies "by sponsoring a new leadership from inside and by focusing . . . energies and interests on socially useful outlets."[25]

The worker has several "tools" at his disposal. Among the most useful is the ability to make referrals of individual adolescents to the person or agency which may best help him. Psychiatric referrals are not uncommon. Referrals are sometimes made to friendly school officials who can modify the school environment of youngsters experiencing difficulty or failure, and who can arrange for tutoring or special education. The worker may also function as an employment referral service, a task which involves not only bringing an adolescent and his potential employer together but also preparing each for the other. In addition, because lower-class youngsters may sometimes fail to understand the nature of a medical problem, or be unaware of the existence of facilities available for help, street workers have the potential to be helpful by making medical referrals as well.[26]

These referrals are important not only because of their inherent usefulness, but also because they generate trust in the worker and facilitate his emergence as an important figure on the street. In achieving that special status which makes it possible for him to affect the attitudes and values of the young people with whom he works, the street worker's most important asset is the force of his own personality. His ability to establish supportive relationships, and to offer affection to young people who are too often lacking it at home, may well be the determining factor in his success.[27] In short, a good worker must have a flair, a kind of instinctive ability to do the right thing at the right time.

The effectiveness of many individual detached workers is downright impressive. Street work with gangs and with alienated and hostile youngsters requires perseverance, professionalism, and a good deal of self-control.

> From a social-psychological point of view, there is a certain amount of conceit in sending a street club worker out into the community to establish relationships with youth groups and confidently expecting that he will exert influence over them in a unilateral fashion. This is especially the case when the worker is a relatively young man with a relatively middle class set of values and the youth group is a delinquent gang reflecting not only a lower class set of values but a definite orientation toward the anti-social and criminal opportunities afforded by a deprived community. Such a set of relationships, in such a context, is fraught with all kinds of ambiguous possibilities. The most obvious possibility is the one that has probably never happened, that is that the street worker goes over to the other side, so to speak, and joins the gang.[28]

Despite this element of conceit, detached-worker programs appear to many scholars to be an effective means through which society can reach out to hostile youth groups. The work of Harold Keltner in St. Louis is illustrative. Keltner, under the sponsorship of the YMCA, worked with juvenile gangs in a slum neighborhood which had been the headquarters of a notorious adult gang. During a period of fifteen years, forty of these youthful gangs became boys' clubs and became engaged in programs of community service. Writing about his work, Keltner stated that the members were seldom in trouble with the police, that older members assisted in developing similar groups for their younger brothers, and that businessmen in the community cooperated with the program whole-heartedly.[29] Similar findings have been reported about projects in many other cities.[30]

There are also findings, however, which indicate that street worker programs are not always effective. The most definitive of these studies was reported by Professor Walter Miller, who evaluated a major programmatic effort (called the Mid-City Project) in Roxbury, Massachusetts, a section of Boston. Professor Miller found that there was *no* significant inhibition of law-violating or morally disapproved behavior as a consequence of the Project efforts.

> All major measures of violative behavior — disapproved actions, illegal

actions, . . . court appearances, and Project control group appearances — provide consistent support for a finding of "negligible impact."[31]

Thus, it is not clear that any program designed to change the attitudes and values of potential delinquents can succeed. Not therapists, nor teachers, nor group workers, nor even street workers seem consistently and predictably able to prevent delinquency by changing individuals. The pervasive assessment of "negligible impact" explains, in part, why theoreticians in the sixties and seventies have thought increasingly about changing environments rather than people.

Prevention Programs Derived from the Community Perspective

Individual-oriented prevention programs are based on theoretical models which hold (1) that delinquents behave differently from nondelinquents, (2) that these differences are caused by "defects" in individuals, and (3) that delinquency can be prevented by programs of individual change. Community-oriented theories agree that delinquents and nondelinquents behave differently, but the differences are seen as created by environmental pressures; thus, it is society rather than individual members of society that must be changed if delinquency is to be prevented.

Community-oriented theories see delinquents as healthy, normal youngsters reacting to the frustrations of life spent in poverty, and learning by the example of others around them in the slums that the greatest prospects for "success" are afforded by crime.[32] Ghetto children have little contact with doctors, lawyers, architects, or businessmen. The "successful" people with whom they have contact are pimps, numbers runners, drug pushers, and prostitutes. According to opportunity theory, the most influential of the community-oriented approaches, it is as natural for ambitious poor youngsters to turn to crime as it is for ambitious middle-class youngsters to turn to business. Delinquency can be prevented only if all children are provided with a meaningful opportunity to achieve success through the legitimate opportunity structure.

Opportunity theory had tremendous influence not only among social workers and sociologists in the 1960s, but also among lawyers and politicians. Consider the following examples of language selected from the Report of the President's Commission on Law Enforcement and the Administration of Criminal Justice, which was published in 1967:

> Before this nation can hope to reduce crime significantly or lastingly, it must mount and maintain a massive attack against the conditions of life that underlie it.[33]

> • • •

> In the last analysis, the most promising and so the most important method of dealing with crime is by preventing it — by ameliorating the conditions of life that drive people to commit crimes and that undermine the restraining rules and institutions erected by society against antisocial conduct. The Commission doubts that even a vastly improved criminal justice system can substantially reduce crime if society fails to make it possible for each of its citizens to feel a personal stake in it — in the good life that it can provide and in the law and order that are prerequisite to such a life. That sense of stake, of something that can be gained or lost, can come only through real opportunity for full participation in society's life and growth. It is insuring opportunity that is the basic goal of prevention programs.[34]

> • • •

> To a population denied access to traditional positions of status and achievement, a successful criminal may be a highly visible model of power and affluence and a center of trainng and recruitment for criminal enterprise.[35]

> • • •

> America can control crime. . . . Crime flourishes where the conditions of life are the worst, and . . . the foundation of a national strategy against crime is an unremitting national effort for social justice.[36]

In a sense, the entire War on Poverty was derived from opportunity theory. Americans were urged to support elaborate programs of poverty relief, manpower training, special education, and community change not merely because such programs were moral, proper, and right, but also because they would improve the quality of life by reducing crime and encouraging social conformity.

Mobilization For Youth (M.F.Y.) in New York City was the archetypal delinquency prevention program upon which many of the

NEW PHASES
I REGIONALIZATION
II COMMUNITY BASED TREATMENT CENTERS
III ~NSION OF FORESTRY PROGRAM
~LOCATION OF DETENTION
V INCREASE PLACEMENT ALTERNATIVES
VI GRANTS-IN-AIDS TO CITIES AND TOWNS
VII INTENSIVE CARE SECURITY UNIT

most exciting efforts of the War on Poverty were based. The story of M.F.Y. indicates both the direction in which community-change programs must develop and the reasons for fearing that such programs may be doomed to failure.

Mobilization For Youth

Mobilization was a demonstration project designed by a team which included representatives of many of the best social services agencies in New York City and several members of the faculty of the Columbia University School of Social Work, including Richard Cloward, one of the co-authors of *Delinquency and Opportunity*.[37] Concerned not with individual pathology but with the failures of the social order, M.F.Y. sought to change the pattern of poverty in an area known as the Lower East Side in Manhattan. Its goal was to reduce delinquency rates by improving the conditions of life, expanding opportunities for conformity, and helping youngsters to exploit these opportunities.[38]

In the period between 1962 and 1968, M.F.Y. received more than $30 million dollars in grants from federal, municipal, and private agencies, such as the National Institute of Mental Health, the City of New York, and the Ford Foundation.[39] The original proposal with which this funding was obtained called for four areas of service: (1) World of Work; (2) World of Education; (3) Services to Individuals and Families; and (4) Group Work and Community Organization.[40]

World of Work.   Mobilization had three main objectives related to work: (1) it sought to create new employment opportunities; (2) it publicized existing opportunities and routes to the achievement of these opportunities; and (3) it tried to make youngsters more employable.[41]

Jobs were created by the Urban Youth Service Corps for young people between the ages of 16 and 21. These jobs, in the areas of construction, maintenance, and service were all designed to improve the quality of life in the community. The Youth Jobs Center was created to publicize existing jobs, to approach prospective employers, and to disseminate information about the availability of work. The Exploratory Work Course was a form of vocational guidance. Under its auspices local youngsters and their parents were taught about the requirements of different types of jobs so they could take the necessary preparatory steps to become qualified for the jobs.[42]

World of Education.   Mobilization For Youth had five main objectives related to education: (1) it sought to increase the responsiveness of existing school programs to the conditions of lower-class life; (2) it wanted to reduce high rates of teacher turnover which occurred because good teachers left for "better" schools at the first opportunity; (3) it tried to improve relations between parents and the schools; (4) it helped to encourage the development of new curricula consistent with lower-class culture; and (5) it provided students with extra tutorial help. It is noteworthy that four of these five objectives were directed toward systems change rather than individual change.[43]

In pursuing these goals, M.F.Y. developed a contract with the Board of Education of the City of New York under the terms of which it was commissioned to work on the creation of new programs to make the schools more relevant to the life experience of poor youngsters. In addition, Mobilization was involved in organizing community groups in support of the decentralization of the school system. Decentralization plans allowed parents' groups and community organizations considerable influence over the development of curriculum and the hiring and firing of teachers. Even the tutoring program developed by M.F.Y. was unusual and interesting. The use of tutors from outside the community was discouraged. Local high school students who were doing well academically were hired to tutor elementary and junior high school students. Thus, the older students were given both financial rewards and status because of their academic success, and the younger students were provided with tutors with whom they could identify.[44]

Individual and Family Services. Programs in this area were directed towards four objectives: (1) to help persons learn the eligibility requirements for welfare assistance; (2) to provide babysitting services to allow mothers free time they could use productively; (3) to teach homemaking skills; and (4) to provide family counseling.[45] While providing counseling is a traditional goal for social service agencies, M.F.Y.'s other goals in this area, particularly helping people apply for welfare benefits, were innovative and untraditional. Unlike most agencies, which seek to help individuals adapt to reality, Mobilization tried to help people change reality.

Mobilization's attempt to achieve these goals involved the creation of several programs. A Neighborhood Service Center provided many services, including babysitting and education about eligibility requirements for public assistance. A Visiting Homemaker Service taught relevant skills to low-income housewives. A Mental Hygiene Referral Service helped find therapists for individuals with mental health problems.[46]

Group Work and Community Organization. M.F.Y.'s four objectives in this area were the agency's most innovative and interesting: (1) to increase the ability of local residents to participate in and influence the social and political life of their community; (2) to dramatize community needs and mobilize social action; (3) to improve communications between local residents and community institutions; and (4) to improve the competence of local leaders.[47]

Many of the agency's organizational efforts centered around the housing needs of the community.[48] Tenants groups were formed and rent strikes were organized in substandard dwellings. Those efforts and others against the unfair business practices of some local merchants and against repressive welfare rules led to the development of a legal services unit, which became the model for many subsequent O.E.O. (Office of Economic Opportunity) Neighborhood Law Offices.

M.F.Y. lawyers were active in the community, seeking out poor people with legal problems and providing vigorous advocacy on their behalf.[49]

Mobilization even "organized" the neighborhood's young people. The plan was to

> encourage attention to social issues among young people, help them develop specific action programs, and provide them with material aids to further their efforts. To channel the anger directed at social injustice away from self-defeating deviant behavior and into constructive avenues of collective social action.[50]

Towards these goals, an organization called the Adventure Corps was created. Like the Boy Scouts, this was a paramilitary organization with uniforms, bands, and the spit-and-polish which often entices youngsters. Projects for the youngsters included raising money to aid other youngsters in more severely depressed areas, such as Appalachia.[51]

Did Mobilization For Youth Achieve Its Goals?

Beyond a doubt Mobilization had considerable impact on the Lower East Side.

> Mobilization For Youth probably helped more people, influenced more professional thinking, and effected more social changes than any other social agency in our time. Tens of thousands of poor people on the Lower East Side were reached by the agency — children were taught to read, school dropouts were given training and jobs, dilapidated apartments were renovated, families on welfare were assisted in demanding adequate allowances, citizens were helped to register and vote, etc. A great many Mobilization staff members went on to teach in Universities; professional journals abound with articles written about Mobilization and about the ideas developed at the agency. And in some measure, changes in policy and procedure in the Welfare Department, school system, and work training programs reflect the activities of Mobilization.[52]

For our purpose, however, it is not sufficient merely to say that Mobilization For Youth did good things. The key question is: Did it reduce delinquency rates? The answer appears to be: Not appreciably!

This conclusion is based on a comparison between the number of arrests of youngsters in the M.F.Y.-serviced neighborhood and the number in surrounding neighborhoods (Table 11.2).

TABLE 11.2. Delinquency Rates for M.F.Y. Areas and Surrounding Areas

	M.F.Y. Serviced Area		Surrounding Areas	
	1962	*1966*	*1962*	*1966*
Juvenile Arrests	603	737	408	416
Arrests per 1,000 youths[54]	97.3	90.6	89.1	91.7

The data indicate that delinquency rates in the M.F.Y. area were slightly higher than those in surrounding areas when the project began in 1962, and that they were slightly lower after the project had been in operation for four years. The change, however, was not so great as to permit the conclusion that Mobilization was particularly effective.[53]

Can Organizations Such As M.F.Y. Ever Really Succeed?

There appear to be three reasons for fearing that organizations such as Mobilization may be doomed to failure from the outset. Each of these can be demonstrated in the history of M.F.Y.

First, the creation of social change is such a large, complex problem that it is not clear that anyone knows how to go about it.[55] There are constantly unexpected consequences of almost every action. Social conditions in slum neighborhoods can be so unsatisfactory that deciding where to start may be an exhausting task.

Second, organizations designed to create social change may prove expensive to run; and clients, who are poor and powerless, can not be expected to support the operation. Mobilization's funds came from government agencies and private foundations. The government, in particular, was often the object of M.F.Y.-organized demonstrations, and frequently found itself being sued by M.F.Y. lawyers. As one of the agency's directors put it:

> As time passed we received our first practical lesson in the unwillingness of government to supply funds to pay the salaries of persons who are attempting to alter basic political and social institutions. Like so many lessons it took a long time to sink in.[56]

Finally, it is clear from the Mobilization experience that crusaders for the poor and powerless must always anticipate that the rich and powerful will fight back. M.F.Y. attempted to change the lifestyle of a whole community. While such change would certainly have been to the advantage of many, it would also have worked to the detriment of some. Landlords, for example, were unhappy about the creation of tenants' organizations. Businessmen were unhappy about consumer's rights litigation. Those powerful groups had political allies who set out to destroy Mobilization For Youth. It was charged the Mobilization's staff was full of communists. When it became clear that there would be little solid evidence to sustain that accusation, charges were made in the press and supported by important political leaders, that M.F.Y.'s executives had embezzled $300,000. That charge also proved unfounded. But the damage had been done.[57] Mobilization lost much of its community support, and staff members began looking for less dangerous places to work.

Mobilization For Youth still exists on the Lower East Side; but it is a much more traditional social service agency now than it set out to be. The magnitude of its task, the uncertainty of its resources, and the power of its enemies combined to render M.F.Y. ineffective as an instrument of community change. In view of the M.F.Y. experience, it is simply not possible to say whether the redistribution of social power can be achieved through community organizations that are designed to change the structure of the society.

Summary Comments Regarding Individual and Community- Oriented Delinquency Prevention

Thus far this chapter has emphasized the differences between types of delinquency prevention programs. There are also important areas of commonality. All types, for example, are hampered by a lack of empirical evidence showing what works and what does not. In addition, all types are inadequately funded. It is rare, indeed, that sufficient resources are available to move an experimental program from the drawing board into actual operation. The American sociologist Clarence Schrag recently spoke to this point:

> . . . it seems to me that most of the guys working in the field of delinquency and crime are agreed that we know really very little about definitions, causes, or control. . . .
>
> I've been concerned about reasons for such ignorance after many years of

research . . . all kinds of prevention programs are instituted without any real evidence of achievement or accomplishment. I'm coming to the view that there are several reasons for our ignorance . . . it's not only the scholars and researchers who share responsibility . . . but I think public officials, administrators, legislators, and others share responsibility for our ignorance in the sense that the programs of delinquency prevention . . . just have never been implemented as far as I can tell. I don't know of any clear case in which a planned or proposed program was truly implemented . . . the way it was planned.[58]

Resources within the juvenile justice system are allocated primarily to institutional rehabilitation programs, with very little left over for prevention efforts. This occurs despite the fact that institutional programs are inordinately expensive and despite the growing belief that such programs may promote, rather than deter, delinquent careers. In some states the cost of maintaining reform schools may run as high as twenty thousand dollars a year per child. As Jerome Miller has pointed out:

That's enough money to send a kid to one of the best private schools in the country, send him to see a private therapist, and still have enough left over for a summer vacation in Europe — and if you do that, what kid won't shape up?[59]

The fact remains, however, that in almost all jurisdictions (local, state, and federal) resources are now committed to institutional programs for many years in advance, because the institutions themselves cost a great deal of money to build and because closing them would mean the loss of many jobs (which is politically untenable). Consequently it is likely that all types of delinquency prevention programs will continue to operate on minimal budgets in the foreseeable future, and that new programs will develop very slowly because of inadequate funds.

The most popular delinquency prevention programs are those with a clinical orientation. Social change programs, the new wave of the 1960s, seem now to be out of vogue. Nevertheless competition among the orientations continues to be keen. With money limited, the types of programs a community develops will determine what types of jobs will be available for professionals. Thus, clinicians, for example, have a stake in fighting for the preservation of clinically oriented programs, and community organizers have a stake in fighting for the development of social change programs. In short, the area of delinquency prevention is characterized by uncertainty about what to do and by inadequate resources with which to do much anyhow.

In recent years, moreover, diversion programs have been receiving a lot of attention in the literature. Derived from the labeling perspective, diversion programs have the objective of preventing not delinquency, but the development of delinquent careers. To a considerable degree, diversionary programs might draw on the types of programs advocated by both individual- and community-oriented theorists. The next section will address some of the theoretical issues regarding prevention as seen from the labeling perspective, and the following chapter will discuss some of the uses to which communities might (and do) channel their available resources toward achieving diversionary goals.

Prevention Programs Derived from the Labeling Perspective

There are fundamental differences between labeling theory on the one hand and individual-oriented and community-oriented theories on the other. Theories of the latter types focus on differences between delinquents and nondelinquents; labeling theory emphasizes similarities. The older theories maintain that the differences between delinquents and nondelinquents bring about delinquency; the labeling theory asserts that such differences as exist are not causes of delinquency, but rather are themselves brought about by the labeling process.[60]

Labeling theorists maintain that all youngsters experiment with antisocial acts; youngsters who are caught and processed by social control agencies, it is argued, begin to develop deviant self-concepts, and become increasingly enmeshed in patterns of lawbreaking behavior. From this it may be implied that labeling theorists are not primarily concerned with the prevention of delinquent *acts*, which they see as healthy, normal, and age-appropriate, but with the prevention of deviant *careers*. From this perspective the challenge is not to keep youngsters from ever misbehaving, but rather to ensure that misbehavior is not responded to in ways that increase the probability that children grow into confirmed delinquents and hardened criminals. The prevention of serious delinquency, interactionsts maintain, can be achieved only if communities are able to tolerate the existence of many types of youthful misbehavior and are able to respond in comparatively nonstigmatizing ways.

Increasing Community Tolerance
for Delinquency

It is a central precept of labeling theory that acts are delinquent not because they are inherently antisocial or malicious, but only because they are identified as delinquent by the dominant forces in a society. Kai Erikson has phrased this proposition as follows:

> Deviance is not a property *inherent* in any particular kind of behavior; it is a property *conferred upon* that behavior by the people who come into direct or indirect contact with it.[61]

To the extent that this is true, delinquency can be prevented by not being identified. This is not merely a semantic argument. Think of all the middle- and upper-class youngsters who participate in law-breaking activities but are never thought to be "delinquent." The community is not particularly bothered by their behavior, which is often seen merely as youthful indiscretion; and the youngsters themselves avoid both punishment and stigma, growing, in the vast majority of cases, into mature, responsible adulthood. It is the poor and powerless youngsters who are caught and labeled and who are most likely to grow into serious delinquents and eventually into confirmed criminals. This is so, labeling theorists argue, not because those kids are really worse but because the labeling process generates pressures towards delinquency. The consequences of labeling are that youngsters begin to think of themselves as being delinquent, that they are isolated from "nondelinquent" society, and that their opportunities for conformity are limited.[62] It may be that children can not be prevented from misbehaving; but misbehaving children, it is argued, can be prevented from growing into committed delinquents if only communities will be more tolerant of their behavior.

Two ways are generally suggested to help increase community tolerance for delinquency. One, called decriminalization, is to change the law so that some behaviors currently defined as delinquent cease to be so defined. The other, called diversion, is to develop apparatus outside the juvenile justice system which can respond to the needs of children in trouble.

Decriminalization

Many "delinquent" acts are thoroughly victimless, involving injury neither to persons nor to property. Indeed, a good number of activities that can result in a finding of delinquency would not be crimes if engaged in by adults. Truancy, for example, is a delinquent act in most states; so, too, is running away from home. While adults may legally imbibe alcoholic beverages, children who do so may be identified as delinquent. Labeling theorists argue that these juvenile "status" offenses ought to be abolished.[63] Status offenders, while they may be troubled youngsters, are not an immediate threat to the community; but treating them as delinquents may generate self-fulfilling prophecies.

It is also thought that treating status offenders as delinquents may breed disrespect for the law, thus contributing to the development of lawbreaking attitudes and values. Children who perceive that they have not done anything seriously wrong but find themselves treated as delinquents may find the law to be unfair, and may see no need to pay any attention to it at all. Decriminalization, by keeping status offenders from becoming enmeshed in the justice system, would minimize the chances that they will come to think of themselves as persecuted outsiders.[64]

While some states have moved to delete status offenses from the behaviors classified as delinquent, they have generally maintained juvenile court jurisdiction over such offenses by redefining them as evidence that a child is "deprived" or "neglected."[65] Real decriminalization, which is depriving the juvenile justice system of jurisdiction over status offenders, has not been tried. Although the argument for decriminalization is attractive, there is good reason to proceed cautiously. If there is no legal mandate for intervention in the lives of status offenders, then a good number of them may not have their behavior dealt with at all.[66] It is not clear that such a course would be desirable. Consider a few examples.

What of a twelve-year-old youngster who is habitually truant, missing as many days of school as he attends, and falling asleep while in class? Should this child be free from any state intervention? What about a nine-year-old whose only offense is that he has run away from home and been living on his own at a beach for several weeks? How about a ten-year-old who habitually drinks wine, beer, and whiskey? Are we really comfortable in saying that because no crime has been committed no intervention is appropriate? If status offenses are eliminated from the law books, there will be no legal justification for requiring such children to submit to care, custody, or treatment. One response to this criticism suggests that children who act out in these ways ought not be ignored, but should be dealt with by institutions outside of the justice system; that is, that they should be diverted from the formal processes of juvenile justice.

Diversion

It was noted in earlier chapters that the vast majority of young people who commit delinquent acts, while not being *prevented* from committing delinquent acts, are in fact *diverted* from the formal processes of juvenile justice.[67] Self-report studies indicate that an overwhelming majority of young people commit delinquent acts, but the vast majority of those offending youngsters never get into legal trouble. Teachers, social workers, policemen, businessmen, neighbors, and parents all make decisions to shield some misbehaving youngsters from the juvenile courts while simultaneously sending others on for adjudication and treatment.

When a teacher sees a youth smoking marijuana, for example, and decides not to call the police, diversion has taken place. When a businessman calls the parents of a young shoplifter rather than the police, diversion has taken place. There is evidence that middle- and upper-class youngsters are disproportionately likely to be diverted.[68] The fact that lower-class and minority-group children are drawn to a greater degree into the custody of the courts is due in part, no doubt, to bigotry and discrimination; but it also is due to the existence of more community facilities geared to service affluent children who are in trouble: private therapists, special schools, psychiatric clinics, recreational programs are all available to the child whose parents can afford to pay and are influential in the community. Even part-time jobs are more readily available to young people whose parents have positions of power and prestige. When "diversion" is talked about as a delinquency prevention strategy, it usually means that resources and facilities available to middle- and upper-class children in trouble ought to be made available to disadvantaged children as well.

This perspective has led in recent years to a search for effective ways to divert increasing numbers of youngsters from the juvenile justice system. This trend is based on the observation that most young people who commit delinquent acts grow up and become mature, responsible adults — unless society intervenes in ways that generate pressure toward delinquent careers. Studies such as those cited in Chapter 5 indicate that schools, social agencies, families, and even policemen often make encapsulating decisions because they do not understand the value of diversion or because of a lack of appropriate diversionary resources in the community. There are growing numbers of people who believe that considerable diversionary resources now exist in practically every community in the United States — if only concerned individuals and community organizations would coordinate their activities. The next chapter addresses models for diversionary programs which have been developed in the United States and in other parts of the world.

References

1. Julian Mack, "The Chancery Procedures in the Juvenile Court," in *The Child, The Clinic, and the Court,* ed. J. Addams (New York: New Republic, 1927), pp. 311 - 12.

2. The uncertainty of knowledge about the causes of delinquency is elaborated on at some length in Chap. 2 of this book.

3. Helen L. Witmer and Edith Tufts, *The Effectiveness of Delinquency Prevention Programs,* Children's Bureau Publication Number 350 (Washington, D.C.: U.S. Government Printing Office, 1954).

4. The lamentable inadequacy of this type of research is well documented in R. L. Morrison, *The Effectiveness of Current Programmes for the Prevention of Juvenile Delinquency* (Strasbourg: Council of Europe, 1963) pp. 7 - 10, 90. The point should be made that the quantity and quality of evaluative research efforts in the United States is generally considered the best in the world; see Leon Radzinowicz, *In Search of Criminology* (Cambridge, Mass.: Harvard University Press, 1962), p. 117.

5. These ideas are discussed at some length in Chap. 2 of this book.

6. Henry D. McKay quoted in E. K. Nelson, *Community Approaches to the Prevention of Crime and Delinquency — Some Research Leads* (1961), p. 1.

7. For an excellent discussion of existing instruments and techniques for predicting delinquency, see Robert E. Stanfield and Brendan ed. Maher, "Clinical and Actuarial Predictions of Juvenile Delinquency," in *Controlling Delinquents,* ed. Stanton Wheeler, (New York: John Wiley & Sons, 1966), pp. 245 - 70.

8. Sybil A. Stone, Elsa Castendyck, and Harold B. Hanson, *Children in the Community,* Children's Bureau Publication Number 317 (Washington, D.C.: U.S. Government Printing Office, 1946), pp. 47 - 8.

9. See, for example, Marion Stranahan and Cecile Schwartzman, "An Experiment in Reaching Asocial Adolescents Through Group Therapy," *Annals of the American Academy of Political and Social Sciences* 322 (March 1959): 117 - 25. See also, G. Lewis Penner, "An Experiment in Police and Social Agency Cooperation," *Annals of the American Academy of Political and Social Sciences* 322 (March 1959): 79 - 88.

10. Edwin Powers and Helen L. Witmer, *An Experiment in the Prevention of Delinquency — The Cambridge-Somerville Youth Study* (New York: Columbia University Press, 1951). See also William McCord and Joan McCord, *Origins of Crime: A New Evaluation of the Cambridge-Somerville Youth Study* (New York: Columbia University Press, 1959).

11. William C. Kvaraceus, "Prevention of Juvenile Delinquency — Evaluation of Different Types of Action," *International Child Welfare Review* 19 (1965): 11.

12. Walter B. Miller, "Lower Class Culture as a Generating Milieu of Gang Delinquency," *Journal of Social Issues* 14, no. 3 (1959): 5 - 19.

13. A good discussion of the role of schools in the prevention of juvenile delinquency may be found in Robert M. MacIver, *The Prevention and Control of Delinquency* (New York: Atherton Press, 1967), pp. 104 - 23.

14. See Jacob Landers, *Higher Horizons Progress Report* (New York: Board of Education of the City of New York, 1963).

15. Adele Franklin, "The All-Day Neighborhood Services," *Annals of the American Academy of Political and Social Sciences* 322 (March 1959): 62 - 8.

16. The extent to which delinquent acts occur at school is considerable. Indeed, in some cities delinquency in the schools is becoming a major social problem. In the year 1973 the New York City Police, for example, received almost 11,000 complaints of crimes on public school property. The offenses ranged from murder, rape, and robbery to false bomb reports. About 900 New York City school teachers were assaulted during the 1973 - 1974 school year. Approximately 640 assaults on students were recorded in the same period. At least half of the assaults on teachers occurred in classrooms. New York's 96 public high schools now employ 950 security guards, and pressure is building for more guards and for the use of electronic surveillance devices. See Diane Ravitch, "Crime-Fighting as Part of Curricula," *New York Times* 4, no. 8 (July 21, 1974): 1.

17. See, for example, Kvaraceus, "Prevention of Juvenile Delinquency," p. 27.

18. Bertram M. Beck and Deborah B. Beck, "Recreation and Delinquency," in President's Commission on Law Enforcement and Administration of Justice, *Task Force Report: Juvenile Delinquency and Youth Crime* (Washington, D.C.: U.S. Government Printing Office, 1967), p. 333.

19. Kvaraceus, "Prevention of Juvenile Delinquency," p. 27.

20. Sheldon Glueck and Eleanor Glueck, *Unravelling Juvenile Delinquency* (New York: The Commonwealth Fund, 1950), p. 399.

21. Ellery F. Reed, "How Effective Are Group Work Agencies in Preventing Delinquency?" *Focus* 28 (November 1959): 170 - 6.

22. See, for example, Roscoe C. Brown, Jr. and Dan W. Dodson, "The Effectiveness of a Boys' Club in Reducing Delinquency," *Annals of the American Academy of Political and Social Sciences* 322 (March 1959): 47.

23. For an excellent discussion of the utility and limitations of recreation programs, see Beck and Beck, "Recreation and Delinquency."

24. Frederick M. Thrasher, *The Gang: A Study of 1,313 Gangs in Chicago,* 2nd rev. ed. (Chicago: University of Chicago Press, 1936), p. 494.

25. Radzinowicz, *In Search of Criminology*, 145 - 6.

26. See Irving Spergel, *Street Gang Work* (Reading, Mass.: Addison-Wesley, 1966), pp. 137 - 40.

27. Ibid., p. 124; see also Nathan S. Caplan et al., "The Nature, Variety, and Patterning of Street Club Work in an Urban Setting," in *Juvenile Gangs In Context*, ed. Malcolm W. Klein, (Englewood Cliffs, N.J.: Prentice-Hall, 1967) pp. 194 - 202.

28. Hans W. Mattick and Nathan S. Caplan, "Stake Animals, Loud-Talking and Leadership in Do-Nothing and Do-Something Situations," in *Juvenile Gangs in Context*, Klein, ed., p. 107.

29. Harold S. Keltner, "Crime Prevention Program of the YMCA, St. Louis," in *Preventing Crime*, ed. Sheldon Glueck and Eleanor Glueck, (New York: McGraw-Hill, 1936), pp. 182 - 98.

30. See Spergel, *Street Gang Work;* Klein, *Juvenile Gangs in Context;* Paul L. Crawford, Daniel I. Malamud, and James R. Dumpson, *Working with Teen-age Gangs* (New York: Welfare Council of New York City, 1950); James R. Dumpson, "An Approach to Anti-Social Street Gangs," *Federal Probation* 13 (December 1949): 22 - 9; Malcolm W. Klein, "Juvenile Gangs, Police, and Detached Workers: Controversies in Gang Intervention," *Social Service Review* 39 (June 1965): 183 - 90; and Solomon Kobrin, "Sociological Aspects of the Development of a Street Corner Group: An Exploratory Study," *American Journal of Orthopsychiatry* 31 (October, 1961): 685 - 702.

31. Walter B. Miller, "The Impact of a 'Total-Community' Delinquency Control Project," *Social Problems* 10, no. 2 (Fall, 1962): 186.

32, Community-oriented theories are discussed at some length in Chapter 2 of this book.

33. President's Commission on Law Enforcement and Administration of Justice, *Report: The Challenge of Crime in a Free Society* (Washington, D.C.: U.S. Government Printing Office, 1967).

34. Ibid., p. 58.

35. Ibid., p. 67.

36. Ibid., p. 279.

37. Mobilization For Youth, "A Proposal for the Prevention and Control of Delinquency by Expanding Opportunities," mimeographed (New York: M.F.Y., 1961), pp. ii - iii.

38. Ibid., pp. 43 - 50; see also Marilyn Bibb, "Gang Related Services of Mobilization For Youth," in *Juvenile Gangs in Context*, Klein, ed.

39. Bertram M. Beck, "Mobilization For Youth: Reflections About Its Administration," in *Justice and the Law in the Mobilization For Youth Experience*, ed. Harold H. Weissman, (New York: Association Press, 1969), p. 150.

40. See Bibb, "Gang-Related Services," p. 178.

41. Ibid.

42. See, generally, Mobilization For Youth, "A Proposal," pp. 91 - 107.

43. See Bibb, "Gang-Related Services," p. 179.

44. See, generally, Mobilization For Youth, "A Proposal," pp. 107 - 26.

45. See Bibb, "Gang-Related Services," p. 179.

46. See Mobilization For Youth, "A Proposal," p. 189.

47. Ibid., p. 133.
48. Ibid., p. 146.
49. Ibid., p. 133.
50. Bibb, "Gang-Related Services," p. 182.
51. Beck and Beck, "Recreation and Delinquency," p. 336.
52. Harold H. Weissman, "Epilogue," in *Justice and the Law*, Weissman, ed., p. 192.
53. Ibid., pp. 196 - 7.
54. The rate of delinquency per 1,000 youths in the area was impossible to determine precisely, since both the M.F.Y.-serviced areas and the other areas in the neighborhood had fairly high tenant turnover rates. During the years of the MFY research, however, several new low-income housing projects were built in the Mobilization area, and it is probable that the total population of children and youths increased appreciably. These figures are based on an estimate of the total numbers of young people on the Lower East Side.
55. There is an extensive and developing body of literature that speaks to this point; see, for example, Raymond A. Bauer and Kenneth Gergen, *The Study of Policy Formulation* (New York: Free Press, 1971); Yehezkiel Dror, *Ventures in Policy Science* (New York: American Elsevier, 1971); Harold D. Lasswell, *A Pre-view of Policy Sciences* (New York: American Elsevier, 1971).
56. Beck, "Mobilization For Youth," p. 148.
57. Ibid., pp. 150 - 5.
58. Clarence Schrag, quoted in William T. Pink and Mervin F. White, eds., "Delinquency Prevention: A Conference Perspective on Issues and Directions," mimeographed (Portland, Ore.: Regional Research Institute, Portland State University, 1973), p. 43.
59. This information was obtained in an interview with Dr. Miller.
60. Labeling theory and the differences between labeling and other orientations are topics discussed at some length in Chapter 2 of this book.
61. Kai Erikson, *Wayward Puritans* (New York: John Wiley & Sons, 1966), p. 6.
62. Edwin M. Schur, *Radical Non-intervention: Rethinking the Delinquency Problem* (Englewood Cliffs, N.J.: Prentice-Hall, 1973).
63. See, for example, Pink and White, "Delinquency Prevention: A Conference Perspective," which is very much committed to the labeling perspective. This compilation is the product of a conference at the Portland State University. Participants in the conference included many of America's most prominent experts on juvenile delinquency and criminology, including David Matza, David Bordua, LaMar Empey, Malcolm Klein, Clarence Schrag, and James Short, Jr.
64. Ibid., pp. 39 - 41.
65. Mark M. Levin and Rosemary C. Sarri, *Juvenile Delinquency: A Comparative Analysis of Legal Codes in the United States* (Ann Arbor: National Assessment of Juvenile Corrections, 1974), pp. 10 - 24.
66. This point was articulately made by David Bordua, who is quoted in Pink and White, "Delinquency Prevention: A Conference Perspective," p. 42.
67. This idea is discussed in Chapters 1 and 4 of this book.
68. See Chapters 4, 5, and 6 of this book.

12 Four Models of Diversion in Juvenile Justice

*A great many young people are in very serious
trouble throughout the technically developed
and especially the Western world. Their trouble,
moreover, follows certain familiar common
patterns; they get into much the same kind of
difficulty in very different societies. But it is
nevertheless strange that they should. Human life
is a continuous thread which each of us spins to
his own pattern, rich and complex in meaning.
There are no natural knots in it. Yet knots form,
nearly always in adolescence.*

— *Edgar Z. Friedenberg,*
Coming of Age in America

Throughout this book it has been demonstrated that *diversion is
the primary characteristic of juvenile justice.* Diversion begins in the
community where delinquent acts occur, and continues in varying
degrees at all stages of the system from identification through disposition; and at each stage, more youngsters are diverted back into the
community than are brought into the custody of the juvenile justice
system. Thus it is social institutions in the broader community —
families, churches, schools, social welfare agencies, etc. — which have
the primary mandate to control and care for young people who commit
delinquent acts. It is only when individuals or institutions in the community fail to divert (or decide not to divert) that the formal processes
of the juvenile justice system are called into action.

Despite these facts about the enormous responsibilities of community agents, it is still true that most programs concerned with
delinquent behavior (and certainly most funds) are concerned with

detention, probation, and institutionalization. Furthermore, there is reason to fear that these programs more often than not contribute to the development of delinquent careers. It is apparent, too, that most youngsters who are diverted typically grow up to be mature, responsible adults. Recent recognition of these discrepancies has led scholars and policymakers alike to search for effective models and programs through which youngsters can be diverted from the formal processes of juvenile justice.

It has also become apparent during our discussion of juvenile justice that the values, philosophies, programs, and institutions which are concerned with youthful behavior (and misbehavior) are highly diverse and fragmented. In fact, the overall system has been characterized as "kaleidoscopic"; that is, the array of organizations and jurisdictions changes from case to case and from community to community. Programs exist at city, county, regional, state, and federal levels; in public, voluntary, and private sectors; and in a variety of categorical program areas — education, child welfare, youth services, health, law-enforcement, employment, corrections, probation, court, etc. The animosities and conflicts that have emerged from this fragmentation have contributed, it seems, to the sad state of affairs regarding the care and treatment of troubled youth and youth in trouble.

The relatively amorphous and conflict-ridden "system" (or non-system) of services for youth is not, however, without its own rationality; and it is possible to describe major clusters or sets of organizations and programs.[1] Moreover, each organization set operates with fairly distinct rules and assumptions about what is and is not proper, and who belongs or does not belong in the particular organizational domain.[2] Both scholars and policymakers have begun to search for effective models to guide the development of programs through which increasing numbers of youngsters can be diverted from the formal processes of juvenile justice. This chapter takes up four models of diversion — the school model, the welfare model, the law-enforcement model, and the youth service systems model. Some of the innovative programs in each are discussed and their confrontation with the conflicting theories and values which historically characterize the juvenile justice system are described. It will be seen that elements of the first three models exist in practically every community in the United States, and that the fourth model (which has been tried in a few places) provides an attempt to rationalize what are otherwise diverse and conflicting efforts.[3]

The School Model of Diversion

Except perhaps for the family, schools are the most ubiquitous institutions of socialization and education in America. In addition to traditional "educational" objectives, schools are now charged with preparing students for social life and for positions in a highly technological economic order. While it is true that schools are sometimes blamed for "causing" delinquency,[4] they are still asked to bear increased responsibility for preparing new generations of American youth for responsible, satisfying, and productive adulthood. Cooper sums up the findings of research on educational attainment and delinquency:

> The educational status of offenders is inferior on the whole to that of the general population, tending to be slightly inferior in respect to illiteracy, somewhat inferior in respect to amount of schooling, decidedly inferior in repeat and school progress, and clearly inferior in respect to educational achievement.[5]

Two current trends may be observed in the schools in respect to delinquency prevention and diversion. Schools are expected both to prevent youngsters from becoming delinquent and to interact therapeutically with youngsters who get into trouble.

In the first area, prevention, the Task Force on Juvenile Delinquency of the President's Commission on Law Enforcement and Administration of Justice placed considerable responsibility on the schools for assuring that young people enter the "mainstream" of American society:

> . . . the public schools must upgrade the amount and quality of education provided today's youth. Specifically, they must do what is necessary to reduce the number of high school dropouts, prepare more youth for college and other post-high school training, and prepare more of those who immediately enter the job market for white collar and highly-skilled blue collar work and for subsequent job mobility and retraining. In short, the schools must increase their "holding power," feed more students into institutions of higher education, and upgrade the quality of non-college preparatory education.[6]

Second, schools are increasingly being required to deal with "exceptional" youngsters. Traditionally, socially or mentally troubled youngsters were excluded from schools; they were left to parents, charities, or public social agencies. As the "right-to-education" movement progresses, however, school authorities bear increased responsibility for education and socialization of practically all youngsters.[7] This expansion means that schools must find ways to cope with youngsters who are chronically truant or chronically disruptive in classrooms. Several recent supreme court decisions found that schools cannot summarily suspend students at the pleasure of teachers and administrators.[8] Again, the words of the President's Commission are a bellwether of this movement:

> [Schools] must develop effective means for "rescuing" students who fail to show normal academic, social, or moral development. When difficulties such as under-achievement and deviation from school or community standards of conduct appear, we assume that the schools must do whatever is necessary to bring the students involved back into the mainstream of educational development.
>
> More specifically, academic failure or underachievement must be met with responses that will serve to improve skills and motivation in order to make success more likely in the future. When pupils violate school or community rules of behavior, the schools must do whatever they can to end such nonconformity, while at the same time reducing the motivation of such students to behave in the same way in the future. When students show an inclination to drop out of school prematurely, the schools should do whatever possible to make education relevant, meaningful, and promising enough that such students will be motivated to remain in school at least through high school.[9]

In this frame of reference, educational and behavioral problems are seen as inextricably intertwined; and school is seen as the appropriate place to deal with them all simultaneously. Thus the school model of diversion regards much of what is considered in this country to be "delinquency" as normal problems of socialization and education. Edwin Lemert's discussion of the system in the U.S.S.R. provides an empirical illustration of this model as applied in practice.

The School Model in the U.S.S.R.[10]

Since the revolutions of 1917 - 1921, education in the U.S.S.R. has been defined as a process of "upbringing" which encompasses the entire personality of children — uniting mental, moral, physical, and aesthetic education. Delinquency is seen as a problem of socialization, and youthful misconduct is generally discounted. Youthful drunkenness, for example, is not treated as a crime; and petty thievery is a minor charge considered to result from insufficient education. In fact, "apart from serious crimes of a more universalistic nature (assault, rape, robbery) and those against the state, Russians seem to regard behavior called delinquent in Americans as normal problems of socialization and education."[11] Thus the Soviet system relies on the schools to provide education for adult life as well as for the creation of honest, productive citizens.

In support of the schools in this regard, the social activities of young people in the U.S.S.R. are organized to provide a locus toward which peer pressure through student groups, and a variety of community (collective) resources are directed.

> Student organization begins as early as the fourth grade in Soviet schools, and is managed to bring any children who "break discipline" into confrontation with their classmates (the nucleus collective), or if that does not suffice, before the student council which represents the whole school. There the student meets face-to-face criticism and is expected to develop self-criticism as well. Wall newspapers also call attention to personal shortcomings of students. Youthful monitors carry on surveillance of the student body to insure compliance with school rules, which are highly explicit and are standardized throughout the entire nation.
>
> Student problems not amenable to peer group controls may cause teachers to contact parents, or bring them to the attention of the school director. The Komsomol, Young Pioneers, youth organizations, parents' groups, tenants' organizations in housing projects, factory groups, and trade unions all can be enlisted at various times and in various ways to help find solutions to children's problems. Besides this, every school or children's home is associated with a patron enterprise on which it can make claims for assistance. There is a standing rule that no child can be expelled from a school without permission of the district or city commission on affairs of minors, which must make plans for his continuing education. Consistent with this policy, transfers between schools are easy to make.[12]

Thus, the Soviet system deals with most youthful misbehavior through the normal processes of the schools. Extracurricular problems are referred to a "Commission on Affairs of Minors" which consists of professional and lay members and is headed by a teacher. "The chief objective at all times is to keep the child in the home and avoid the stigma of appearance in court."[13] Children under twelve may not be prosecuted. Older youngsters may be tried in ordinary courts, but only for specific offenses of theft, violence, assault, murder, and destroying state property.[14] In this system the schools are a focal point for unifying community action in coping with youth problems and in effectuating diversion from the courts.[15]

Some Trends in the U.S.

In 1972 the U.S. Supreme Court found that under the U.S. Constitution every child, regardless of handicap or disability is guaranteed a right to a free and equal educational opportunity. In *Mills v. Board of Education of District of Columbia,*[16] the court found that adequate public education suited to each exceptional child's special needs or the alternative of public payment of tuition for appropriate private education is required. This right-to-education principle has been reiterated in a variety of state decisions holding that all children are capable of benefiting from a program of education and training and that adequate programs must be provided by school authorities.

Nevertheless, a recent study by the Children's Defense Fund found the record of school performance in this regard falls far short of the law. The study found not only that schools fail children in school but also that they fail to have any contact with many youngsters.

Most Americans assume that all children go to school. This is not true.

According to our analysis of the 1970 U.S. Bureau of the Census data on nonenrollment, nearly two million children 7 to 17 years of age were not enrolled in school. Over one million were between 7 and 15 years of age. More than three quarters of a million were between the ages of 7 and 13.

• • •

[Moreover,] the nearly two million children the Census counts as nonenrolled only reflect the surface of how many children are out of school in America. Not included are:

The hundreds of thousands of children expelled and suspended and otherwise thrown out of school for disciplinary reasons.

The countless truants who elude Census enumerators and school officials alike.

The many children whose parents do not understand English and who therefore did not correctly answer the Census nonenrollment questionnaire.[17]

The project also found that there are additional thousands of students who are excluded by reason of pregnancy, extreme poverty, mental retardation, emotional illness, learning disabilities, or inability to speak English. And there are nearly 100,000 children in detention or other institutions — and between 250,000 and 400,000 who are jailed for short periods — for which no adequate educational program is provided.[18]

We found that if a child is not white, or is white but not middle-class, does not speak English, is poor, needs special help with seeing, hearing, walking, reading, learning, adjusting, growing up, is pregnant or married at age 15, is not smart or is too smart, then in too many places school officials decide school is not the place for that child.

It is as if many school officials have decided that certain groups of children are beyond their responsibility and are expendable. Not only do they exclude these children, they frequently do so arbitrarily, discriminatorily and with impunity.[19]

Facts such as these combine with right-to-education principles and the increasing volume of youth crime to spur communities to seek new ways to keep youngsters in school and to require that schools cope effectively with exceptional and problem youngsters. Increasingly schools are attempting to create special programs for problem youngsters, habitual truants, "predelinquents" and even delinquents. Most cities in the U.S. now have some school programs which remove youngsters from competitive situations and try to meet special individual needs; they usually have smaller class sizes and special selection and training of teachers. Many times sessions are shorter than in regular schools, attendance may not be compulsory, and there are often arrangements for the youngsters to work or train for a job. According to Lemert:

The "600" and "700" schools of New York city are the best known examples of special schools for student deviants. They provide intensive services for "disruptive" and delinquent children. The 600 schools concentrate on those with severe behavior problems, the 700 schools service children with "consistent" problems, especially those with court records. Actually these schools are a "system within a system" and have fairly elaborate procedures for referrals and admissions. Altogether in 1959 there were 22 units and annexes ranging from day schools to special units for children within psychiatric hospitals. Chicago's two special schools, Montefiore and Mosely, are less differentiated than those in New York, and in the case of Montefiore seems to be tied closely with the Family Court. Direct referrals come from school transfers or from welfare agencies.

A compromise arrangement midway between the retention of deviant students in regular classes along with recognition of their problems through provision of special services, and total separation in special schools, is the institution of special classes. These can be for slow learners, truants, delinquents and others with residual problems making them unresponsive to ordinary classroom methods.[20]

While definitive evaluations of these programs are not yet in, there is some evidence that these schools and special classes do tend to lead to decreases in truancy, vandalism, and confrontations with teachers.[21] There, are, however, problems to overcome: increased costs, special training, and isolation of teachers. Moreover, assignment of youngsters to these schools may become as stigmatizing as referral to the court. In this regard, a statement of Anton Makarenko, the founder of the Soviet system, demands careful reflection:

> I am absolutely convinced that creating a special abnormal pedagogy to deal with delinquents tends to foster deviation in youngsters, while on the other hand, a positive, purposeful approach to them transforms their collective very quickly into a normal one.[22]

In conclusion, it seems fair to say that schools are being asked to take an increasingly active role in dealing with troubled youngsters and youngsters in trouble; but also that, in the words of the President's Commission, "although there is a stir in the air, the schools — and the public that supports them — have largely failed to respond, resulting in serious lags between the educational system and other parts of society."[23] Thus the school model, to the degree that it is applicable in the U.S., constitutes not *the* system of diversion, but one group of fragments in the larger societal network. Consideration of the welfare model in the next section will illuminate still another approach and another set of pieces in the larger system.

The Welfare Model of Diversion

The school model just described is based on the idea that because children are away from parental and neighborhood experiences for such a large part of the time, schools should have a primary responsibility for "upbringing." Thus schools would replace the family as a primary institution of socialization and control. The welfare model, however, retains the family as the central societal institution; it seeks to support, supplement, and strengthen (or, if necessary, replace) the natural family. To these ends, a wide variety of social services are provided (see Chapter 5). Under a pure welfare model, social service agencies are given the authority and responsibility to "promote wholesome child development, strengthen family life and preserve the child's own home, and reduce the incidence of circumstances that deprive children of the requirements for their optimal development."[24] Their mandate often goes so far as to allow child welfare agencies to

. . . intervene in the "normal", "natural", or routine functioning of family life. It may curtail the control of parents over their children, it may remove children from the home, or even treat the home as unfit and formally divest parents of all authority over their children.[25]

Should child welfare agencies, or any agency, have this degree of authority over families and their children? Should these be solely administrative decisions, or should full due process rights be afforded to all parties involved? What would be the advantages and disadvantages in each case?

Child Welfare Councils in Sweden[26]

The welfare model for dealing with the needs and problems of youngsters originated in Norway, Sweden, and Denmark in the same period that the juvenile court movement began in America.

In purest form the welfare model completely replaces or functions in lieu of a juvenile court. This, for example, is the arrangement in Scandinavian countries, such as Sweden, which has no system of juvenile courts. In modified form the special welfare councils share authority or jurisdiction over childrens' problems with juvenile courts; this will be the situation in England when new legislation there is put fully into effect. Jurisdiction over children up to the age of criminal responsibility may be plenary or it may be qualified in instances of serious crimes, such as murder, which must be tried in criminal courts. Councils also may share jurisdiction with regular criminal courts over older youth.

There is a strong element of positivism in the welfare model, expressed in the idea that for children below the age of criminal responsibility, the application of measures to overcome problems of neglect, waywardness, and violations of laws should be part and parcel of a comprehensive child and youth welfare service. Justification for the administrative cast to the welfare model comes from the necessity to construct, staff, maintain, and supervise a variety of childrens' institutions. Along with this there must be procedures to select and regulate foster homes, and facilities for the examination, observation, and specialized treatment of more complicated cases must be established. Finally, administrative organization is needed to uphold standards among workers given responsibility for the supervision of children.[27]

Lemert suggests that differences between America and Scandinavia may have occurred because the focus in the latter was on how to treat delin-

---

FIGURE 12.1. Sweden's System of Handling Juvenile and Youth Offenders

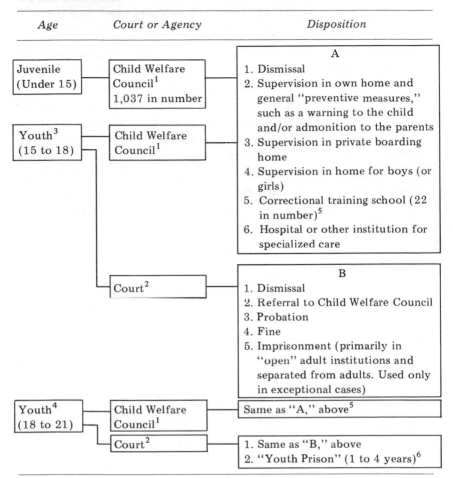

Age	Court or Agency	Disposition

A
1. Dismissal
2. Supervision in own home and general "preventive measures," such as a warning to the child and/or admonition to the parents
3. Supervision in private boarding home
4. Supervision in home for boys (or girls)
5. Correctional training school (22 in number)[5]
6. Hospital or other institution for specialized care

B
1. Dismissal
2. Referral to Child Welfare Council
3. Probation
4. Fine
5. Imprisonment (primarily in "open" adult institutions and separated from adults. Used only in exceptional cases)

Juvenile (Under 15) — Child Welfare Council[1] 1,037 in number

Youth[3] (15 to 18) — Child Welfare Council[1]

Court[2]

Youth[4] (18 to 21) — Child Welfare Council[1] — Same as "A," above[5]

Court[2]
1. Same as "B," above
2. "Youth Prison" (1 to 4 years)[6]

[1] "Child Welfare Council" is the name generally applied to this social welfare council. The name "Youth Welfare Council" may, according to law, however, be applied when the agency is dealing with youth, i.e., those about 15 to 18 years of age.

[2] Ordinary criminal court of first instance.

[3] The choice between the Child Welfare Council and the Court depends on the decision of the prosecuting authority.

[4] Youth offenders in this age group are as a rule first brought before court.

[5] Placement in correctional training schools is the most common disposition of the Councils for the age group 18 to 21 years.

[6] Correctional training institutions for this age group only.

Source: Ola Nyquist. How Sweden handles its juvenile and youth offenders. *Federal Probation*, 1956, XX. 36–42; *Social Services for Children and Young People in Sweden*, Stockholm: The Swedish Institute, 1948, pp. 3–16.

quents and their problems, while in the U.S.
people were concerned more about "the sorry
plight of children in jails and youth in prisons."[28]

Ideally the welfare model assigns complete responsibility for problems of children and youth to a public social service agency comparable to child welfare or social welfare departments in many U.S. cities and states or the federal Department of Health, Education and Welfare. In Sweden, for example, the Social Welfare Administration and local child welfare councils have absolute jurisdiction over all children under 15 years of age *(no* such child can be sent to court). Youngsters from 15 to 21 years of age may come before either child welfare councils or the court; however, even if charges are proved in court, youngsters may still be referred to a child welfare council. Figure 12.1 presents a diagrammatic representation of Sweden's system.[29]

Rehabilitation Goals and Others

Thus the welfare model suggests that programs for young people should be based on rehabilitative goals and that youthful misdeeds should not be considered crimes. In practice, this approach is not unproblematic; however, there are always proponents of social protection especially in situations in which young people commit serious acts against individuals or the community. Even in Scandinavian countries, the fact that there is no sure way to affix the legal age of responsibility (after which "youthful misconduct" becomes a "crime") leads to conflict between welfare agencies and public prosecutors. In Sweden, for example:

> The actions of public prosecutors in disputed cases have their roots in their commitments to protect society by preventing crime through the use of deterrent measures. Hence, while they may be willing to have a youth benefit from the special measures available for use by the child welfare councils, the prosecutors may want some degree of punishment added to them. For example, the prosecutor may request that a warning be issued by the council as a condition to waiving prosecution. There is, however, no assurance that this will be done. The council may proceed differently with each of three youths involved in a common offense, two being subjected to supervision, while the third is dismissed, whereupon the prosecutor may elect to prosecute the third.[30]

In addition, the welfare model, by proceeding informally (without a court trial) may deprive children of their freedom (and parents of their children) without full due process of law. Thus the perennial conflict between the major values of social rehabilitation and those of due process creates additional dilemmas. Furthermore, in some cases, the kinds of dispositions made by welfare agencies seem to be little different from those usually made by juvenile courts, for example, special homes or correctional institutions.

There is also concern about the degree to which the time, money, and effort invested in social work methods ameliorates problems. Studies such as the Cambridge-Somerville Project,[31] the Chicago Area Project,[32] Mobilization For Youth in New York,[33] and the Los Angeles Youth Project[34] are scarcely encouraging. The small amount of research on such projects is inconclusive as to the effects on delinquency rates of project youngsters compared with control groups. They certainly do not show dramatic improvements in youngsters who receive social work help. In fact, one study in New York, as far as could be determined, was counterproductive because the program introduced a labeling process of its own and invaded personal liberties:

> . . . the singling out of individuals and their confrontation in casework interviews stimulated great anxiety and resistance among the girls, so much that it was deemed necessary to abandon traditional casework methods in favor of a kind of group mental hygiene presentation. Even more significant than the poverty of results from the project was its revelation of the lack of insightfulness of social workers into the sociological implication of their activities and their apparent willingness to impose treatment in a way that invaded privacy and was implicitly degrading to the client.[35]

Research does show, however, that (1) the younger an individual is when first involved with the juvenile justice system, the more likely it is that he or she will persist in crime, and (2) the farther youngsters proceed into the juvenile justice system, the less the chance there is that they will be diverted.[36] Thus there seems to be strong evidence to suggest that even if social welfare programs cannot be shown to be a "sure cure" for youthful misconduct, nonjudicial interventions are more appropriate for youngsters and, most importantly, they tend to avoid the creation of delinquent careers.

Youth Service Bureaus

A recent trend in the U.S. is to seek to provide a diversionary counterbalance to the formal processes of juvenile justice by creating local-level child welfare-oriented organizations with a mandate to divert. These new programs, usually called *Youth Service Bureaus,* are explicitly external to the traditional juvenile justice system and are intended to serve as an alternate source for referrals from parents, schools, businessmen, clergy, and social agencies, as well as from probation officers and the police.

> The problem to be addressed is how to reduce the imbalance of power between the juvenile justice system and those with whom it deals. Two important facts about the clientele of this system need to be made explicit. First, in most communities, official delinquency tends to be impacted in limited geographic sections. It is not uniformly distributed across the geographic face of the community. Such ecological concentration seems to reflect simply the geographic distribution of minority groups, the white poor, and other powerless groups whose children make up most of those handled by the juvenile justice system.
>
> Second, most of the official delinquency and youth crime cases dealt with by the police, courts and corrections involve relatively minor law violations, essentially unthreatening to the common interests.
>
> These facts make the development of locally based agencies whose function would be to divert cases out of the juvenile justice system both logical and practical devices. Perhaps the best known mechanism being offered at present along these lines is what are now called Youth Services Bureaus. As recommended by the President's Commission on Law Enforcement and Administration of Justice, these would be local, community-based, youth serving agencies situated *outside* of the juvenile justice system. The police, juvenile courts, parents, schools, and others would refer adolescents, delinquent *and* nondelinquent, who are in need of special attention to such bureaus. Properly staffed and managed, such bureaus could be used to divert cases out of the juvenile justice system, thus avoiding many of the negative consequences which face individuals who in fact remain under the care of the system.[37]

Target Group and Location

A first characteristic of youth service bureaus as an instrument of diversion (which seeks to avoid the stigmatization of contact with the juvenile justice system) is the provision of services to several categories of youngsters — the target group. The primary target group of youth service bureaus (YSBs) corresponds closely to the group of youngsters served by the existing welfare system or courts; that is, young people who are in danger of becoming delinquent.[38] More specifically, these are youngsters who are referred by schools, parents, the police, or others and whose conduct could bring them within the jurisdiction of the juvenile court.[39] Youth service bureaus go further, however, and seek to serve three additional categories of young people. One secondary target group consists of young people who seek help on their own volition; these walk-ins, or self-referrals, are youth with economic, personal, or social problems or handicaps who are not able to get help through their families, friends, school, or traditional agencies. A third group is composed of youth who are adjudicated delinquent, for whom services are requested by an official of the juvenile justice system. Finally, and perhaps most important from a diversionary perspective, YSBs should be open to *all other youth in the area.*

> A YSB should not limit its activities to providing services *only* to youths in danger of becoming delinquent or who have been adjudicated delinquent. Any such limitation might stigmatize all of a YSB's activities as being directed solely toward serving "youths in trouble" — a policy which might very well inhibit some referrals as well as voluntary requests for service.
> It has been said that in order to avoid or lessen any stigmatization of recipients which might develop if the program is limited to the two primary groups, that there be some activities which should be open to *all* youth in the area. These might include recreational or leisure time programs, "rap" sessions, and the use of youth as volunteers in a variety of capacities.[40]

This last aspect of the YSB target group is meant to ensure that youth service bureaus are nonstigmatizing. In this way, YSBs seek to present an image, and a program, to the community which makes it seem to be the place for all youth to go, for a variety of services.

It is precisely for those reasons that YSBs should also be located in neighborhood community centers or in some location in close proximity to the regular activities of young people.[41]

> The YSB should preferably be organized on a town-, city-, or county-wide basis with neighborhood-based branches in high-delinquency areas. It should be independent of other agencies and systems.[42]

Thus the intent is that YSBs be accessible to, available to, attractive to, and used by a cross-section of the youth in the community.

The Role of YSBs in the Community

Essentially the task of a youth service bureau is to function in lieu of or in addition to the family. It is a modern mechanism providing some of the functions of the extended family (that web of relatives and friends which traditionally existed), and some of the functions served by "influential contacts" in the community who in modern times have assisted middle-class families in an arrangement of reciprocal favors.

> The Youth Service Bureau is a noncoercive, independent public [sometimes private] agency established to divert children and youth from the justice system by (1) mobilizing community resources to solve youth problems, (2) strengthening existing youth resources and developing new ones, and (3) promoting positive programs to remedy delinquency-breeding conditions.[43]

Thus the key service (and perhaps the distinguishing characteristic) of youth service bureaus is that they should provide *advocacy linkages* to the community. In addition, youth service bureaus often find a dearth of certain services or facilities which they then seek to stimulate in the community; or, lacking a successful response, to provide themselves. The concept of advocacy linkages and service delivery are discussed next.

Advocacy Linkages

Through the implementation of the concept of advocacy linkages, the YSB takes on the role of a concerned parent who attempts to divert. It has been noted throughout this book that practically all youngsters commit acts for which they could be adjudicated delinquent, and furthermore that a considerable portion of these youngsters, and their behavior, are known to someone in the community. Most of these youngsters, however, are not brought to the court but rather are left to a third party such as parents, schools, and social agencies who, in a sense, take up their case (advocate for them) in order to divert them from the formal process of juvenile justice. It has also been demonstrated that when such third-party "advocates" fail youngsters, the court becomes the referral of last resort; that is, encapsulation processes tend to be set in motion (mostly for youngsters from poor and minority-group families). Finally, we must note that no community organization exists which has a mandate to synchronize community programs on behalf of youngsters.

> Many juvenile offenders, especially those from minority groups living in poverty pockets, are trapped in situations from which they cannot escape without help. The existing procedures for providing assistance are

haphazard, since schools, social agencies and police differ widely in philosophy, understanding of behavior, and approach. There is no single agency that (1) provides assistance to parents and troubled youngsters by coordinating community services on their behalf and mobilizing concerned citizens to correct delinquency-breeding conditions, (2) identifies and statistically records gaps in urgently needed youth services in order to promote their establishment and obtain the necessary local, state, and federal funds, and (3) coordinates the effort of community residents — professionals, private citizens, and youth — to change those attitudes and practices of established institutions that contribute, directly or indirectly, to delinquent behavior.[44]

In addition, two trends have emerged in recent years: a decline in community tolerance for delinquency, and an increase in delinquent behavior, with a spread to the middle class. In either case, for want of another alternative, many young men and women are referred to the police for minor infractions of the law and for status offenses. These youngsters may be given "station adjustments" by police officers; be referred to other agencies (often inappropriate and without followup); be placed in jail or other detention; or be referred to court, in which case the process of court custody has begun.

Many youngsters who are picked up repeatedly are told, in effect, "Come back when you are more delinquent; we can do nothing for you now." When they do come back, they are either rejected or punished. As hundreds of juvenile court surveys have demonstrated, many of those who are declared delinquent by the court and most who are detained and sent to institutions should have received a variety of helping services in their own homes and in their own neighborhoods without having been branded delinquent.[45]

Youth service bureaus take on the task of intervening on behalf of youngsters by providing a noncoercive place for youth to turn and for referral agents to send youth. In concept, YSBs are intended to be the referral-of-first-resort for all except the most dangerous youngsters. YSBs are responsible for intervening with the youngster or with parents, community agencies, the police, or others as appropriate in order *to ensure that optimum diversionary action takes place;* YSBs also provide linkages to appropriate community services so as to avoid any future encapsulation as well.

This service is often called "intake" or "information and referral". YSBs should take

*additional steps in providing follow up and
advocacy, however, if the intention is to ensure
that services are indeed provided.*

Service Delivery: A Concerted Community Effort

In addition to their primary role as linkage mechanism in the community, youth service bureaus also seek to ensure a cooperative stance on the part of existing agencies, and to precipitate or provide additional programs where gaps or deficiencies exist. The realization that many community services fail to present themselves as attractive sources for referrals, and that others ought to be providing more services to youngsters, has led to general policy that YSBs should not duplicate existing services but rather should work to make existing agencies responsive to young people. The statement of the Youth Development and Delinquency Prevention Administration of the federal Department of Health, Education and Welfare exemplifies this policy:

> Certainly a basic rule should be that a YSB is designed primarily to supplement community services for its target group rather than to supplant them. Under this principle the YSB, with the exception of Information and Referral services, should resort to the direct provision of services only when it has been determined that the needs of its target group cannot be met by formal agreement or contract to purchase with an existing community service. Even if the YSB directly provides a service, it should do so only for a period necessary for it to be made a part of an already existing service.
>
> In other words, an effectively operating YSB should eventually "work itself out of business." It should avoid any attempt to provide those basic community services which are necessary to the healthy development of all youth, including general health services, education, housing, employment. Its function is essentially remedial in nature, designed to help its target group have ready access to such service.
>
> By its very nature the YSB program assumes an advocacy role for its target group.[46]

Thus youth service bureaus seek to ensure: (1) that existing agencies are attuned to the preferences of young people; (2) that a diversionary orientation is taken by community agencies and that they are open to referrals from the YSB as well as from the police, schools, and other agencies; and (3) that a full range of appropriate services are available in the community.

To date, it is federal policy of both the Youth Development and

Delinquency Prevention Administration (YDDPA) of the Department of Health, Education and Welfare, and the Law Enforcement Assistance Administration (LEAA) of the Department of Justice that YSBs originate from local initiatives and community concern. This policy is intended to foster local commitment and cooperation in organizing and implementing youth service bureaus and thus to increase the probability of success. Typically, youth service bureaus originate when citizens in a community, or officials of local government or social agencies (or a combination), decide that existing programs are inadequate to deal with youth in trouble, rising rates of antisocial activity, and rising arrest and adjudication rates among young people. A concerted community effort — which draws representatives from various cultural, ethnic, racial, religious, and professional groups, with a special emphasis on young people — is then organized. Citizens, local government officials, child welfare workers, school personnel, the police, representatives of the court, staffs of drug and alcohol programs, employment services, mental health and health workers are all involved in determining what to do in the particular community. Thus when the outcome is a decision to establish a youth service bureau, most community interests are committed to the program.

Sponsorship and direction of YSBs are typically designed to further broad community and agency support and participation. YSBs usually are established with a mix of resources — public and private, local, state, and federal. The director is provided with a council or advisory board composed of representatives from various agencies and professions in the community. The characteristics of organization, implementation, operation, and support are designed to give a broad range of community citizens and groups an interest in assuring the successful operation of the YSB.

YSBs seek to make available a wide range of services either directly or by YSB staff. This is accomplished by referrals to other agencies, through formal agreements or contracts with community organizations, or by direct operation of programs by the YSB. This variety of service-delivery mechanisms allows YSBs to draw on existing programs such as personal and family counseling, remedial education and tutoring, vocational counseling and job placement, medical and maternity care, drug and alcohol abuse programs, temporary shelter and foster care, and recreation and social activities. Obviously the types of services available through referral, agreement, or purchase will vary from community to community. Moreover the problems of community agencies mentioned in Chapter 5 continue to exist, which often makes effective use of YSB programs for troubled youngsters a difficult ideal to achieve.

A useful class project would be to determine the range of services available in your community, and then to determine what additional services might be needed.

Thus, YSBs often find it necessary to develop and provide some services themselves.

Some Special YSB Programs

The youth service bureau in State College, Pennsylvania (with which the authors are most familiar), provides a good example of a YSB having a variety of special youth-oriented programs. Established and organized by a private citizen's group, the YSB now receives funds from the United Way, local government, the state Department of Public Welfare, and the Governor's Justice Commission of the Department of Justice, as well as from many private donors. The program has established branches of the youth service bureau in three communities, which makes it directly accessible to most young people in the county.

The health, welfare, justice, education, and voluntary social service subsystems of the community all receive and act on advocacy referrals made by the YSB. In addition, the YSB has found it appropriate to establish a variety of special youth-oriented programs itself. Their Youth Employment Service helps young people from ages 13 to 18 find part-time employment throughout the year; and a Youth Corps arranges for full-time summer jobs. A program called "Opt Out" helps young people who have dropped out of school to get jobs, to prepare for the high school G.E.D. (high school equivalency certificate) if they desire, and to learn simple budgeting, housekeeping, and employment-related skills. Drop-in centers have been established in all three communities, where all youngsters can come for social and recreational activity. These contain a pool table, table tennis, and music center; they are staffed by counselors and other helping personnel; and they feature camping, hiking, and canoeing trips as regular activities. The YSB also has a "drag club" where young people learn auto mechanics and safety and are encouraged to participate in organized competitive events.

The youth service bureau has other programs as well. A truancy program receives referrals from schools; it works with youngsters and families concerning problems with schools and provides tutoring, counseling, and other services as required. An "Attention Home" provides full-time family living arrangements for small groups of young people (the court would call them "incorrigibles") while working to establish better relations with the families. Big Brother and Big Sister programs provide parent surrogates for appropriate youngsters. Another program makes arrangements for temporary care for runaways and other young people who need a temporary home. A program for pregnant teenagers and teenage mothers provides counseling and referral to local agencies, prenatal instruction and care, family planning information, furniture and housing accessories, or whatever is appropriate to aid the young person and her family to deal with the situation. A 24-hour crisis intervention program is available for both young people and referral agents. Thus the youth service bureau provides specially tailored services for a broad cross-section of young people in a manner intended to divert them before and after contact with the juvenile justice system.

There are many additional types of special programs provided by youth service bureaus throughout the nation. The Winston-Salem, North Carolina, youth service bureau, for example, provides training for youth leaders which enables young people to develop plans, find resources, and establish programs themselves. A program, "You and the Law," for junior high students explains their rights and responsibilities under the law. "Project Return" provides a bridge between institutions and the community for young offenders on release.

In La Puente, California, the Bassett YSB adds to the list of possible services a free medical clinic oriented to drugs, venereal disease, pregnancy, and other health problems of young people. This YSB, because the county is multicultured, also has a Human Relations Service to deal with problems of discrimination, racial unrest, and rumor control. The San Diego, California, Youth Service Bureau provides a variety of public education programs directed toward educating the community about youth and youth services; it also aids in the evaluation of youth-serving agencies in the community. In New York City the Youth Services Agency provides a city-wide program of education, recreation, and cultural activity. An "Educational Incentive Program" helps disadvantaged youngsters gain admission to colleges and technical schools. A program in "Dances and Instruction in the Variety Arts" focuses on neighborhood activities including dances, variety shows, and family nights. A "Ticket Bureau" makes free and reduced-price tickets to Broadway plays and athletic events available for youngsters. A variety of summer programs provides supervised cultural, educational, and recreational activities for young people.[47]

In these ways, the YSBs seek to be attractive to youngsters who just want some socializing and relaxation as well as to those seeking help in deciding about an abortion versus parenthood, dropping out of school or re-entering, working to earn spending money, working to support a family, help with drug or alcohol problems or with personal, social, or family problems. These kinds of help, traditionally associated with family or clergy, must now be provided by communities, via new institutions. Youth service bureaus are one type of program being considered in many localities. Thus youth service bureaus are designed to advocate the cause of young people both with individual agencies in seeking service for particular youngsters, and with the community in seeking to precipitate more and better youth-related services. The advocates of YSBs foresee benefits accruing to a variety of groups.

> For the *court,* the YSB provides a reduction in many "nuisance cases" and a source of follow-up services for nonadjudicated children.
> For *probation officers,* the YSB provides a reduction in time-consuming "informal adjustment" cases, which are more effectively worked with outside an authoritative framework.
> For *police officers,* the YSB provides an alternative to detention and court referral when, in the officer's judgment, release with warning is insufficient but filing a petition is not imperative.
> For the *public schools,* the YSB provides a link with the social work community so that truancy and other school behavior difficulties may be handled through cooperative problem-solving with other agencies.
> For *citizen volunteers,* the YSB provides a chance to turn from frustration over juvenile delinquency to constructive efforts on behalf of youth and youth-serving agencies.
> For private *social agencies,* the YSB provides an extention of youth services through citizen action.
> For the *Welfare Department,* the YSB provides an advocate for troubled youth and support for protective services available to young children.
> For *youth,* the YSB provides the listening ear of someone who can cut establishment "red tape" in an effort to solve their problems.

For the *community* as a whole, the YSB provides an opportunity to accept responsibility for assisting its troubled and troubling youth by coordinating services on their behalf rather than relying on court authority.[48]

Youth Service Bureaus: Some Reality Perspective

Youth service bureaus present perhaps the most attractive and promising new program for young people of the social welfare system. They are one of the more talked-about and advocated programs in the nation today. YSBs were recommended in 1967 by the President's Commission; and two major federal agencies, the Youth Development and Delinquency Prevention Agency and the Law Enforcement Assistance Administration (YDDPA and LEAA), have made YSBs a top priority. Despite these pronouncements, however, it is estimated that in 1975 fewer than two hundred YSBs existed in the entire United States. Moreover, research tends to question even this figure for it appears that the label "youth service bureau" has been attached to many types of programs whether or not they exhibited the appropriate characteristics.

Several questions must be asked about youth service bureaus. Is the label "in need of services" imposed by a youth service bureau really less stigmatizing than the label "delinquent" imposed by a juvenile court? What sorts of services do these children actually need? What will happen to a child who refuses to accept the services of a youth service bureau: will he be compelled against his will? if so, how is a youth service bureau different from a coercive juvenile court? This last question raises a very serious civil liberties issue. Consider this scenario: A policeman apprehends a youngster who appears to have committed a crime and tells the youngster that rather than press charges he will merely take him to a youth service bureau for counseling if the youngster promises to cooperate. On the one hand, the policeman is diverting the youngster from the potentially obstructive and stigmatizing juvenile justice system. On the other hand, he is also holding out leniency in return for a promise not to exercise the constitutional rights to a fair trial, to a lawyer's assistance, and to the privilege against self-incrimination. Are youth service bureaus to intervene in youngsters' lives without first holding a fair hearing to determine guilt or innocence? If so, are they not just what the original juvenile court reformers intended to create at the turn of the century?

While there is a considerable body of literature about youth service bureaus, there are in reality fairly few such programs. Most of these programs are not involved in ongoing research and evaluation. Consequently there are virtually no data available with which to answer the questions of the last paragraph. We simply do not know how diversion programs of this type are actually functioning.

Until questions such as these have definite answers — and perhaps even after — there will be a continual demand for a juvenile justice system in the United States. The law-enforcement model, which is discussed in the next section, most closely parallels the American juvenile justice system; it will be seen that even within this model there are attempts at reform and improvement, with an emphasis on diversion.

The Law-Enforcement Model of Diversion

Essentially the law-enforcement model of diversion is concerned with the exercise of police discretion.[49] Diversionary programs seek to influence the way police officers use their authority to arrest or not arrest young people, and further, to encourage police dispositions that do not draw the suspect into the aegis of the juvenile justice system. It is a fact that the police are the primary conduit through which young people enter the juvenile justice system. They determine which youngsters are returned to the community and which are sent on for further processing. It seems reasonable to assume, therefore, that if the police can be cultivated as a diversionary agent, even fewer youngsters will become encapsulated.

> The police are society's agents through which the criminal justice process is initiated. They are, in a sense, legal and social "traffic directors." They have very wide discretion and may send a child on through the court and ultimately into a "correctional institution." Or, using their discretionary powers, they may "detour" the criminal justice "highway" by choosing any of numerous alternatives. A judge has remarked that the sentencing process, in which he is the one who makes the pronouncement, really begins with the initial decision of the policeman.[50]

Mechanisms appropriate to this model of diversion emphasize (1) specialized police organization and (2) techniques available to police, sheriff's or probation departments to "adjust" youngsters without court action. The usual approach is to employ specialized juvenile bureaus or juvenile specialists who make station adjustments and utilize social work techniques. More recent developments include police-community education programs, probation subsidy, and a number of court-based programs.

Police Probation and Station Adjustments

A law-enforcement model of diversion is almost entirely dependent on the interaction of police and youngsters concerning suspected or anticipated delinquent behavior. In this regard, many police departments have established specialized juvenile bureaus or juvenile specialists to deal authoritatively, but informally, with youngsters (See Chapter 6). A recent nationwide study found that 72.5 percent of the reporting police departments have a juvenile bureau or juvenile specialists.[51] (There were, however, only 2.7 juvenile officers per 100 officers nationwide, with a high of 3.8 in the North Central states and a low of 1.9 in the Middle Atlantic region.[52]) Such programs are "motivated by beliefs of police that youthful offenders have a great potential for reformation or that they deserve a "second chance".[53]

The presence and authority of police officers in conjunction with youthful misbehavior or illegal activities is often enough to frighten youngsters so as to deter repetition of the behavior. In addition, many police jurisdictions have established relatively formalized (but "informal") programs of station adjustment or police probation in which parents and friends may be called in, and a courtlike procedure is employed to "adjust" the youngster. Informal police probation, where youngsters agree to mend their ways (including regular visits to the police station) may also be utilized.[54] These methods depend on dramatic emphasis to work: they utilize the respect and fear many youngsters (and their parents) have regarding the police as the authoritative instrument of force in the community.

Dramatization of authority may be done in the field by patrolmen or squad car officers, who engage in a range of behavior, from clever through heated acting to acute personal involvement. In many American police jurisdictions dramatization of authority takes place through well-structured hearing procedures, which in many respects are the analogues of probation intake or juvenile court hearings. There are formal notices to parents and minors setting the time and place for the meeting with a "hearing officer" who is seated impressively behind a desk. Such officers are chosen for their special ability to charm (con) adolescents; sometimes there are two, one who plays the "bad guy," the other the "good guy."[55]

Although the police have the legal authority neither to require attendance at adjustment hearings nor to impose restrictions on the freedom of children, the leverage available to the police is quite compelling. Police have only to make clear that the alternative is referral on to the court, the creation of a formal record, and perhaps even institutionalization. It is not surprising to find, therefore, that in most cases the parents and the youngster choose the more informal procedure.[56]

To what degree is this form of coercion an infringement on individual rights and an assault on due process values?

The manifest purpose of such hearings is to allow police officers to determine whether to terminate cases in the police station or to refer them on to the juvenile court. In fact, such procedures give police officers the adjudicatory and dispositional responsibility for deciding what is best for the child and for the community. Thus a latent function of these procedures is to put a large degree of power and control over the lives of youngsters in the hands of police officers. Factors which have been found to be keys to such decisions include age, seriousness of the offense, prior contact with the police, the attitude of the youngster, the need for professional assistance, the parents' recognition of their responsibility, and the rights of the complainant.[57] Kobetz reports that police use their discretionary powers in both felonies and misdemeanors committed by juveniles. "In some jurisdictions, offenses such as involuntary manslaughter, rape, serious assault and battery, armed robbery, burglary, and many other felonies are adjusted by the police at the station. . . ."[58] Police hearings provide a forum wherein a quasi-judicial "adjustment" can be made and the police can "counsel" youngsters for the purpose of deterring further misbehavior.

The outcome of such informal procedures can be outright release of the youngster, release with an official report ("look out next time"), or release to a parent or social agency. All of these alternatives may also involve some conditions — police probation.

Often there may be requirements for restitution (where something was stolen or damaged) or restrictions on the behavior of the youngster — e.g., in one city a youth must attend school unless excused by a doctor, leave his home only with parents, and keep certain patterns of dress and grooming.[59] Because the police have no formal power to make such adjustments, it is usually necessary to secure an admission of guilt and demonstration of repentance. Lacking such an admission, the police will simply conclude that the youngster will not be "helped" by a station adjustment, and will refer the case on to court.[60] If the officer does not utilize any of these options, a referral is made to the juvenile court.

These practices are condoned, and even encouraged, by many judges and professionals as relieving the burden on overcrowded court dockets and providing a less encapsulating method of disposition for many young people. The President's Commission, for example, stated its recognition of the practices:

> Informal and discretionary pre-judicial dispositions already are a formally recognized part of the process to a far greater extent in the juvenile than in the criminal justice system. The primacy of the rehabilitative goal in dealing with juveniles, the limited effectiveness of the formal processes of the juvenile justice system, the labeling inherent in adjudicating children delinquents, the inability of the formal system to reach the influences — family, school, labor market, recreational opportunities — that shape the life of a youngster, the limited disposition options available to the juvenile judge, the limitations of personnel and diagnostic and treatment facilities, the lack of community support — all of these factors give pre-judicial dispositions an especially important role with respect to juveniles.[61]

In these ways, many police departments have adapted their use of discretion to decide whether or not to arrest and to refer to court, and have created fairly routinized (although highly subjective) quasi-diversionary programs.

Police Social Work

In addition to developing quasi-judicial procedures wherein the police act as prosecutor, jury, and judge, many police departments (beginning in the 1930s) became involved in what is known as police social work. Here the police, usually juvenile specialists, take on the social work functions of counseling and referrals to community agencies and the development of diversionary programs in the community.

Some of the direct services police undertook for minors and their families were in the form of social investigations and casework-type treatment in which women police workers played an important role. Big Brother programs were organized by police on the assumption that avuncular-type relationships between a juvenile and a policeman or other adult would keep the youth from delinquency. Capitalizing on the prevalent though questionable idea that participation in recreational activities would have a preventive effect on those inclined toward delinquency, police also sponsored athletic leagues for youth in city areas where risk of delinquency was statistically high. Finally, systematic surveillance was undertaken of special community institutions typically associated with delinquency and child neglect — junk yards, pawn shops, pool rooms, and liquor outlets.[62]

Some juvenile police officers function as detached street workers. They interact informally with gangs and other groups of young people to direct them away from violence and delinquency into more acceptable community activities. In this regard, police officers also provide counseling and linkages with community agencies for youngsters in need of particular types of help. A recent statewide study of juvenile police officers in Pennsylvania, for example, found that 74 percent of the officers responding indicated that they "consult with or give advice to kids" quite frequently, and 66 percent indicated that they very frequently "attempt to change the behavior of kids in trouble."[63] The same study found that most referrals by juvenile police officers are back to parents, and only relatively infrequently to social service agencies (which were viewed as being largely unresponsive to police referrals). While many argue that such programs detract from the law-enforcement role of the police, such activities are intended to provide timely intervention at critical points of youthful careers so as to prohibit their drift into more permanent delinquent patterns.

Although police social work is a long-established aspect of the profession, a number of police agencies have also recently begun experimenting with the use of policemen or police aides in crisis teams. In view of the fact that a large part of police work involves noncriminal types of emergencies and other calls, these programs seek to make police departments more responsive to the actual demands placed on them by citizens. For example, the police-community aide project in Oakland, California, trains aides to mediate in neighborhood quarrels, to get youth involved in clubs or part-time work, to work with schools, and to advocate for youngsters in obtaining early release from probation. In several cities, crisis teams have been established for which

police officers receive social work training. Police-youth dialogues and "Officer Friendly" programs provide contacts between police and young people toward identifying problems and the development of mutual respect and understanding.

Police-Community Education: A Two-Way Street

A more recent thrust in police work is concerned with fostering better understanding and communications between police and citizens, in particular, young people. A wide variety of research has demonstrated that the police role and image are ambiguous and conflict-laden. Police are expected to be both *law officers* (strict enforcers of law and order) and *peace officers* (an ever-present help in time of need).

> The policeman is a friend and a protector. He assures safety on the streets and keeps the peace. You call him when you are in trouble, when your neighbors are making too much noise, or when your cat is caught in a tree. At the same time, the policeman is foe and repressor. He inhibits your freedom, tickets you when you are speeding or illegally parked, comes to your house to quiet you down when your neighbors complain about noise, investigates, and interrogates you when you are suspected or involved in some illegal activity.[64]

Police training (and the community image) however, has traditionally focused on what Stanley Brodsky calls the "inspector" and "soldier" roles. The police are told that their role is surveillance and combat with "the criminal enemy in action."[65] When this role is manifest in conjunction with youngsters, interactions are clouded with suspicion, hostility and distrust — hardly an atmosphere conducive to enhancing diversionary efforts.

Furthermore, a number of research projects have demonstrated that the reality of police work is that perhaps eighty to ninety percent of the daily activity requires the policeman to be a helping agent.[66] This phenomenon is true for the community as a whole. It is most striking in poor and minority communities.

> In these concentrated minority group areas, police are often hated and feared. They are perceived as soldiers of a White occupation army in a bitterly hostile country. Yet, the amazing paradox is that the police are the ghetto resident's most important source of help in times of sickness, injury, and trouble. The poor and uneducated, it seems, use the police in the same way that middle-class people use family doctors and clergymen.[67]

The studies that support these conclusions are drawn from a variety of contexts. They suggest that, as was the case with schools and community agencies, the police are being called upon increasingly to deal with social and human problems. Parnas's study of police calls in Chicago, for example, found that only 17 percent of the police calls involved criminal incidents; the remaining 83 percent were calls for help in other areas. Epstein estimates that 90 percent of the police role is unrelated to strict law and order issues. Misner reports that more than 80 percent of police work involves noncriminal matters. And Cumming et al. found that a majority of the calls to one urban police department involved family crises or other personal and social problems.[68]

Other studies suggest that the police are often called on in practically every type crisis or emergency situation.[69] In one city, for example, Lieberman found that almost 50 percent of the mentally ill patients and their families use the police because other community resources were not perceived as being responsive.[70] Such contacts place the police in a position to anticipate problems and to initiate diversionary action.

These facts, combined with realization that young people tend to have a negative image of the police,[71] have led to an emphasis on police-community education directed toward two goals: changing the image of the police in the eyes of youngsters and changing the attitudes of police toward youth problems. Several types of programs have been tried experimentally, some being implemented more widely throughout the United States. For example, in 1966, the Cincinnati Police Juvenile Attitude Project found that young people were "ignorant of the nature of law and the mission and function of law enforcement", *and* that "police officers who have initial contacts with these youngsters were ignorant of the nature of early adolescence."[72] The study also found: (1) that the further young people proceed in high school, the more negative their attitude toward the police; (2) that attitudes are more negative at the lower socioeconomic levels; and (3) that youngsters from racial minorities are more negative toward the police. They also found that school curricula have little education on the nature and role of law-enforcement officers in the community, and that police training has little to inform the officers on the nature of early adolescence.[73]

As a result of these findings, an educational program was developed and instituted in the three junior high school grades. Seventh graders study the "World of Rules" which introduces them to the nature of rules and the law in the home, school, and community. Eighth graders study the "World of Games" which demonstrates the need for rules in sports, games, and social activities, as well as the need for someone to officiate. Ninth graders study the "World of Laws" which involves discovering the necessity for laws and enforcement. These sessions are integrated into the regular social studies programs of the schools.

Prior to the experiment, and eight weeks following the initial programs, tests to determine attitudes toward law and law enforcement were given to all students in the classes where the programs were piloted and to a control group. The experimental classes, both as a group and for every individual youngster, showed an improved attitude toward the police and law.[74] The success of this program led to the initiation of experiments in the following year in Rochester, New York, Tampa, Florida, Fort Smith, Arkansas, and more than five hundred other schools throughout the nation. In each case, the results were the same. Since then, many hundreds of additional school systems have established similar programs.[75]

The extent to which such programs exist in the nation was probed in 1970 by the International Association of Chiefs of Police (IACP) in a nationwide survey of police departments. The IACP survey found that 19 percent of the departments responding indicated that they participate in one or more programs to increase community responsibility and awareness. "These activities for juveniles attempt to engender a collective responsibility for neighborhood environment, personal safety and prevention of crime. . . ."[76] Safety programs for youth constituted another 11 percent of the programs. These programs involve films and lectures on traffic safety, first aid, water safety, and "dangerous strangers." There is also drug abuse counseling, auto Road-A-Os, and motorcycle rider clinics. Six percent of the police departments responding indicated that they sponsor programs designed to "bridge the generation gap." Thus police departments are involved in parent education and advisory programs, storefront community relations programs between teenagers and adults, police-youth dialogues, "rap" sessions, and "hang-out patrols" to help police gain acceptance and understanding of teenagers.[77]

The apparent success of such programs, and the availability of new sources of federal funding through LEAA and YDDPA, led to their rapid spread throughout the United States in the late sixties and early seventies. That these programs could be successful has been demonstrated by research. Many police departments, however, used their new encounters with young people as an opportunity for increased surveillance and investigation. Such practices led, in turn, to a decrease in credibility for the programs, reinforcement of negative attitudes toward police, and eventual disillusionment with the programs on the part of many people. These reversals underscore the fact that communications is a two-way street and that programs to change police attitudes and practices are also required.

Throughout the nation, a variety of programs seek to teach policemen that *prevention* of delinquency and *diversion* are the goals of police-youth interactions. Such programs have a difficult task because traditional training centers on surveillance, arrest, investigation, pistol practice, etc. Moreover, where young people are involved, the entire attitudinal system of police officers may be a significant barrier. The International Association of Chiefs of Police (IACP), for example, has stated:

> Police officers, many of them parents themselves, often have a difficult time communicating with teenagers because the officer represents parental authority outside the home. Two different worlds exist and two different languages are spoken, even though the officer may live in the same house with a teenager. Police officers need to take time to know teenagers, work with them, and talk *with* them, never *down* to them.[78]

A preservice juvenile officer training program offered by the Chicago Police Department through the city colleges in Chicago, for example, provides the equivalent of six college credits in the following topic areas:[79]

I. SOCIALLY ORIENTED TOPICS

    A. Adolescent Behavior
    B. Alcoholism Factors in Delinquency
    C. Common Problems in Adolescence
    D. Defining and Measuring Delinquency
    E. Gangs and Gang Activity
    F. General Principles of Psychology
    G. Mental Health
    H. Perceptually Handicapped Child
    I. Principles of Juvenile Research
    J. Principles of Social Work
    K. Socially Maladjusted Child
    L. Theories of Delinquency Causation
    M. Theories of Delinquency Prevention
    N. The Puerto Rican and Appalachian Communities

II. TECHNICALLY ORIENTED TOPICS

    A. Interviewing the Juvenile Offender/Victim
    B. Juvenile Case Study
    C. Narcotics and Youths
    D. Organization of the Youth Division
    E. Panel Discussion
    F. Principles of Speech
    G. Processing Procedures
    H. Railroad Vandalism and the Juvenile

I. Role of the Youth Officer
J. Schools and the Juvenile

III. LEGALLY ORIENTED TOPICS

A. Dependent/Neglected Child
B. Family/Child Legal Concepts
C. Fingerprinting/Photographing Juveniles
D. Juvenile Related Law/The Juvenile Court Act
E. Organization and Function of the Juvenile Court
F. Principles of Probation

IV. REMEDIALLY ORIENTED TOPICS

A. Illinois Department of Children and Family Services
B. Illinois Department of Corrections
C. Informal v. Formal Referral Agencies
D. Juvenile Court Probation Department
E. Principles of Community Agencies

The same IACP survey of 1970 which was mentioned above found that eighty-eight percent of the responding police departments indicated that some training in juvenile procedures is offered to all police recruits. The number of classroom hours devoted to police juvenile operations, juvenile law, and related subjects varies in recruit academies but averages only about six to nine hours, around one to two percent of the total curriculum hours.

Consider this in light of the fact that over half the arrests in the U.S. are of young people.

Special programs of in-service training that is related specifically to juvenile police work, however, are offered in many places throughout the United States. The University of Southern California, the University of Minnesota (St. Paul), Northeastern University, The Pennsylvania State University, the University of Georgia, Florida State University, Michigan State University, the University of Kansas, Louisiana State University, Texas A&M University, the University of Nevada, the University of Arizona, and Colorado State University are among those mentioned in the IACP survey.[80]

The authors, for example, are involved in a project to develop new techniques for training juvenile police officers. The project teaches basic helping skills, communications in counseling, and empathic listening. Simulations of difficult situations are utilized to provide practice in applying the new skills to actual difficult situations involving youngsters. In addition, a variety of topic areas regarding drugs, the retarded offender, using community referral agencies, development of youth service bureaus, etc., are explored.

Through programs such as these, police officers are being made aware that they are often the first community institution to which youngsters in need of help are sent, and that this contact can be the crucial decision point in the career of the youth. It is the police contact that can be (and usually is) the turning point toward increased involvement in the juvenile justice system and the beginning of a delinquent career. Thus policemen must become aware of negative forces in the community and of the characteristics of the socioeconomic environment which present barriers for youngsters. They must become alert to the needs and problems of youngsters. They must be open to providing appropriate linkages between youngsters and appropriate diversionary agents in the community. If such lofty objectives could be achieved, the police could provide a great deal of creative diversion on the beat (prior to arrest) and in the station house (station adjustment).

Probation Subsidy

The police are but one element of the juvenile justice system which makes diversionary decisions. Probation officers, or intake to the court, is another. A recent trend here, probation subsidy, is a program that seeks to precipitate less encapsulating interactions between young people and the juvenile justice system by encouraging communities to develop more adequate (and more widely used) probation programs. Probation subsidy seeks to provide financial incentives to encourage local communities to keep youngsters in the community rather than sending them away to institutions.

Because most institutional programs are state operated while probation departments are locally operated, supporters of probation subsidy suggest that there is a local incentive to institutionalize youngsters. Probation subsidy seeks to reverse the incentive and to provide funds for more adequate probation and other services at the local level. In California, the Youth Authority is authorized to pay counties up to $4000 for each juvenile offender *not committed to an institution*. Inasmuch as California estimates that probation costs only about $600 per year for each person on probation compared to over $5000 for institutionalization, the program results in substantial savings for taxpayers while keeping youngsters in the community. For example, from 1966 to 1972, California saved about $186 million through closing institutions and ending construction; probation subsidy during those years cost only $60 million. Moreover, expected commitments (based on the past year's performance) declined by more than 20,000. Although there has been a general nationwide trend for institutionalization to decline, the decrease in participating California counties was twice that of those not participating.[81] (A similar program in the state of Washington led to a decline of 55 percent in commitments in only the second year of operation.[82])

In addition, when funds become available to local communities through incentive schemes like probation subsidy, it is possible for them to make probation a more effective quasi-diversionary tool and to experiment with new approaches. For example, in San Bernardino County, California, a probation-oriented program called "Project Thunder" is experimenting with a group-work approach to probation. Project Thunder provides intensive informal treatment utilizing short-term family-group counseling. When an application for petition to the court is filed, the youngster and his or her family are introduced to the program. If the family agrees to complete a series of group sessions (two hours a week for six weeks) the petition is not filed. If the family misses more than one session, the petition is filed. If the sessions are completed, the petition is settled out of court. This program is reported to be cheaper than processing young people on through the court, it results in slightly fewer future contacts with the court than the court route, and it leads to smaller probation caseloads and to less encapsulation.[83]

> *Consider, however, the pressures on parents and young people to accept this type of program without due process of law, even in cases in which they are falsely accused. Would you protest your innocence and go on to trial or agree to "plead guilty" in order to assure lenient treatment?*

An interesting variant on probation subsidy involves incentives to police departments to divert youngsters from further involvement in the juvenile justice system. The "601 Diversion Project" in Santa Clara County, California, seeks to divert almost 80 percent of the youngsters arrested and previously referred to the probation department. This project provides law-enforcement agencies a "reward" commensurate with the degree of reduction in referrals of children to the court. Administered by the probation department, all twelve local law-enforcement agencies in the county participate in the program. The funds received are used to purchase services from appropriate community agencies for the youngsters.[84]

The experience with programs such as these suggests that if communities are willing to support adequate local-level resources, many youngsters can be diverted effectively from the more stigmatizing aspects of the juvenile justice system.

Court-Based Diversion Programs

There are a number of diversion programs which operate much as the police hearing or police probation do, but which address youngsters who have already been referred to the court by the police or probation officers. Operating in similar fashion to the aforementioned programs, these "pretrial intervention programs" seek to screen children who have been referred to court (are on the calendar) and to divert as many as possible. The nature of the interviews, or hearings, varies and may involve volunteers, public defenders, court staff, legal services attorneys, law students, community service workers, etc.

> Pretrial intervention projects basically operate in two ways. In a number of the projects, no formal charges are lodged. Instead, after an individual has been arrested, he is screened on a number of criteria to determine whether he is eligible for participation in a formal diversion program. Such screening criteria vary, depending on the scope and range of the particular project. . . .
>
> * * *
>
> In the other model, formal charges are lodged but individuals are screened for eligibility in a particular intervention project. If they and the court agree, further criminal proceedings are suspended pending the outcome of the individual's participation. Completion of the program results in a request that charges be dropped. Unsuccessful participation results in regular proceedings on the charges.[85]

Like police probation, these programs usually require that the youngster and his parents agree to participate in certain "remedial" activities. Project Crossroads in Washington, D.C., and the Manhattan Court Employment Project in New York City, for example, provide a variety of counseling, supervision, job training and remedial education programs toward a goal of experience in a lifestyle of worthwhile employment and stability. To date, offenders accused of petty larceny, auto theft, forgery, solicitation for prostitution, attempted burglary, simple assault, unlawful entry, and destruction of property have been accepted.[86]

The National Advisory Commission on Criminal Justice Standards and Goals reports that of 753 young first offenders enrolled in one project, charges were dropped for 468 (62 percent) who completed the program, and 285 (38 percent) were returned for prosecution. In addition, the recidivism rate for the fifteen-month period following arrest was 14 percent lower for project participants than for a control group. Similar projects have been established in Baltimore, Boston, Cleveland, Minneapolis, San Antonio, New Haven, the San Francisco Bay Area, and Newark.[87]

The Law-Enforcement Model of Diversion vs. the Goals of Juvenile Justice

The law-enforcement model of diversion is predicated on the assumption that police officers, and to an extent probation officers and court personnel, will use their decision-making authority (discretion) to divert youngsters from the formal processes of juvenile justice. Such actions would be rooted in the rehabilitative ideal of protecting the child from the negative effects and labeling which frequently accompany placement in custody.

It is a fact, however, that police officers and others who act within the juvenile justice system typically take an oath to enforce and to uphold the laws of the community. Thus their job may be said to be first and foremost oriented toward social protection goals. Most police training reflects this latter goal. The attitudes and orientations of most police officers reflect such values. Moreover, it would seem patently unwise to divest the juvenile justice system of these ideals because such action would leave the community with no responsibility for civil order and control.

In other words, unless communities can determine how to prevent all lawbreaking, a balance of power between the several sets of values of juvenile justice is desirable. Furthermore, the police and the courts are the most likely candidates to uphold the social protection ideals.

> Police encounter youth problems more frequently than other community agencies; they meet the problems at the time of their occurrence, and they wield a great deal of coercive and symbolic authority to make deviance costly to juveniles and parents, as well as to define it on their own terms. Police methods, such as cautioning, counseling, supervision, threats, dramatized hearings, and suspended action, usually proceed from relatively uncomplicated moral conceptions of right conduct and respect for law (authority), without much specialized knowledge of human behavior and its treatment. Insofar as the net result of these is unofficial action, normalization takes place. Their effectiveness in preventing subsequent deviance probably is greatest among middle class youths or those whose family situation and resources support remedial action. Police predictions that this will occur, in turn, affect discretion and the likelihood that adjustment rather than referral to court will be their choice.[88]

It is clear that at present youngsters who pose little or no threat to the community are sometimes selected for more intense interactions and are involved in the processes of adjudication.

> Two important facts about the clientele of this system need to be made explicit. First, in most communities, official delinquency tends to be impacted in limited geographic sections. It is not uniformly distributed across the geographic face of the community. Such ecological concentration seems to reflect simply the geographic distribution of minority

groups, the white poor, and other powerless groups whose children make up most of those handled by the juvenile justice system.

Second, most of the official delinquency and youth crime cases dealt with by the police, courts and corrections involve relatively minor law violations, essentially unthreatening to the common interests.[89]

Thus consideration of programs to implement a law-enforcement model of diversion does not take away from the social-problems role of the police. Rather, one goal of such programs is to ensure uniform enforcement of laws pertaining to young people throughout the entire community. A second goal is to develop programs for diversion or non-stigmatizing dispositions for youthful misbehavior that is "essentially unthreatening to the common interests" (e.g., status offenses, summary offenses, and many misdemeanors).

It seems appropriate to impose a requirement that the police, probation officers, and judges balance social protection ideals with rehabilitative ideals so as to promote the "best interests of the child." Programs of community education, police training, station adjustment, probation subsidy, and other diversion-oriented programs in the law enforcement system have the goal of addressing the current imbalance of power which the social protection goals enjoy regarding certain groups of youngsters and certain types of offenses. Given the pronouncements and recommendations of the President's Commission, the Task Force on Juvenile Delinquency, and other such national goal-setting bodies, it can be expected that efforts of this type will continue and that new directions will evolve.

In fact, a police-sponsored youth service bureau has been established in Pleasant Hill, California. Similar to YSBs described in the previous section, the program is designed to divert young offenders and potential delinquents from the juvenile justice system. It is staffed by three policemen and two aides. About 80 percent of the young people arrested by the Pleasant Hill police are handled within the police department, and only 20 percent are sent on to court or probation. (These figures indicate a larger degree of police diversion when contrasted to the 50 percent figure cited earlier.)[90]

There is no doubt that law-enforcement-based diversion programs can and do divert youngsters from the more stigmatizing aspects of the juvenile justice system. Thus these programs take into account the rehabilitative and social protection goals of the juvenile justice system. When due process ideals are considered, however, many of the programs mentioned above may bear serious questioning. In considering the role of the police in working with young people, especially in situations in which no crime is committed, or those in which there is some reason to suspect that misbehavior is about to occur, and perhaps in many less serious misbehaviors, questions are raised concerning violation of individual and civil liberties and undue police interference in the lives of individuals. Many groups, including churches, PTOs, the American Civil Liberties Union, and the federal YDDPA have raised questions regarding the propriety of police officers trying to form or change attitudes of young people in the schools. There is also the possibility (in fact, the actuality) that police presence in the schools leads to the police becoming the disciplinarian and thus stigmatizing the youngsters whom the police seek out. The same would apply to police involvement in social agencies and youth service bureaus.

Due process ideals may also be compromised when police, or probation officers, utilize station adjustments and informal probation. Here the police use their discretionary authority as a lever to gain confessions and agreements that the youngsters will conform to certain types of behavior without due process of law. In fact, these practices are designed to avoid further considerations of due process provided by the juvenile justice system by "adjusting" youngsters in a police "hearing." These are serious factors to consider for people who profess to live in a "nation of laws, not of men."

There is also the question of the degree to which police involvement in school, social work, and community education programs detract from the police role. In addition, we must ask whether communities have the capacity to support police in such a role. For example, Kenney and Pursuit indicate that if there were police-school liaison officers in only 15 percent of the more than 7000 junior high schools in the U.S., more than 1000 highly-trained officers would be required.[91] Furthermore, the availability of the police for helping-type activities tends to work to the detriment of certain types of youngsters.

> For one thing lower class parents more than others are prone to seek police assistance in the disciplining of their children; also, misconduct of youths in slum or ghetto areas has a higher visibility than elsewhere because these areas are more heavily policed. Too, shabbily dressed youths or Negroes moving outside of their own areas may be suspect

because of their appearance. Outcomes of police hearings are more unfavorable to lower class youths because they are less apt to have intact families or families which can mobilize resources to solve the problems of their deviance. Negro youth not only more than share the handicaps of low social status, they more frequently make the system work against them by their hostile and enigmatic manner in the presence of the police.[92]

It can thus be shown that law-enforcement-based diversion can lead to less encapsulating activity on the part of the police. It is doubtful, however, that a large portion of police work regarding young people should ever be processed by the police. Problems of neglect and abuse, runaways, incorrigibility, sex-related problems, truancy, drinking alcoholic beverages, etc. (to the extent that they do not harm other people or property) might well be handled by other types of community agencies. It is also possible that police diversion may not provide help to many youngsters who need it.

Realization of these facts has in recent years led to a trend toward development of a model of diversion which seeks to orient whatever services and agencies exist in communities toward the goal of helping youth: the "Youth Services System Model" discussed in the next section.

Youth Services Systems as a Model of Diversion

It is clear that every community in the United States contains a wide variety of resources which have the capacity for diversion. The institutions and agencies which administer the programs that exist are in the domain of several community subsystems: the educational subsystem, the social services subsystem, and the law-enforcement subsystem. It is also apparent that these subsystems do not work as well as they could regarding troubled youth and youth in trouble nor do they work well with each other. The wide variety of programs described throughout this book have the potential to divert many additional young people from the vagaries of the juvenile justice system and to normalize the lives of youngsters who are adjudicated delinquent — if, and perhaps only if, they are interrelated properly.

Community agencies and schools must be prepared to accept responsibility for many youngsters whom they now refer into the juvenile justice system. Police officers and the courts must be prepared to demand that diversionary resources be amenable to referrals. Community leaders must act to create appropriate interactions among the several community subsystems. What this means is that all parties involved with youth in trouble or troubled youth must work together to create an overall community system that has the capacity to act more nearly in the best interests of young people than any of the existing subsystems.

The urgency of this requirement is underscored by the rising tide of youth crime and the undesirability of creating large numbers of criminal careers. The International Association of Chiefs of Police, for example, cites the importance of reconciling the diversity and fragmentation which characterize juvenile justice in the United States:

> Can our juvenile justice system survive in a society that appears to be getting out of control? Not in its present state. The juvenile justice system as it functions today is actually a "non-system" — a collection of agencies striving to reach the same goals yet functioning autonomously with little cohesive direction or purpose. The multitude of agencies which comprise our present juvenile justice system are accountable to no one except themselves.
>
> All agencies in the juvenile justice system should be accountable to each other. Our present system, with its nonaccountability to its subparts, often leaves the juvenile offender out in the cold, and, as a result, perpetuates its own existence and the existence of the entire criminal justice system by recycling human beings first through the juvenile justice system and then into the criminal justice system itself. The agencies may mean well, but meaning well and actually doing well are two entirely different concepts. As our nation advances into the future, with the juvenile delinquency problem increasing at an alarming rate, it becomes imperative that juvenile justice agencies wake up to reality and start doing something to curb delinquency. Good intentions alone no longer suffice. The age of independent endeavors to eliminate one of the nation's most menacing problems is dying.[93]

Many people — citizens, scholars, and practitioners alike — have come to similar conclusions in recent years. In fact, it is the policy of both the federal Department of Health, Education and Welfare (whose Youth Development and Delinquency Prevention Administration has recently been renamed the Office of Youth Development) and the Department of Justice (which runs the Law Enforcement Assistance Administration) that concerted efforts to reconcile organizational conflicts be given high priority. In this regard, it is suggested that communities place a priority on shifting the emphasis from the far end of the juvenile justice funnel (institutionalization) toward programs of diversion and normalization. To these ends, a fourth model of diversion has been proposed. This model recognizes the fact that no one of the previous models is likely to become dominant. It recognizes that no single community subsystem could deal with all youngsters. It seeks to take advantage of the large number of programs which exist and which have the capacity to divert or to help youngsters (rather than inventing a new wheel for an old job). Called the "Youth Services Systems Model", this model focuses on bringing available resources into a concerted community effort wherein each has a part and each is willing to allow the others to have a part.

The Youth Services System Model of Diversion (YSS) is based on the most fundamental principle of systems: the interaction of a number of diverse units toward a common goal or set of goals. It recognizes that the predominant characteristics of the existing non-system are: (1) that each group of related agencies seeks to form and pepetuate its own subsystem for the prevention and control of delinquency, (2) that no one such organization set has been able to do so, (3) that one outcome of the resulting conflict over organizational domain ("turf") is that many youngsters are poorly handled and inadvertently pushed in the direction of delinquent careers, and (4) that many community resources are expended with little measurable impact. Youth Services Systems seek to provide a full range of community services for youngsters by bringing together available programs and resources into a more concerted community effort. They do this by working to have each subsystem and its constituent agencies recognize, and be assured a guaranteed, viable role in the overall community effort, *and at the same time*, to recognize the legitimacy and contributions of the others.

In describing what local communities can do, the U.S. Department of Health, Education, and Welfare's Office of Youth Development envisions a "comprehensive network of community-based programs enabling youth-serving agencies to focus their combined efforts on helping all youth."[94]

> Every community has some form of youth services available. With rare exception, however, the services are fragmented. Frequently one agency does not know what the other is doing — even for the same client being served.
>
> *Under an integrated services approach, agencies work together to achieve common objectives to assure a coordinated effort.*

Many agencies today are finding it increasingly difficult to adapt their services and methods of operation to the constantly changing social scene. For example, a school counseling program may find it difficult to refocus its efforts on dealing with the sudden phenomenon of a drug abuse problem.

Under a system of coordinated programs, local agencies can have enough flexibility to change program emphasis and focus when the needs arise.

One failure of most youth-serving programs is that they are geared to help only those youth with overt problems. Young people who have not come to the attention of the authorities can find few places to go for help. Others involved in relatively minor offenses are frequently released without any provision of services.

A coordinated approach could provide services to all youth — regardless of the problem — and without the "stigma" attached to many youth services now provided by individual community agencies.

Most past efforts to coordinate services have failed. The principal reason has been the lack of sufficient financial support.

A system of integrated community services involves joint funding and mutual support to assure that agencies which should work together can remain working together.

In most communities, service programs are operated individually by units of local or State governments and private non-profit agencies. Such programs frequently overlap.

An integrated, comprehensive system has multi-governmental participation in planning and executing programs — thereby avoiding unnecessary duplication of services.

Still another problem with individual youth services programs is that the knowledge, information, and experience gained by each individual agency is frequently not transferred to other agencies. There is no formal mechanism for such transfer.

A coordinated system assures that agencies working together can share experiences — learning from one another's successes and avoiding a repetition of mistakes.

There is considerable criticism — most of it frequently justified — that youth themselves are rarely consulted and utilized in planning and carrying out programs and services directly affecting them.

A coordinated community program involves youth advocacy agencies, assuring appropriate involvement of youth in the planning and operation of integrated programs.[95]

The chart in Figure 12.2 is one example of a youth services system. Essential components are: (1) the involvement of a variety of referral sources; (2) a common source for referrals, which is youth oriented and can draw on available community resources (such as a youth service bureau); (3) the commitment of existing community resources to definitely provide services on demand; and (4) the involvement of young people in developing, operating, and evaluating the entire system.

The model in Figure 12.2 is based on the assumption that many of the problems of the juvenile justice system and associated subsystems in the community are due not so much to a lack of resources as to a failure on the part of the subsystems to adequately focus on the needs of young people and the appropriate ways in which each subsystem can make its services effective. The objective of youth services systems is to bring together in a concerted manner all appropriate programs in a community — federal, state, county, city, private, volunteer — in a way which is appropriate to the local organizational milieu. That is, there is no one organization or organizational form envisioned. Rather, the arrangement of organizations and agencies through which action can be channeled may take a variety of forms and prove successful.

The Office of Youth Development reports that shortly after the model was developed (in 1971), some twenty-three communities began to adopt it. "By mid-1972, Youth Services Systems were at some stage of development in 49 communities, including the eight cities selected by the Law Enforcement Assistance Administration for an intensive effort to reduce street crimes by 20 percent in five years."[96]

Early statistics reflect the impact of Youth Services Systems in communities where such Systems have been in existence long enough and where data have been compiled uniformly enough to indicate how well this approach has succeeded in achieving its first goal, namely, diversion of youth from the juvenile justice system. A two percent reduction in juvenile court referrals was the goal set when the Youth Services System was developed. The rate of decrease realized in the areas served by the ten systems for which complete data is available for the period October 1971 - September 1972 in fact significantly exceeded this objective, as the statistics on juvenile court referrals measured a 21 percent decrease against the number of referrals for the previous twelve-month period.[97]

Not only have the two major federal administrative departments

FIGURE 12.2

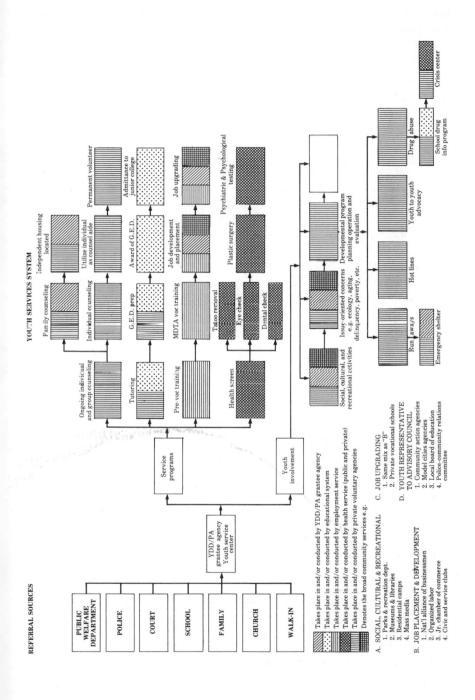

and the many state and local agencies which have agreed to experiment with youth services systems indicated support for this model, so too has the U.S. Congress recognized that this may be a viable direction. The 1972 Juvenile Delinquency Prevention and Control Act ended the practice of providing separate grants for various types of service (which reinforced fragmentation), and authorizes support only when services to young people are part of a coordinated system.

> Specifically, the Act authorizes grants to State, county, municipal or other public or nonprofit agencies to plan, develop, and operate coordinated Youth Services Systems. These Systems, as defined in the Senate report on the Act, are "comprehensive delivery systems separate from the system of juvenile justice, for providing youth services to an individual who is delinquent or is in danger of becoming delinquent and to his family." Provisions relating to technical assistance and training also focus on the goal of developing coordinated programs.[98]

Thus the youth services systems model and the programs based on it, seek to take advantage of the benefits of all three of the other models of diversion — and more. It is expected that each of the community subsystems concerned with young people will be able to draw on the others; this in itself would be a welcome change. It is expected that this will free each subsystem to concentrate more on the task with which it is most immediately concerned; this too is seen as a desirable outcome. Most importantly, however, it is expected that all community subsystems will develop a better understanding of young people and will discover how communities might most appropriately deal with the "knots of adolescence." Whether or not the people of the United States and the organizations which have been established to deal with troubled youth and youth in trouble can rise to this challenge is one of the more important issues in the 1970s, for the youth of today are the inheritors of the society which emerges.

References

1. William M. Ewan, "The Organization Set: Toward a Theory of Interorganizational Relations," in *Approaches to Organizational Design,* ed. James D. Thompson (Pittsburgh: University of Pittsburgh, 1966), pp. 73 - 98.

2. Rita Braito, Steve Paulson, and Gerald Klonglon, "Domain Consensus: A Key Variable in Interorganizational Analysis," in *Complex Organiza-*

tions and Their Environments, ed. Philip R. Kunz, (Durane, Iowa: William C. Brown Co., 1972), pp. 176 - 92.

3. Much of the material on the first three models is drawn from Edwin M. Lemert, *Instead of Court: Diversion in Juvenile Justice* (Washington, D.C.: U.S. Government Printing Office, National Institute of Mental Health, Center for Studies of Crime and Delinquency, 1971).

4. See Chapter 5 in this book; also President's Commission on Law Enforcement and Administration of Justice, *Task Force Report: Juvenile Delinquency and Youth Crime* (Washington, D.C.: U.S. Government Printing Office, 1967), Appendixes M and N. See also Richard A. Cloward and James A. Jones, "Social Class, Educational Attitudes and Participation," in *Education in Depressed Areas,* ed. A. Harry Prasow (New York: Teachers College Press, 1963); Robert D. Vinter and Rosemary C. Sarri, "Malperformance in the Public School: A Group Work Approach," *Social Work* 10 (January 1965): 3 - 13; and Jackson Toby and Marcia Toby, *Low School Status as a Predisposing Factor in Subcultural Delinquency,* U.S. Office of Education: Cooperative Research Project, No. 526 (Washington, D.C.: H.E.W., U.S. Office of Education, 1961).

5. Clara C. Cooper, *A Comparative Study of Delinquents and Non-Delinquents* (Portsmouth, Ohio: The Psychological Service Center Press, 1960), p. 207.

6. President's Commission on Law Enforcement, *Task Force Report: Juvenile Delinquency,* p. 225. See also Wilbur B. Brookhover and David Gottlieb, *A Sociology of Education,* 2nd ed., (New York: American Book Co., 1964); and Educational Policies Commission of the National Education Association, *The Central Purpose of American Education,* (Washington, D.C.: the Comission, 1961).

7. See, for example, *Children Out of School in America* (Cambridge, Mass.: Children's Defense Fund of the Washington Research Project, 1974).

8. At this writing the decisions regarding Supreme Court actions on truancy and misbehavior in schools have been announced by the press but official citations have yet to be published.

9. President's Commision on Law Enforcement and the Administration of Justice, *Task Force Report: Juvenile Delinquency,* p. 225.

10. This discussion is drawn in large part from Lemert, *Instead of Court,* Chap. 2, "The School Model," pp. 19 - 34.

11. Ibid., p. 22.

12. Ibid., p. 20.

13. Ibid.

14. Ibid.

15. In this regard, the White House Conference on Children 1970, *Report to the President* (Washington, D.C.: U.S. Government Printing Office, 1970), pp. 374 - 5, has stated:

Much could be done in our public schools to prevent crime, delinquency and other problems of children in need. Elementary school teachers often see the symptoms as early as the first or second grade, but just providing a good, basic education for children can be difficult today. Recent studies suggest that schools can cause delinquency. Most reform children are one to five years behind their age group academically, and more children are committed to some reform schools and mental hospitals during the school year than during vacation periods. . . .

16. *Mills* v. *Board of Education of District of Columbia,* 348 F. Supp. 866 (D.D.C. 1972).

17. *Children Out of School in America,* pp. 1 - 2.

18. Ibid., Introduction and Chap. 1.

19. Ibid.

20. Lemert, *Instead of Court,* pp. 27 - 8.

21. Paul Hoover Bowman, "Effects of Revised School Program on Potential Delinquents," *The Annals of the American Academy of Political and Social Science* 322 (1959): pp. 53 - 61.

22. Anton S. Makarenko, "Problems Inherent in Soviet School Education," in *Soviet Educators on Soviet Education,* Helen B. Redl, ed. (New York: Free Press of Glencoe, 1964), p. 151.

23. President's Commission on Law Enforcement *Task Force Report: Juvenile Delinquency,* p. 226.

24. See Chap. 5, Reference number 51.

25. Lemert, *Instead of Court,* p. 36.

26. *Much of this section is drawn from Lemert, Instead of Court,* Chap. 3, "The Welfare Model," pp. 35 - 53.

27. Ibid., p. 35.

28. Ibid., pp. 36 - 37.

29. Ibid., p. 38.

30. Ibid., p. 40.

31. See Chap. 11 of this book.

32. Clifford Shaw and Henry MacKay, *Juvenile Delinquency in Urban Areas* (Chicago: University of Chicago Press, 1942), and Solomon Kobrin, "The Chicago Area Project — a 25-Year Assessment," *Annals of the American Academy of Political and Social Science* 322 (1959): 20 - 9.

33. See Chap. 11 in this book.

34. *Los Angeles and the New York City Youth Board* (Los Angeles: Welfare Planning Council, 1960).

35. Henry J. Meyer et al., *The Girls at Vocational High,* (New York: Russell Sage Foundation, 1965).

36. See, for example, Donald R. Cressey and Robert A. McDermott, *Diversion from the Juvenile Justice System* (Washington, D.C.: National Criminal Justice Reference Service, LEAA, U.S. Department of Justice, 1974).

37. John M. Martin, *Toward a Political Definition of Juvenile Delinquency* (Washington, D.C.: U.S. Department of Health, Education and Welfare, Youth Development and Delinquency Prevention Administration, 1970), p. 11.

38. U.S. Department of Health, Education and Welfare, Youth Development and Delinquency Prevention Administration, *Youth Service Bureaus and Delinquency Prevention* (Washington, D.C.: U.S. Government Printing Office). Publication No. DHEW (SRS) 73-26022.

39. Ibid.

40. Ibid., pp. 3 - 4.

41. President's Commission on Law Enforcement and Administration of Justice, *The Challenge of Crime in a Free Society* (Washington, D.C.: U.S. Government Printing Office, 1967), p. 83.

42. Sherwood Norman, *The Youth Service Bureau* (Paramus, N.J.: National Council on Crime and Delinquency, 1972), p. 8.

43. Ibid.

44. Ibid., p. 10.

45. Ibid., p. 11.

46. HEW, YDDPA, *Youth Service Bureaus and Delinquency Prevention.*

47. Norman, *The Youth Service Bureau*, "Appendix F.: Five Existing Programs."

48. Ibid., pp. 11 - 12.

49. See Chapter 6 of this book.

50. Richard W. Kobetz, *The Police Role and Juvenile Delinquency* (Gaithersburg, Md.: International Associaton of Chiefs of Police, 1971), p. 74.

51. Ibid., p. 53.

52. Ibid., p. 55.

53. Lemert, *Instead of Court*, p. 55 - 6.

54. David R. Barrett et al., "Juvenile Delinquents: The Police, State Courts and Individualized Justice," *Harvard Law Review* 79, (February 1966): 784.

55. Lemert, *Instead of Court*, p. 61.

56. Kobetz, *Police Role*, p. 116.

57. Ibid., p. 118.

58. Ibid., p. 115.

59. Barrett et al., "Juvenile Delinquents," p. 784.

60. Ibid.

61. President's Commission on Law Enforcement, *Challenge of Crime*, p. 82.

62. Lemert, *Instead of Court*, pp. 55 - 6.

63. Frederick Hussey and John Kramer, "A Research and Development Program for Enhancing the Performance of Juvenile Police Specialists: Phase I Report," mimeographed (University Park, Pa.: The Pennsylvania State University, Institute for the Study of Human Development, 1974), p. 23.

64. Deborah Johnson and Robert J. Gregory, "Police-Community Relations in the United States," *Journal of Criminology, Criminal Law and Police Science* (March 1971), pp. 94 - 106.

65. Stanley L. Brodsky, "Models of Police Behavior," *Police* (May-June 1969), pp. 27 - 28; see also M. Banton, *The Policeman and the Community* (New York: Basic Books, 1964).

66. Brodsky, "Models of Police Behavior."

67. Johnson and Gregory, "Police-Community Relations," p. 352.

68. Charlotte Epstein, *Intergroup Relations and Police Officers* (Baltimore: William and Wilkins, 1962); Elaine Cumming, Ian M. Cumming, and Laura Eden, "Policeman as Philosopher, Guide and Friend," *Social Problems* 12 (Winter 1965): pp. 276 - 84; Raymond I. Parnas, "The Police response to the Domestic Disturbance," *Wisconsin Law Review* (1967), pp. 914 - 60; Gordon E. Misner, "The Urban Police Mission," *Issues and Criminology* 1 (1967): 35 - 46.

69. David H. Bayley and Harold A. Mendelsohn, *Minorities and the Police: Confrontation in America* (New York: Free Press, 1969), p. 111.

70. Robert Lieberman, "Police as a Community Mental Health Resource," *Community Mental Health Journal* 2 (April 1969): p. 111.

71. David Epstein, "The Treatment of the Police by the Negro Press," *Criminologica* 30 (1967): 37 - 59; Burton Leny, "Cops in the Ghetto: A Problem of the Police System," *American Behavioral Scientist* (March-April 1968); 31 - 4; Phillip H. Ennis, "Crime, Victims and the Police," *Transaction* 7 (1967): 36 - 44; Henry Milander, "Local Police Department — School System Interaction and Cooperation," *Police* 9 (1967): 72 - 5.

72. Robert Portune, et al., *The Cincinnati Police-Juvenile Attitude Project: Final Report*, LEAA Dissemination Project, Grant #0521. (Undated).

73. Ibid.

74. Ibid.

75. Howard James, *Children in Trouble* (New York: David McKay, 1969), p. 57.

76. Kobetz, *Police Role*, p. 208.

77. Ibid., p. 209.

78. Ibid., p. 239.

79. Ibid., pp. 239 - 240.

80. Ibid., p. 185.

81. Allen F. Breed, "The Youth Authority in 1972," *Youth Authority Quarterly* (State of California, Department of the Youth Authority) (Fall 1972), pp. 3 - 11.

82. National Advisory Commission on Criminal Justice, Standards and Goals, *Corrections,* (Washington, D.C.: U.S. Government Printing Office, 1973), p. 315.

83. Kenneth M. Austin and Fred R. Speidel, "Thunder: An Alternative to Juvenile Court Appearance," *Youth Authority Quarterly* (State of California, Department of the Youth Authority) (Winter 1971), pp. 13 - 17.

84. National Advisory Commission, *Corrections,* p. 85.
85. Ibid., p. 84.
86. Ibid., p. 85.
87. Ibid.
88. Lemert, *Instead of Court,* p. 68 - 9.
89. Martin, *Toward a Political Definition,* p. 11.
90. National Advisory Commission, *Corrections,* p. 82.
91. John P. Kenney and Daniel G. Pursuit, *Police Work With Juveniles and the Administration of Juvenile Justice,* 4th ed. (Springfield, Ill.: Charles C. Thomas, 1970), p. 367.
92. Lemert, *Instead of Court,* pp. 61 - 62.
93. Kobetz, *Police Role,* pp. 219 - 20.
94. U.S. Department of Health, Education and Welfare, Office of Youth Development, "Challenge, Action, Change: a Community Guide for Youth Development," pamphlet (undated, circa 1974).
95. Ibid.
96. U.S. Department of Health, Education, and Welfare, Youth Development and Delinquency Prevention Strategy," *Delinquency Prevention Reporter* (Special Issue, February 1973), p. 7.
97. Ibid.
98. Ibid.

Index

Criminology. *See* Community-oriented criminology; Individual-oriented criminology; Labeling perspective; Postivism

Darrow, Clarence: on criminal law, 61; criticism of retribution, 257 - 258
Darwin, Charles: 33 - 34
Davidson, Bill (on Cook Country Jail): 230 - 232
Decriminalization: 397 - 398
Defense attorney. *See* Counsel
Delinquency. *See* Causes of delinquency; Deviance; Identification of delinquents; Race; Social Class; Socioeconomic status; *and following entries*
Delinquency, definition of: 12 - 20, 23 - 24, 28 - 29; ambiguity in, 16 - 20, 25, 28, 208, 215 - 216, 348 - 349, 377 - 380; in crime-control model, 96 - 97; in due process model, 108, in rehabilitative model, 101; variations among states, 16, 17 - 19, 129, 286
Delinquency, extent of: 11 - 14, 20 - 23; reported, 11 - 12; unreported or undetected, 11, 12, 133 - 134
Delinquency, as failure: of parents, 262 - 263; of social institutions, 4, 6, 45 - 56, 159, 180. *See also* Rehabilitative model
Delinquency, public's image of: 25 - 26, 27, 170 - 175
Department of Health, Education, and Welfare: 203; 414; National Center for Social Statistics, 195; Youth Development and Delinquency Prevention Administration (Office of Youth Development), 420 - 421, 434, 445, 446 - 448
Department of Labor: 202
Dependent child: 20; defined, 19
"Deprived child." *See* Person in need of supervision
Detention: 7, 229 - 246, 318 - 319; alternatives to, 243 - 246; community-based programs of, 243 - 244; correlation with adjudication, 135, 283 - 284; in crime-control model, 97 - 98, 239 - 240; decisions concerning, 7, 135, 237 - 238, 244 - 245; in due process model, 110, 239; justifications for, 238 - 242; labeling perspective on, 243; legal safeguards, 7; of PINS and status offenders, 241, 243; as punishment, 240; in rehabilitative model, 102, 241
Detention facilities: abuse of juveniles in, 230, 231 - 233; effects of conflicts within system on, 235 - 242; effects of staff inadequacy on, 236; effects of underfinancing on, 236; improvement of, 245 - 246; inadequacy of, 229 - 235, 246; number of youth held, 238; overcrowding, 242; separation of juveniles and adults in,

230; standards for, 235; variations among states, 234, 236, 237 - 238
Deterrence: 98 - 99, 138, 251 - 254; assumptions underlying, 252; general, 251, 252 - 254; specific, 251
Deviance: 57 - 58, 59, 62 - 63, 176; defined, 60, 397. *See also* Labeling
Diane M., case study: 123, 131
Differential association theory: 45 - 46
Dismissal and suspended judgment: 301 - 302, 337, 338 - 339
Dispositions: 9, 139, 161, 299 - 306; correlated to seriousness of offense, 336, 341; in crime-control model, 98 - 99; decision making on, 303 - 306; in due process model, 112 - 113; legal limitations on, 349 - 350; options for, 300 - 303, 322 - 329, 336 - 353; in rehabilitative model, 103 - 104, 300, 336
Diversion: 10 - 11, 73 - 74, 132 - 137, 199 - 200, 399 - 400, 404; by community agencies, 193 - 199, by courts, 136, 439 - 440; defined, 10; by families, 181 - 185; law-enforcement model of, 426 - 444; school model of, 406 - 411; by schools, 185 - 193; welfare model of, 411 - 426; youth services systems model of, 444 - 450. *See also* Community decision making; Nonreporting; Police (discretionary power of)
Dix, Norman (on causes of delinquency): 142
Drop-in centers: 422
Drug abuse: 78 - 79, 126 - 127, 205
Due process of law: 94, 102, 239, 266 - 270, 320 - 322; extension to juvenile courts, 271 - 276, 291 - 293; and rehabilitative ideal, 264 - 266, 270, 443
Due process model of juvenile justice; 105 - 114; case studies, 130 - 132; goals of, 105 - 106, 114; relation to other models, 114 - 116
Durkheim, Emile: 52

Edwin M., case study: 122 - 123, 130 - 132, 288
Eichmann, Adolph: 258 - 259
Emerson, Robert (on court clinic): 304
Encapsulation: 10 - 11, 169, 313 - 318; defined, 10
Erikson, Kai *(Wayward Puritans):* 57 - 58, 60 - 61, 63, 397
Evidence: in crime-control model, 97, 98; in due process model, 105, 109, 110, 111, 112; in rehabilitative model, 102
Eysenck, H. J. (neuropsychological study of delinquents): 40 - 41

Family: delinquency within, 181 - 182; failure to divert, 182 - 183; as instrument

243. *See also* Child abuse; Deprived child; Neglected child; Status offenses

Peter B., case study: 125 - 126, 131

Philadelphia Enquirer: 186 - 187

Piliavin, Irving (study of police discretion): 216, 217

Platt, Anthony (on development of reformatories): 103

Plea bargaining: 282

Police: "cognitive lenses" of, 222 - 223; conflict with other elements of system, 215, 225, 440 - 444; decisions on detention, 7, 97, 237, 244; demands on, 213, 214 - 215, 222, 432; discretionary power of, 7, 10 - 11, 27, 214, 215 - 216, 221, 426, 443; diversion by, 6, 7, 10, 134 - 135, 212, 430; effectiveness, public view of, 179; fraternity among, 223; as gatekeeper of juvenile justice system, 211, 226, 246; as helping agent, 432 - 433; improving communications with community, 431 - 437; informal adjustment by, 427 - 429; intensified coverage of poor areas by, 27 - 28, 219, 226; juvenile specializaton, 223 - 225, 427, 429 - 431, 435 - 436; power in crime-control model, 97; power in due process model, 109; power in rehabilitative model, 101; professionalism of, 223 - 225; recruitment and training of, 221 - 226, 441; referrals to, 6, 211, 213 - 215; reliability of judgment, 97, 109, 217 - 218; restrictions on, 141; socialization of, 221 - 226, 432

Polier, Justine Wise (on accountability of private agencies): 150

Politics: effect on criminal law, 61 - 62; and institutional reform, 234

Porterfield, Austin L. (self-report study): 20 - 23

Positivism: criminological, 31, 32, 38 - 39, 42, 58, 65, 376, 412; scientific, 33, 45, 261

President's Commission on Law Enforcement and the Administration of Justice: 177 - 178, 340, 388, 429; Task Force on Juvenile Delinquency, 191, 406, 407, 411, 416

Prevention of crime and delinquency: 373; National Advisory Commission recommendations, 201 - 203; primary, 374; programs for, 376 - 400; secondary, 374. *See also* Deterrence

Private agencies: 150, 193 - 199, 302

Probation: 9, 74 - 76, 99, 302, 339, 341 - 345; effectiveness of, 344 - 345; subsidy, 438 - 439

Probation officer: and the community, 341 - 344; and detention decisions, 237, 244; and informal adjustments, 8, 146 - 147, 285, 438; as prosecutor, 8 - 9, 82, 123; qualifications of, 307, 342; role in court,

127, 296, 308, 321; and waiver decisions, 288 - 289; workload, 342 - 344, 345

Prosecution in juvenile courts: 293 - 296; and *parens patriae*, 295 - 296; by probation officer, 8 - 9, 82, 123, 293; by prosecuting attorney, 294 - 296

Protection of public from crime: use of detention for, 239 - 240. *See also* Crime-control model; Incapacitation

Psychoanalytic theory: 42 - 44, 45

Psychodynamic approaches: 41 - 45

Psychological explanations of delinquency: 38 - 45; and preventon of crime, 377 - 380

Psychopathic criminality: 43 - 44

Psychophysiological characteristics of delinquents: 41

Public defender: 124, 125, 296 - 297; compared with private counsel, 62, 79

Punishment: justification for, 250 - 260, 346 - 348; objectives of, 98 - 99. *See also* Retribution

Race: correlated with delinquency, 26 - 27, 218 - 220

Racism: 26, 72

Radical treatment strategies: 104, 368 - 372

Raisen, Bernice (on probation): 146 - 147

Randi B., case study: 124, 131

Ravitch, Diane (on crime in schools): 188 - 189

Recidivism: 152, 202 - 202, 252, 350

Recreation programs: and prevention of delinquency, 383 - 386

Reform school: 74 - 75, 269, 270, 350

Rehabilitation: as excuse for retribution, 260; as goal of juvenile court, 8, 138, 146, 260 - 264, 414 - 415; as myth, 161, 269 - 270, 358

Rehabilitative model of criminal justice: 100 - 105, 261 - 263; case studies, 130 - 132; goals of, 100 - 101, 104 - 105; relation to other models, 114 - 116

Reiss, Albert, Jr. (study of police-citizen interaction): 218

Removal of delinquents from community: 9. *See also* Incapacitation

Reporting of delinquency. *See* Identification of delinquents; Nonreporting

Restitution: 8, 302, 428

Retribution: 138, 256 - 259. *See also* Punishment

Richette, Lisa Aversa (on Youth Study Center): 233

Robert S., case study: 127 - 128, 130 - 132

Rockland State Hospital (N.Y.): 154

Salem, Massachusetts: witchcraft hysteria, 57 - 58

School: delinquency in, 185, 186 - 187, 188 - 189; failure to divert, 190 - 193; as instrument of diversion, 185 - 193, 406 -